I0198472

Songs of Our Pilgrimage

365 Daily Devotions
on the Psalms

Songs of Our Pilgrimage

JOHN A. HEYS

**REFORMED
FREE PUBLISHING
ASSOCIATION**

JENISON, MI

©2024 Reformed Free Publishing Association

Originally published in 1988 by the Men's Society of Hudsonville Protestant Reformed Church in Hudsonville (MI).
Reprinted with permission by Hudsonville Protestant Reformed Church.

Printed in the United States of America.

No part of this publication may be reproduced, stored in a retrieval system, or transmitted in any form or by any means—electronic, mechanical, photocopying, recording, or otherwise—without the prior written permission of the publisher. The only exception is brief quotations in printed reviews.

Scripture cited is taken from the *King James (Authorized) Version*.
Italics in Scripture quotations reflect the author's emphasis.

Cover design by Erika Kiel
Interior design by Pear Creative.ca

REFORMED
FREE PUBLISHING
ASSOCIATION

Reformed Free Publishing Association
1894 Georgetown Center Drive
Jenison, Michigan 49428
616-457-5970
mail@rfpa.org
www.rfpa.org

ISBN 978-1-959515-20-3
Ebook ISBN 978-1-959515-21-0
LCCN 2024934245

TABLE OF CONTENTS

A WORD FROM THE PUBLISHER

This book is a compilation of 12 pamphlets which were originally collected and printed in 1988 by the Men's Society of Hudsonville Protestant Reformed Church in Hudsonville (MI). These small monthly booklets, at one time also available in paperback book form, were published under the title *Daily Devotions from the Psalms*. This new version's title, *Songs of Our Pilgrimage*, was inspired by the theme of journeying and pilgrimage that is repeated often in these meditations.

In order to remain faithful to the words and ideas of the author, changes made to this version were primarily stylistic in nature. Deity pronouns were lowercased and Scripture citations were abbreviated. In addition, Psalmic, Psalter, and topical indexes have been included to better guide the reader in studying and growing from these meditations. Because the meditations were originally written in 1988, some references are made to outdated technology and the like. These references have been preserved in order to respect the context in which the devotionals were written.

Rev. John A. Heys was a musician and composed multiple tunes for *The Psalter*. He is remembered, too, for his love of the psalms and for his prayers, ending often with the phrase "We ask it for our Redeemer's sake alone, Amen."

We pray that the music of the author's original writing and love for the subject material shines through in this publication, such that the reader may be edified by its contents. *We ask it for our Redeemer's sake alone, Amen.*

GLORY AT THE END OF THE ROAD

Thou shalt guide me with thy counsel, and afterward
receive me to glory. —Psalm 73:24

What lies in store for us in the year we entered today we know only in broad, general terms. But we know not how long we will continue in this valley where the shadow of death is cast. For some, today will be the last day in this vale of tears. Others may be here for another week or month. Some of us will live through this whole year and beyond. And having been created as thinking, willing creatures, we have faculties whereby we can and do plan, and whereby we judge whether what we desire to see happen this year is threatened by what takes place round about us.

The big question, however, is not whether the wishes of our flesh will be fulfilled. The all-controlling question is not what the year will bring to us, but *where* the year will bring us. And the word of God contains such comfort for the child of God, because it not only tells us where we are going but also assures us that all that the year brings us will, without one exception, bring us to the glory of the kingdom of God's dear Son. For the psalmist declares in Psalm 73:24, "Thou shalt guide me with thy counsel, and afterward receive me to glory."

Take that truth with you today and every day throughout the years of your life. The all-wise and almighty God has the glory of those whom he purchased by the blood of his Son planned to the smallest detail. If you belong to that innumerable host that he gave to his Son, you will find heavenly glory at the end of the road you now travel on this earth.

Sing then that truth of Psalm 73:24 as versified with these words:

My soul with Thy counsel through life Thou wilt guide,
And afterward make me in glory abide.[1]

Sing it as soon as you wake up in the morning and face a new day. Sing it no matter what the day may bring you. For all that happens is bringing you to the glory that Christ himself now has and has purchased for his people.

Read: Psalm 73
Psalter versification: 202:1

---

1 Throughout the book, all the versifications of the psalms that the author references are from *The Psalter with Doctrinal Standards, Liturgy, Church Order, and added Chorale Section*, reprinted and revised edition of the 1912 United Presbyterian *Psalter* (Grand Rapids, MI: Wm. B. Eerdmans Publishing Co., 1927; rev. ed. 1995).

POLISHED IN TENDER MERCY

*Nevertheless I am continually with thee: thou hast holden me
by my right hand. —Psalm 73:23*

What do you have planned for today? It may or may not take place. It all depends on what the all-wise God of all mercy has planned in his eternal, unchangeable counsel. And that counsel is not a dead blueprint but a living plan that he eternally has in mind and that is constantly before his consciousness.

All in that counsel is designed to realize the day when the kingdom of Christ is established upon the new earth and God is all in all. Then the church of Christ is crowned with the glory that he now has at God's right hand. And the exact measure of glory, as well as the exact way it will be realized for each individual believer, and the exact moment of his entrance into it with his soul, is all unchangeably decreed in that counsel or living plan.

Asaph did not see that before he wrote Psalm 73. He envied the wicked in their earthly prosperity. His own poverty, afflictions, and difficulties made him question God's love and tender mercy for him. He could not see how the rough road on which he was traveling could lead to heavenly glory. He wanted earthly glory as an evidence of coming heavenly glory. Being chastened every morning and plagued all the day long, he could not see that "God is good to Israel, even to such as are of a clean heart" (v. 1). Later on he did see this and began his psalm with those words. But for a time he questioned where the days of his years were bringing him. It seemed useless to walk in God's law and to have faith in his covenant faithfulness.

Do not borrow his unbelief today or ever in the future when the going is rough. Instead, take hold of his words after God caused him to see the light. In Psalm 73:23 he writes: "Nevertheless I am continually with thee: thou hast holden me by my right hand." This is versified beautifully in the words:

In doubt and temptation I rest, Lord, in Thee;
My hand is in Thy hand, Thou carest for me.

Yes, God does care for us in our afflictions. For with these he is polishing us and getting us ready for that heavenly glory in Christ.

Read: Romans 8:18–39
Psalter versification: 202:1

A PERFECT GUIDE

Whom have I in heaven but thee? and there is none upon earth that
I desire beside thee. —Psalm 73:25

Do you think that you know what is best for you today? Would you like to have the universe in your hands, to control and use all that is in it for your fleshly advantage?

Let me urge you to forget it. The universe could not be in better hands than it is and has always been. Not only has the God of our salvation complete control of every molecule and atom of creation, so that he can move and remove them as it pleases him, but he knows and reads the hearts and minds of every rational, moral creature. Yes, he knows what the devil is thinking at any given moment. God knows the devil's plans, and where he and his helpers are, and what they are trying to do. All this God does not learn but knows because eternally he planned it all. All that every creature in heaven and on earth, rational and irrational, animate and inanimate, does, he eternally decreed. What is going to happen today—in every split second thereof—he determined and will execute on time, in the right place, and in the exact way that he decreed.

Could you then want a better guide through this valley wherein the shadow of death is cast? Should we not say with Asaph:

Whom have I, Lord, in heav'n but Thee,
To Whom my tho'ts aspire?
And, having Thee, on earth is nought
That I can yet desire.

In the Scriptures it reads like this: "Whom have I in heaven but thee? and there is none upon earth that I desire beside thee" (Ps. 73:25).

Indeed, the cross was no mistake, even though it looked that way when it took place. And what happens today may look as though "clean hands are worthless and pure hearts are vain" (Psalter 201:5), but they are not. He who designed that cross did so in love for all his people, as we can now see. But look at all that happens in your life: it is designed by that same infallible guide. He will guide your steps so that you do arrive in his glory. On earth we cannot find a more loving and perfect guide.

Read: Psalm 48
Psalter versification: 203:3

LIVING CLOSE TO GOD

Truly God is good to Israel, even to such as are of a clean heart. —Psalm 73:1

One truth we must hold on to with both hands and never let go. With Asaph we must say: "Truly God is good to Israel, even to such as are of a clean heart" (Ps. 73:1). That truth we must take with us wherever we go and no matter what happens to us. Come what may, God is good to his people. And a clean heart is not vain; nor are hands washed in the blood of Christ worthless.

Cleansing our hearts and fighting against sin, washing our hands and believing that our sins have been blotted out by the blood of Christ, reveals the goodness of God. In his goodness he causes us to believe. It is in his goodness that we receive his Spirit who enables us to fight against the sin that still resides in our flesh.

Let not the prosperity of the wicked deceive you. Think not that God is good to those whose hearts beat only with the love of sin and who have no interest in the forgiveness of sins, just because you see their eyes stand out with fatness and they have more of this earth's goods than the believers. Let not their pleasure-filled lives and prosperity make you judge God to be unfaithful to his promises to his church. Be sure, as we approach the end of time, with its greater persecution and deprivations, that God has not forgotten us and is not blessing our enemies.

Be sure that you see things correctly. Therefore, do as Asaph did: go to God's house. Draw nigh to him where he reveals to us that the "victory" of his Son's enemies, when they crucified him, actually was the victory for the church over sin and death; and that he is always working all things together for good to those who love him.

Our trust in God grows stronger or weaker in the measure that we do or do not draw nigh to him. Our faith must be fed to grow, and its food is the word of God. There you will see of the wicked that surely he "set them in slippery places" (Ps. 73:18). Then you can sing:

> To live apart from God is death.
> 'Tis good His face to seek;
> My refuge is the living God,
> His praise I long to speak.

Read: Psalm 84
Psalter versification: 203:5

THANKFUL PRAISE

Truly God is good to Israel, even to such as are of a clean heart. —Psalm 73:1

To ask for something is seldom difficult, especially when the need is great and the desire is strong. But to give thanks so often is hard to do and easily forgotten, because the thrill of enjoying what we have gotten overwhelms us. We will not easily forget to ask; but to give thanks is quite a different matter.

It is no wonder then that we are so lacking in praise and thanksgiving to God. When rain becomes a desperate need, churches will set aside a day to pray for it. But do they set aside days during the week to praise and thank God for all he bestows upon us? The nation sets aside a day of thanksgiving for crops and prosperity. Do the churches set aside days to thank God for his mercy, love, and grace, for salvation and all its benefits? Do we take time in the day, and do our prayers express praise and thanksgiving? Or are our prayers mere requests?

Follow in the footsteps of Asaph after he had gone to God's house and understood the goodness of God. He had found it so easy to complain and to accuse God—at least in his thoughts—of unfaithfulness. But when he understood God's works, after going to his sanctuary, he praised God with those words: "Truly God is good to Israel, even to such as are of a clean heart" (Ps. 73:1). And well may we sing that versification of this psalm that contains this beautiful chorus:

> My God, I will extol Thee
> And ever bless Thy Name;
> Each day will I give thanks to Thee
> And all Thy praise proclaim.

Do that today. Pray for blessings, for they are promised by God in his goodness. But thank him for sending his Son so that showers of blessings may fall upon us. Live in the shadow of the cross, and because of it cry out of the goodness of God to his people. Too often our prayers are complaints. Not often enough are they praise. Yet because of all his goodness, we have even reason to praise him by thanking him as the God of our salvation.

Read: Psalm 113
Psalter versification: Chorus of 202

A BLESSED COVERING

Blessed is he whose transgression is forgiven, whose sin is covered. Blessed is the man unto whom the LORD imputeth not iniquity, and in whose spirit there is no guile. —Psalm 32:1–2

How blest is he whose trespass
hath freely been forgiv'n,
Whose sin is wholly covered
before the sight of heav'n.
Blest he to whom Jehovah
imputeth not his sin,
Who hath a guileless spirit,
whose heart is true within.

Thus we sing from our Psalter versification of Psalm 32:1–2. What David wrote and our King James Version of the Bible hands down to us is: "Blessed is he whose transgression is forgiven, whose sin is covered. Blessed is the man unto whom the LORD imputeth not iniquity." The word *blessed* can be translated *happy*. And knowing David's grievous sins, we can understand why he called it blessed to have these sins forgiven. But what about our sins?

Usually we do not consider our sins to be as great as David's. And so often we find that, if we were called to write a psalm, we would not begin by bursting forth with happiness that our sins are covered, so that we would not list this first as blessedness. There is instead a host of earthly treasures and pleasures which, if we obtain them, we would classify as rich blessedness.

Yet here is the blessing that opens the door to all of heaven's blessings. And though the statement is negative in that something is taken away from us, there is a positive truth. Our sins are covered by the righteousness of Christ through his cross. No, they are not covered in the sense that his blood hides them from God's eyes. That is impossible. But we are given robes of righteousness to cover us, because all our sins were paid for in full. The cross covers us more fully than any insurance policy can. And Christ's righteousness becomes ours.

When we are clothed with those robes of righteousness, we become beautiful in God's eyes. He sees us as the beautiful bride of Christ. For the beauty of him, of whom it is said that God is well-pleased, shines forth from us. We reflect his beauty, belonging as we do to him.

Is that not great blessedness? Does that make you happy? Do you know that blessedness? Think about it today and every day.

Read: Psalm 32
Psalter versification: 83:1

ASSURANCE OF FORGIVENESS

Blessed is the man unto whom the LORD imputeth not iniquity, and in whose spirit there is no guile. —Psalm 32:2

Yesterday we took note of the fact that:

Blest is he to whom Jehovah
imputeth not his sin,
Who hath a guileless spirit,
whose heart is true within.

This is the versification that we sing of Psalm 32:2, "Blessed is the man unto whom the LORD imputeth not iniquity, and in whose spirit there is no guile."

But our attention today must be called to that last part, for it contains a rich truth for us. They in whose spirit there is no guile have this great blessedness of not having their sins imputed to them. This may sound strange at first. If their spirit has no guile, they have no iniquity. Why then does David speak of their sins being forgiven them? Is he perhaps referring to past sins, which they committed before their spirit was cleansed of all guile?

That could never be the case. For then no one would ever obtain pardon for sin. We keep our evil nature till we die. Even that great man of faith, namely Paul, states in Romans 7:18 that in his flesh still dwells no good thing. No, our Psalter versification explains what a spirit without guile is. It is a heart that is true within. It is a heart that sincerely desires salvation from sin. The words "without guile" mean without deceit, a spirit that is sincere. He who sincerely wants a pardon, who from the bottom of his heart wants to be robed with the righteousness of Christ and enjoy fully what the blood of Christ realized on the cross, has this blessedness of forgiveness.

Why do these have such a blessing? Not because their desire earns it for them. David makes it very emphatic that God forgives. He covers us and imputes to us Christ's righteousness. Sincerely desiring is no prerequisite to forgiveness. We do not earn it by our sincere desire.

The idea is that this sincere desire is the evidence that our sins have been—not will be—blotted out. On the basis of that blotting out we are born again and are given hearts that are true within.

Read: Psalm 51
Psalter versification: 83:1

BREAKING A SINFUL SILENCE

When I kept silence, my bones waxed old through my roaring all the day long...I acknowledged my sin unto thee, and mine iniquity have I not hid. I said, I will confess my transgressions unto the LORD; and thou forgavest the iniquity of my sin. Selah. —Psalm 32:3, 5

There are times when we keep from sin by keeping silent. But there are also times when to keep silent is to sin. David speaks of one of those instances when he declares in Psalm 32:3, "When I kept silence, my bones waxed old through my roaring all the day long." Then in verse 5 he speaks of breaking his silence. He writes: "I acknowledged my sin unto thee, and mine iniquity have I not hid. I said, I will confess my transgressions unto the Lord; and thou forgavest the iniquity of my sin." We must confess our sins and not keep silent about them before God. To keep silent about them is to add to our sins.

What is more, while we defend our sins we cannot be sure that we have forgiveness. For we do not manifest a spirit that is without guile. If we are God's elect children, our sins have been blotted out by the blood of his Son; but we can have no legal basis for believing that they are not imputed to us. And we will have to say with David:

> While I kept guilty silence
> My strength was spent with grief,
> Thy hand was heavy on me,
> My soul found no relief;
> But when I owned my trespass,
> My sin hid not from Thee,
> When I confessed transgression,
> Then Thou forgavest me.

The idea is that David became sure that God forgave him his sins. He had a God-given sign, the undeniable evidence of God's love for him. For it is God's eternal love for his people that brings them to confession.

Never need we be afraid of confessing our sins unto God. We had better be afraid of keeping silent and refusing to confess them. Confessing them means that we hate them and love God. And our love for God reveals that he eternally loved us and gave us that love for himself.

Before you go to bed tonight, confess all the sins of the day. But confess them also during the day as soon as they have been committed and you realize that you sinned against God. Confession will bring you peace of mind and assurance of God's love.

Read: Luke 18:9–14
Psalter versification: 83:2

THE ONLY WAY

For this shall every one that is godly pray unto thee in a time when thou mayest be found: surely in the floods of great waters they shall not come nigh unto him.
—Psalm 32:6

There is a time when we can find God. There is also a time when we cannot find him and his pardoning mercy. This is not due to the fact that God is not everywhere present. Nor is it due to the fact that he changes and makes impossible what once was possible. When David wrote in Psalm 32:6, "For this shall every one that is godly pray unto thee in a time when thou mayest be found: surely in the floods of great waters they shall not come nigh unto him," he was teaching us that there are times when we are not walking properly and therefore cannot find God.

When you enjoy the warmth of the sun, it is not while you walk in a cave or deep coal mine. Then the sun has not ceased to give off its warmth, but you have gone where you cannot enjoy it and find its comfort. So, if we do not confess our sins but continue in them, we are walking in a dark, damp spiritual coal mine where God's forgiving mercy cannot be found. God is still forgiving, but we are not looking for it, and the time for us to receive it is not present. When we have turned from our sins and then pray for forgiveness, we will find it.

Then no rushing floods of guilt will sweep over our souls and give us terrifying fear. The time for us to know his mercy is there, when we sincerely confess our sins. Our prayer is heard, and we can sing:

> So let the godly seek Thee
> In times when Thou art near;
> No whelming floods shall reach them,
> Nor cause their hearts to fear.

Then only will these floods of what we deserve not hurt us, but the warmth of that mercy of God will flow over us. Then we will not be swept back into sin. Satan will try—for he hates us and wants to get us back into sin—but confessing our sins and praying for God's mercy, seeking God's favor with a spirit in which there is no guile, we are where we shall find these blessings from God.

Fill your day then with prayer while confessing your sins. The time is there for you to find forgiveness and heavenly blessedness.

Read: Luke 15:11–32
Psalter versification: 83:3

OUR PERFECT HIDING PLACE

Thou art my hiding place; thou shalt preserve me from trouble; thou shalt compass me about with songs of deliverance. Selah. —Psalm 32:7

We must come out of our spiritual cave where we cannot enjoy God's pardoning grace. But we do need a hiding place to be safe in the midst of countless troubles. Does not David confess in Psalm 32:7, "Thou art my hiding place; thou shalt preserve me from trouble; thou shalt compass me about with songs of deliverance"?

If we are sincerely sorry for our sins—and not merely relieved that we need not suffer their punishment—we will want to have a hiding place so that we are kept from sinful thoughts, desires, and actions. That is what a spirit without guile yearns for. Enjoying the sunshine of God's mercy, we do not want to be enticed and drawn away from the place where we can enjoy it. We want a hiding place from Satan's fiery attacks. We want to keep clean spiritually. Clad with the robes of Christ's righteousness, we do not want to lose the smallest part of them. Enjoying God's protecting care, we will sing of deliverance and safety. We will have echoing in our souls the versification of Psalm 32 that declares:

> In Thee, O Lord, I hide me,
> Thou savest me from ill,
> And songs of Thy salvation
> My heart with rapture thrill.

Note that God receives the honor and praise. Songs of his salvation fill the hearts of those who confess their sins. Some years later Paul wrote that of him, through him, and to him are all things (Rom. 11:36). That is true also of our salvation. From him comes all of it. Through him it all is realized. It is all unto his glory. Songs of deliverance will fill our souls. But take note of the fact that God is the one who compasses us about with songs of deliverance. Our praise then is of the Deliverer.

How important that every day we search our souls to see how much of a song of praise there is therein for the cross of Christ. He is our hiding place but also the one who puts a song in our hearts. How wonderful when in the new Jerusalem we shout for joy and praise him for all he did for us. But there must be a beginning of this singing in our souls today.

Read: Psalm 91
Psalter versification: 83:3

TRUE BLESSEDNESS

Blessed is the man that walketh not in the counsel of the ungodly, nor standeth in the way of sinners, nor sitteth in the seat of the scornful. But his delight is in the law of the LORD; and in his law doth he meditate day and night. —Psalm 1:1–2

It certainly is a blessing to have one's sins forgiven. But with that blessedness always comes a life that flees from sin and walks in God's law. No, our flesh does not consider hatred of sin to be a blessing. Our flesh is happy when we walk in sin. It never wants to sing:

That man is blest who, fearing God,
From sin restrains his feet,
Who will not stand with wicked men,
Who shuns the scorners' seat.
Yea, blest is he who makes God's law
His portion and delight,
And meditates upon that law
With gladness day and night.

Now, when it comes down to it, he who simply counts it a blessing to escape the punishment his sins deserve, and calls that heaven, does not really want forgiveness. Yes, he wants to escape misery and have joy for his flesh, but in the measure that he delights in sin he hates God. Listen! He who is only interested in escaping the punishment of sin is interested in sin. Such love self and not God. Being happy with sin and being happy about forgiveness of sin just cannot go together. You can hate the bitter taste of the medicine but be happy that it is bringing relief from a far more serious condition. But you cannot love sin and love being clothed with the righteousness of Christ. And that is the positive side of forgiveness of sins.

God, who sent his Son to fulfill the law for us and to suffer the punishment of our sins, not only removes our guilt but implants his love in those for whom Christ died. Such will not sit with those who ridicule God and his law. Of them David says in Psalm 1:1–2, "Blessed is the man that walketh not in the counsel of the ungodly, nor standeth in the way of sinners, nor sitteth in the seat of the scornful. But his delight is in the law of the LORD; and in his law doth he meditate day and night."

Remember that not to keep God's law is to scorn and ridicule it. Those who ridicule his law do not want to be covered with Christ's law-abiding righteousness but simply with an armor—which does not exist—to keep them from God's holy wrath while they continue in sin. No, a sincere desire for forgiveness also wants a life that loves God.

Read: Psalm 1
Psalter versification: 1:1–2

A WORTHY WALK

Blessed is the man that walketh not in the counsel of the ungodly, nor standeth in the way of sinners, nor sitteth in the seat of the scornful. But his delight is in the law of the LORD; and in his law doth he meditate day and night. —Psalm 1:1–2

Regardless of our occupation and whether we be man or woman, we either walk, stand, or sit to perform our work. And it is also while walking, sitting, or standing that we commit our sins. That is why David in Psalm 1:1–2 declares: "Blessed is the man that walketh not in the counsel of the ungodly, nor standeth in the way of sinners, nor sitteth in the seat of the scornful. But his delight is in the law of the LORD; and in his law doth he meditate day and night."

The positive side of this is walking in God's counsel, standing in the way of the righteous, and sitting with those who praise God and delight in his law. Now, God's counsel is his advice; and that advice you will find in his law. The advice there is that you love him with all your being. The way of the righteous is to do that—love him—every moment of your life. And sitting with those who praise him and delight in his word is being friends with those who walk according to his advice and stand foursquare upon his holy law. It is enjoying their company and seeing eye to eye with them, working with them to praise and extol God's name. It is meditating in God's law day and night.

Shame should cover our faces then when we realize how little there is of this in our lives. By God's grace there is a small beginning. Therefore, we are able to sing sincerely:

> Blest is he who loves God's precepts,
> Who from sin restrains his feet,
> He who will not stand with sinners,
> He who shuns the scorners' seat.
> Blest is he who makes the statutes
> Of the Lord his chief delight,
> In God's law, divinely perfect,
> Meditating day and night.

We do well therefore to examine ourselves to see how true this is of us. It will be there to some degree in every believer. But we must find growth through the years. We should strive to walk more vigorously in the counsel of Jehovah, to stand more firmly in his law with the righteous, and to sit down meaningfully with those who praise and extol his holy name.

Never, no never, should we be satisfied until we are perfect, and our walking, standing, and sitting please God every moment of our lives.

Read: Proverbs 4
Psalter versification: 2:1–2

January 13

MEDITATING IN GOD'S LAW

But his delight is in the law of the LORD;
and in his law doth he meditate day and night. —Psalm 1:2

What a small beginning of that new obedience that God gives to his children do we have! David, speaking of the man who is truly blessed, says that "his delight is in the law of the LORD; and in his law doth he meditate day and night" (Ps. 1:2).

That is not the picture that we see of ourselves, if we take a good look into the mirror of God's law. Meditating in the law is one thing. Doing so day and night is something else. Yes, we do sing:

> Yea, blest is he who makes God's law
> His portion and delight,
> And meditates upon that law
> With gladness day and night.

But singing these words is one thing, and living them is quite another. We do well today to search our hearts. Do we really take as much time to read and meditate in God's word as we do to read our newspaper? Are we really so interested in that word that we not only read it but meditate upon it? Is that true also of God's law?

Meditating in God's law is thinking about what we read, turning it over in our minds, asking ourselves what is required of us in the present situation and circumstances, trying to delve more deeply into the meaning of that law for us personally. It means that what God demands of us does not get a quick thought, which is soon brushed aside because we have "more important" things to do. It means that we study his law so that we are sure that today and tomorrow, yea the rest of our lives, we will walk in love to God. It means that we delight in that law and want to walk in it more perfectly than yesterday. Meditating in God's law means that we want to know our calling in every circumstance of life so that we can improve our walk in it. We do not merely want to see what that law says of our past deeds, but also what we are to do tomorrow, should we meet with adversity. Yea, we must also know how to react to prosperity and an increase in this world's goods.

And surely it means that we meditate in the fulfillment of that law of God by his own Son. Surely day and night that truth brings us comfort as our sins so rise up before us day and night.

Read: Psalm 119:97–112
Psalter versification: 1:2

WORKS THAT ABIDE

And he shall be like a tree planted by the rivers of water, that bringeth forth his fruit in his season; his leaf also shall not wither; and whatsoever he doeth shall prosper. —Psalm 1:3

One prospers when one succeeds in what he sets out to do. We call it prosperity when everything goes well and we go forward in enjoying life. The opposite of prosperity is adversity. Then all goes against us, and we lose the things we were enjoying.

David in Psalm 1:3 gives us a beautiful picture of prosperity. He writes of the man who delights in God's law: "And he shall be like a tree planted by the rivers of water, that bringeth forth his fruit in his season; his leaf also shall not wither; and whatsoever he doeth shall prosper."

This does not mean that we are going to prosper materially when we keep God's law. It does not mean that our flesh is going to have a good time and that we are going to succeed financially. The very opposite will in most instances be true. Walk in God's law and you may be ridiculed. That is especially true when you keep the first table of the law. Hallow the Sabbath and you may lose your job, when the unbelieving employer insists that you desecrate the Sabbath by working for him. Be honest in your business dealings and you will not be able to compete with those who break God's law. But even apart from what men may do to us, we have no promise from God that if we keep his law we will not have sicknesses and diseases. And we all are going to die and lose all our earthly goods.

Yet note that David speaks of a tree planted where it will get plenty of water and bring forth abundant fruit. It gets what it needs for life and does what it was created and designed to bring forth, and remember that we depend upon God's grace and were created and designed to love and serve him every minute of our lives. The ungodly are not so. They receive none of God's grace and bring forth not one good work.

Of the one who keeps God's law we may sing:

> That man is nourished like a tree
> Set by the river's side;
> Its leaf is green, its fruit is sure,
> And thus his works abide.

That man will receive God's grace and prosper in good works.

Read: Jeremiah 17:1–14
Psalter versification: 1:3

A CALL TO PRAISE GOD

Praise ye the LORD. Praise God in his sanctuary: praise him in the
firmament of his power. —Psalm 150:1

Psalm 150 speaks of the calling of every one of us. In verse 1, the psalmist says: "Praise ye the LORD. Praise God in his sanctuary: praise him in the firmament of his power." And we ought to take note of the fact that he speaks of two groups of persons and of two places where they abide. He speaks of those in God's sanctuary here below and of those in heaven, where he reveals himself more fully. This is beautifully expressed in our Psalter with these words:

Hallelujah! Hallelujah!
In His temple God be praised;
In the high and heav'nly places
Be the sounding anthem raised.

Surely this includes you and me today. We are quite ready, when troubles come, to run to God for help. But did you lift your heart and soul in praise to him today? You may have praised your employer or employee, your children, or a friend for his or her kindness. But have you praised God for all the blessings of salvation which he has showered down upon you? Did you, the first thing this morning, praise him for the care and protection he gave you last night?

Your newspaper may have informed you of a fire that destroyed a home last night, of a person rushed to the hospital, or of a family bereaved of a loved one. You and I did not suffer any of these disappointments. But did we thank God for watching over us and our loved ones? Or did we just take it all for granted? Truly God is not in all our thoughts. For that matter, he is so seldom in our thoughts.

And what about all the rich gifts of salvation that he unceasingly gives to us? He keeps us in the faith and preserves in us the life from above that he gave us the moment we were born again. He deals with us from moment to moment on the basis of what his Son did for us on the cross. And today his Son is working all things, without exception, together for our good. What a multitude of reasons there are to praise him.

Praise him then. And if you want music in your home or at work, let it not be silly noise the world makes and calls music, but let it be songs of praise. With the angels sing: "Hallelujah, praise Jehovah."

Read: Psalm 150
Psalter versification: 409:1

MIGHTY ACTS AND FITTING PRAISE

Praise him for his mighty acts: praise him according
to his excellent greatness. —Psalm 150:2

We do well today to take note of the fact that the psalmist in Psalm 150:2 exhorts us to lift our voices to God and "Praise him for his mighty acts: praise him according to his excellent greatness." Let it not be misunderstood, however. We are not to praise him merely for those works that make this life more comfortable and enjoyable. That is the tendency of our flesh; and that creeps so easily into our prayers. Then, too, his mighty act of bringing up the sun every morning, after guiding the stars in their courses all night, can fill us with amazement. All this is so very superhuman. But the mighty act of God in our salvation calls for endless and heavenly praise.

What a mighty act that God sent his Son by a virgin birth! How marvelously he sent him as our representative. What an awesome and mighty act that he poured on him all the vials of his wrath against our sins! What excellent greatness he manifested in raising him from the dead and in lifting him to his right hand in heavenly glory, giving him power over all things in heaven and on earth! Surely all this calls for constant lofty praise.

Do you know of anything that reveals his "excellent greatness" more richly and brings us more blessedness? His creating the universe and all its multitude of creatures was a mighty act. No one else could do that and sustain it as he does. Surely the works of his providence are mighty acts. However, what reveals the greatness of his love, mercy, and grace is the salvation he wrought for us in his Son. Creation reveals the greatness of his wisdom and power. Salvation draws us close to him to enjoy his love, mercy, and grace in covenant fellowship. Here are mighty acts which eye (including Adam's) has not seen, ear has not heard, and that were never revealed to man apart from Christ.

Did you give much thought to this today? Have you praised God for it today, or have you reserved only Sunday for singing his praises?

Let this be your daily song:

Hallelujah! Praise Jehovah
For His mighty acts of fame;
Excellent His might and greatness;
Fitting praises then proclaim.

Read: Psalm 33
Psalter versification: 409:2

A CALL TO SING GOD'S PRAISES

Praise him with the sound of the trumpet: praise him with the psaltery
and harp. Praise him with the timbrel and dance: praise him with stringed
instruments and organs. Praise him upon the loud cymbals: praise him upon
the high sounding cymbals. —Psalm 150:3–5

What an array of musical instruments our symphony orchestras have today! What rich music they are able to produce compared with the instruments the psalmist mentions in Psalm 150:3–5! There, concerning God, he writes: "Praise him with the sound of the trumpet: praise him with the psaltery and harp. Praise him with the timbrel and dance: praise him with stringed instruments and organs. Praise him upon the loud cymbals: praise him upon the high sounding cymbals."

How emphatic then is the exhortation in verse 2, to praise him for his mighty acts and excellent greatness! The piercing sound of the trumpet, the softer music of the timbrel, harp, stringed instruments, and organs, and the emphatic accentuation by the cymbal must all be used to sound his praises. And to make it very emphatic, the psalmist adds in the next verse: "Let every thing that hath breath praise the LORD" (v. 6).

That personal note brings this call to praise God to you and me. Do not look at your neighbor and tell him to praise God. With emphasis say that to yourself. Never mind if you have no talent to play those instruments. Do not excuse yourself because you were not born with a beautiful singing voice. Yea, even if you were born as a monotone, this word comes to you. It is the content of your singing and the words that are accompanied by those instruments that count.

Fittingly the versification of these words declares:

Hallelujah! Hallelujah!
All that breathe, Jehovah praise;
Let the voices God hath given
Joyful anthems to Him raise.

Did you notice how this includes you? Those instruments enrich the music, but praising God means extolling him for his virtues, and that must be in the minds of those who accompany with musical instruments. Music and musical instruments were designed by God, and we can praise him for his wisdom, his mighty acts and excellent greatness that give those to us. But they must be used to praise him as our God and savior in Christ. Fill your day then with praise to him for his love and works of love to those whom he chose in Christ and saved by his blood.

Read: Psalm 81
Psalter versification: 409:5

OUR NEED FULLY SUPPLIED

The LORD is my shepherd; I shall not want. —Psalm 23:1

After his profound, powerful confession that "The LORD is my shepherd," David in Psalm 23:1 expresses with absolute confidence: "I want nothing." That is a better translation than "I shall not want." For what we need above all is a shepherd who will supervise our whole life, take constant care of us, protect us from all our enemies, and lead us to the glory of the kingdom of heaven. Having Jehovah as our shepherd, all these needs will be taken care of in full. We shall not want because of what we now have. Having Jehovah as our shepherd, we want nothing. All we need is him, and having him we want nothing.

This is true because he is the I AM. That is what his name means, and to the believer that means volumes. That name tells us that he depends upon no one and upon nothing. Every creature—and that includes the devil—depends upon him for all its existence. All creatures must say: "I will be, if it pleases him." Only God can say "I AM," because he has in himself all he needs for his life. He is therefore also unchangeable and cannot be changed or influenced by any creature. All creatures depend upon him completely. Therefore also, he has absolute control over them all.

He then is the one who can and does take care of us, the shepherd who will unerringly lead us to the kingdom of heaven. Put your trust in him completely. Doubt not for the slightest moment the safety of your body and soul. The first thing to do when you awake every morning is to sing:

> My Shepherd is the Lord Who knows my needs,
> And I am blest;
> By quiet streams, in pastures green, He leads
> And makes me rest.
> My soul He saves and for His own Name's sake
> He guides my feet the paths of right to take.

And because Jehovah has given us to his Son, so that we are the sheep of his flock, all is well. Giving us his Son, he supplied all our needs. We may not get all that our flesh desires and all that we think we need. But we will receive everything we need to arrive presently in the kingdom of his dear Son, where we will not know what want is and will ever be full.

Read: Psalm 23
Psalter versification: 56:1

ALL IS WELL

*He maketh me to lie down in green pastures: he leadeth me
beside the still waters. —Psalm 23:2*

The day is coming when we will not be able to buy or sell, because we refuse to take the mark of the beast. We will then be faced with starvation. Yet the child of God will with David be able to say of Jehovah: "He maketh me to lie down in green pastures: he leadeth me beside the still waters" (Ps. 23:2).

Now, a sheep lies down when it has eaten sufficiently. And to lie down in green pastures means that there is still an abundance of food far beyond the present needs. Still waters represent peace, tranquility, complete freedom from fear of any harm.

And although such a wonderful life seems impossible, and we can only wonder how David, a man with such a troubled life, could say this, he does in verse 3 say that God restores his soul. How can he speak that way? How can we sing this truth? Well, remember that David says that Jehovah is his shepherd. And we do well to write that truth in our souls and daily sing:

> The Lord's my Shepherd, I'll not want;
> He makes me down to lie
> In pastures green; He leadeth me
> The quiet waters by.

Yes, all that which we need will be supplied. All is well, and all will be well every step of our way, because Jehovah is our shepherd.

Just glance ahead a few verses and note that in the last verse David says: "And I will dwell in the house of the LORD for ever." Keep that in mind all day and every day. Come what may, even in the days of the antichrist, we will be supplied by our shepherd with all that we need to reach and enter into that house of God. Remember that it is to that house that he is leading us, and he is supplying us with that which is necessary for us to reach glory.

What terrible agony his Son suffered to earn a place for us in that house! But it brought him there and gave him power over all our enemies. Behold him there and put your trust in him. At God's appointed time he will return and take you out of this vale of tears and into that house.

Read: Ezekiel 34:11–31
Psalter versification: 53:1

FED WITH SPIRITUAL BREAD

The LORD is my shepherd; I shall not want. —Psalm 23:1

Another versification of the truth in Psalm 23:1 which we sang yesterday is the beautiful confession:

> Thou, Jehovah, art my Shepherd,
> Therefore I no want shall know;
> In green pastures Thou dost rest me,
> Leadest where still waters flow,
> And, when fainting,
> Sweet refreshment dost bestow.

And truly every crumb of bread our earthly lives need and every drop of water upon which our earthly life depends will be given us, until the moment when our Good Shepherd brings us to his Father's house, that we may dwell there with him.

But can you, and do you, sincerely sing that your shepherd makes you lie down in pastures of *spiritual* food and leads you beside still waters of *spiritual* refreshment? These, and these above all, our Good Shepherd provides. Therefore, regardless of what day in the week it is, two questions must be answered today. Did you feed in those pastures and lie down in them in your church this past sabbath day? Are you with hunger and thirst looking forward to enjoying both these green pastures and that cool, refreshing, still water this coming sabbath day?

Remember that Christ is the bread of life and supplies us with the water of life. Our spiritual life needs him. We need the preaching of him. And we need to eat and drink him with our souls. The question is whether we have an appetite for them and are faithful in seeking them.

Then, too, how often during the waking hours of the day do you find yourself in these green pastures of God's word and do you seek refreshment by those still waters that assure us that being justified by faith, we have peace with God through our Lord Jesus Christ? We need spiritual food and drink far more than the bread and water our bodies crave and enjoy.

Is it really true that Jehovah is your shepherd? Is then your Bible an open book out of which you eat and drink daily? In the measure that it is, your soul is restored. Your body may be filled with aches and pains, but your soul shall sincerely say: "I want nothing. God's word assures me that my Shepherd cares for all my needs."

Read: Revelation 7
Psalter versification: 52:1

BLESSED ASSURANCE

He restoreth my soul: he leadeth me in the paths of righteousness
for his name's sake. —Psalm 23:3

Frail and helpless creatures that they are, sheep are easy prey to the wolves. Attacked by wolves, the sheep are filled with terror and tremble. But having a shepherd who makes them lie down in green pastures and leads them beside still waters, the sheep have their souls restored to the calm confidence they had before the attack. Of this, one of our versifications of Psalm 23:3 sings:

> He tenderly restores my soul
> When I am in distress,
> And for His name's sake guides my feet
> In paths of righteousness.

But understand that this truth, as applied to us, refers to much more than human wolves that threaten us. It is God's wrath, because we have left the paths of righteousness and earned for ourselves everlasting punishment, that troubles our souls.

However, because Jehovah is our shepherd, our souls are restored to the assurance of the innocency wherein Adam was created. For our Shepherd, whose name is Jesus, which means "Jehovah saves," suffered fully the wrath of God for our sins and removed all our guilt.

This Good Shepherd not only blotted out our guilt and supplies us with all the things of this present life that we need, but he also supplies all that which our souls need. And this David expresses so beautifully when he states that our shepherd leads us in paths of righteousness. Thus not only does he take away our fears by dying in our place, but he enables us to walk again in righteousness. What blessed assurance that is for one whose soul is also disturbed because it hates sin.

And remember that we must find this in our lives, if we are going to be freed from the fear of punishment. Even the devil wants to be assured that he will not be cast into the lake of fire. All who will be cast in have that fear and desire a way out. But walking in the paths of righteousness is the evidence that our Good Shepherd died for our sins. For he died for them in order that we might live in a way that glorifies God's name. He saves us not merely for our good, but his deepest motive is his love for God and the glory of his name.

Read: Psalm 5
Psalter versification: 54:2

ALL FEAR DISPELLED

Yea, though I walk through the valley of the shadow of death, I will fear no evil: for thou art with me; thy rod and thy staff they comfort me. —Psalm 23:4

Although a shadow is impossible where there is no light, a shadow is always caused by an object that stands between that light and the place where that light would otherwise fall. In Psalm 23:4 David speaks of a huge mountain that exists between us and God, who is the light. We are in the valley at the bottom of that mountain. And daily in one way or in another we are reminded of that mountain, for not only do we every day hear of death, but in our bodies we feel or see evidence of coming death. And even as a mountain cannot be moved by man, the awesome reality is that the mountain of our guilt cannot be removed by man and calls for the wrath of God. That mountain is our awesome load of sin!

How wonderful then that God restores our souls so that we do not fear this evil, because we believe that our Good Shepherd paid the price for our sins and has begun in us the work of making us walk in the paths of righteousness. Although we still live in that valley, we are sure that the day will come when we will be before God's face, because all our guilt and all our old man of sin will be taken away, and we will have covenant fellowship with God in Christ, who is the Light of the world.

And though we still see death, which is the shadow this mountain of guilt causes, and will see it all the rest of this life, we can sing:

Yea, though I walk thro' death's dark vale,
Yet will I fear no ill,
For Thou art with me, and Thy rod
And staff me comfort still.

Now, we can see why David declares that God has restored his soul. All fear is dispelled, and he can face death with confidence. For in his Son God has come into our flesh, dwelt with us, died for us, arose because he had justified us, and then ascended to heaven to prepare the way for us to come there; returned in the Spirit; and assures us by his Spirit that death will not bring us to the lake of fire but into the light and blessedness of life with God. He is with us in his Spirit and will lead us through death and the grave to life and everlasting blessedness. Let not that shadow of death frighten you. Look at him who became one of us and will never leave or forsake us but bring us through death to glory.

Read: Psalm 27
Psalter versification: 53:3

AN OVERFLOWING CUP OF JOY

Thou preparest a table before me in the presence of mine enemies: thou anointest my head with oil; my cup runneth over. —Psalm 23:5

The sheep that has a faithful and powerful shepherd fears no evil. It knows that the shepherd will watch over it and is able to defend it from the fiercest enemies. And for the sheep of Christ's flock this is far more certain than for any earthly sheep that depends upon a human shepherd. All of Christ's sheep can and do sing:

My food Thou dost appoint me,
Supplied before my foes:
With oil Thou dost anoint me,
My cup of bliss o'erflows.

So easily we forget that truth. However, we had better keep in mind every day that God prepares a table for us. Did you see that the last time you sat down to eat? Did you see all your food furnished by God? And did you thank him for it?

David changes the figure a bit here in Psalm 23:5. Sheep have no table, and although we do, we depend upon God for all our food. And we are more really surrounded by enemies than earthly sheep are. We have the wicked enemies not only of Satan and his host of fallen angels, but also the world that far outnumbers the church. Yet in their presence God fully supplies all our needs.

And since our shepherd's rod and staff hold off all our enemies, we can sit down at our table and in comfort eat what God provides. We can be sure that we will lack nothing that we need to reach his heavenly house.

If now you see what David could not yet see, it is true that not only in the presence of our enemies does he fully supply all our needs, but he uses these enemies to prepare us a heavenly table. They broke the earthly house of flesh of his Son, nailing him to his cross. Yet God was using them so that heavenly dainties might be prepared for us to such a degree that our cup runs over.

With a tremendously liberal hand our Good Shepherd prepares a table for us and soothes us with the oil of his Spirit, so that our human language cannot fully express it. And never in eternity will that cup be anything less than a cup that is still overflowing with blessedness.

What bliss lies in store for us by God's boundless grace!

Read: Psalm 3
Psalter versification: 55:3

HEAVENLY GLORY ABSOLUTELY SURE

Surely goodness and mercy shall follow me all the days of my life: and I will dwell in the house of the LORD for ever. —Psalm 23:6

In the concluding remarks in what is called David's best-known psalm, he states: "I will dwell in the house of the LORD for ever" (Ps. 23:6). He began the psalm with the words: "The LORD is my shepherd." And although he says much between those statements, the fact that he shall dwell in the house of the Lord is the glorious climax of the truth that the Lord is his shepherd. Until he arrives in that glory of God's house, he will need food and protection, for he does live in the valley where the shadow of death is cast; but in that house are all the blessings that make his cup overflow. There he no longer is surrounded by enemies, but he is with God in the most intimate way that the creature can enjoy his covenant fellowship.

And the expression "Surely goodness and mercy shall follow me all the days of my life" (v. 6) explains why David is so sure that he will dwell in the house of the Lord forever. We therefore do well to pay attention to those words of David. For we do not deserve to live in that house. It is only because of the goodness and mercy of God that in his Son he cares for us in this life and makes sure that we arrive in his house.

That those follow us means that they are behind us and beneath us to push us and lift us up to that house consistently. It is God's good and merciful hand that will not let us slide back into Satan's clutches and lifts us out of this vale of tears and sorrows. And that hand of God is his Son in our flesh.

How beautifully stated is this truth in the versification:

Goodness and mercy all my life
Shall surely follow me,
And in God's house forevermore
My dwellingplace shall be.

Can you unequivocally say that? Can you say, "Surely," not, "Maybe"? "Surely," not, "I hope so"? "Surely, all the days of my life that goodness and mercy will be there."

If you cannot say that at the moment, go to the cross of Christ where God's goodness and mercy are so clearly and powerfully displayed. His enemies lifted him to his cross, but by it he lifted us to heavenly glory.

Read: John 14
Psalter versification: 53:5

A CRY FOR MERCY

Have mercy upon me, O God, according to thy lovingkindness: according unto the multitude of thy tender mercies blot out my transgressions. —Psalm 51:1

Although David, to hide his own sin, dealt very cruelly with the husband of the woman whom he had defiled, he in Psalm 51:1 cries out: "Have mercy upon me, O God, according to thy lovingkindness: according unto the multitude of thy tender mercies blot out my transgressions."

There are two things which we ought to see in this cry, because they hold true also for us. First of all, we ought to hold fast to the truth presented here that it takes a multitude of God's mercies to wipe away our guilt, or else we will perish under God's holy wrath. Forgiveness of our sins requires mercy for each sin.

It took only one sin of Adam to bring down the curse upon the whole human race; and as Paul writes in Romans 6:23, "The wages of sin is death." Each sin then calls for death and everlasting punishment in the lake of fire.

What a multitude of mercies is then required for us to escape God's holy wrath, by having our sins wiped out of his book! What a multitude of loving-kindness it was then also that God sent his own Son for such a multitudinous punishment, so that we might be judged to be righteous in God's sight!

But consider also that a cry for mercy with a confession of sin earns us no mercy, but underscores the need for God to show us mercy. The word *confess* means literally *to say with*. In this instance it means to say with God that we are vile sinners and deserve no mercy but should be cast into the torments of hell. In our confession of sin we earn nothing. And a sincere confession agrees with God that we deserve everlasting punishment.

Cry to him then, but not with the idea that your confession will move him to be merciful. Cry at the end of every day, but base your request on the multitude of mercies which his Son purchased. And with confidence sing:

God be merciful to me,
On Thy grace I rest my plea;
Plenteous in compassion Thou,
Blot out my transgressions now.

Read: Psalm 51
Psalter versification: 140:1

A THOROUGH CLEANSING NEEDED

Wash me throughly from mine iniquity, and cleanse me from my sin. For I
acknowledge my transgressions: and my sin is ever before me. —Psalm 51:2–3

To judge that David's sins of adultery and murder were heinous sins is certainly correct, but Scripture does not want us to stop there. David himself wholeheartedly declares in one of our versifications of Psalm 51:

O wash me wholly from my guilt
And make me clean within,
For my transgressions I confess,
I ever see my sin.

The words as David wrote them are: "Wash me throughly from mine iniquity, and cleanse me from my sin. For I acknowledge my transgressions: and my sin is ever before me" (Ps. 51:2–3).

It ought to be noted then that not even once does David in this psalm cry out for escape from the punishment he deserves. The desire for this is certainly implied in his cry for mercy. But the emphasis throughout the psalm is on the sin, not on the punishment called for by his sin. There is no spiritual value in a mere desire to escape punishment. All sinners want that, and if this is all that we want, there will be no mercy for us. We must, as the versification expresses it, want to be made clean within. We must want sinful thoughts and desires washed out of our souls. Note that David confesses that his sin is ever before him. His sin bothers him, and from it he wants to be set free.

How is that in your life? A prayer for nothing more than escape from punishment will not be heard or fulfilled. There must be a sincere desire to be set free from the power as well as from the punishment of sin. David sets a beautiful example for us here in this psalm. Yes, the David who committed such heinous sins also sets a good example afterward.

Follow then in David's footsteps which are presented here. Pray for a thorough cleansing from sin in every aspect of it. It must all be there, if we are to be assured that the cross of God's Son blotted out all our guilt and that his Spirit will set us free from the power of sin. He brought salvation for the body, but also for the soul. He saves us to the uttermost.

Read: Hebrews 9
Psalter versification: 143:1

THE HEART OF THE MATTER

Against thee, thee only, have I sinned, and done this evil in thy sight: that thou
mightest be justified when thou speakest, and be clear when thou judgest.
—Psalm 51:4

When David in Psalm 51:4 confessed: "Against thee, thee only, have I sinned, and done this evil in thy sight," he was not forgetting the sin that he had committed when he killed Uriah, after defiling the man's wife. No, he was getting at the heart of the matter. And we do well to bear in mind that we so often and quickly forget our sins and minimize them.

We disobey the authorities, entertain thoughts of hatred, covet the neighbor's goods, and forget that in breaking the second table of the law we broke the first table as well. We are inclined to behave as though all we need to do is to say to the neighbor: "Against thee, thee only, have I sinned." Such is always the case with the unbeliever, when he pleads guilty in court. He admits only of doing evil to his neighbor. But sin in every form is sin against God; and to God we ought to sing:

> Against Thee only have I sinned,
> Done evil in Thy sight;
> Lord, in Thy judgment Thou art just,
> And in Thy sentence right.

We really do not see our sins unless we see them as hatred against God. Whenever we sin, and regardless of how we sin, we always have another god instead of Jehovah. Regardless of which of the last nine commandments we break, it is because we are already breaking the first commandment. For our flesh has become our god, and we do its bidding, even though to do so is rebellion against the one true God.

We must not overlook or minimize our sins against our neighbor. To do that is to add to our sin. But we must get to the heart of the matter and in sincere humility before God confess that we have sinned against him.

A true confession of sin agrees with God and with David says that when God judges our deeds, his judgment is right. A sincere confession declares that only God's will must be obeyed. Our flesh must be put down. If only God's will counts and is heeded by us, we will not sin against the neighbor. As Jesus said, the great commandment is that we love God. If we love him, we will also love the neighbor for his sake. Do you?

Read: 1 John 1
Psalter versification: 143:2

WHITER THAN SNOW

Purge me with hyssop, and I shall be clean: wash me, and I shall be whiter than snow.
—Psalm 51:7

Conceived and born in sin, we are blacker than coal. And David had just confessed that God had to put truth in his inward parts, because he was born without it. But now in Psalm 51:7 he speaks of the tremendous change from being blacker than coal to becoming whiter than snow. He writes: "Purge me with hyssop, and I shall be clean: wash me, and I shall be whiter than snow."

Now, snow is the whitest of all earthly creatures. How then can David pray to be whiter than snow? Very simply: the blood and Spirit of Christ raises us to a higher spiritual level than Adam and Eve enjoyed when they came forth from the hand of God. Snow has earthly whiteness. The blood of Christ brings heavenly whiteness and purity. In other words, to be whiter than snow means that although Adam and Eve had a righteousness that was perfect, they could fall into sin and did. We are going to have the righteousness of Christ, which is a righteousness that is perfect and can never be lost. Wonderful as it would be to be like righteous Adam and Eve, it is far more wonderful to be like Christ.

Now, God must wash us and does wash us by the blood of Christ, and David's words point to that cross. For he speaks of hyssop, a twig of which was used to sprinkle the blood on the doorposts before Israel left Egypt and Pharaoh's clutches. So we by the blood of Christ escape the hold of Satan upon us. That cross we should have in mind when we sing:

> Thou alone my Saviour art,
> Teach Thy wisdom to my heart;
> Make me pure, Thy grace bestow,
> Wash me whiter than the snow.

What a blessing then flows forth from that cross of Christ! And what a love of God David speaks of and seeks, when he prays to be so clean that he can never sin again. David's adultery and murder were terrible sins which he now sees as God sees them. But he is not simply interested in being delivered from their guilt. He wants every single sin removed and wants to be like Christ, so that never in any way does he sin again.

Do you want that, and is this your prayer? You may not pray for anything less.

Read: Isaiah 1:1–18
Psalter versification: 140:3

AN AWESOME EXPLANATION

Behold, I was shapen in iniquity; and in sin did my mother conceive me. —Psalm 51:5

Although it is certainly true that we learn how to commit new sins, and children learn to sin by what they see and hear—especially on TV—the fact that we sin has a far deeper explanation. David gives us that explanation in Psalm 51:5 when he writes: "Behold, I was shapen in iniquity; and in sin did my mother conceive me." Or as the versification has it:

> Behold, in evil I was formed,
> And I was born in sin,
> But Thou wilt make me wise in heart,
> Thou seekest truth within.

Here we have the awesome reason why we have such a multitude of sins and need a multitude of mercy to have our sins forgiven.

No, David is not blaming his mother or father. He is explaining why every man, woman, and child with an earthly father is a sinner. The awesome fact is that no one has been born without sin except the Son of God who came by a virgin birth. Adam and Eve were created righteous, but from Cain onward each child came into this world with a heart that hated God. God's truth was not in his inward parts. That is why David says that God will have to make us wise in heart with truth in our inward parts. We do not come into this world with it. All are born totally depraved.

Now, David is not trying to defend himself by this reason for his sin. He is confessing the deep-seated reason why he is so sinful in order to accentuate the truth that all of our salvation comes from God, and that our only hope of salvation is God's mercy in Christ. Still more, he gets to the very heart of the matter. God must not merely work upon our hands and feet, our eyes and ears, and bridle our tongues. We must have heart surgery. Truth must be implanted in our hearts; and then eyes, ears, hands, and the like will perform works of righteousness.

Here is a humility that must be found in us. There is no room for us to boast. A corrupt seed always brings forth a corrupt plant. The seed of a weed never brings forth wheat. How necessary then that God's Son comes by way of a virgin birth! And how important that he must come into the depth of our being to free us from sin.

Read: Job 14
Psalter versification: 143:2

JOY AND GLADNESS RESTORED

Make me to hear joy and gladness; that the bones which thou hast broken may rejoice. Hide thy face from my sins, and blot out all mine iniquities. Create in me a clean heart, O God; and renew a right spirit within me. —Psalm 51:8–10

What would it take to bring you joy and gladness today? What work of God above all would make you sing? Would it be this:

> Blot out all my iniquities,
> And hide my sins from view;
> Create in me a spirit right,
> O God, my heart renew.

What God takes away from us can be very much more important than some of the things which he gives us. At other times what he gives us can be far more important than what he takes away from us. When he takes away our guilt, all the miseries, pains, and even death that he gives us cannot keep us from endless, heavenly joys Christ prepared for us. When he gives us a clean heart and a right spirit, that is, one that delights in righteousness, then all that which he takes away from us, be it even all our earthly goods and this present life, will serve to bring us where we will have treasures that never fade and where we will forever be satisfied.

David was crushed by the knowledge of his sin when God through the prophet Nathan rebuked him. Figuratively, not literally, his bones were broken, and he could not sing. Therefore, in Psalm 51:8–10 he cried: "Make me to hear joy and gladness; that the bones which thou hast broken may rejoice. Hide thy face from my sins, and blot out all mine iniquities. Create in me a clean heart, O God; and renew a right spirit within me."

He prays that God will take away his guilt, but also that God will give him a life that loves righteousness and holiness.

Thus when you pray, be sure that you pray not only for forgiveness of the sins of the day, but also for strength to do what is pleasing in God's sight. Be concerned about the punishment and desire its removal; but be deeply interested in walking in a sinless way to be pleasing in God's sight.

Search your soul. Does your guilt and love of evil crush you? Or do you need a Nathan to point it out to you? You must see and hate it, if your joy and gladness is to be restored. And that hatred of sin reveals that you are the object of God's love and that he has begun salvation in you.

Read: Isaiah 61
Psalter versification: 143:3

LIPS OF PRAISE

Deliver me from bloodguiltiness, O God, thou God of my salvation: and my tongue shall sing aloud of thy righteousness. —Psalm 51:14

To pray for something is to ask for a gift. Therefore, when we pray to God, we do not try to bargain with him. That is not praying. Praying is throwing ourselves completely upon God's mercy and grace. It contains no promises whereby we try to induce him to give us what we seek. God does have a heavenly storehouse full of blessings; but God does not run a store. He does not exchange blessings for works of men.

When David in Psalm 51:14 writes, "Deliver me from bloodguiltiness, O God, thou God of my salvation: and my tongue shall sing aloud of thy righteousness," he is not bargaining with God, offering him praise if he will only take away David's guilt. For note that this very prayer is full of praise. He calls God the God of his salvation. He already speaks of God's righteousness. And in the next verse he adds: "O Lord, open thou my lips; and my mouth shall shew forth thy praise." It is not something he is going to do for God, if he is saved. God will have to give him the desire and ability to sing his praises. No, David's reason for speaking of praising God, if his bloodguiltiness is removed, is that to give thanks unto God, there must be a reason. And in this instance it is not only that the guilt of murder is taken away, but that the desire to walk in sin has been removed by God. Doing this, God will open our lips and cause us to praise his name.

And what an abundant reason we have to praise God, as we live on this side of the cross of Christ. There is the undeniable evidence of the blotting out of all our sins. Ought we not then be very busy singing of his love, of his wisdom and power, of his righteousness and faithfulness to his promises? As David sang, so should we in the versification:

> Saviour, all my guilt remove,
> And my tongue shall sing Thy love;
> Touch my silent lips, O Lord,
> And my mouth shall praise accord.

By nature our lips are closed. Or far worse, they utter folly and evil. But God opens the lips of his people. And to be sure we are his children, we must find that praise on our lips every day.

Read: Psalm 98
Psalter versification: 142:4

A SACRIFICE OF THANKFULNESS

For thou desirest not sacrifice; else would I give it: thou delightest
not in burnt offering. —Psalm 51:16

One truth taught throughout Scripture is that salvation is a gift, and that we cannot buy the smallest part of it. We are aware of the fact that in a time of drought we cannot buy one drop of rain. Much less can we buy one drop of the blood of Christ to wash away even the smallest part of one sin.

When then in Psalm 51:16 David writes, "For thou desirest not sacrifice; else would I give it: thou delightest not in burnt offering," he plainly is speaking of sacrifices we make and of burnt offerings we present, and which cannot buy any part of salvation from God.

There are, however, sacrifices and offerings that do please him and in which God does find delight. The sacrifice of Christ on the cross God not only desired and delighted in, but he decreed it for our salvation. And by it he did pay the full price of our salvation and satisfied fully his justice.

Another sacrifice that pleases him David speaks of in the next verse in Psalm 51. Our versification which we sing presents it thus:

A broken spirit is to God
A pleasing sacrifice;
A broken and a contrite heart
Thou, Lord, wilt not despise.

For here we deal not with a sacrifice to *obtain* salvation but with sacrifices and offerings that express thankfulness for salvation that *has been obtained*, because God graciously gave it to us.

This pleases God because it renders to him the praise that is due to his name. It acknowledges him as the merciful giver and not as the demanding seller of salvation. And today we had better have that cross of Christ clearly before our eyes. In the measure that we see the sacrifice that God made for our salvation, we will bring to him offerings of praise and thanksgiving. We will cry out: "O God, how good thou art!"

The question is not as to how well you fared in earthly things yesterday. The question is not how well you were physically and what your flesh enjoyed. The question is whether you appreciate as much as you should and thank God for the salvation he freely gives.

Read: Psalm 34
Psalter versification: 144:4

CONCERN FOR ZION'S GOOD

Do good in thy good pleasure unto Zion: build thou
the walls of Jerusalem. —Psalm 51:18

If your sins are blotted out, and you know it because of the faith and love for God that always is bestowed upon those for whom Christ died, you will also love God's whole church. If you hate sin, you love God. And if you love God, you will love his whole church.

That is why David, having prayed for the blotting out of his sins in God's mercy, is concerned with his mercy upon his whole church. And having prayed for the forgiveness of his own sins, David in concern for the whole church of God prays in Psalm 51:18, "Do good in thy good pleasure unto Zion: build thou the walls of Jerusalem." Our versification goes thus:

> Do good to Zion in Thy grace,
> Her ruined walls restore;
> Then sacrifice of righteousness
> Shall please Thee as of yore.
> Thy people then with willing hands
> And hearts that Thou hast blessed
> Shall bring in thankful sacrifice
> Their choicest gifts and best.

It is true that David had set a very bad example before the whole church of that day, here called Zion and Jerusalem. The versification speaks of ruined walls. Walls in that day protected the city. David had broken down the walls, so that Satan now had easy access to the whole church, because of that bad example which he set. Therefore, David prays that God will do good to Zion, protecting his church from Satan's arrows and causing the church to bring sacrifices of righteousness.

The question is whether your sins bother you in that way. The sins you committed before others in your family, at work, among the members of God's church, did they make you sad in the thought that you may have encouraged others to walk in your sins?

Confess your sins before God, but also before men. Never defend them. And pray that your sins may not break down the walls of your church and give Satan easy access to the hearts of the members of your church. Go then, as David did, to God and pray that he may protect his church from the sins you performed before her members, and that they may bring their choicest and best gifts of thanksgiving and praise to him.

Read: Psalm 4
Psalter versification: 144:5–6

OUR GOD, THE GOD OF ALL GLORY

The heavens declare the glory of God; and the
firmament sheweth his handywork. —Psalm 19:1

Glory is the radiation or shining forth of virtue, so that when you see virtue, you see glory. Solomon says this plainly when in Proverbs 20:29 he writes: "The glory of young men is their strength." Thus when they display their strength, they show forth their glory.

God's glory shines forth also when he reveals his strength, wisdom, love, mercy, grace, and all his other virtues. Of his glory David speaks in Psalm 19:1 when he says: "The heavens declare the glory of God; and the firmament sheweth his handywork." And the idea is that the heavens, that is, the heavenly bodies, show God's glory because they show his wisdom and power, for they are his handiwork. Indeed, what a wisdom and power the heavens do reveal!

That glory of God may be summed up in one word, namely, that he is God. That above all is his glory. The name of God that David uses here is the Mighty One. And what a might and wisdom it took to bring forth and uphold that vast expanse that we call the heavens! What creature could do that? What idol made by man's hands could make and hold all those heavenly bodies in their exact courses? Indeed, the God of Scripture is God alone.

Our versification of the psalm speaks of this glory thus:

The heav'ns in their splendor declare
The might and the glory of God;
For day unto day speaks His praise,
And night tells His wisdom abroad.

Look at the sky today and tonight, and let no one tell you, or teach your children, that all this came by an evolutionistic process! We reckon time by the position of the heavenly bodies. Upon them we depend and receive our seasons. And how well we know that we cannot move or remove these bodies nor alter their courses through the heavens. How amazing it also is that we can today state when the sun will arise and the moon be full at any future date that man may pick. What wisdom and what power God reveals! How loudly he shouts to the whole human race that he is God!

Do you hear him, and do you see his glory every day?

Read: Psalm 19
Psalter versification: 39:1

A CALL TO PRAISE GOD

Day unto day uttereth speech, and night unto night sheweth knowledge. There is no speech nor language, where their voice is not heard. Their line is gone out through all the earth, and their words to the end of the world. In them hath he set a tabernacle for the sun. —Psalm 19:2–4

In Psalm 19:2–4 David, speaking of the heavens, states that "Day unto day uttereth speech, and night unto night sheweth knowledge. There is no speech nor language, where their voice is not heard. Their line is gone out through all the earth." Correctly our versification of these lines sings:

They speak not with audible word,
Yet clear is the message they send;
Their witness goes out thro' the earth,
Their words to the world's farthest end.

And another versification presents this significant addition:

Yet through the world the truth they bear
And their Creator's power declare.

Even as a red traffic light speaks, even though it utters no word that you can hear, so the heavens speak with words that are without sound. And what is important for us to maintain and hold on to is that they speak the truth not only of God's power but of the fact that he is God alone upon whom all creatures depend, and who must be served and worshiped.

That truth is spoken on both sides of the earth, the sun declaring it on one side while, at the same time, the moon and stars declare it on the other side.

Because of this fact no man has an excuse for not serving and worshiping him every split second of life. Even as the red traffic light says to you that you are guilty of sin if you do not stop as it demands, so no man anywhere at any time can escape the truth that he must serve and worship God day and night.

We cannot make God richer, and we have nothing that he needs. But he delights in having man, because he depends so completely upon God, serves and worships him, rendering him praise and thanksgiving.

The heavens declare his glory, but do you? The heavens do with words that are not audible. Do you sound out his praises? Do the songs you sing render him the praise that is due unto his name? Listen to the heavens sing his praises to you, and then with audible words sing those praises to God.

Read: Psalm 147
Psalter versification: 39:2, 37:2

SOULS THAT GLORIFY GOD

The law of the LORD is perfect, converting the soul: the testimony of the LORD is sure, making wise the simple. —Psalm 19:7

There is not a man on earth who does not hear the speech of the heavens. Powerfully the sun comes up to every man every day. Nothing is hid from its heat. All men know therefore that there is a God who made that sun and moves it exactly according to a predetermined schedule of time and on a predetermined course.

Knowing that there is a God, all men must live according to his law. No one is a law unto himself. The heavenly bodies all move according to a law set down by God. And man, made in the image of God, as a thinking, willing creature, must live according to God's ethical, moral, spiritual law. In other words, he must love God and in that love serve him day and night. He must glorify God by his works as well as by his words.

And having fallen into sin, man needs God's law to teach him how to serve and glorify the one true God of whom the heavens speak. David therefore wrote in Psalm 19:7, "The law of the LORD is perfect, converting the soul: the testimony of the LORD is sure, making wise the simple." When man came from the hand of God in paradise, he did see God's glory and did glorify him by his walk and words. But man fell and now needs to be converted and made wise in regard to Satan's lie and his own God-given calling. And in his grace God has given us that perfect law. It shows us perfectly our calling, and it serves to make us perfect.

Consider that the heavens declare the glory of God because it is God who is speaking through them. The same is true of his law. It is his law, and he speaks through it. Therefore, we can be sure that this law is perfect, making wise the simple, to give them souls that glorify God.

When we sin, we say that God's law is imperfect and foolish. What shameful pride sin displays! Let us instead with David sing:

> Most perfect is the law of God,
> Restoring those that stray;
> His testimony is most sure,
> Proclaiming wisdom's way.

Read: Psalm 111
Psalter versification: 42:1

APPRECIATING GOD'S LAW

The statutes of the LORD are right, rejoicing the heart: the commandment of the
LORD is pure, enlightening the eyes. —Psalm 19:8

Man fell into sin when he accepted Satan's word and rejected God's. Then he was no longer able to hear God speak through the heavenly bodies. But then he also lost all ability to keep God's law according to which he was created. Satan taught man to think only of his own glory and to turn his back upon God's holy law.

But in his grace God came to speak to man and to restore him to his calling to glorify God. And the reborn child of God who listens to that law of God becomes wise. His eyes are enlightened by that law, and his heart rejoices. Serving God does not become a painful chore but a delightful work.

David says that in Psalm 19:8 with these words: "The statutes of the LORD are right, rejoicing the heart: the commandment of the LORD is pure, enlightening the eyes."

However, David is not simply thinking of the ten commandments. He has in mind God's word, the Scriptures wherein the law given at Mount Sinai is found. He means all that God speaks to us in human language. The whole purpose of God's word is to restore us to our calling to glorify him consciously and willingly.

The question is whether we listen to that word and want to listen to him speak to us from it. The question is whether we can sincerely sing:

The precepts of the Lord are right;
With joy they fill the heart;
The Lord's commandments all are pure
And clearest light impart.

Only as we hear God speak in his law are we able to hear him speak through heavenly bodies. That is why only in his church do you find those who confess him to be God and do so with delight. Here is a sign that you have been born again: if your heart is filled with joy when you hear God's law, the life of Christ has been instilled in you. He delighted in that law and gives that delight to those whom the Father gave him. And you will sing: "O how love I Thy law! It is my meditation all the day" and night (Ps. 119:97). Then you, as well as the heavens, will declare the glory of God.

Read: Psalm 119:97–120
Psalter versification: 41:2

THE UPWARD LOOK

More to be desired are they than gold, yea, than much fine gold: sweeter also than honey and the honeycomb. Moreover by them is thy servant warned: and in keeping of them there is great reward. —Psalm 19:10–11

The god that is worshiped by most men is gold. And if gold is not in the literal sense that for which they live, their god is that which gold can buy. And the sweetest thing that they know is honey. Such people cannot agree with David when in Psalm 19:10–11 he writes concerning God's judgments: "More to be desired are they than gold, yea, than much fine gold: sweeter also than honey and the honeycomb. Moreover by them is thy servant warned: and in keeping of them there is great reward." By *judgments* David means that which God judges to be true and righteous. In other words, his law, his statutes are a very precious possession. If we have them in our hearts, we are very rich. If we delight in them, they are sweeter to us than any earthly food or drink.

Made in God's image and created to glorify him, man, when his soul is converted by the Spirit of God's Son, will see gold and all that it can buy, and all the food delicacies of this earth, as God-given means to serve and glorify him. He will look beyond the gold and honey. He will desire the gold only as an instrument wherewith to serve and glorify God. Tasting the sweet delicacies God gave him, he will taste the richer love and grace of God in Christ. These earthly creatures, when God's law has made us perfect and converted our souls, will cause us to lift our eyes above these temporary creatures to look through the heavens to the God who made all things for his own glory.

By that law man will be warned not to make gold his god, and not to live for the pleasures of the flesh. He will be given the upward look, so that his enlightened eyes see the Creator and not simply the creatures which he made for his own transcendent glory. And of these judgments of God he will sing:

> They are to be desired
> Above the finest gold;
> Than honey from the comb
> More sweetness far they hold;
> With warnings they Thy servant guard,
> In keeping them is great reward.

Read: Joshua 7
Psalter versification: 38:3

WARNED AND REWARDED

Moreover by them is thy servant warned: and in keeping of
them there is great reward. —Psalm 19:11

Warnings protect our lives. The buzzing sound of the smoke detector, the screaming of the siren of the fire engine speeding toward us from behind, and the red light indicating that the automobile ahead has its brakes applied all serve to make us aware of danger. These warnings are given to keep us from possible harm. Unless we are foolish, we are thankful that there are such devices for our protection.

But do you react with thankfulness because God gave us his law? Are you thankful when relatives, or friends, or officebearers warn you when you are breaking one of God's laws, and that in light of the fact that the wages of sin is death?

One who warns you is concerned with your well-being. Even more so, God displays his love when he warns us in his testimonies and statutes. Never lose sight of the fact that the admonitions, or warnings, in his word have been put there in his love to spare us the punishment that the transgression of his law demands.

Still more, God sets his law before us because in his grace he rewards our works of love toward him. He gave us his law for our good, not for our harm; in love and not in hatred. And when you thank him for food and drink, for life and health, be sure to thank him also for his law, which shows us how to keep from harm and what works he in his grace rewards.

Say it with David: "By them is thy servant warned: and in keeping of them there is great reward" (Ps. 19:11). Sing it with these words:

> They warn from ways of wickedness
> Displeasing to the Lord,
> And in the keeping of His word
> There is a great reward.

The reward his Son earned for us through his death and perfect obedience. There is a reward for those who keep God's law, because their guilt has been removed by his Son's cross, and he earned blessedness for his people.

Thank God for his law, and for his law-abiding Son.

Read: Matthew 6:19–34
Psalter versification: 41:4

ACCEPTABLE IN GOD'S SIGHT

Let the words of my mouth, and the meditation of my heart, be acceptable in thy sight, O LORD, my strength, and my redeemer. —Psalm 19:14

The heavens declare the glory of God, but in a way that they are not heard by the human ear. Man, however, was created in such a way that he could, with words that his fellow men could hear, speak of the glory of God. And he who truly hears the heavens declare God's glory will with his mouth speak words that glorify him. The more he hears the heavens declare God's glory, the more he will want strength and desire to open his mouth to extol God for that glory. He will with David pray: "Let the words of my mouth, and the meditation of my heart, be acceptable in thy sight, O LORD, my strength, and my redeemer" (Ps. 19:14).

David gets to the heart of the matter when he prays that the meditations of his heart may be acceptable to God. Words that are simply spoken by the mouth, and that come not out of a heart that loves God, are mockery and do not glorify God. Simply speaking the words with the lips is doing less than the heavens, for such words are spoken for the glory of self and not of God.

The heart is the spiritual center of our being; and our glorifying of God must come from that center and move the lips, or we sin against God by our words. Then we are by no means acceptable in his sight by the words we speak. And our prayer must be for the desire and strength to glorify him from the bottom of our hearts.

David expresses this when he prays to God as his strength and redeemer. As our strength he must give us the ability. As our redeemer he must deliver us from seeking self and fill us with the life that desires to glorify him.

How important, as well as beautiful, it is for us, in the midst of a world that denies God, to confess him and his glory, and to do this not only on the Sabbath in his house of prayer, but daily before the family and neighbors. Make this then your prayer:

> I pray that my words and my thoughts
> May all with Thy precepts accord,
> And ever be pleasing to Thee,
> My rock, my Redeemer, my Lord.

Read: James 3
Psalter versification: 40:6

SEEING OUR REDEEMER'S GLORY

Let the words of my mouth, and the meditation of my heart, be acceptable in thy sight, O Lord, my strength, and my redeemer. —Psalm 19:14

When our lives are spared, in what we call a miraculous way; when a loved one recovers remarkably after serious surgery; when things go exceptionally well for our flesh; the words of our mouths often are: "O God, how good thou art." We need no prodding or exhortation to do that. When we receive earthly treasures and fleshly joys, we, as believers, recognize this as his work, see his glory, and give expression to it.

Sad to say, however, that same enthusiasm, that same loose tongue, often is not there when we taste God's work of saving us from our sins. We are ready to confess him as our strength when all goes well physically, but we are not so enthusiastic and ready to confess him as our redeemer. The smile on our faces is not as broad when we speak of our salvation.

How happy are you in the knowledge that your sins are forgiven? How much is your soul thrilled when you think of what Christ did for you on his cross? How enthusiastically can you pray: "Come, Lord Jesus, come quickly"? Is there not so much that you still want to enjoy in this life?

The need is there, but is there the desire to pray with David: "Let the words of my mouth, and the meditation of my heart, be acceptable in thy sight, O Lord, my strength, and my redeemer" (Ps. 19:14)?

There is indeed so much room for us to pray, as versified, those words of Psalm 19:14,

> The words which from my mouth proceed,
> The thoughts within my heart,
> Accept, O Lord, for Thou my rock
> And my Redeemer art.

Sing of God as your redeemer as well as your strength. And pray for the grace to see his glory as your redeemer. Pray that the things here below do not make you forget the washing away of your guilt and the precious gift of a God-glorifying life like that of his Son. Pray that you may be more and more spiritual, to seek the things above and be pleasing in God's sight in all that you do.

Read: Revelation 7
Psalter versification: 41:7

MOUTHS FILLED WITH LAUGHTER

When the LORD turned again the captivity of Zion, we were like them that dream.
Then was our mouth filled with laughter, and our tongue with singing: then said they
among the heathen, The LORD hath done great things for them. The LORD hath done
great things for us; whereof we are glad. —Psalm 126:1–3

Yesterday we were reminded of the fact that God is our redeemer, and that we should praise and thank him more emphatically in regard to the spiritual gifts of our salvation.

This truth is expressed again in Psalm 126:1–3, where the psalmist writes: "When the LORD turned again the captivity of Zion, we were like them that dream. Then was our mouth filled with laughter, and our tongue with singing: then said they among the heathen, The LORD hath done great things for them. The LORD hath done great things for us; whereof we are glad."

Although this captivity was physical, when the Israelites were taken into Babylon, the return of which the psalm speaks was a type and shadow of our deliverance from the captivity and bondage of Satan. It was a picture of our redemption through the cross of Christ. And although the church's deliverance from the bondage of Satan does not in this life bring us all the joy that it should and calls for, we will in the day of Christ, when our bodies and souls together are freed from all sin and the curse, sing of this blessedness in these words:

> When Zion in her low estate
> Was bro't from bondage by the Lord,
> In ecstasy we sang for joy,
> By grace and wondrous love restored.
> The Lord in greatly blessing us
> Before the world His pow'r displays;
> Yea, great things God has done for us,
> And filled our hearts with joy and praise.

That laughter, and that singing, give evidence that we have the beginning of that deliverance from Satan's bondage. And then, indeed, the Lord has done great things for us. Let your mind dwell on that spiritual deliverance today. The captain of our salvation has wrought a wonderful victory for us. Let your mouth be filled with laughter that will not cease, but will in the new Jerusalem increase and never end.

Read: Psalm 126
Psalter versification: 357:1–2

WITNESSING OUR SPIRITUAL JOY

When the LORD turned again the captivity of Zion, we were like them that dream. Then was our mouth filled with laughter, and our tongue with singing: then said they among the heathen, The LORD hath done great things for them. The LORD hath done great things for us; whereof we are glad. —Psalm 126:1–3

The world may, and often does, ridicule God's church. Think of how the King of the church was ridiculed upon his cross. Think of how they scoffed at those upon whom the Spirit was poured out on Pentecost, accusing them of being filled with new wine. But there are also times when they have to and do admit what the psalmist says in Psalm 126:1–2, namely: "When the LORD turned again the captivity of Zion...Then said they among the heathen, the LORD hath done great things for them." And the idea is that the unbelievers also saw what God did for his church, and admitted it. One of our versifications has it thus:

> The nations saw with fear
> The might of God displayed,
> When He at last drew near
> To give His people aid;
> Great things for us the Lord has wrought,
> And gladness to our hearts has brought.

This does not mean that today unbelievers will praise God and reveal faith in him when they see what he has done. His works they ascribe to their god, whom they call Mother Nature, or at times Providence. So often—and sad to say this even happens in the church—they ascribe it to a god they call Luck.

Not only must we watch our speech and ascribe all things to Jehovah, the one and only true God, but we must fight against our tendency to keep silent and to fail to witness and confess God to be the one who is behind all that takes place, not only in heaven, but also here on this earth.

Our calling is to rebuke the world for its language and unbelief. Our calling is to witness and let the world know that we are glad because of the work of salvation which God has wrought for us. Our calling is to say before the world, as the psalmist does: "The LORD hath done great things for us; whereof we are glad" (Ps. 126:3).

How glad are you for your salvation? How openly do you show that joy before the world? Let your light shine before men. God may be pleased to use it to cause others to glorify him with you.

Read: Joel 3
Psalter versification: 358:2

DAILY CONVERSION ALWAYS NECESSARY

Turn again our captivity, O LORD, as the streams in the south. —Psalm 126:4

Our sins have been blotted out. The cross has wiped them completely out of God's book. But until we die, we still have the old man of sin, and we also have the motions of sin in our flesh. Therefore, we so quickly go back to the sins from which we turned. We fall again into sin.

The history of Israel reveals this so clearly. They turned to idolatry, and God sent them into the captivity in Babylon. There they repented, and God returned them to the promised land. It did not take long before they were back in idolatry. That is why the psalmist in Psalm 126:4, after speaking of the great things God did for them by returning them to Palestine, now prays: "Turn again our captivity, O LORD, as the streams in the south." Our versification states it this way:

> Again refresh us, Lord,
> With Thy reviving love,
> And be Thy blessing poured
> In mercy from above;
> By grace revive our hearts again,
> As streams refreshed by copious rain.

Did you notice that word *again*? It is used twice. And truly time and again we need to have hearts that are revived. We do, by God's grace, become sorry for our sins; but as Paul writes in Romans 7:19, 24, "For the good that I would I do not: but the evil which I would not, that I do...O wretched man that I am! who shall deliver me from the body of this death?"

So it is, day after day. We must flee daily to God and ask him to turn our captivity, our bondage in sin and in Satan's clutches, and to turn us back to obedience and works of love to him.

If we do not see this need, then it is even more evident that we have returned to the bondage of sin. Then the riverbed of service to God is dry, and we need the copious rain of God's grace and mercy to refresh us. If we do see this, we will earnestly pray for the putting down of the old man of sin and the reviving of the new man in Christ. Do that. By all means do that today!

Read: Romans 7
Psalter versification: 358:3

A SURE SALVATION

They that sow in tears shall reap in joy. —Psalm 126:5

Be sure that you take the words of Psalm 126:5 in their context and setting. The psalmist writes: "They that sow in tears shall reap in joy." Scripture here does not teach us that there will be no crop failures for those who weep, for one reason or another, while they sow their seed.

The psalmist had been speaking about the sin into which we fall so easily because of our old man of sin, who is with us until the day of our death. And he who in sorrow for his sins, with a soul that is weeping in sincere grief because he loves God, prays for conversion and deliverance from the bondage of sin shall reap in joy. He will reap conversion and complete deliverance from sin in the day of Christ.

In that sense we may sing this versification:

Although with bitter tears
The sower bears his seed,
When harvest time appears
He shall be glad indeed;
For they that in the sowing weep
Shall yet in joy and gladness reap.

Here you and I have God himself—for this is his word—assuring us that every sincere prayer for spiritual growth and full triumph over our sinful flesh will be fulfilled. And, to return to the first part of the psalm, great things will be done for us, and he will make us glad.

We can be sure that in the new Jerusalem our mouths shall be filled with laughter and our tongues with singing. We will be like those who dreamed of heavenly blessedness and found that their dreams became true. For they were God-given dreams proclaimed in the gospel as it is in Christ.

The gospel is good news. The angel who told the shepherds of the birth of Jesus said: "I bring you good tidings of great joy" (Luke 2:10). And because all the blessings of salvation and all the glory of the kingdom of heaven are realized by Christ, the king of the church, the harvest will be full. Every elect shall reach it. Every elect child of God shall be given the full measure of glory designed for him. We shall reap the harvest which Christ has sown and comes to reap. Our salvation is sure because our Savior is the almighty God who loves us and keeps all his promises.

Read: Jeremiah 31:1–17
Psalter versification: 358:4

A CALL TO PRAISE JEHOVAH

O praise the LORD, all ye nations: praise him, all ye people. —Psalm 117:1

Psalm 117 is the shortest psalm and the briefest chapter in the Bible, consisting in only two verses, and in our translation having no more than thirty-three words. But size does not always indicate value. A small diamond is worth far more than a piece of coal that is ten times larger. And this psalm, though very brief, expresses a very important truth.

In this psalm the call comes to all men: "O praise the LORD, all ye nations: praise him, all ye people" (v. 1). And to get the idea of its significance, listen to what we read in Isaiah 43:21, namely: "This people have I formed for myself; they shall show forth my praise." Turn also to 1 Peter 2:9, where we read: "But ye are a chosen generation, a royal priesthood, an holy nation, a peculiar people; that ye should shew forth the praises of him who hath called you out of darkness into his marvellous light."

Because of our sinful flesh, it may not seem important or delightful to praise God; but the three texts above reveal how important it is in God's eyes and how much he delights in it.

God sent his own Son that a people might be formed to praise him. He poured out the vials of hellish agonies, which our sins called for, upon that Son, in order that we might be called out of darkness into his marvelous light in order to praise him. Having done all this, he surely considers praise to his name important and finds delight in it.

Well therefore may we sing this versification of the psalm:

With thankful voice praise ye the Lord,
Jehovah's praise in song record;
Yea, all ye people ev'rywhere,
Jehovah's worthy praise declare.

When all the work of salvation is completed in the day of Christ, our lives will be filled with praise to God. And how advanced we are in the blessings of salvation reveals itself in how greatly we delight in praising him. Examine your life. Praise to God will reveal whether he is forming you for himself and whether you belong to that chosen generation, royal priesthood, holy nation, and peculiar people.

Read: Psalm 65
Psalter versification: 314:1

UNIVERSAL PRAISE OF GOD DEMANDED

O praise the LORD, all ye nations: praise him, all ye people. For his merciful kindness is great toward us: and the truth of the LORD endureth for ever. Praise ye the LORD. —Psalm 117

All men on earth that live,
To God all glory give,
Praise ye the Lord;
His lovingkindness bless,
His constant faithfulness
And changeless truth confess;
Praise ye the Lord.

That is a very comprehensive call. "All men on earth" excludes no one. The psalmist in Psalm 117 puts it this way: "O praise the LORD, all ye nations; praise him, all ye people. For his merciful kindness is great toward us: and the truth of the LORD endureth forever. Praise ye the LORD." And although the reason for that praise is listed as the merciful kindness of God toward his church, that call comes to unbelievers as well.

The idea is not that only those who tasted that mercy are to praise him for it. Nor does it mean that believers alone in every nation and people are called to praise God for his mercy. "All men" means all who live on this earth. Every living person must praise God for his mercy that is limited to his people.

Rightly understood, God's mercy is all concentrated and displayed in Christ. And no man is excused from praising God for sending him to save us from our sins. And when he returns, all people in all nations will praise him for his merciful kindness in Christ. From that day onward all finding fault with God by the unbeliever will be brought to an end. Then all shall confess him to be God—which is an act of praising God—but also confess that he was mercifully kind to those whom he chose in Christ. Did not the rich man in the parable of the rich man and Lazarus by implication do so, when he asked Abraham to send Lazarus to his brothers so that they could be taught that merciful kindness of God (Luke 16:27–28)?

Here is an added reason, for those who tasted this mercy, to praise God. He has formed individuals and families to be the host that enjoys this loving-kindness which he revealed and pours out through his Son.

All men must praise God for *all* his works. Do you do that, with gladness in your soul, for what he has done for you in his only begotten Son? Every knee shall bow and confess that he is Lord. Have you done so today?

Read: Psalm 100
Psalter versification: 316

ALL IS WELL

O praise the LORD, all ye nations: praise him, all ye people. For his merciful kindness is
great toward us: and the truth of the LORD endureth for ever.
Praise ye the LORD. —Psalm 117

Can you mention one work of God that does not call for praise? To praise is to commend or to extol. And the idea is that we see good of one kind or another in someone or in something. To praise God is to see that he is good and that his works are not only without fault, but always serve a good purpose. In that light can you find one work of God that is not good?

Indeed, there are works of God that do not bring us what we judge to be good. He sends rain on the day we planned to have a picnic. He lays us low with a painful disease. He snatches a loved one away from us by the cold hand of death.

The question is not, however, does this bring us what we call good? Rather it is, does this serve God in the fulfillment of his sovereign counsel? Can you name one work that delayed God in getting done what he planned for a particular moment? Does Paul not teach us that all things work together for good to those who love him (Rom. 8:28)? What God wants done is what counts, not what our flesh craves. The minute we judge that God is not doing good, because his work does not serve our flesh, we, rather than praising him, are denying him the praise due to his name. Then we are praising our flesh and saying that God must be our servant, while our calling is to bow before him and confess him to be God.

But all is well and in the day of Christ we will see that everything that happened worked together for good, to bring us to the exact place in God's house that he eternally decreed for us, and that we owe him everlasting thanks and praise, and that all his works were perfect.

There in God's house we will, from the bottom of our hearts, sing the versification of Psalm 117:1–2,

Praise Jehovah, all ye nations,
All ye people, praise proclaim;
For His grace and lovingkindness
O sing praises to His Name.
For the greatness of His mercy
Constant praise to Him accord;
Evermore His truth endureth;
Hallelujah, praise the Lord.

Read: Psalm 145
Psalter versification: 315

CONSTANT COVENANT FAITHFULNESS

O praise the LORD, all ye nations: praise him, all ye people. —Psalm 117:1

One of the virtues of God that calls for praise from our lips is often kept in the background of our minds and not frequently expressed in our prayers and songs. That virtue is God's faithfulness. Yet all the good God does for us is there, because he is everlastingly faithful to his covenant promises given in Christ.

The idea expressed by the psalmist is that God is true to his word. The psalmist states it this way: "The truth of the LORD endureth forever" (Ps. 117:2). And the versification of Psalm 117:1 therefore has it correctly when it states:

His lovingkindness bless,
His constant faithfulness
And changeless truth confess;
Praise ye the Lord.

This fits in so beautifully when in the original we find not "Praise the Lord," but "Praise Jehovah." That name literally means "I AM." There is then no change in him. He is the same yesterday, today, and forever. Never does he say, "I was." Never does he say that he will be different from what he eternally has been. He has kept his word because nothing can make him change his mind or will. What he eternally decreed he will do. What he promised us in Christ will surely come to pass.

The things round about us keep changing. The seasons come and go. The sun rises and sets. The days, weeks, and years fly by and never return. But God is not only here exactly as he eternally was, but his thoughts and desires are eternally the same. He will fulfill every covenant promise in its smallest detail.

Praise him then today for his merciful kindness; but have no doubt in your mind as to whether he will deal in loving-kindness tomorrow and into everlasting life.

When sickness and disease come, when weakness and forgetfulness on your part manifest themselves, do not accuse God of unfaithfulness. Instead, praise him for uninterrupted faithfulness that will bring you through all these shortcomings and woes to what he promised in Christ.

Rest assured that his faithfulness will bring you to his kingdom, where you will faithfully sing his praises.

Read: Psalm 19
Psalter versification: 316

A TREMENDOUSLY IMPORTANT QUESTION

LORD, who shall abide in thy tabernacle? who shall dwell in thy holy hill? —Psalm 15:1

From the days of our early childhood we learned by asking questions. But the answer had to be correct, or we were deceived, and instead of being instructed we were misled. The question had therefore to be asked of one who had the correct answer and could be trusted. And a most important question is the one we find in Psalm 15:1, namely: "LORD, who shall abide in thy tabernacle? who shall dwell in thy holy hill?"

The significance of dwelling with God in his house is expressed in one of the versifications of this psalm in these words:

> Who, O Lord, with Thee abiding,
> In Thy house shall be Thy guest?
> Who, his feet to Zion turning,
> In Thy holy hill shall rest?

We may note two words in this versification that explain the question. Dwelling in God's house is being his *guest* and enjoying a heavenly *rest.*

We all look for physical rest, for we are all weary, because we lie under the curse, having fallen into sin in Adam. And we all, therefore, consider the psalmist's question one of great importance. But consider it in the light of Jesus' words in Matthew 11:28, "Come unto me, all ye that labour and are heavy laden, and I will give you rest." Our deepest concern should be that heavy load of sin, which we carry with us and strive to get rid of and want removed. From that point of view we do have a tremendously important question.

Is that your question? So far today, how heavy has that load of sin felt? And do you really want to get rid of that load of guilt as well as that force of sin that is within you?

To be sure, you want to get from under the punishment of sin that has been upon this world since Adam fell. But do you want to get from under the power and drive of sin that is in your flesh?

You cannot be a guest in God's house as long as you walk in, think, and will sin. The question is whether your sins bother you. If they do, this question of the psalmist will be very important to you. If not, you will be satisfied to dwell in the tents of wickedness.

Read: Psalm 15
Psalter versification: 24:1

AN ONLY POSSIBLE ANSWER

LORD, who shall abide in thy tabernacle? who shall dwell in thy holy hill? —Psalm 15:1

In reading and studying Scripture, one must always take careful note of the words which God uses in the passage. Scripture is his word, and we miss the message in the measure that we slide over any of the words which he uses.

In that important question in Psalm 15:1, "LORD, who shall abide in thy tabernacle? who shall dwell in thy holy hill?" we could easily slide over that word *holy*. But if we do, we will not understand the answer to that question that is given in the remaining verses of the psalm. Because God's house is a holy house, we are given the answer that appears in the psalm.

Look at the question and at the beginning of its answer as we sing it from our Psalter:

> Who, O Lord, with Thee abiding,
> In Thy house shall be Thy guest?
> Who, his feet to Zion turning,
> In Thy holy hill shall rest?
> He that ever walks uprightly,
> Does the right without a fear,
> When he speaks, he speaks not lightly,
> But with truth and love sincere.

It is because God is holy, and we by nature are so unholy, that this is the only possible answer to that question the psalmist asked. Only the holy will be guests in God's house. And to be holy is to be like God, completely cut off from sin and hating sin as completely as he does. Otherwise the door is tightly shut against us. There is no rest for us until there is no sin in us.

That blessedness is promised us, but surely not because we are worthy of it. Appreciate the fact then today that God's Son earned it for us, and that he has already begun the work of making us holy by implanting the seed of a heavenly life in us. As we read in 1 John 3:9, "Whosoever is born of God doth not commit sin; for his seed remaineth in him: and he cannot sin, because he is born of God." The new man in Christ is holy. He reveals this in his constant fight against the old man of sin.

Read: 1 John 3
Psalter versification: 24:1

THE HEART OF THE MATTER

He that walketh uprightly, and worketh righteousness, and speaketh the truth in his heart. —Psalm 15:2

To enter a house whose doors and windows are locked requires a key. To get an audience with a high governmental official demands documents of identification. And in this day of terrorism, you may even have to be searched to see whether you carry dangerous weapons. How much more are there severe requirements to come before the holy God and to be a guest in his house.

Wisely does the psalmist ask in Psalm 15:1, "Lord, who shall abide in thy tabernacle? who shall dwell in thy holy hill?" There also is a reason why Jesus spoke of the keys of the kingdom of heaven.

What the psalmist writes after his question ought to be before our minds daily. He writes: "He that walketh uprightly, and worketh righteousness, and speaketh the truth in his heart" (v. 2). In the verses that follow, the psalmist tells us what an upright walk and doing righteousness are. But the heart of the matter is speaking truth in the heart. There will be no upright walk and works of righteousness unless we speak the truth in our hearts.

Out of the heart are all the issues of our life. Even as every cell in our bodies must receive blood from the heart in order to live, so our whole being is controlled by the spiritual "blood" that comes out of our spiritual center, which Scripture calls the heart.

Since by nature our hearts are spiritually dead—Adam died the day he disobeyed—the answer to the psalmist's question is: "No one!" No one has the right to be a guest in God's house.

Listen to this versification and ask whether it describes you:

> He who walks in righteousness,
> All his actions just and clear;
> He whose words the truth express,
> Spoken from a heart sincere.

How much then ought we to appreciate the love of God that sent his Son to take away all our unrighteousness and to implant in us by his Spirit that beginning of holiness. And the evidence that this life is in us is the confession that we have no righteousness of ourselves.

Read: Matthew 5:1–20
Psalter versification: 26:2

LIVING IN LOVE TO THE NEIGHBOR

He that backbiteth not with his tongue, nor doeth evil to his neighbour, nor taketh up a reproach against his neighbour. —Psalm 15:3

If one speaks the truth in one's heart, one will walk uprightly and work righteousness. This one will then be living in love toward the neighbor. For love toward God always produces love toward the neighbor. And if we live in hatred of the neighbor, it is because we are acting in hatred of God. So serious is the matter.

One cannot face toward the north and toward the south at the same time. One cannot open one's mouth and keep it shut that very same moment. And because God demands that we love the neighbor, it is an act of hatred against God to hate the neighbor.

For that reason David, in Psalm 15:3, in answer to the question as to who will dwell with God in heavenly glory, states: "He that backbiteth not with his tongue, nor doeth evil to his neighbour, nor taketh up a reproach against his neighbour." And one of our versifications declares:

> He that slanders not his brother,
> Does no evil to a friend;
> To reproaches of another
> He refuses to attend.
> Wicked men win not his favor,
> But the good who fear the Lord;
> From his vow he will not waver,
> Tho' it bring him sad reward.

Plainly, what we do today here below reveals whether we will dwell above and taste God's love when we are called out of this life.

No, we will not earn a place in God's house by our works here below. We can earn nothing from him upon whom we depend for everything. But to those whom God has chosen to live with him in covenant fellowship, he gives that new principle of life that causes them to love him. And in that love we will watch our tongues and fight against slander, backbiting, gossip, and foolish speaking of every sort. And we will call all these deeds acts of hatred against God.

Then we will agree with David that holiness must be found in us, if we are to live with our holy God. And we will fight against all the unholiness that still remains in us.

Read: Ephesians 4:17–32
Psalter versification: 24:2

A BLESSED ASSURANCE

He that putteth not out his money to usury, nor taketh reward against the innocent. He that doeth these things shall never be moved. —Psalm 15:5

You are a member of an established congregation. You are called a Christian by those outside as well as by those within the church of God here below. But note the words of David wherewith he closes Psalm 15, namely: "He that doeth these things shall never be moved" (v. 5).

He had asked who shall dwell with God in covenant fellowship in his house of many mansions; and he had answered that it was only those who walk uprightly and work righteousness because they spoke the truth in their hearts. And now he points out that we must *do* these things, if we are to be God's blessed guests. We must do more than agree with David. We must do what is holy to live with our holy God.

Sing the versification that goes thus:

> Doing this, and evil spurning,
> He shall nevermore be moved:
> This the man with Thee sojourning,
> This the man by Thee approved.

Did you note the comfort here? Because of our flesh we will slip and slide into sin. But while we walk uprightly, we have God's word for it that we shall not be moved. And the idea is that our names will not be removed out of the book of life. We will have the forgiveness of our sins, through the blood of God's Son. And if we fall into sin we will be brought back to sorrow and an upright walk, because "he which hath begun a good work in you will perform it until the day of Jesus Christ" (Phil. 1:6).

However, we will have this comfort only while we are doing the things David listed. If no sorrow for sin arises, and we do not feel bad about our sins, we do not even want to live with the holy God in heaven. Then we do not even want the assurance of enjoying the rest Christ prepared.

If you do hate sin and are fighting your sinful flesh, this comfort is yours. Satan cannot recapture you. There is a place for you in God's house of many mansions prepared by Christ and reserved for you. And once you get there, you will never have to move or be removed. It is an everlasting blessedness God has for his people.

Read: 2 Peter 1
Psalter versification: 24:3

A JOYFUL FORETASTE

Make a joyful noise unto the LORD, all ye lands. Serve the LORD with gladness: come before his presence with singing. —Psalm 100:1–2

When in Psalm 100:1–2 the psalmist writes, "Make a joyful noise unto the LORD, all ye lands. Serve the LORD with gladness: come before his presence with singing," there is a matter that we ought to take note of, for a right understanding of these words.

Although it was in God's temple that Israel came before his face, the statement "come before his presence" for us today means "come into his house of prayer upon the sabbath day." And we do well to bear in mind that it is God himself who is speaking these words to us through the psalmist. Remember that he says to us today:

> All people that on earth do dwell,
> Sing to the Lord with cheerful voice;
> Him serve with mirth, His praise forth tell,
> Come ye before Him and rejoice.

We have here a command of God to his people in every nation, tongue, and tribe. And indeed, these have every reason to rejoice and sing. For in his house they meet God in a special way and to a special degree. There they meet him not only in his word preached, but also in his word as it is sung, and while it is sung by the sheep of his flock. And the Sabbath ought to be the happiest day of our week. We ought to look forward to it; and the joy of it ought to carry us through the week ahead. There, indeed, we should be glad that we can join hearts and voices with others to sing his praises.

Regardless of our physical condition, even though we are in financial straits, yea, even when in the last days we cannot buy or sell because we refuse to take the mark of the beast, we will have reason to make a joyful noise and to come before God's presence with singing. For there he gives us spiritual food and drink, assures us that our sins are blotted out by the blood of his Son, reminds us of his faithfulness to his promises, enriches us in our faith, and in all this gives us reason to come before his face singing of his work and grace.

Read: Psalm 100
Psalter versification: 268:1

A REASSURING REASON

Know ye that the LORD he is God: it is he that hath made us, and not we ourselves; we are his people, and the sheep of his pasture. —Psalm 100:3

The psalmist states in Psalm 100:3, "Know ye that the LORD he is God: it is he that hath made us, and not we ourselves; we are his people, and the sheep of his pasture." Plainly he is not referring to the work of creation but to bringing the church into being. For note that he speaks of us as being God's people and the sheep of his pasture.

Truly that is an undeniable reason for coming before his presence with praise and singing. His work of creating calls for praise when we see the smallest creature that is made so delicately, or when we look up into the vast expanse of the heavens. But to come before him as our covenant Father in Christ, as well as our creator, calls for boundless joy and songs.

He has given us church buildings to use, even as he gave Israel a temple where they could meet him. That should fill us with gladness. But what he says there in his house should overwhelm our souls with the truth that he loves us and sent his Son to make us his people, who by nature are Satan's slaves. Indeed, there is reason to come before his presence with singing. And that he cares for us as such a wonderful shepherd should move us to make a joyful noise.

Have this in mind when you enter his courts today, tomorrow, or whenever the next Sabbath arrives. Commit to memory and take with you, as you leave home to come before his presence in his house, these words:

> Know that the Lord is God indeed;
> Without our aid He did us make;
> We are His flock, He doth us feed,
> And for His sheep He doth us take.

What a truth and what a comfort we have in those words! Almighty in power, not in the least dependent upon us, as God he can and will fulfill every word of every promise that he has given us. As sheep of his flock there is nothing we need to fear. We have absolute protection and supply of all that we need and really counts. Make then a joyful noise as you enter his courts. May the confidence of the truth that our shepherd is the almighty God, upon whom all creatures depend, move you to sing with gladness his praises in his house.

Read: Psalm 23
Psalter versification: 268:2

THANKFUL PRAISE

Enter into his gates with thanksgiving, and into his courts with praise: be thankful unto him, and bless his name. —Psalm 100:4

Our singing in God's house must be singing his praises and thanking him for all the blessings of salvation that he gives us. The psalmist in Psalm 100:4 states: "Enter into his gates with thanksgiving, and into his courts with praise: be thankful unto him, and bless his name."

Here we have three words of similar and yet complementary meaning. The broadest word is *praise*, for thanking God and blessing his name are forms of praise. To praise God is to extol him for his virtues. To thank him is to praise him for the virtues which he displays in what he does for us. Blessing his name is praising him for what he is. Therefore, the main thought of the verse is that we praise God when we enter his courts.

We must be a God-praising people. Therefore, we must thank him for all the blessings of salvation which he freely gives us, beginning with sovereign, eternal election in Christ, worked out for us through his Son from Bethlehem through Calvary to heavenly glory, where he is seated as our head and redeemer who is preparing the way for us to come before God's presence in the new Jerusalem.

Therefore also, we must bless his name, as the psalmist does in verse 3. We must bless him as God alone, who saves us without our help and by his own almighty power.

How careful then we ought to be in choosing the songs that we will sing together in his house, but also in our own homes. He made us to be his people and his sheep. And the meaning is that he made us to be a God-centered people. And a God-centered people will also be a God-praising people. The silly songs, the words of unbelief that the world sings, should never be on our lips. And we must not provide our children with God-denying songs. He created music for his own glory and so that we might sing:

With thankfulness enter His gates,
His praise in His temple proclaim;
Your voices in thanksgiving raise,
And bless ye His glorious Name.

Read: Isaiah 51
Psalter versification: 269:3

EVERLASTING MERCY

For the LORD is good; his mercy is everlasting; and his truth
endureth to all generations. —Psalm 100:5

Having called us to praise God, to thank him and bless his name, the psalmist in Psalm 100:5 gives us the reason why he is worthy of our praise. He writes: "For the LORD is good; his mercy is everlasting; and his truth endureth to all generations."

Take note of the fact that he speaks of God's goodness, and then explains that this goodness consists in God's mercy and faithfulness. His mercy covers the whole realm of our salvation. Most of the time the word here translated *mercy* is translated as *kindness* or *loving-kindness*. This covers all the work that God performed for us in Christ, the Son of his love. His faithfulness is the virtue that makes our salvation so very, very sure. Now, back of that faithfulness is his almighty power, because of which he can do as he pleases. Thus behind his faithfulness is the truth that he is God, upon whom every creature depends for every breath of life. We cannot bless his name more fully than to say that he is God.

Because of God's faithfulness we can sing sincerely:

For gracious and good is the Lord,
His mercy to us never ends;
His faithfulness, true to His word,
Thro' ages unending extends.

Be careful then that you do not complain today about any of God's works. Grumbling does not become a child of God. Singing his praises does. And fear for the future will never bring forth joyful singing of thankfulness to God. Unshaken faith in God, as one whose truth endures forever, will produce thanksgiving.

Good and faithful is our God; and our calling is to be good, in that we bless his name and praise him with thanksgiving, and in that we are faithful in coming into his house on the Sabbath with joy in our hearts and songs on our lips that praise him.

If we come that way to God's house, we will, after meeting him, go home even happier than we were when we came. Before you leave home next Sabbath, and on your way to church, think of God's everlasting mercy.

Read: Psalm 136
Psalter versification: 269:4

DAILY PRAISES

Serve the LORD with gladness: come before his presence with singing. —Psalm 100:2

Although the psalmist in Psalm 100:2 exhorts us to serve God in his house of prayer, this also applies to our entire walk of life and to our serving him wherever we are. One of our versifications of "come before his presence with singing" is:

> O make a joyful noise, ye lands,
> And serve the Lord with fear;
> With gladness wait His high commands,
> And with a song draw near.

The psalm does indeed speak of God's gates and courts, referring to the temple. But, as in this versification, we must in all our walk of life, also during the week, wait God's high commands. We must serve him every day and sing his praises seven days a week.

It is so much easier to serve him and sing his praises when we are with other sheep of his flock. But we must not hesitate to do so when we are with those who never step into his house of prayer. The simple truth of the matter is that if we praise God only on the Sabbath, and do not serve his high commands the other six days, our praise is mockery. It certainly is not with sincere gladness.

Not keeping God's commandments means that we deny that he is God. And actions speak louder than words, when our life is one of sin all week. Then we make a noise on the Sabbath that only *sounds* like praise to God. The unbelievers round about us put more stock in what we do than in what we say. Both cannot be true. And we should bear in mind that during the other six days of the week, we are just as surely in God's presence as in his house of prayer on the Sabbath. He is God, and from him we cannot hide.

Very important then it is that we come to his house of prayer to learn more and more of his mercy and faithfulness, but also of our calling to bless his name before those with whom we come in contact during the week and that we show thankfulness to God for his mercy and faithfulness by a walk of love to him. While we walk in sin, our words of thankfulness for salvation from sin are not true. God blesses us daily. And in the measure that we enjoy our salvation we are going to sing praises and walk in love to God.

Read: Psalm 96
Psalter versification: 270:1

AN EXTRA DAY WITH EXTRA CARE

The day is thine, the night also is thine: thou hast prepared the light
and the sun. Thou hast set all the borders of the earth: thou hast
made summer and winter. —Psalm 74:16–17

Every fourth year the whole world becomes aware of what the psalmist wrote in Psalm 74:16–17. There Asaph wrote: "The day is thine, the night also is thine: thou hast prepared the light and the sun. Thou hast set all the borders of the earth: thou hast made summer and winter."

No, every man on earth does not on February 29 confess that leap year is the work of God's hands, and that he controls the days and the nights, by means of the sun and its light, so that we have an extra day in the second month of some years. But no man can deny that there is a difference here, over which man has no control, and that man must abide by what it pleases God to do.

But the child of God sings:

> The day is Thine, and Thine the night,
> And Thine the shining sun;
> At Thy command earth's bounds are set
> And changing seasons run.

And to that truth we must hold.

The thought of the psalmist behind all this is that the church must have no fear of her enemies. God has not lost control when his church is ridiculed, mocked, and persecuted. Things have not slipped out of God's hands when a child of God is desperately ill and dies in what we call the prime of his life. Everything happens exactly on time. The sun rises at the exact moment because God controls it, and the moon is full or new the exact minute of every month and year. What amazing control!

When this day is added to our year, stop to appreciate the fact that Asaph writes in verse 12: "For God is my King of old, working salvation in the midst of the earth." There you have it! God is working salvation in the earth as king over all creation, including Satan and his wicked host.

The time will never be too short for us to get salvation. The days will never be too long, so that we slip away from Christ and the work he accomplished on his cross.

An extra day speaks of extra care that God has for his church. There is no confusion in God's works but perfect order, so that presently we will be brought into heavenly perfection.

Read: Psalm 74
Psalter versification: 205:10

March 1

GOLDEN SILENCE

Truly my soul waiteth upon God: from him cometh my salvation. He only is my rock and my salvation; he is my defence; I shall not be greatly moved. —Psalm 62:1–2

Psalm 62 has been called "David's only psalm." And there is a measure of truth in that title. Surely he wrote many other psalms. But the reason why this one is called his only psalm is the fact that he uses the word *only* so often in it.

The words in our translation of verses 1 and 2 are these: "Truly my soul waiteth upon God: from him cometh my salvation. He only is my rock and my salvation; he is my defence; I shall not be greatly moved." However, that word *truly* can be, and here ought to be, translated as *only*. Then we find him using that word *only* five times in the first six verses of the psalm.

What David means when he states that his soul waits upon God is explained in our versification with these words:

> My soul in silence waits for God,
> My Saviour He has proved;
> He only is my rock and tow'r;
> I never shall be moved.

Notice that we sing: "My soul in silence." That is what David did write. And waiting upon God is being silent before him in the sense that we do not grumble and complain in dissatisfaction at what God has done to us or around us. Indeed, at times we dare to call him unfair and forgetful. No, not with our lips; but notice that David is speaking about what his soul is doing, not his lips. With his lips David is not silent in praying to and praising God. In this psalm he is by no means silent as far as God's praise is concerned. But real trust in God reveals itself in silence as far as faultfinding is concerned.

And surely when we are thinking of our salvation, our trust must be in God alone. He is our salvation, and apart from him there is no hope, as we lie in the midst of sin and death.

Examine your soul today. Is it silent? Is all its trust in God? Can you silently wait for him to show you in the day of Christ that *all* things work together for good to those who love God?

That is golden silence, a silence that pleases God.

Read: Psalm 62
Psalter versification: 161:1

A SURE SALVATION

Truly my soul waiteth upon God: from him cometh my salvation. —Psalm 62:1

David's reason for trusting God for all his salvation is the fact that it all comes from God. So he states it in Psalm 62:1, in these words: "Truly my soul waiteth upon God: from him cometh my salvation."

Surely the most important gift bestowed upon man, since the fall of Adam, is salvation. Rain and sunshine, food and drink, health and life are valuable gifts man receives *from* God. But these all men receive to a degree in God's providence. Salvation, however, brings us to an everlasting life that contains the richest and most blessed fellowship with God that the creature can enjoy. Salvation makes us children of God; and though we were created a little lower than the angels, we will be closer to God than they are now.

Sad to say, however, we are most of the time interested in earthly things. They come first in our minds rather than the blessings of salvation. And we do not see and use them as means wherewith to serve God. But if we are going to appreciate David's words, we must wait for Christ to bring us to holiness, and to a covenant life of fellowship with God that is higher than Adam knew before he fell.

That salvation is absolutely sure. For note that David calls God his rock, his salvation, and his defense. As our rock he is unmovable, and as our defense he is our mighty fortress and high tower. Once again, our versification has it thus:

> My soul in silence waits for God,
> My Saviour He has proved;
> He only is my rock and tow'r;
> I never shall be moved.
> My honor is secure with God,
> My Saviour He is known;
> My refuge and my rock of strength
> Are found in God alone.

Waves of men and evil spirits may assault us. Floods of enemies may sweep over us. But waiting on God, all is well with us. The forces that attack us will be shattered as the waves of the sea are upon the rocks on the shore. Our salvation is sure, for the almighty, unchangeable God is our rock and our salvation.

Read: Romans 8:22–39
Psalter versification: 162:1

SAFE IN GOD'S KEEPING

*He only is my rock and my salvation; he is my defence; I shall
not be greatly moved. —Psalm 62:2*

It would be foolish as well as sinful to claim that we will never fall into sin, and that our faith never wavers. Satan is there to attack us time and time again; and our flesh wants what he dangles before our eyes. If we say that we never slip or slide, we are slipping and sliding in that haughty speech. Then we cannot honestly repeat David's words, which are God's word, when he says of God in Psalm 62:2, "He only is my rock and my salvation; he is my defence; I shall not be greatly moved."

David does not here boast that his soul will not at times fail to wait upon God. But he states that because God is his salvation, his rock, and his defense, he will not fall away and lose his salvation. The idea is that our safety is sure, because it is God who protects us. We do not and cannot stand in our own strength. We can never defend ourselves against an enemy who has had almost six thousand years of experience. A clever, crafty Satan, who could make righteous Adam and Eve fall, can surely make us, who have an old man of sin, turn our backs upon the righteous and holy God.

But he cannot make us fall away from God's grace. He cannot make God hate us, and he cannot keep God from bringing us to a sincere sorrow over our sins. If it all depended upon us, Satan could in a moment kill us spiritually. But he cannot obtain the slightest, most temporary victory over God, who is our rock, salvation, and defense.

Because God is our rock, he with his little finger can crush Satan and grind him to powder. We will not be *greatly* moved. Satan will never strike a fatal blow upon us. He made Peter fall deeply into sin; but our God made the cock crow and caused Peter to weep bitterly over his sin. We will often be moved to commit sin. But to be moved greatly, so that we fall away and God's grace is withdrawn from us, is impossible. The almighty God is our defense.

My soul in silence waits for God,
My Saviour He has proved;
He only is my rock and tow'r;
I never shall be moved.

He proved himself as our Savior in the cross of his only begotten Son.

Read: 2 Corinthians 4
Psalter versification: 161:1

OUR ENEMIES' CERTAIN DEFEAT

How long will ye imagine mischief against a man? ye shall be slain all of you: as a bowing wall shall ye be, and as a tottering fence. They only consult to cast him down from his excellency: they delight in lies: they bless with their mouth, but they curse inwardly. Selah. —Psalm 62:3–4

Although we must love our neighbor, this does not mean that we will have no enemies here below. According to the promise that God gave Adam and Eve after they fell, the world was divided into two groups of people, namely, the seed of the woman and the seed of the serpent. And a fierce unending enmity exists between them, because the seed of the serpent cannot stand those who love God. They cannot love God, and therefore they cannot love those who put their trust in God.

The result is that we are going to suffer at their hands. David knew this and expressed it in Psalm 62:3–4 with those words: "How long will ye imagine mischief against a man? ye shall be slain all of you: as a bowing wall shall ye be, and as a tottering fence. They only consult to cast him down from his excellency: they delight in lies: they bless with their mouth, but they curse inwardly. Selah."

All this became clear when the wicked tried to cast Christ down from his excellency, outwardly claiming that this Seed of the Woman was a blasphemer, while inwardly they were cursing. And that hatred and evil all those for whom Christ died will experience. David is not the only one. All the seed of the woman will know it when they manifest themselves as members of his body.

As we are, or soon shall be, in the season when we consider in a special way Jesus' suffering and death, let us find comfort in David's words. Not we but our enemies shall be as a bowing wall and tottering fence. Our victory is sure. If the enemy slays us, he is only serving as God's tool to bring us to everlasting blessedness. He, not we, will be defeated.

Sing it then in these words of our versification:

> My enemies my ruin seek,
> They plot with fraud and guile;
> Deceitful, they pretend to bless,
> But inwardly revile.
> My soul, in silence wait for God;
> He is my help approved,
> He only is my rock and tow'r,
> And I shall not be moved.

Read: Psalm 46
Psalter versification: 161:2–3

TRUST THAT IS A MUST

My soul, wait thou only upon God; for my expectation is from him. —Psalm 62:5

Trust in God will always be characterized by looking away from self. David revealed this very plainly in Psalm 62. Having stated that his soul trusted in God alone for his salvation, he commands his soul to wait upon God. In verse 1, he stated: "Truly my soul waiteth upon God," and then after reviewing the woes of the wicked's attack upon him, he gives in verse 5 this command to his soul: "My soul, wait thou only upon God; for my expectation is from him."

And it is so important that we say this to our souls. For our souls must say this to our whole being. That our mouths say that we trust in God means nothing, if the soul does not say it. And when the soul says that it trusts in God, it commands our whole being to look up to him for all of our salvation. That soul does not simply say that it is a good idea to trust only in God. Our souls must not simply suggest to our whole being that we look nowhere for salvation but unto God. Our soul must command our whole being to wait in silence upon God.

Our versification exhorts such trust in these words:

On Him, ye people, evermore
Rely with confidence;
Before Him pour ye out your heart,
For God is our defense.

Tell your soul then to trust in God when the unbeliever attacks you or Satan tempts you. Say it when it looks as though God has forsaken and forgotten you. Say it when all goes well, as far as your flesh is concerned. For then you are in danger of forgetting and forsaking him and of trusting in self or in earthly things.

Trust in God is a must. There is not one moment when this is not absolutely essential for our well-being. Our souls must be ordered to trust in God alone. David speaks of his expectation or hope. But there is no hope of salvation unless our souls wait upon God. Rely on him with confidence, for he is our defense. And a more sure and safer defense you cannot find than the almighty, unchangeable God.

Read: Psalm 118
Psalter versification: 161:5

TRUST IN GOD ALONE

Trust not in oppression, and become not vain in robbery: if riches increase, set not your heart upon them. —Psalm 62:10

The standard of living today is so much higher than when David wrote Psalm 62. Even Solomon in all his glory did not have many of the things our flesh enjoys today. He may have had servants to fan him on a hot, sultry day, but he did not know the comfort of air conditioning. He had means to warm his body on a cold wintry day, but he did not enjoy central heating. His chariot ride did not equal the speed, comfort, and smoothness of our automobiles, and he could not fly to a distant point in his realm by jet aircraft as we can. We have so much more than David or Solomon.

How much more necessary then today are David's words in Psalm 62:10, namely: "If riches increase, set not your heart upon them." Or as one of our versifications has it:

> Trust not in harsh oppression's power
> Nor in unrighteous gain;
> If wealth increase, yet on your gold
> Ye set your hearts in vain.

We may enjoy the conveniences God gives us, but we must not let these lessen our trust in him. These earthly treasures do not bring us one smallest step toward our everlasting home. And instead of bringing us into closer fellowship with God, they so often make us forget him. As our earthly goods increase, so often our trust in God will decrease. We look around at these earthly treasures instead of looking up to him who is our rock, salvation, and defense.

How true it is that "If wealth increase, yet on your gold ye set your hearts in vain." These cannot take away one sin. They cannot give us the shortest breath of spiritual life. These cannot enrich our fellowship with God or buy us the smallest part of a place in his house of many mansions. All this is purchased by the blood of Christ; and our trust for it must all be in God and in what he did through his Son.

The only hope we have of not being swept into the lake of fire and of escaping Satan's clever attacks is trusting in God alone. Tell your soul then not to let these earthly things turn you away from God, but to see these earthly objects as God-given means whereby we are to serve him. From him they came. In his service they must be used.

Read: Matthew 6:24–34
Psalter versification: 161:7

THE FOOLISHNESS OF THE WORLDLY WISE

The fool hath said in his heart, There is no God. Corrupt are they, and have done abominable iniquity: there is none that doeth good. —Psalm 53:1

One may be very rich in earthly goods and desperately poor in spiritual life. And one may be honored as one full of worldly wisdom and by God be called a fool. Men there are who teach in colleges and universities and have high-sounding titles and a string of degrees behind their names. Yet, through David, God calls them fools in Psalm 53:1. There we read: "The fool hath said in his heart, There is no God."

These men deny that God created the world. Their explanation of the world's existence is that intense heat and cold acted upon gaseous vapors. But they make no attempt to explain where that gaseous vapor, cold, and heat came from, and thus only push the question back without answering it.

Such men take God's name in vain in order to emphasize their words even while they insist that he does not exist. What folly it is to spend time and money to fight an enemy whom you declare nonexistent!

Very correctly our versification of David's words has it:

Fools in their heart have said,
There is no God of might;
Corrupt are they and base their deeds,
In evil they delight.

We had better be careful, however, because there is so much of this sinfulness and foolishness in us. In our hearts, as we are by nature, is this same folly, and often it comes across our lips.

How often have you ascribed this or that to luck or called this or that good luck or bad luck? You never said: "I was lucky"? Or: "It was just a case of tough luck"? Whenever we ascribe anything to luck, David is used by God to point his finger at us and to tell us that we are behaving as fools.

It is sin and folly to deny God in anything that happens. And by that word *luck* we deny that the everywhere present and almighty God has caused this or that to take place. We rule him out, and our god is luck!

By all means let us start today to praise God, and never let that word *luck* fall from our lips, except when we condemn its use.

Read: Psalm 53
Psalter versification: 146:1

A FOOLISH DELIGHT

The fool hath said in his heart, There is no God. Corrupt are they, and have done abominable iniquity: there is none that doeth good. —Psalm 53:1

It is not difficult to agree with David when in Psalm 53:1 he declares that those who say in their hearts that there is no God are fools. But we ourselves so often need to be warned of our own folly. For there are times when we also say that there is no God.

To realize this, we ought first of all to note that David is speaking of those who say *in their hearts* that there is no God. His words are: "The fool hath said in his heart, There is no God. Corrupt are they, and have done abominable iniquity: there is none that doeth good" (Ps. 53:1).

We ought also to note further that when one says in one's heart that there is no God, that one behaves in a corrupt way, does abominable iniquity, and does nothing that is pleasing in God's sight.

We ought then to hang our heads in shame when we realize that every time we commit a sin, we do so because our hearts say that there is no God whose laws we must keep. Never mind in what form that sin comes, every sin is an act that results from a heart that says that there is no God whom we must serve. Every sin is abominable iniquity. In every sin we say in our hearts that we are God and have no one above us who can tell us what to do.

Listen then once again to the versification in our Psalter:

Fools in their heart have said,
There is no God of might;
Corrupt are they and base their deeds,
In evil they delight.

The very reason why the heart says that there is no God is that this heart delights in evil and finds no joy in doing God's will.

What is more, such a heart also says that there is no Christ. For if there is no God, there is no Son of God, who came in our flesh to save us from our sins and to make us sons of God. In fact, that heart says that it wants no salvation from sin. What a foolish delight that is!

The question, therefore, is whether it is only with our lips that we say that we are Christians. Let us also say it with the heart and reveal in our walk of life that we delight in that which is good in God's eyes.

Read: Proverbs 4
Psalter versification: 146:1

March 9

WHEN A CORRUPT HEART SPEAKS

The fool hath said in his heart, There is no God. Corrupt are they, and have done abominable iniquity: there is none that doeth good. —Psalm 53:1

With the lips one can say what one with the mind knows is not true. Satan knew full well that there is only one true God and what God had told man about the trees of the garden. Yet with the lips he told Eve that eating the fruit of the tree of knowledge of good and evil would not bring death but a wonderful blessing.

And we ought again to bear in mind that David in Psalm 53:1 is speaking of what one says in the heart, and not in his mind. Satan knows full well that there is one God. But that did not keep him from denying God. In his mind he was convinced, in fact so convinced that there is a God that he uses the same name of God, namely, Elohim, the Almighty One, when he spoke to Eve as David does here in Psalm 53:1.

The very fact that all men have an idol reveals that they all know in the mind that there is a God, with power above them and upon which they depend. They even take his name on their lips in their songs, such as "God Bless America."

But what they say in their hearts controls their lives. In that spiritual control center, they say that they hate God. That is why David says that they are corrupt, have done abominable iniquity, and do no good, when in their hearts they say that there is no God.

Saying in the heart that there is no God is to say to all our members that we need not and should not obey God, and that we are a god unto ourselves. That is why the versification sings:

They all are gone aside,
Corruption doth abound;
There is not one that doeth good,
Not even one is found.

Do not then expect the unbeliever to do good. Do not expect the world to improve and crime and sin to be put down by man. We are headed for the days of the antichrist, who is called "that man of sin" in 2 Thessalonians 2:3.

Never mind how much knowledge increases and man understands more of this creation wherein God has placed us. The vile heart of man will make him do more abominable iniquity than we now know.

Read: 2 Thessalonians 2
Psalter versification: 146:3

HATED FOR CHRIST'S SAKE

Have the workers of iniquity no knowledge? who eat up my people as they eat bread: they have not called upon God. —Psalm 53:4

Yesterday we noted that to say in the heart that there is no God is to say in the depth of our being that we hate God. And this means that in the heart we also hate those who confess God and serve him.

As David writes in Psalm 53:4, "Have the workers of iniquity no knowledge? who eat up my people as they eat bread: they have not called upon God." Or as our versification sings it:

> These men of evil deeds,
> Will they no knowledge gain,
> Who feed upon my people's woes,
> And prayer to God disdain?

Do you know this hatred of the unbeliever who says that there is no God? If not, you should seriously search your own heart and look carefully at your walk of life. Are you saying before the world with your words, but also with your deeds, that there is a God and that you love him?

These fools who say that there is no God, David says, do not call upon him. Or as the versification has it, they "prayer...disdain." But what about you? Yes, in your home with your family and in church among fellow saints, you bow your head in prayer and call upon God. But do you do that before unbelievers as well? Do you do so in public places, at work or in a restaurant? Do you openly look to him to bless that food, and give thanks to him for his gifts?

In the measure that you do, the world will have no use for you and will feed upon your woes. You will soon begin to suffer their ridicule and find that they want no fellowship with you.

And the closer we come to the end of time, the more David's words will be our experience. Figuratively they will eat us up as they eat bread.

Jesus said it in John 15:18, "If the world hate you, ye know that it hated me before it hated you." The world hates us because we display Christ before them. And they who crucified Christ will think nothing of eating us up as they eat bread. But there is a God, and he will bless us. He will make the world know its folly and reveal to the unbelievers what wisdom he gave to us in his grace.

Read: Matthew 5:1–16
Psalter versification: 146:4

LOOKING TO GOD IN PRAYER

Have the workers of iniquity no knowledge? who eat up my people as they eat bread: they have not called upon God. —Psalm 53:4

During so-called World War II (a truly worldwide war will not come until the days of the antichrist), it was repeatedly said: "There are no atheists in foxholes." Then God's name came upon men's lips, and they cried to God for help and protection. Yet what David says in Psalm 53:4 is true. Those who say in their hearts that there is no God do not call upon God in prayer. A heart that says that there is no God will surely not call upon him. Such a heart calls it folly to pray to a "nonexistent being."

This is to be understood, for when a man looks heavenward to view the fleecy clouds, he is looking away from the grass at his feet. When he tries to find a coin which he dropped in the beach sand, he is turned away from the clouds above him. And that man who tramples God's law underfoot, because in his heart he says that there is no God, is surely correctly described in the versification we considered yesterday:

These men of evil deeds,
Will they no knowledge gain,
Who feed upon my people's woes,
And prayer to God disdain?

With their minds they know better, and therefore in their desperate situations, when death seems very close, they will cry out for help and safety. With their lips they will call him almighty and confess that they depend upon him. They will clearly reveal that they believe that he is Elohim, that is, the Almighty One who can save them from physical woes. But in their hearts they will still deny him. No sooner is the danger over and their cursing and evil deeds reappear.

Examine your life. Do you confess God in your moments of trouble, and at once? While all goes smoothly for your flesh, do you forget him, or thank him for all his works? This past minute he gave you sixty to eighty heartbeats. Do they go by without thanks at the close of the day, but also at times between your arising and retiring at night?

Say it, as implied in David's words, that in him you "live, and move, and have [all] your being" (Acts 17:28). And call upon him to thank him for all the spiritual life as well as physical life he gives you.

Read: Psalm 121
Psalter versification: 146:4

A HOLY LONGING

Oh that the salvation of Israel were come out of Zion! When God bringeth back the captivity of his people, Jacob shall rejoice, and Israel shall be glad. —Psalm 53:6

Having said that one is a fool if one says in one's heart that there is no God, David clearly reveals that his heart beats loudly with the truth that there is an almighty God whom he loves.

In Psalm 53:6 David brings this psalm to a close with the words: "Oh that the salvation of Israel were come out of Zion! When God bringeth back the captivity of his people, Jacob shall rejoice, and Israel shall be glad." The point is that David by those words reveals not only his confidence that God is able to keep his people safe from those who eat them up as bread, but also his love for that people. And if we love God, we will love his people. Their well-being, yea their full salvation, will be the desire of our hearts. Not out of custom, or because we are forced to do so, but sincerely and with joy we will sing the versification:

> O would that Israel's help
> Were out of Zion come!
> O would that God might early bring
> His captive people home!
> When God from distant lands
> His exiled ones shall bring,
> His people shall exultant be,
> And gladly they shall sing.

Do you have that trust in God? Are you sure that he will come, as he promised, to deliver us completely from the captivity of sin, wherein the devil lured us? The question is not whether we long for, and would be so glad, if only we would be delivered from our aches and pains, from our physical miseries and woes. It is not a question as to whether we would like to escape the lake of fire. There is not a person, including Satan and the fallen angels, who would not rejoice to escape that! But are you interested in deliverance from the captivity of the power of sin, yea from the foolishness of acting as if there is no God and as though Satan's lie is true, that by sinning we become like gods, knowing good and evil?

If in your heart you say, "*That* is what I want!" you are by no means a fool, but an extremely wise person filled with the wisdom of God through the Spirit of his Son. That is a holy longing that will be answered.

Read: Psalm 126
Psalter versification: 146:7–8

KNOWING OUR DEPENDENCY UPON GOD

Except the LORD build the house, they labour in vain that build it: except the LORD keep the city, the watchman waketh but in vain. —Psalm 127:1

From the day they are born, children reveal that they know they are dependent upon their parents. Much of their crying is a call for help in what they cannot do themselves. They want food that they cannot prepare or get and comfort in situations that they cannot change.

As they get older, begin to walk, and grow physically and mentally stronger, they do less asking, and they grow in confidence as to their own abilities. When they become fathers and mothers, they are the ones who must answer such cries and serve the needs of their children.

And we, as children of God, are really put to shame so often by our children. Indeed, boisterous cries can be sinful and are not to be commended. But awareness of, consciousness of our complete dependency upon God is a must. The child's heart can beat without help from the parent. The parent need not give it strength to cry. But there is nothing, no nothing, that we can do without strength given us by God. Every heartbeat comes from him. "In him we live, and move, and have our being" (Acts 17:28).

The psalmist in Psalm 127:1 states this in broader terms, but teaches us our utter dependency upon God. He writes: "Except the LORD build the house, they labour in vain that build it: except the LORD keep the city, the watchman waketh but in vain." And the question for us today is, do we live in the consciousness of the fact that behind everything we do is God, giving us the physical and mental strength to do it? Do we, before we set out to do anything, look to God for strength, or do we go ahead as though we have no need of him? Can we sincerely sing:

Unless the Lord the house shall build,
The weary builders toil in vain;
Unless the Lord the city shield,
The guards a useless watch maintain.

Remember today that even our crying for help, and the desire for it, must come from God. Boast not of what you did, but thank God for what he was pleased to do through you. See all that you have as God's gift, and all you did as his work through you.

Read: Psalm 127
Psalter versification: 359:1

BOWING BEFORE GOD'S WILL

Except the LORD build the house, they labour in vain that build it: except the LORD keep the city, the watchman waketh but in vain. —Psalm 127:1

To know our dependency upon God is important, but there is another side to the picture that the psalmist paints in Psalm 127:1. It is true that "Except the Lord build the house, they labour in vain that build it: except the Lord keep the city, the watchman waketh but in vain." And we are fools if we set out to do anything apart from God. For the word *vain* does mean foolish as well as empty.

Jesus taught us the other side of the truth when he taught us to pray: "Not my will but thy will be done on earth as it is in heaven." For unless it pleases God to have this or that happen, it is absolutely impossible that it will take place. Bear that in mind all day.

God is so often so far away from our thoughts, and we make all kinds of plans as though he does not exist, or at least as though we need not be concerned with his will.

Instead we find ourselves grumbling and complaining because of what he was pleased to have happen. He wanted rain, and we wanted sunshine. He wanted us to be ill, and we wanted health.

So often our works, but also our prayers, spring forth from the proud notion that God must listen to us, rather than that we must bow before his will, no matter what that will is. And we do well to commit that versification of Psalm 127:1 to memory and take it with us every step of our earthly life:

> Unless the Lord the house shall build,
> The weary builders toil in vain;
> Unless the Lord the city shield,
> The guards a useless watch maintain.

Let the cross of Christ speak loudly to you. This was not what we planned, or even understood when it took place. Jesus' disciples all forsook him and fled, thinking all was going wrong.

Yet he was building the house of many mansions and the glorious city called the new Jerusalem. The cross was no vain work but that which brings everlasting blessedness.

Read: Mark 14:26–42
Psalter versification: 359:1

FLEEING FROM FOLLY

It is vain for you to rise up early, to sit up late, to eat the bread of sorrows: for so he giveth his beloved sleep. —Psalm 127:2

A word may be used twice for emphasis. And surely when the word *vain* is used three times in Psalm 127:1–2, we should take careful note of it. Building a house is vain if God is not building it through you. Watching over a city is vain if God is not keeping it safe. And now: "It is vain for you to rise up early, to sit up late, to eat the bread of sorrows: for so he giveth his beloved sleep."

Surely there are times when one must rise up early for a particular work; and we cannot always retire early at night, because of circumstances. Our food is sometimes obtained through difficult toil, even to the point that we are so weary, we would rather sleep than eat. Yet it is folly to do these things, if we are doing so to keep up with the neighbors who have a higher standard of living than we do.

The tragedy is today that we already have so much higher a standard of living than men did in the days of the psalmist. We have it so good compared with men in those days, who had not our labor-saving devices: electricity, furnaces and air conditioners, comfortable, swift automobiles, to mention only a few advances that we have. Yet the versification of the psalmist's words we do well to heed:

In vain you rise ere morningbreak,
And late your nightly vigils keep,
And of the bread of toil partake;
God gives to His beloved sleep.

The simple truth is that we must not ruin our health to increase our wealth. We must not work to seek the things below, to build a house, and to defend a city as the goal of our life. We are to seek the kingdom of God and its righteousness. The natural must serve the spiritual. Life must be protected. The necessary sleep must not be put aside in order to obtain the dainties Satan dangles before our eyes.

We depend upon God and must bow before his will. But we must also thank him for what he does give unto us and not misuse one bit of it. We must serve him and use the sleep that he gives us, so that tomorrow we may have the strength to do his will.

Read: Matthew 6:19–34
Psalter versification: 359:2

March 16

GOD'S FRUITFUL TREES

Lo, children are an heritage of the LORD: and the fruit of the
womb is his reward. —Psalm 127:3

All the houses that were built are there because God built them through men. Every city that escaped the attacks of an enemy or terrorists still stands because God kept it safe. And how true is it not that every child conceived and born appeared on this earth because God brought it forth through a man and woman. As we read in Psalm 127:3, "Lo, children are an heritage of the LORD: and the fruit of the womb is his reward." Men are God's trees who bring forth his fruit by the strength that he gives them.

Even as an inheritance is that which is not earned, so children are a free gift from God. Men and women are active, thinking, willing agents, and children are God's reward to them for their deeds. But children are given, not purchased or earned.

Is there any work of God performed through men that is more amazing? What a wonderful house for the soul is the body! What a gift is the mind and soul that lift man above all the earthly creatures and make him God's image-bearer!

But hold on to the truth that you have children because God willed to give them and brought them forth through you. He decided whether it would be son or daughter and have these or those talents. There is nothing that has life that did not receive it from God. There is no one with this or that nature and ability who did not get it as an inheritance rather than by man's work or wish.

How much thanks then do we not owe to God for giving us children, but also for our own existence and place in this world. Daily we should sing:

Lo, children are a great reward,
A gift from God in very truth;
With arrows is his quiver stored
Who joys in children of his youth.

All boasting is ruled out about the house we built and the city we kept intact. But put aside all boasting also about the children God gave you. And every day, as you see them and their children, look up to God on high and bring your thanks to him. As God's fruitful trees we must also be a God-praising people. He gave us his Son as our savior. But he also gave us children as a free gift that we might praise him.

Read: Genesis 18:1–14
Psalter versification: 359:3

A COVENANT PARENT'S TREASURE

As arrows are in the hand of a mighty man; so are children of the youth. Happy is the man that hath his quiver full of them: they shall not be ashamed, but they shall speak with the enemies in the gate. —Psalm 127:4–5

As the psalmist wrote in Psalm 127:1, "Except the Lord build the house, they labour in vain that build it," so it is true that they who build a household must give God all the credit. Children are God's gift; and even as no one has room to boast of bringing himself into being, no one can rightfully boast of having brought children into being. God brings them into being through man and gives them to man. Man gives God nothing. All is his eternally.

And what a gift children are! As we read in Psalm 127:4–5, "As arrows are in the hand of a mighty man; so are children of the youth. Happy is the man that hath his quiver full of them: they shall not be ashamed, but they shall speak with the enemies in the gate." We may sing it thus:

> Lo, children are a great reward,
> A gift from God in very truth;
> With arrows is his quiver stored
> Who joys in children of his youth.
> And blest the man whose age is cheered
> By stalwart sons and daughters fair;
> No enemies by him are feared,
> No lack of love, no want of care.

God may not have given you a house. You may not own a city. But if he gave you a covenant child, he made you rich with a most precious gift. Many children do not make a man poor. No covenant parent has room to complain about how much it costs to bring up a child. He may not be able to buy or build a house. Many of the dainties of this earth may never be his. But if God gives him a child, he has made him rich with that which lasts beyond this earth and all its treasures. As a covenant parent with covenant children, he will have with him in the house of many mansions, and in the holy city, a gift of God, while the multi-millionaires have seen all their wealth go up in smoke.

Before those who have and fight for gold and silver, he need have no fear, and by all means need not be ashamed of the gift God gave him. No one with gold and silver can take them from him. They are his children forever. Gold and silver are ours only for a few years.

Read: Mark 10:13–16
Psalter versification: 359:3–4

EXTREMELY RICH AND ENDLESS PRAISE

Who can utter the mighty acts of the LORD? who can shew
forth all his praise? —Psalm 106:2

In this season when our thoughts are directed in a special way to the suffering and death of our Savior, we ought to listen to the psalmist in Psalm 106:2. There he states: "Who can utter the mighty acts of the LORD? who can shew forth all his praise?"

And undoubtedly the greatest wonder, the mighty deed of God behind all that which his Son did for us, and that causes his glory to shine forth most beautifully, as well as calls for praise, is the fact that God himself came into our flesh to become one of us. Indeed, his virgin birth was an amazing miracle, a mighty wonder that calls for endless praise. It was a miracle that man cannot begin to duplicate; and there is just nothing like it in all the history of mankind. But more wonderful, more amazing is the fact that through this wonder of the virgin birth God himself became flesh and tabernacled with us so that we could see him and touch him. The Infinite One became finite. The Creator of all became a creature so that he might be our covenant head and represent us.

Truly our salvation is a wonder, and as we consider for a few days what God's Son did for our salvation, our wonder ought to grow, and our praise to God ought to increase. The implications and significance of that incarnation of the Son of God are so great that God himself prepared an everlasting life, so that his people might utter his mighty acts and never come to an end of doing so, nor ever lose the implication and significance of it. Not one of the elect in that new Jerusalem will ever run out of words or think that he sees less reason for praising God.

Do you not see the truth the psalmist declares here in this psalm? Do you not agree with him that, as we have it in our Psalter versification,

> What tongue can tell His mighty deeds,
> His wondrous works and ways?
> O who can show His glory forth,
> Or utter all His praise?

It takes an innumerable host to do that, and an everlasting life. But we should begin that praise today, and by a wonder of his grace we will do so.

Read: Psalm 106
Psalter versification: 290:2

CHRIST CAME TO SAVE US

Give ear, O Shepherd of Israel, thou that leadest Joseph like a flock; thou that dwellest between the cherubims, shine forth. Before Ephraim and Benjamin and Manasseh stir up thy strength, and come and save us. —Psalm 80:1–2

From the day that man fell into sin and God promised to send Christ as the seed of the woman to save us, the believers have looked and prayed that Christ would come. And although the Old Testament saints did not see the Son of God come into our flesh, they did pray for him to come.

We sing their prayers in this versification of Psalm 80:1–2,

> Great Shepherd Who leadest Thy people in love,
> 'Mid cherubim dwelling, shine Thou from above;
> In might come and save us, Thy people restore,
> And we shall be saved when Thy face shines once more.

This was not a literal prayer for Christ's coming in Bethlehem. It was not in their minds a prayer for the wonder of the virgin birth of Christ. But it was a prayer to God that he would visit us with salvation. Literally the psalmist said: "Give ear, O Shepherd of Israel, thou that leadest Joseph like a flock; thou that dwellest between the cherubims, shine forth. Before Ephraim and Benjamin and Manasseh stir up thy strength, and come and save us."

Nevertheless, the very fact that they pray to him, as the Shepherd of Israel, reveals that in effect they were praying for Christ to come. For he himself states in John 10:11, "I am the good shepherd: the good shepherd giveth his life for the sheep."

What about you then? Christ has now come and suffered and died for our sins. Do you daily look back at his cross? Do you mention him in your prayers? Do you ever close your prayers without mentioning this Good Shepherd? Do you plead without a "For Jesus' sake, amen"?

Leave Christ and his cross out of your prayers, and you leave out the only possible ground for the smallest part of the salvation which he earned for his people.

We can and must still pray that he will come again with the full salvation of body and soul. But since he came once and blotted out our sins, we must come to God on the basis of that mighty and important work. The work he did then makes his final coming possible and wonderful.

Read: Psalm 80
Psalter versification: 220:1

HEAVENLY JOY

Then said I, Lo, I come: in the volume of the book it is written of me, I delight to do thy will, O my God: yea, thy law is within my heart. —Psalm 40:7–8

A truth concerning Jesus' coming in our flesh, and concerning his ministry until he was crucified, that is often overlooked or brushed aside is stated prophetically in Psalm 40:7–8. There we read: "Then said I, Lo, I come: in the volume of the book it is written of me, I delight to do thy will, O my God: yea, thy law is within my heart."

Here we have characterized not only his work, during his whole life here below, but also the indispensable requirement for him to be our savior. God's love must be written in his heart, and he must do God's will without one moment of interruption and without one sinful thought or desire.

If Jesus is guilty of only one sin, he cannot save us from our sins. Then he must die for his own sin. If Adam's sin is handed down to him through an earthly father, salvation is hopeless for us. But no, God's law is written in his heart. As the Son of God, no evil thought or desire has arisen in his heart. His heart wants to keep God's law perfectly, even after he came into our flesh. Only such a savior will God accept as the sacrifice for our sins.

This also speaks volumes of what he will do in us. For us he suffered and died. In us he will implant God's law, which is a perfect love for God. He has earned for us, and will when he returns give to us, bodies and souls completely freed from sin. He will make us sing with him:

> Then, O my God, I come, I come,
> Thy purpose to fulfill;
> Thy law is written in my heart,
> 'Tis joy to do Thy will.

He will cause us to come before God's face in the new creation, and there our only desire will be to serve him fully. We will serve with perfect and unceasing joy, doing what he wills to have us do.

What a change that is going to be! Now, we have only a small beginning of that joy and obedience. But keep before your minds that Christ came to make us like himself, and not simply to take away our guilt. He came to take away the power of sin that now rules us, and to make us love God with our whole being. That heavenly joy is in store for us.

Read: Jeremiah 31:31–34
Psalter versification: 109:2

THE ACCEPTABLE SACRIFICE

Sacrifice and offering thou didst not desire; mine ears hast thou opened: burnt offering and sin offering hast thou not required. Then said I, Lo, I come: in the volume of the book it is written of me. —Psalm 40:6–7

Depending on what day the moon is full at that time of the year, the church observes in either March or April the crucifixion of our Lord and Savior. That day is usually called Good Friday. Its significance, however, is expressed far more fully and clearly if we call it Crucifixion Friday. And we do well to bear in mind that what happened on that cross of Christ, that Friday of which Scripture speaks, has significance for us every day of our lives. It is not the day that we observe but the work Christ performed on that day. For it brought us salvation. And though we have a Lenten season, this work speaks of a constant, unending blessedness.

David spoke prophetically of it in Psalm 40:6–7 when he said: "Sacrifice and offering thou didst not desire; mine ears hast thou opened: burnt offering and sin offering hast thou not required. Then said I, Lo, I come: in the volume of the book it is written of me."

The idea here is not that God did not desire or find delight in the sacrifices and offerings of the Old Testament saints. He did, for they revealed their faith in salvation through the shedding of blood and were types of Christ and his cross. But the idea is that these sacrifices were only pictures and did not take away as much as one sin. They pointed to a work of God that would blot out all our sins forever and was required if we were to be justified before him.

That is why David is speaking here of Christ when he says: "Lo, I come: in the volume of the book it is written of me."

Look then to Christ and see all those Old Testament sacrifices and offerings as pictures which God hung up to teach his people that Christ was coming, according to his book, or counsel, and would blot out all our sins. And in that light sing our versification:

> Not sacrifice delights the Lord,
> But he who hears and keeps His word;
> Thou gavest me to hear Thy will,
> Thy law is in my heart;
> I come the Scripture to fulfill,
> Glad tidings to impart.

Read: Matthew 26:36–46
Psalter versification: 111:4

EARS THAT HEAR GOD SPEAK

Sacrifice and offering thou didst not desire; mine ears hast thou opened: burnt offering and sin offering hast thou not required. —Psalm 40:6

The reason, as we saw yesterday, why David in Psalm 40:6 said, "Sacrifice and offering thou didst not desire; mine ears hast thou opened," is that the blotting out of our sins has two requirements. The everlasting punishment our sins call for must be suffered and brought to an end; and the ceaseless obedience he demands of us must be brought to him in full measure.

This no man can begin to do. Only the eternal Son of God can bring an everlasting punishment to an end. He only can bring a full measure of obedience for all of us to the Father. What a gift then it is that God gave, as stated in John 3:16, "God so loved the world, that he gave his only begotten Son, that whosoever believeth in him should not perish, but have everlasting life."

How beautiful then are those words of our versification:

> The off'ring on the altar burned
> Gives no delight to Thee;
> The hearing ear, the willing heart,
> Thou givest unto me.
> Then, O my God, I come, I come,
> Thy purpose to fulfill;
> Thy law is written in my heart,
> 'Tis joy to do Thy will.

Can you say with David: "Mine ears hast thou opened"? From the day that man fell into sin, God said that he would crush Satan's head and save us from his power. In time he sent his Son to do this through his cross. In Ephesians 2:10, through the apostle Paul, he tells us that "we are his workmanship, created in Christ Jesus unto good works," and not because of the good work of believing in his Son.

Has he opened your ears so that you have heard this truth and received it into your heart? Have you heard him say that Christ fulfilled all the conditions that our salvation requires?

If he has opened your ears, you will not boast of your works, but thank him for a free gift. And your offerings will express that thankfulness. You will then say: "All that I am I owe to Thee, Thy wisdom, Lord, hath fashioned me" (Psalter 383:1).

Read: Ephesians 2:1–10
Psalter versification: 109:1

THE REASON FOR JOYFUL SINGING

O sing unto the LORD a new song; for he hath done marvellous things: his right hand, and his holy arm, hath gotten him the victory. —Psalm 98:1

You can suggest singing. You can even command it, as a choir director does when he gives orders to go back to do a line over to get it correctly sung. But you cannot make a sad person sing a joyful song. Singing expresses the condition of the heart. Singing is not merely making sounds with the vocal cords and lips. Sincere singing expresses what is in the heart. You have to have a reason in the heart to sing joyfully.

The psalmist had abundant reason and therefore urges us to join him when in Psalm 98:1 he says: "O sing unto the LORD a new song; for he hath done marvellous things: his right hand, and his holy arm, hath gotten him the victory."

What a reason that is for us to join him! Do I need to urge you to join with him in singing our Psalter versification:

> Unto God our Saviour
> Sing a joyful song;
> Wondrous are His doings,
> For His arm is strong.
> He has wrought salvation,
> He has made it known,
> And before the nations
> Is His justice shown.

Indeed, what a reason for singing! God's right hand and his holy arm has gotten him the victory over sin and death! And that right hand and holy arm is his only begotten Son. He is now seated at God's right hand in our resurrected flesh. But in his person he is God, and the right and holy arm of God that saves us from sin and death.

What a wonder that salvation is, for we do not deserve it. In fact, we deserve the opposite. What a wonder also, for his Son came to us by a virgin birth, and in that flesh brought an everlasting punishment to an end! The holy God dealt with an unholy people in most tender love and mercy!

Appreciate what he did for you. Thank him for it. And sing a new song to him in the season when we consider his Son's suffering for us. But also do that every day of the year. That salvation is a wonderful reason for singing his praises, and for singing joyfully.

Read: Psalm 98
Psalter versification: 262:1

AMAZING FAITH

He hath remembered his mercy and his truth toward the house of Israel: all the ends of the earth have seen the salvation of our God. —Psalm 98:3

It is an amazing faith; and it ought to fill us with awe to notice what faith God wrought in his people years before his Son came in our flesh to save us. The psalmist in Psalm 98:3 writes: "He hath remembered his mercy and his truth toward the house of Israel: all the ends of the earth have seen the salvation of our God."

If the saints in that day could speak and sing thus, is there not a more powerful reason for us to do so today? When, on this side of the cross of Christ, we see what awful, holy wrath God poured out on his Son, and hear him cry out because of the hellish agonies he was suffering on that cross, feeling also the thick, intense darkness that for three hours covered that place where he hung, do we not have a much clearer and more powerful manifestation of God's mercy, and an undeniable reason to sing a new song unto him?

Mercy is kindness, pity, compassion. And if we consider what we deserve and was poured upon Christ, what kindness it was, what mercy upon us, when God poured all that agony on his Son, so that we might escape every single bit of it!

Long before that cross, believers in the Old Testament times spoke of God's mercy, when God delivered Israel from far more limited suffering that men tried to inflict upon them. Long before the Atlantic Ocean was crossed and the Americas were discovered, the saints sang that "all the ends of the earth have seen the salvation of our God" (Psalm 98:3). And today with the Scriptures translated into so many languages, the church being found in countless nations, tongues, and tribes, that salvation has truly been universally made known.

Shall we not then in the Lenten season, but also all the year around, loudly and lustily sing our Psalter versification:

> Truth and mercy tow'rd His people
> He hath ever kept in mind,
> And His full and free salvation
> He hath shown to all mankind.
> Sing O earth, sing to Jehovah,
> Praises to Jehovah sing;
> With the swelling notes of music
> Shout before the Lord, the King.

Read: Matthew 27:33–50
Psalter versification: 261:2

SINGING A MOST DIFFICULT SONG

O sing unto the LORD a new song; for he hath done marvellous things: his right hand, and his holy arm, hath gotten him the victory. The LORD hath made known his salvation: his righteousness hath he openly shewed in the sight of the heathen. —Psalm 98:1–2

In our natural life it is so much easier to learn a new song than to learn an equal number of lines that do not have rhyme and rhythm. Yet to sing, as the psalmist exhorts us in Psalm 98:1–2, with these words, "O sing unto the LORD a new song; for he hath done marvellous things: his right hand, and his holy arm, hath gotten him the victory. The LORD hath made known his salvation: his righteousness hath he openly shewed in the sight of the heathen," is a most difficult thing to do. Note carefully that we are exhorted to sing of salvation and of God's righteousness.

Indeed, to sing this with the lips is not difficult. But to sing it with the heart and unto God is something else. Those two facts must be borne in mind. We must sing, with the heart and unto God, of the salvation we have in the righteousness of Christ, who is God's holy arm.

This song is not new in that it has different music and has in it new thoughts that have not been sung before by others. God's work is unchangeably what he promised the day we fell with Adam into sin. Salvation is one sure work God's people have known since Adam and Eve heard it. But to sing of salvation with the heart is something new to him whose songs, as he is by nature, express the lust of his flesh, the lust of his eye, and the pride of life.

And even though we may know all about that salvation and righteousness of God, singing it to him is not only difficult but, as we are by nature, impossible. We must be born again by his right hand to

Sing a new song to Jehovah
For the wonders He hath wrought;
His right hand and arm most holy
Triumph to His cause have brought.
In His love and tender mercy
He hath made salvation known,
In the sight of ev'ry nation
He His righteousness hath shown.

Be honest with yourself. What is it you like to listen to over your radio, off the tapes and records which you buy? What songs rise up in your mind and do you sing at work and in the home? Is it Christ and what he did for us to bring us the righteousness of God? Do you sing of his cross?

Read: Psalm 96
Psalter versification: 261:1

HIS AGONY OF GETHSEMANE

Save me, O God; for the waters are come in unto my soul. I sink in deep mire, where there is no standing: I am come into deep waters, where the floods overflow me. —Psalm 69:1–2

We can understand Jesus' prayer in Gethsemane, and that his sweat fell as great drops of blood to the ground (Luke 22:44), when we realize that he stood at the top of the stairway leading down to hell; and he saw what he would have to suffer on his cross for our sins.

This is also expressed in Psalm 69:1–2, where David, as the type of Christ, writes: "Save me, O God; for the waters are come in unto my soul. I sink in deep mire, where there is no standing: I am come into deep waters, where the floods overflow me."

No wonder then that Jesus prayed for another way to save us than this way of suffering God's holy wrath. His love for God made it so hard for him to be cut off from God's fellowship that we can understand the versification:

> Save me, O God, because the floods
> Come in upon my soul;
> I sink in depths where none can stand,
> Deep waters o'er me roll.

What agony he must suffer for us in his soul! Those floods of waters are the awful, holy wrath of God against sin. Jesus sees already that he will suffer that which will make him cry out: "My God, why hath thou forsaken me?" (Matt. 27:46).

Even the anticipation of being forsaken of God was intense agony for him. It was what God would take away from him and not what men would do to him that gave him so much agony. He would not enjoy God's love but would be cut off from his fellowship.

But what does heaven mean for you and me? Is it merely being cut off from physical aches and pains, bodily miseries? Could fellowship with God, living with him in his house of many mansions, seeing him smile down upon us in his love, be lacking, and we would still call it heaven?

When you pray, "Save me, O God," be sure that you are seeking joy for your soul, the joy Jesus spoke of when he said to the penitent thief: "To day shalt thou be with me in paradise" (Luke 23:43). The joy of being with Christ is heaven. To be cast away from God is the agony of Gethsemane.

Read: Psalm 69
Psalter versification: 184:1

FRIEND OR FOE?

Yea, mine own familiar friend, in whom I trusted, which did eat of my bread, hath lifted up his heel against me. —Psalm 41:9

To have enemies who openly oppose is one thing; but it is quite another thing to have enemies with a false front. Satan as such an enemy approached Eve in paradise, thus also through Judas Iscariot he approached Jesus in the garden of Gethsemane, and today he attacks us through crafty, deceitful enemies.

We sing of that in our versification with these words:

> Yea, he who was my chosen friend,
> In whom I put my trust,
> Who ate my bread, now turns in wrath
> To crush me in the dust.

Or as David wrote it in Psalm 41:9, "Yea, mine own familiar friend, in whom I trusted, which did eat of my bread, hath lifted up his heel against me."

Anger can easily arise in our souls when we read of the deceitfulness of Judas, when he betrayed Jesus with a kiss (Matt. 26:49). But the question is, Are you angry with the devil? Do you loathe him, or consider him your friend?

It is easy to be angry with Judas and stop right there. Satan who moved and used Judas seems like such a mystical being. We talk about him and may even with the mouth condemn his works. Yet do you see him as a person and hate him as an enemy of Christ? Is he your friend or your foe?

The sad reality is that we are so often pleased with him and consider him as our friend. We like the things into which he leads us. Is he not the one who so often makes life enjoyable for us?

But remember that what he did to Jesus through Judas he is continually doing to us, and he lifts his heel against us. He uses men who pose as Christians and lovers of Christ seemingly concerned with our spiritual well-being. Through them he comes with such crafty, subtle false doctrines. Is not the world full of doctrines, while only one is what God says?

Remember then Gethsemane and the treachery of Judas. Be on your guard and keep in mind that from the beginning Satan's approach and attack is deceitful. But remember, too, that God used him to bring his Son to the cross for our salvation. Satan cannot win. God's counsel stands.

Read: Matthew 26:47–57
Psalter versification: 113:8

THE SWEETNESS OF GOD'S LOVE

They gave me also gall for my meat; and in my thirst they gave
me vinegar to drink. —Psalm 69:21

Exhausted after not getting one wink of sleep the night before, having had a crown of thorns pressed into his brow, Jesus was weary and undoubtedly showed it upon his face. For we read in Matthew 27:34, "They gave him vinegar to drink mingled with gall."

This was also prophesied in Psalm 69:21, where David spoke of his own persecution. There we read: "They gave me also gall for my meat; and in my thirst they gave me vinegar to drink." These words are versified in our Psalter thus:

They gave me bitter gall for food,
And taunting words they spake;
They gave me vinegar to drink,
My burning thirst to slake.

Outwardly to onlookers this might have seemed an act of mercy to a thirsty one; but the contents of the cup spoke of hatred and base cruelty. That gall and that vinegar revealed how bitter the hearts of those who gave them were toward God's Son and thus toward God.

However, let it be borne in mind that Jesus had to taste far greater bitterness than all the men in the world could produce. Yes, he must suffer the hatred of man. That, too, is part of the punishment he must suffer for our sins. But this is only a small part of the punishment. All the bitterness of hell must be endured and brought to an end. And all that bitterness he must not refuse and spit out after tasting it. He must and did drink the full vial of God's wrath.

But because he did drink every drop of that bitterness, we will taste God's love and mercy. We will drink of the water of life, because God has through Christ and his cross prepared for us the fountain of everlasting life that will never run dry.

Though we in this life will know the bitterness in men's hearts that makes peace on earth impossible for man to realize, we will have peace on earth, because we already have peace with God. And soon we will enter a world that has no gall or vinegar but has joys and blessings to taste and enjoy without end.

Read: Matthew 27:29–38
Psalter versification: 185:7

AN AWFUL AND REVEALING PICTURE

Many bulls have compassed me: strong bulls of Bashan have beset me round. They gaped upon me with their mouths, as a ravening and a roaring lion. —Psalm 22:12–13

A camera was unknown in the day when Jesus was nailed to his cross. What happened there, however, is pictured by words which God gave to man to write. There must have been a large crowd and shameful noise!

Our Psalter versification, where David paints a picture of his own experiences as a type of Christ, expresses it thus:

> Unnumbered foes would do Me wrong,
> They press about Me, fierce and strong,
> Like beasts of prey their rage they vent,
> My courage fails, My strength is spent.

David says it in Psalm 22:12–13 with these words: "Many bulls have compassed me: strong bulls of Bashan have beset me round. They gaped upon me with their mouths, as a ravening and a roaring lion."

What an awful picture! And remember that it is the Son of God hanging there on that tree, one who never committed one sin and had done so much good: healing the sick, casting out evil spirits, and preaching the gospel of God's kingdom. It is not putting it too strongly with David to say that beasts, strong bulls, and roaring lions attacked him.

No man can touch or see God. But when God came into our flesh, man revealed clearly, and painted an awful picture that clearly reveals, what he thinks of God. Yea, Calvary shows clearly that if he could, man by nature would kill God and get rid of him!

What a wonder then that salvation gives us hearts that love him, seek him, and praise him. What an amazing grace that the God whom our natures wanted to kill has given us faith to see our devilish natures and to want the salvation which he realized by that cross.

This calls for everlasting thanks and praise. And God has prepared a kingdom where we will unceasingly forever, in an everlasting life, thank and praise him for what he did for us through the cross of his Son.

The cross is an awful and revealing picture of man's heart. But God in his Son paints for us a beautiful and everlasting picture of his love.

Read: John 19:1–18
Psalter versification: 47:7

FROM EARTHLY SHAME TO HEAVENLY GLORY

They part my garments among them, and cast lots upon my vesture. —Psalm 22:18

It was not only what the wicked gave Jesus, but it was also what they took away from him that revealed the devilishness of their hearts. They gave him a crown of thorns, stripes upon his back, blows upon his head, a purple robe, and a reed in his hand. But also, as David said in Psalm 22:18, "They part my garments among them, and cast lots upon my vesture."

Now, surely this was a humiliating thing. But it is also quite evident that they were looking forward to his death. For it is at the moment of death that one loses all one's earthly possessions. The enemy was doing before his very eyes what may be done only after death. What is more, they took from his mother, brothers, and sisters what they had a right to divide and distribute. Even if he were a criminal worthy of death, these clothes were still his. And if after his death his nakedness is exposed to the eyes of all who passed by, it is one thing, but an entirely different thing to do so while he was conscious and still alive. Fitly we sing:

> While on My wasted form they stare,
> The garments torn from Me they share,
> My shame and sorrow heeding not,
> And for My robe they cast the lot.

Indeed, shame and sorrow are heaped upon him. The wicked have absolutely no use for him. They heaped upon him all the suffering and shame that they could in that day, while still, behind a false front, acting as though outraged by what they called blasphemy.

But we ought to appreciate the fact that he lost everything, including his life, so that we might gain everything in an everlasting life that brings us above and beyond all the cruelty and hypocrisy of Satan and of men whom he uses.

To us God gives robes of righteousness and bodies that know no sorrow or shame. Jesus deliberately lost all earthly things so that we might gain heavenly blessings that are indescribably rich. As Paul writes in 1 Corinthians 2:9, "Eye hath not seen, nor ear heard, neither have entered into the heart of man, the things which God hath prepared for them that love him."

Read: John 19:19–24
Psalter versification: 47:9

A SIGNIFICANT QUESTION

My God, my God, why hast thou forsaken me? why art thou so far from helping me, and from the words of my roaring? —Psalm 22:1

Before the three hours of darkness fell, while Jesus hung on the cross, he answered a question; but during those hours of darkness he asked a very significant question. In answer to the penitent thief, who requested being remembered when Jesus would come into his kingdom, Jesus assured him that he would be with him in paradise that very day. But his own question is the one David asked in Psalm 22:1, namely: "My God, my God, why hast thou forsaken me?"

This question expresses the awfulness of the agony that he was suffering for our sins. It was not a physical, bodily misery about which he cries. Nor was he questioning God's justice in pouring all this upon him. He knew full well that he must lay down his life for his sheep, and he was willing to do so. No, the question expresses his anguish, or if you will, the extreme cost spiritually for him to blot out our sins.

He loved God perfectly and delighted in God's fellowship. Even a momentary or partial denial of that fellowship would be agonizing for him. And now he was completely cut off from enjoying that love of God and sweet communion with him.

Note that he has not forsaken God. For he cries out, "My God, my God." And as our versification has it:

> My God, My God, I cry to Thee;
> O why hast Thou forsaken Me?
> Afar from Me, Thou dost not heed,
> Though day and night for help I plead.

We have, no doubt, many a time run to God in prayer, seeking his help to benefit our earthly lives. But the question is whether we are Christlike in this respect, that we want to taste God's love and would consider it a tremendous loss to be cut off from enjoying his fellowship.

Would your days be dark and gloomy if you knew that God would withdraw his love from you? You forsook him many a time and laughed and sang during those moments. Would you laugh and sing if you knew that God had no covenant fellowship for you? What means most to you, your physical or your spiritual miseries?

Read: Matthew 27:39–53
Psalter versification: 47:1

FIRST THINGS FIRST

My strength is dried up like a potsherd; and my tongue cleaveth to my jaws; and thou hast brought me into the dust of death. —Psalm 22:15

Down unto death Thou leadest Me,
Consumed by thirst and agony;
With cruel hate and anger fierce
My helpless hands and feet they pierce.

Such is our versification of Psalm 22:15, where David wrote: "My strength is dried up like a potsherd; and my tongue cleaveth to my jaws; and thou hast brought me into the dust of death." Plainly here we have a prophecy of Jesus' words on the cross: "I thirst" (John 19:28).

It is, however, interesting to note that in John 19:28 we read it like this: "After this, Jesus knowing that all things were now accomplished, that the scripture might be fulfilled, saith, I thirst." Undoubtedly, then, he spoke these words after the three hours of darkness and his cry: "My God, my God, why hast thou forsaken me?" (Matt. 27:46). For John states that the Scriptures were fulfilled, and his suffering the hellish agonies fulfilled the requirements for our salvation. He had completely suffered the wrath of God against our sins and began to feel the miseries of his body again. For almost twenty-four hours he had not had a drop of water to drink while under tremendous physical strain.

What an example we have here! By some it is claimed that Jesus cries of thirst for God's fellowship. However, John points to the fact that all was accomplished. The agony of being forsaken of God is past. We should therefore see that Jesus rates the spiritual suffering of being forsaken of God above his physical miseries. Not till all the misery of being forsaken of God is past does he become aware of his bodily woes.

Are you ready to put the spiritual first? Can you put your physical, material needs behind you to seek and enjoy the spiritual things of God's kingdom? Is God's love to you more important than this world and its gold and silver and fleshly pleasures? Are first things first in your life? Remember that Jesus told us first to seek the kingdom of heaven and its righteousness. A good example he certainly reveals here to us.

Read: John 19:25–42
Psalter versification: 47:8

A BLESSED HOPE

For thou wilt not leave my soul in hell; neither wilt thou suffer thine Holy
One to see corruption. —Psalm 16:10

The child of God believes not only what has taken place, but also what surely will take place in God's appointed time. He also sings of this in our versification of Psalm 16:10 in these words:

> I know that I shall not be left
> Forgotten in the grave,
> And from corruption, Thou, O Lord,
> Thy holy one wilt save.

David states it this way: "For thou wilt not leave my soul in hell; neither wilt thou suffer thine Holy One to see corruption" (Ps. 16:10).

These words contain a truth that we should hold to especially on the day between Jesus' death and resurrection. For the word *hell* is here more clearly translated as *grave*. And the word *for* reveals that here we have the reason for David's statement in the preceding verse that "my flesh also shall rest in hope" (v. 9). When we die, our flesh rests in hope of being raised again. For we believe in the glorious truth of Christ's death and resurrection as our covenant head. On Crucifixion Friday he had triumphantly cried out: "It is finished" (John 19:30). Our salvation was purchased. God's Son had earned it for us!

Therefore, today, no matter what happens and how badly our bodies are ravaged by disease, wasted away by fierce fevers, crushed and even blown to pieces by an explosion, or burned by fire, we have hope that our bodies will not remain in their graves, but be raised and be like the glorious body of Christ, incorruptible, immortal, powerful, spiritual, and honorable.

What a blessed truth then the cross and death of Christ presents us! What a blessed hope we have because of that work finished on the cross! Because our justification was finished, our glorification is absolutely sure. Our hope is not a wish, but it is a confident expectancy based upon the word of our God, who cannot lie, and upon a finished work that gave us the right to it.

Let this blessed significance of what took place almost two thousand years ago be with you today and every day, so that you can close your eyes in sleep of death with this blessed hope of waking up in heavenly glory.

Read: Psalm 16
Psalter versification: 28:4

A SONG OF GLORIOUS VICTORY

O sing unto the LORD a new song; for he hath done marvellous things: his right hand, and his holy arm, hath gotten him the victory. —Psalm 98:1

Three short words, spoken the day Jesus rose from the dead, should have tremendous significance for us today. The angel said to the women who came to Jesus' open tomb: "Fear not ye" (Matt. 28:5). The soldiers appointed to watch the tomb were so frightened when the angel appeared that they fell to the ground as if they were dead men. And they had reason for fear. The women, however, because they were of Christ's sheep, had reason to sing:

> Come, let us sing before the Lord
> New songs of praise with sweet accord,
> For wonders great by Him are done,
> His mighty arm has vict'ry won.

And the angel had told them this as well, for he said: "He is not here: for he is risen, as he said" (Matt. 28:6). The psalmist had stated this prophetically in Psalm 98:1 with these words: "O sing unto the LORD a new song; for he hath done marvellous things: his right hand, and his holy arm, hath gotten him the victory." Yes, it was a victory over sin and death.

When sin is conquered, death is destroyed! When guilt is gone, punishment vanishes into thin air. And Christ, as God's holy arm, removed that guilt by his death. Christ, as God's right hand, had broken the shackles of death and the grave, because our sins were paid for in full. What a victory! What a day to remember with songs of praise to God!

As Paul wrote in Romans 4:25, "Who was delivered for our offences, and was raised again for our justification." And the word *for* means *because of* or *on account of*, so that it was on account of our justification that he was raised. He was not raised in order to justify us, but because he had done so.

The world has its Easter rabbits and Easter eggs, which have nothing to do with the removal of sin. They in no way even suggest this marvelous work of God accomplished through the cross of his Son. They sing the old song of sin that Satan gave them to sing, turning their thoughts away from Christ and his cross.

Fear not ye, but sing this new song of a glorious victory over sin.

Read: Matthew 28:1–10
Psalter versification: 264:1

WALKING IN GOD'S LAW

Blessed are the undefiled in the way, who walk in the law of the LORD. —Psalm 119:1

From a spiritual point of view there are only two places to walk. We either walk in God's law, or we walk outside of that law. Men who, in the early days of our country's settlement, lived outside the laws of men were called outlaws. But Scripture calls those walking outside of God's law transgressors or trespassers. For sin is always a going into places where our feet may not go, or from another point of view, it is a passing over the line drawn by God.

The psalmist puts it this way in Psalm 119:1, "Blessed are the undefiled in the way, who walk in the law of the LORD." And did you notice that walking outside of God's law causes one to be defiled?

It is not simply a case of being where we ought not be. It is a case of having a blemish, a mark of imperfection. When we sin, we lose our clean slate and get a mark of guilt upon it. That is why our versification of this psalm has:

How blest the perfect in the way
Who from God's law do not depart,
Who, holding fast the word of truth,
Seek Him with undivided heart.

Our flesh does not agree with these words. For our flesh it is bliss to walk in sin. And we will, if we only can, go as far away from God's law as we can. The sad truth is that we are always happy when we are breaking God's law. For our flesh, to walk in God's law is boring. How much, for example, does not the sabbath day deny our flesh! How much more pleasure do we not get when we disobey the authorities put over us?

But the word of God stands! The only place where we will have and enjoy that which is truly a blessing is to be in the sphere marked off by God's law. And that sphere is that of walking in love to God and to the neighbor.

Walk in love to God, and you will enjoy God's love for you. Walk as his Son did, and you will know the joy of what that Son did for you. Only while walking in the light can you enjoy it.

Read: Psalm 119:1–16
Psalter versification: 321:1

SEEKING GOD WHOLEHEARTEDLY

Blessed are they that keep his testimonies, and that seek him with the whole heart. —Psalm 119:2

Many words are used in Scripture to call attention to the great significance of God's law for us. A very unique and interesting one is found in Psalm 119:2. There we read: "Blessed are they that keep his testimonies, and that seek him with the whole heart." The ten commandments are called God's testimonies.

Did you ever think of God's law that way? A testimony is a statement a witness makes in court. And it makes no difference whether you think now of the ten commandments or, as Jesus gave it to us in a few words, that we love God and for his sake love our neighbor; the testimony of his law is that he is God.

One fundamental truth that runs through God's law is that he, and he only, is God and must be served by all continuously. Does not the law begin with the words: "And God spake all these words, saying, I am the LORD thy God" (Ex. 20:1–2)? And the first commandment therefore calls to us and tells us: "Thou shalt have no other gods before me" (v. 3).

That he alone is God you must say with your whole heart and in every deed you perform, whether it be of the mind, will, or strength. That is why we must heed what we sang yesterday, namely:

How blest the perfect in the way
Who from God's law do not depart,
Who, holding fast the word of truth,
Seek Him with undivided heart.

For our heart is the spiritual control center of our being. It determines what every member and faculty of our being performs. Out of it comes every deed that we perform.

Let me counsel you, therefore, to live according to and to keep God's testimony that he is God. Hold fast his word of truth and not Satan's lie, as Adam did and led us into the curse. Follow in the steps of Christ, who is the last Adam; and then you will enjoy the blessedness that he realized for us. He kept God's testimonies and called him God in all his deeds, even while suffering hellish agonies on his cross. And now he is living proof that they who serve God with their whole heart are blessed and will receive everlasting glory in God's kingdom.

Read: Matthew 5:1–20
Psalter versification: 321:1

DIRECTED BY GOD'S LAW

O that my ways were directed to keep thy statutes! Then shall I not be ashamed, when I have respect unto all thy commandments. —Psalm 119:5–6

When one is in a strange city and desires to find a certain building, or park, or any other point of unique interest, one does well to follow carefully the instructions given and the signs that mark the way.

And to enjoy true, lasting blessedness, we must follow God's law as the compass to bring us there. When God's testimonies tell us to go north, and we go east, west, or south instead, we will not reach that blessedness. It is for that reason that the psalmist in Psalm 119:5–6 cries out: "O that my ways were directed to keep thy statutes! Then shall I not be ashamed, when I have respect unto all thy commandments."

Here we find another word for God's law, namely, statutes. And statutes are things fixed or established, something decreed. Here it is that which is decreed for God's image-bearer to perform here on this earth.

If we turn to our Psalter versification, we find this interesting interpretation:

> My wav'ring heart is now resolved
> Thy holy statutes to fulfill;
> No more shall I be brought to shame
> When I regard Thy holy will.

How true it is that we have wavering hearts that do go south, east, and west, when God orders us to go north. But also how true it is that by God's grace, our ways begin to be directed to keep his statutes. And then we are not brought to shame. The idea is that, no longer foolishly disregarding God's statutes, we are not walking in a way wherein we ought to be ashamed of ourselves. Depart from God's statutes, and we walk foolishly as well as sinfully. Then shame must cover our faces. Have respect to God's commandments, and there is no need to be ashamed of our deeds.

Will you, when you go to bed tonight, be ashamed of your walk? If so, then make this prayer of the psalmist yours: "O that my ways were directed to keep thy statutes!"

The word *respect* literally means *look*. Do that. Look at God's compass, and then go with it and not against or away from its reading. Arriving at the blessedness at the end of that way, you will not be ashamed and disappointed but reach everlasting joy and gladness.

Read: 1 John 2:18–29
Psalter versification: 321:3

PRAISE FROM AN UPRIGHT HEART

I will praise thee with uprightness of heart, when I shall have learned thy righteous judgments. I will keep thy statutes: O forsake me not utterly. —Psalm 119:7–8

Plant a live seed properly, and you are going to see results. Plant an assortment of seeds, and each one will bring forth its own kind of plant with its own peculiar leaves, flowers, and fruits. So it is when God plants in us the new life of Christ. Then a life that keeps God's statutes will appear.

The psalmist in Psalm 119:7–8 says this in these words: "I will praise thee with uprightness of heart, when I shall have learned thy righteous judgments. I will keep thy statutes: O forsake me not utterly." And the point is that when God gives us an upright heart, by implanting the life of Christ in us, we are going to do what Christ did. We are going to be plants whose leaves are God's statutes and whose flowers and fruit are praise to God. And by our keeping God's statutes, our deeds speak louder than our words. They, too, say that God is God alone, and that we are his humble, willing servants. These flowers, this praise, will be seen in us.

Now, it takes the seed of that new life to make us learn God's commandments and call them righteous judgments. Having the life of Christ, we say with him that what God judges to be right is right, and what he judges to be sin we condemn and hate with him.

Still more. If we really have that new life in us, we will delight so much in it that we will pray to God that he never take it from us. Our Psalter versification has it beautifully this way:

To Thee my praise sincere shall rise
When I thy righteous judgments learn;
Forsake me not, but be my guide,
And from Thy truth I will not turn.

There you have it! Knowing God's law because we have been given an upright heart, we will want God to continue to be our guide. We will not want him to forsake us, that is, take away that new life in Christ from us. But we will want to be led ever more deeply into keeping his law and into praising God.

How about it? What leaves, flowers, and fruit does your life display? Do your actions say that you want God to be your guide, or is it more delightful to have Satan mislead you?

Read: John 15
Psalter versification: 321:4

A COMPLETE LOSS

The LORD looked down from heaven upon the children of men, to see if there were any that did understand, and seek God. They are all gone aside, they are all together become filthy: there is none that doeth good, no, not one. —Psalm 14:2–3

Do you realize that there is not one basic truth of Scripture that we must believe, if we are to understand and appreciate our salvation, that is not taught in the book of Psalms?

One of these is the very humiliating truth that we come into this world spiritually dead. Not spiritually sick, weak, or paralyzed but *dead*, which means that we must be given a new life before we can even want to be saved. For God clearly teaches this in Psalm 14:2–3, where he tells us: "The LORD looked down from heaven upon the children of men, to see if there were any that did understand, and seek God. They are all gone aside, they are all together become filthy: there is none that doeth good, no, not one." Notice that *all* are gone aside and become filthy—and the Hebrew word here means that they stink like a dead body—and that there is *not one* that does good. Had man kept just a little spiritual life, he would have performed at least one good work.

But here is the truth God told Adam before he fell. He would die the *day* that he sinned. That day he did not die physically, although death began in his body, but he did die spiritually that day. And that is why Paul writes in Ephesians 2:1 that God quickens—that is, makes alive those "dead in trespasses and sins."

Remember that when you sing the versification of David's words:

From righteousness they all depart,
Corrupt are all, and vile in heart;
Yea, ev'ry man has evil done;
Not one does good, not even one.

Hold on to that truth. Ours was a complete loss. We lost all ability to love God and serve him. We do not help God save us. He even has to give us the desire to be saved. For dead men do nothing, even as children contribute nothing to their conception or birth. They neither ask for it nor help make it possible.

Take that truth with you today. Let it humble you before God and help you to be thankful for what he has done for you. How much is it not then that we owe him? By all means do not think that we help God and let him save us. Dead men have nothing to say about what happens to them.

Read: Psalm 14
Psalter versification: 23:3

ASCRIBING TO GOD ALL HIS GLORY

O sing unto the LORD a new song; for he hath done marvellous things: his right hand, and his holy arm, hath gotten him the victory. The LORD hath made known his salvation: his righteousness hath he openly shewed in the sight of the heathen. —Psalm 98:1–2

It would not only be unfair but plainly untrue to say that although Jesus healed many of their painful diseases, he never raised one person from the dead. Scripture clearly ascribes to him the resurrection of Jairus' daughter, of the widow of Nain's son, and of Lazarus.

Yet it is not a rare thing today to hear men deny that God raises us from spiritual death. Man, they say, did not die spiritually when he fell in paradise. He still kept the ability to want salvation, before God caused him to be born again with a new spiritual life.

Actually this is an attempt to rob God of his glory. It paints a picture of God wherein he is less glorious than he is in the picture Scripture gives us of him. But listen to what God says himself through the psalmist in Psalm 98:1–2, "O sing unto the LORD a new song; for he hath done marvellous things: his right hand, and his holy arm, hath gotten him the victory. The LORD hath made known his salvation: his righteousness hath he openly shewed in the sight of the heathen."

Note that we are to sing a new song, a song we just could not sing and did not want to sing because we were spiritually dead. God did a marvelous thing when he made us spiritually alive again. He has gotten the victory, and the point is that we were fighting him and did not want salvation. Being spiritually dead, we could not want to be given love for him.

Rather than try to rob God of one bit of his glory, let us:

> Sing a new song to Jehovah
> For the wonders He hath wrought;
> His right hand and arm most holy
> Triumph to His cause have brought.
> In His love and tender mercy
> He hath made salvation known,
> In the sight of ev'ry nation
> He His righteousness hath shown.

Robbing the neighbor of some of his goods is one thing. How much more vile and godless is it to try to rob God of some of his glory? Let us confess that he has done that marvelous thing of causing us to be born again with a new spiritual life. Let us say with Jesus that except God gives us spiritual life, we cannot even see the kingdom of heaven, and surely cannot then want it (John 3:3).

Read: Psalm 98
Psalter versification: 261:1

BLESSED AS A CHOSEN PEOPLE

Blessed is the nation whose God is the LORD; and the people whom he hath chosen for his own inheritance. —Psalm 33:12

Did you ever hear of a dead man asking for something? Before he died, he may have chosen where he would be buried and in what type of coffin. But after he died, he could not ask for a drink of water, ask to be brought back to life, or for that matter for anything of any person here below. And so it is with all of us who by nature were born spiritually dead. We cannot ask to be chosen, to be those God would save from their sins and bring to heavenly glory. Dead men do nothing.

God, however, chose some whom he would save and to whom he would give spiritual life. The psalmist wrote of this in Psalm 33:12 in these words: "Blessed is the nation whose God is the LORD; and the people whom he hath chosen for his own inheritance." He chose us. We did not choose him. By nature, being spiritually dead, we can only do what Adam and Eve did. We can choose to follow Satan in his lie and seek to satisfy our sinful flesh. But God chose to change us and to make us members of a nation that bows before him and worships him as their God.

Sing it then with the psalmist in our versification of his words:

O truly is the nation blest
Whose God before the world confessed
Jehovah is alone;
And blest the people is whom He
Has made His heritage to be,
And chosen for His own.

Here in the psalms we read of the truth of predestination, the truth that God eternally chose some to make them spiritually alive, and as a kingdom or nation that loves and glorifies him.

Surely we owe God everlasting thanks, and he owes us absolutely nothing. Keep that in mind all day. Give him all the glory due unto his name. Confess him to be the "Alpha and Omega... the first and the last" (Rev. 22:13), the one who planned all things and worked them out exactly according to that plan.

Do we not read in Ephesians 1:4 that we were chosen in Christ "before the foundation of the world"? Surely we owe God endless thanks.

Read: Psalm 33
Psalter versification: 86:3

103

SAVED IN A MARVELOUS WAY

For thou art great, and doest wondrous things: thou art God alone. Teach me thy way, O LORD; I will walk in thy truth: unite my heart to fear thy name. —Psalm 86:10–11

As a versification of Psalm 86:10–11 we sing:

> In all Thy deeds how great Thou art!
> Thou one true God, Thy way make clear;
> Teach me with undivided heart
> To trust Thy truth, Thy Name to fear.

And the Scripture version reads: "For thou art great, and doest wondrous things: thou art God alone. Teach me Thy way, O LORD; I will walk in thy truth: unite my heart to fear thy name."

We do well to give serious thought to this truth today. For the greatness of God in the work we considered yesterday is so universally denied.

No one can deny that God chose some to everlasting life and not others. As we noted yesterday from Psalm 33:12, "Blessed is the nation whose God is the LORD; and the people whom he hath chosen for his own inheritance." But we must not make this choice one made in time and on the condition that one believes. That limits God's greatness and takes away from the wonderful work he has wrought upon us and for us. For it makes God's desire dependent upon man's help. Man must save himself from his unbelief, and then God will save him from his guilt and the curse.

Surely, as we saw three days ago, man is spiritually dead and cannot then fulfill any conditions. Dead men do not make it possible for the living God to do what he wants to have done. If they can, then what the psalmist in Psalm 86:10 wrote is not true.

Let us make the psalmist's prayer in verse 11 ours: "Teach me Thy way, O LORD; I will walk in thy truth: unite my heart to fear thy name." Pray that you may see the way in which God saves us, and that it is a great and marvelous way, a miracle of his grace. Pray that you may walk in that truth that our salvation is a miracle and that we contributed absolutely nothing to it and owe God all the thanks and praise. Pray that your heart may be united to fear him as such a sovereign and powerful God, who wrote our names in the Lamb's book of life before the foundation of the world.

Read: Psalm 86
Psalter versification: 233:6

OUR SINS FULLY COVERED

Blessed is he whose transgression is forgiven, whose sin is covered. —Psalm 32:1

If there is one thing that we all need, it is the forgiveness of our sins. Since "there is none that doeth good, no not one" (Rom. 3:12), we all need to have our sins blotted out, or everlasting punishment lies before us. As Paul wrote in 1 Corinthians 15:22, "For as in Adam all die, even so in Christ shall all be made alive." In Adam all of us are guilty, and the wages of sin is death. Unless we have our guilt removed, we will enter everlasting punishment.

But thanks be to God, those whom he chose in Christ have their sins covered, as we read in Psalm 32:1, "Blessed is he whose transgression is forgiven, whose sin is covered." And that one's sin is covered does not mean that it is hidden from God's eyes. No one and nothing can be hidden from his everywhere-present and powerful eyes. Psalm 139:4–12 states that loudly and clearly. And in Psalm 32:1 David says that our sins are forgiven. God sent his Son to suffer fully the punishment and to do fully the work of love we failed to begin to do. Therefore, our sins are covered, as an insurance policy covers all the damages and expenses. Our sins will cost us nothing, for the Son of God paid the full price of our salvation.

One truth clearly and repeatedly taught in the book of Psalms is that we have atonement, the blotting out of our sins. And one of the beautiful songs God gives us to sing is this versification of David's words:

> How blest is he whose trespass
> Hath freely been forgiv'n,
> Whose sin is wholly covered
> Before the sight of heav'n.
> Blest he to whom Jehovah
> Imputeth not his sin,
> Who hath a guileless spirit,
> Whose heart is true within.

Learn that song and take it with you all the rest of your life. Sing it every day for your comfort, for we add to our sins every day of our lives. Atonement is reconciliation and means that God's justice is satisfied. Full payment has been made for all our sins by God's Son. And that gives us the right to sing that we are blessed by God's grace. But then let us bless and praise God for this wonderful gift that is so freely given us. It cost his Son his life. It costs us nothing. Salvation is a free gift.

Read: Psalm 32
Psalter versification: 83:1

OUR GOD, A PARTICULAR GOD

Praise the LORD; for the LORD is good: sing praises unto his name; for it is pleasant. For the LORD hath chosen Jacob unto himself, and Israel for his peculiar treasure. —Psalm 135:3–4

God is particular. Let us take hold of and maintain that truth with all our strength. Every day we are bombarded with a denial of this truth. On bumper stickers, over the radio, from off the pulpit, and displayed where passersby may read it, these unscriptural words are presented: "Smile, God loves you."

Whosoever reads or hears these words is supposed to be the object of God's love; and it is shouted out that Christ died so that everyone who hears them has a chance to be saved. But let us get it deeply into our souls that God is not a gambler or a beggar. He is not one who strives to get his way and to save as many as he can. He chose certain definite people and sent Christ to die only for their sins. As clearly as you could want it, he through Paul tells us in Romans 9:11–13 that before they were born or had done good or evil, it was stated that "the elder shall serve the younger," for "Jacob have I loved, but Esau have I hated."

The psalms also speak of a particular atonement. For we read in Psalm 135:3–4, "Praise the LORD; for the LORD is good: sing praises unto his name; for it is pleasant. For the LORD hath chosen Jacob unto himself, and Israel for his peculiar treasure." And plainly Israel consisted of a relatively small part of the human race in the Old Testament dispensation. God's election then was very particular. And the blood of Christ would be shed for a very particular people.

Jesus said that same truth in John 10:15, "As the Father knoweth me, even so know I the Father: and I lay down my life for the sheep." *That* is very particular, for there were wolves as well as sheep, and the atonement is only for the sheep.

Sing this truth then in the words of our versification:

O praise ye the Lord for His goodness;
'Tis pleasant His praises to sing;
His people, His chosen and precious,
Your praises with gratitude bring.

Read: Psalm 135
Psalter versification: 374:2

GRACE THAT CONQUERS

Praise ye him, sun and moon: praise him, all ye stars of light. Praise him, ye heavens of heavens, and ye waters that be above the heavens. Let them praise the name of the LORD: for he commanded, and they were created. He hath also stablished them for ever and ever: he hath made a decree which shall not pass. —Psalm 148:3–6

All the heavenly bodies have their God-given places and move in a divinely prescribed course. Therefore, man can tell just when the sun shall arise or set on a particular day in the future, and when the moon shall be full or a new moon appears. God has it all under his perfect control. And the psalmist declares this in Psalm 148:3–6 with these words:

Praise ye him, sun and moon: praise him, all ye stars of light. Praise him, ye heavens of heavens, and ye waters that be above the heavens. Let them praise the name of the Lord: for he commanded, and they were created. He hath also stablished them for ever and ever: he hath made a decree which shall not pass.

Note that they came into being by his command, were established by him, and were made by a decree that shall not pass away. And since this is true of his work of creating, how much more wonderful and comforting is it to know that what he does in his grace comes by a command and not by a wish, is established, and cannot be made to pass away or fail by man and his sinful will.

Why then should we say that God pleads with man to accept Christ, rather than that he commands it, and that man decides how many God will save? Look at the last verse of the psalm, which is versified thus:

> By all let God be praised,
> For He alone is great;
> Above the earth and heav'n
> He reigns in glorious state;
> Praise Him, ye saints, who know His grace
> And ever dwell before His face.

How comforting to know that all those who were eternally written in the Lamb's book of life will irresistibly be drawn by God's grace out of unbelief into faith, and out of spiritual death into everlasting spiritual life.

Surely we have undeniable reason to praise God for the salvation which he works in us by irresistible grace. Do that then today and every day of your life here below. You will do that in glory.

Read: Romans 9:1–21
Psalter versification: 404:5

ALL OF OUR SALVATION, GOD'S WORK

I will praise thee for ever, because thou hast done it: and I will wait on thy name; for it is good before thy saints. —Psalm 52:9

It is not without good reason that God in his word warns us not to boast of our faith and new life. Through Paul he tells us in Ephesians 2:8–9 that we are saved by grace in such a way that faith also is a gift, so that there is no room for us to boast of having contributed even the desire for salvation. That, too, he gives us through his Son.

This truth he gave us the very day we fell into sin. For then he told us that through his Son he would put enmity in us against the devil and the sin into which he led us. David says this, too, in Psalm 52:9, where we read: "I will praise thee forever, because thou hast done it: and I will wait on thy name; for it is good before the saints."

A few lines we may fruitfully commit to memory are the versification:

> I put my trust in God alone,
> For evermore I trust His grace,
> And like the trees within His courts
> I flourish in a favored place.
> With endless thanks, O Lord, to Thee,
> Thy wondrous works will I proclaim,
> And in the presence of Thy saints
> Will ever hope in Thy good Name.

Yes, in the most absolute sense, when we speak of salvation we must say with David: "Thou hast done it: and I will wait on thy name." Always and every step of our way we must sing: "I put my trust in God alone, for evermore I trust His grace."

Be conceited and think that you stand in your own strength, and you have already fallen. And your trust in God has been replaced by trust in self. Boast of having accepted Christ before he came into your heart, and you cannot sing: "I will praise thee forever, because thou hast done it."

No, let us love the truth we sing every sabbath day: "Praise God from whom *all* blessings flow." Let us wait on God's name and then confess that even this waiting is his gift unto us. May our thanks to God be endless so that it includes the desire for salvation. One of the things from which we must be saved is the idea that we let Christ come into our hearts. May we receive grace to say of his entrance: "I will praise thee forever, because thou hast done it."

Read: John 10:14–29
Psalter versification: 145:5–6

PRESERVED FOR PERFECTION

I have set the LORD always before me: because he is at my right hand, I shall not be moved. Therefore my heart is glad, and my glory rejoiceth: my flesh also shall rest in hope. For thou wilt not leave my soul in hell; neither wilt thou suffer thine Holy One to see corruption. —Psalm 16:8–10

Once a believer, always a believer. Once a child of God, always a child of God. Once on the way to heavenly glory, always on the way to that unending glory. That is the comforting assurance in the word of God.

This does not mean that we will never sin anymore and will look always like believers and never as those on the way to the lake of fire. In all our life here below we will still have the old man of sin and, like Peter, may even by word or deed deny all connection with Christ and say that we do not know him. It does not mean that we will never doubt our salvation and always be strong in our faith.

It does mean what Paul says in Philippians 1:6, namely: "Being confident of this very thing, that he which hath begun a good work in you will perform it until the day of Jesus Christ." It means what the psalmist says in Psalm 16:8–10, "I have set the LORD always before me: because he is at my right hand, I shall not be moved. Therefore my heart is glad, and my glory rejoiceth: my flesh also shall rest in hope. For thou wilt not leave my soul in hell; neither wilt thou suffer thine Holy One to see corruption." What God began, he will finish. He is the unchangeable, almighty God. Having begun the work of salvation in us, he will continue it until we are perfect in every respect.

The proof that he did begin a good work in us is our sorrow over our sin. If we find that in us, he has begun the work of salvation in us. Then the Spirit of his Son came into us, and he will bring us back from every sin.

Do you hate your sins? Do you desire to be sinless and so fully freed from sin that you can walk in perfect love to God? Then sing:

I keep before me still
The Lord Whom I have proved;
At my right hand He guards from ill,
And I shall not be moved.
My heart is glad and blest,
My soul its joy shall tell;
And, lo, my flesh in hope shall rest,
And still in safety dwell.

Read: Ephesians 2
Psalter versification: 29:2

CLEANSING OUR WAY

Wherewithal shall a young man cleanse his way? by taking heed thereto
according to thy word. —Psalm 119:9

Throughout the day we wash our hands. Our clothes also need periodic washing to remove the grime they collect. But far more important is it that we cleanse our way. And cleansing our way is straightening out our walk of life so that we walk in love toward God.

That is why the psalmist writes in Psalm 119:9, "Wherewithal shall a young man cleanse his way? by taking heed thereto according to thy word." And it is not because young men sin more than older people that the psalmist writes these words. It is because if we do not learn how to cleanse our way in the days of our youth, we will spend our whole pilgrimage here below walking to destruction.

Now, it is God's law that points out for us the way of life. And since we are born on the way that leads to everlasting woe in the lake of fire of God's holy wrath, we need to know this and where to walk to be pleasing in the sight of him who created us in his own image and calls us to walk in love to him.

We all, whether we are young or old, wisely sing:

How shall the young direct their way?
What light shall be their perfect guide?
Thy word, O Lord, will safely lead,
If in its wisdom they confide.

And although in his grace God will reward us for such a walk, we do not earn anything by serving him. Consider once that we walk on his earth, breathe his air, eat his food and drink his water, are given every heartbeat by him, and have received bodies and souls from him with their talents and abilities. We owe him for everything we have and are. Yea, we owe him for his Son and the salvation we have in him. Can we earn something by our good works? No, we are everlastingly indebted to God and owe him everlasting and continuous thanks. We need, therefore, to be cleansed of our pride whereby we think that we have given God something. Cleanse your way of that conceit by taking heed to his word that teaches us that "in him we live, and move, and have our being" (Acts 17:28).

Read: Psalm 119:9–24
Psalter versification: 322:1

SEEKING GOD WHOLEHEARTEDLY

*With my whole heart have I sought thee: O let me not
wander from thy commandments. —Psalm 119:10*

To find a particular object one must go in a definite direction and upon a particular way. Go north when the object is south of the place where you are, and you will not reach that object. And the same is true about things spiritual. Therefore, the psalmist in Psalm 119:10 writes: "With my whole heart have I sought thee: O let me not wander from thy commandments."

Two truths are evident here: we must seek God with our whole heart; and if we wander from his commandments, we are not going to find him and enjoy his covenant fellowship. Wander the slightest bit from one of his commandments, and we are going away from God, for we are going in the wrong direction.

Consider once that if on a stretch of highway you drive your automobile only one inch toward the lane of the oncoming traffic, and keep that up for a few minutes, you are headed for a head-on collision. Even more so, if we wander for just one moment from one of God's commandments, we are on a collision course with the almighty, holy God. And instead of finding him in his love and mercy, we will have him find us in his holy wrath. For that law is a very, very narrow path.

Therefore, it is essential that we seek God with our whole heart, that is, constantly, by walking in his commandments, which call us to love God.

Listen to the versification of the psalmist's words:

Sincerely I have sought Thee, Lord,
O let me not from Thee depart;
To know Thy will and keep from sin
Thy word I cherish in my heart.

In order to keep on the path that leads to God's fellowship and the assurance of his love, our hearts must be directed to God. That steering wheel in your automobile will determine the direction in which you go. Your heart will determine the spiritual direction of your whole being.

Seeking God sincerely, seeking him in his Son who fulfilled that law for us, you will find his love. Beware, therefore, of wandering, and pray with the psalmist that God may keep you walking where you may know and enjoy God's love.

Read: Isaiah 55
Psalter versification: 322:2

SIN PREVENTION

Thy word have I hid in mine heart, that I might not sin against thee. Blessed art thou, O LORD: teach me thy statutes. —Psalm 119:11–12

Of fire prevention we have all heard. Crime prevention likewise is not only a matter we desire but one whose need we become aware of more and more every day. Sin prevention, however, is far more necessary and, sad to say, of very little concern even in the church world today.

Yes, we can make a distinction between crime and sin. Crime is sin, but not all sin is crime. Crime is what the world calls any deed that breaks a man-made law, and that is sin before God when that law is made by the authorities God placed over us. But there are sins against the first table of the law of God which do not bother the world. Trust in a creature, make an idol to worship, take God's name in vain, and desecrate the Sabbath, and the world will not call it a crime.

We ought to be concerned about such sins and seek to prevent them and all other sins, as the psalmist writes in Psalm 119:11–12 in these words: "Thy word have I hid in mine heart, that I might not sin against thee. Blessed art thou, O LORD: teach me thy statutes." Or as we sang yesterday:

Sincerely I have sought Thee, Lord,
O let me not from Thee depart;
To know Thy will and keep from sin
Thy word I cherish in my heart.

Quite plainly sin prevention requires knowing God's statutes, or if you will, having God's word in our hearts. How important then is the reading and studying of God's word in our homes.

You may have smoke detectors and take many fire prevention actions. You may vote for higher taxes to get more policemen for crime prevention. But are you interested in stopping and preventing all sin in your home and life?

God's word will show you which of your thoughts, desires, and actions are sin in his sight. His word is a mirror, and when you stand before it, you will see yourself as God sees you. You will in it see his Son in all his righteousness and holiness. Take heed to what his Son calls you to do, even if it costs you your earthly life. Trust in him to bring you into his kingdom when he returns upon the clouds of heaven. There you will everlastingly be prevented from all sin forever.

Read: James 1
Psalter versification: 322:2

April 20

DELIGHT IN GOD'S LAW

With my lips have I declared all the judgments of thy mouth. I have rejoiced in the way of thy testimonies, as much as in all riches. —Psalm 119:13–14

"Like father, like son." So the expression goes, and very often this is true. Sons often resemble their fathers to such a degree that you do not need to ask the child who his father is. Then, too, fathers' mannerisms, talents, and the like show up in sons.

Now, there is one instance where the son will always look exactly like the father in thinking, willing, and acting. When God the Father begets a child through his Son and his Spirit, that child will look exactly like God from a spiritual point of view. Do we not in Psalm 17:15 read: "I shall be satisfied, when I awake, with thy likeness"?

The psalmist in Psalm 119:13–14 declares a similar truth when he writes: "With my lips have I declared all the judgments of thy mouth. I have rejoiced in the way of thy testimonies, as much as in all riches." Did you note that what God speaks, the psalmist declares with his lips? That he rejoices in God's testimonies means that he thinks as God thinks and wills what he wills.

Therefore, if you are a child of God, this will be true also of you, not only in the new Jerusalem but also in principle in this present life. You will love what God loves, think as he thinks, will what he wills, judge to be good what he calls good. In this life already you will sing:

> O blessed Lord, teach me Thy law,
> Thy righteous judgments I declare;
> Thy testimonies make me glad,
> For they are wealth beyond compare.

In this life already you will with your lips declare all his judgments to be right. You will not go against or speak against his testimonies, but will with joy keep them. You will with your lips and walk say that you are glad to be one with him in thought, word, and deed.

How about it? Do your words and works make plain that God is your Father? Do you find in yourself a delight in God's law that is above joy in earthly treasures? We were created in the image of God but fell into accepting Satan's lie and becoming his children. Do you long to awake with God's likeness and be like his holy and righteous Son?

Read: Psalm 19
Psalter versification: 322:3

A WALK THAT TALKS

I will meditate in thy precepts, and have respect unto thy ways. I will delight myself in thy statutes: I will not forget thy word. —Psalm 119:15–16

Actions speak louder than words. And proof that we have meditated in God's precepts is that we have profound respect for them. That is why, when the psalmist wrote in Psalm 119:13–14, "With my lips have I declared all the judgments of thy mouth. I have rejoiced in the way of thy testimonies, as much as in all riches," he continues in verses 15–16 with these words: "I will meditate in thy precepts, and have respect unto thy ways. I will delight myself in thy statutes: I will not forget thy word."

Now when he says that he will not forget God's word, he does not merely mean that he will keep that word in his mind, but that he will do what that word presents as man's calling. As our versification has it:

> Upon Thy precepts and Thy ways
> My heart will meditate with awe;
> Thy word shall be my chief delight,
> And I will not forget Thy law.

Plainly, sincere and serious meditation in God's precepts will produce awe in us; and that awe will bring forth not only words that our lips utter, but works that reveal that we know what God demands of us.

For not forgetting his word is not merely being able to say what he says in it, but is doing what he demands of us. If we really stand in awe and have respect for God's precepts, we will have that law constantly before us as something we desire to do and keep doing.

What then does your walk of life say? The question is not what your lips say, even though that is important, and we must be careful what our lips declare. The question is, What do your works say? Do they say that you stand in awe before God's law, or that you do not delight in his statutes and have not meditated in his precepts? Do you, as Adam did, remember what God said but still go contrary to it?

Meditating in God's precepts, we will know what is required of us in every circumstance of life. And if it is true that we rejoice in the way of God's testimonies, we are going to meditate in them and by our deeds as well as by our lips declare that his testimonies are "wealth beyond compare."

Read: Matthew 5:21–48
Psalter versification: 322:3–4

A CALL TO PRAISE GOD

O praise the LORD, all ye nations: praise him, all ye people. For his merciful kindness is great toward us: and the truth of the LORD endureth for ever. Praise ye the LORD. —Psalm 117

In the book of Psalms we find the longest and the shortest chapters in the Bible. Psalm 119 is the longest, having 176 verses; and Psalm 117 the shortest, having only 2 verses. But do not brush this psalm aside as having little to say to us. It presents to us a very, very important calling, one we must not for one minute forget.

Three times in this brief psalm we are told to praise the Lord. That is a tremendously important calling for man who is made in the image of God. Did he not himself say in Isaiah 43:21, "This people have I formed for myself; they shall shew forth my praise"? And the psalmist calls our attention to the fact that all nations and peoples without exception must heed this call. He writes, "O praise the LORD, all ye nations: praise him, all ye people. For his merciful kindness is great toward us: and the truth of the LORD endureth forever. Praise ye the LORD" (Ps. 117).

Consider that to praise God is to extol him for his virtues. And it means that we tell *him* that he is good. Praising God certainly includes telling other people how great and good he is. But praising him means basically that we tell him how good he is. Our Psalter versification states that clearly in these words:

Praise Jehovah, all ye nations,
All ye people, praise proclaim;
For His grace and lovingkindness
O sing praises to His Name.
For the greatness of His mercy
Constant praise to Him accord;
Evermore His truth endureth;
Hallelujah, praise the Lord.

Take note of the fact that we sing, "O sing praises to His Name," and "Constant praise to Him accord." The idea plainly is that we must praise him in our prayers as well as in our songs. It is one thing to sing about a person's virtues. It is quite another to go to that person and let him know your good thoughts of him. We are quick to attack someone with our words rather than to extol him for his goodness to us. We are quick to complain about God's works but slow to thank him.

Speak to others about God's goodness, but by all means speak to him and "constant praise to Him accord."

Read: Psalm 147
Psalter versification: 315

ALL GLORY TO GOD

O praise the LORD, all ye nations: praise him, all ye people. For his merciful kindness is great toward us: and the truth of the LORD endureth for ever. Praise ye the LORD. —Psalm 117

If there is one gift of God for which we should praise him, it is the gift of his Son as our savior. Quite naturally the Old Testament saints could not do that the way we can. For Christ was not yet born, and his cross had not yet become the altar on which he was sacrificed for our sins. Nevertheless, in essence all the saints, from Adam onward and in every nation and people, did and should praise God for that precious, all-important gift.

Note once again that in Psalm 117 we are told to praise God for his merciful kindness and for the fact that his truth endures forever. All of God's merciful kindness is in Christ. And the truth concerning him and what he did for us will never wear out or become out-of-date.

What mercy it was for God to give up his only begotten Son whom he loved with all his infinite being. How can we ever brush aside that evidence of God's mercy? How kind he was to place all the punishment that we deserve on his Son! How great then is that merciful kindness! So great it is that it will never run out but "endureth forever."

But note that linked with that mercy is his truth. Our versification explains this when it states:

> All men on earth that live,
> To God all glory give,
> Praise ye the Lord;
> His lovingkindness bless,
> His constant faithfulness
> And changeless truth confess;
> Praise ye the Lord.

God is faithful, true to his word; and he is this because he is changeless. He is Jehovah, the I AM, who is the same yesterday, today, and forever.

Upon his word we can depend. His merciful kindness once bestowed upon us will never be removed. What a reason, therefore, we have for praising him. And here in our versification is the beautiful explanation of our praising him. For praising God is telling him that he is glorious. It is ascribing all glory to him. And glory is the radiation, the shining forth, of virtue.

Praise him then for supplying all your earthly needs; but by all means praise him for the gift of his Son and the salvation in him.

Read: Psalm 100
Psalter versification: 316

WITH GOD'S SMILE UPON US

Give ear, O Shepherd of Israel, thou that leadest Joseph like a flock; thou that dwellest between the cherubims, shine forth. —Psalm 80:1

Not every smile reveals love. An enemy can smile at you because he got the victory over you and is happy about his victory. Satan often uses a "friendly" smile upon the face of one he uses to try to lead you into a particular sin and to depart from a particular truth of Scripture.

But when God smiles upon us, it is a manifestation of his love to us. And in Psalm 80:1 Asaph speaks of God's smile upon his people when he writes: "Give ear, O Shepherd of Israel, thou that leadest Joseph like a flock; thou that dwellest between the cherubim, shine forth." And rightly our versification has it this way:

> Great Shepherd Who leadest Thy people in love,
> 'Mid cherubim dwelling, shine Thou from above;
> In might come and save us, Thy people restore,
> And we shall be saved when Thy face shines once more.

God's smile is rooted in and caused by his love that brings us safely to a life of most wonderful, covenant fellowship with him. And Asaph speaks of this when he calls God our shepherd who leads us like a flock. For a shepherd cares for his sheep and strives to bring them where all is well with them.

Then, too, that he shines forth from between the cherubim means that he smiles in a love that sent his Son to the torment of hell, that we might be led like a flock into the new Jerusalem and its glories. For those cherubim were on the covering of the ark, and it was on that mercy seat that the typical blood of Christ was sprinkled to cover our sins. And oh, how that death of Christ revealed God's love to us, and why God can smile down upon us, who by nature are vile, filthy sinners, worthy of being destroyed by him.

Call then to that shepherd, that Great Shepherd, on the basis of that cross of his only begotten Son. Never try to come to him in any other way.

If you want to see and enjoy God's smile of love upon you, seek him in the blood of his Son. If you want to live in the joy of having a shepherd who is leading you to glory, look to that cross of Christ.

Read: Psalm 80
Psalter versification: 220:1

TURNED IN GOD'S LOVE

Turn us again, O God, and cause thy face
to shine; and we shall be saved. —Psalm 80:3

A sheep is a very helpless creature and needs a shepherd. Especially was that true in the Old Testament dispensation, when there were many wolves and lions in the vicinity, from whom the sheep needed protection. Yet today we are in a far more serious danger than sheep were in the day when Asaph wrote, calling God the Great Shepherd. "Turn us again, O God, and cause thy face to shine; and we shall be saved" (Ps. 80:3).

We have a wolf in sheep's clothing (Matt. 7:15) and "a roaring lion…seeking whom he may devour" (1 Pet. 5:8). The devil is an invisible enemy against whom we cannot stand in our own strength. What is more, we are so prone to stray where he lurks. We may bodily be in church, but with our minds we stray from Christ, our shepherd. And we like to run after teachings and doctrines that satisfy our flesh and open doors for us to walk in the sins our flesh enjoys.

That is why Asaph calls to God to turn us and, if you please, to turn us *again*, for we are straying so often and going where Satan wants us to be. We need to be turned and be brought back to the flock to feed in green pastures. Straying causes our backs to be turned to our shepherd, and we cannot see his face shining with the smile of love. Instead we are doing that which greatly displeases him.

We need to be turned, or as our versification has it, we must be restored. Remember what we sang yesterday?

Great Shepherd Who leadest Thy people in love,
'Mid cherubim dwelling, shine Thou from above;
In might come and save us, Thy people restore,
And we shall be saved when Thy face shines once more.

We must be restored in the sense that we must be brought back to the path of righteousness, where the light of God's smile falls. Because of his love, which is behind that smile, we will be turned back again to where we can see what he did for us in his Son.

Pray that you may be turned. But then thank him for turning you again and for what he did in his Son.

Read: 1 Peter 5
Psalter versification: 220:1

HOLY ANGER AGAINST UNHOLY PRAYERS

O LORD God of hosts, how long wilt thou be angry against the
prayer of thy people? —Psalm 80:4

That God is angry when we break one of his commandments we understand. That he is angry with our prayers is another matter. Yes, if we pray for sinful things, it is understandable that God is angry; but if we pray for salvation, will God be angry?

Yes, even that can make God angry. For not only are our best works—and that includes our prayers—polluted with sin, but so often in our prayers our method and motive are wrong. We can pray to be healed from our sicknesses, not so that we can serve God more fully, but to seek the things here below.

No wonder then that Asaph in Psalm 80:4 writes: "O LORD God of hosts, how long wilt thou be angry against the prayer of thy people?" Consider that Asaph writes about God's people in the ten tribes who no longer went to God's temple in Jerusalem to pray there, but went to the two places where Jeroboam set up golden calves. Therefore, our versification reads:

How long, O Lord, wilt Thou disdain our prayer?
For Thou hast fed us with the bread of tears,
And bitter sorrow Thou hast made us share;
The nations round us mock with scornful jeers.

Remember that God is holy and cannot be happy with any sin, no matter in what form it comes. Adam only ate a forbidden piece of fruit; but God sent death! But understand that God does not hate his people whom he gave to Christ, and for whose sins his Son died. But he is angry with our sins and often keeps us in difficult situations in order to turn us away from these sins and to bring us where his face shines and we enjoy his smile. The ten tribes had to be captured and mocked with scornful jeers so that God's people in those tribes might be turned again to him who dwells between the cherubim on the ark in the temple in Jerusalem.

And we, too, so often need afflictions to bring us back to the Lord of Hosts, so that we may be where his face shines upon us. We need chastisement, and as our Great Shepherd he supplies it. He does this because he loves us and intends to turn us and save us.

Read: Psalm 119:65–80
Psalter versification: 218:2

SAVED BY GRACE

Turn us again, O Lᴏʀᴅ God of hosts, cause thy face to shine; and
we shall be saved. —Psalm 80:19

Although Asaph begins Psalm 80 by picturing God's church as a flock of sheep that he leads and protects, he changes the figure at verse 8 and now calls the church the vine God brought out of Egypt, placed in the promised land, and later afflicted grievously because the ten tribes had turned from him. He speaks of the vine having its branches broken down, being wasted by the boar of the woods, burned with fire, and cut down. And in our versification it is presented thus:

> The branch of Thy planting is burned and cut down,
> Brought nigh to destruction because of Thy frown;
> The man of Thy right hand with wisdom endue,
> The son of man strengthen Thy pleasure to do.

We do well to remember Asaph's words which for the third time he writes in Psalm 80:19, namely: "Turn us again, O Lᴏʀᴅ God of hosts, cause thy face to shine; and we shall be saved."

That frown on God's face, which in verse 16 is called "the rebuke of thy countenance," and the urgent necessity that we be turned again both reveal that we deserve God's curse upon us and are sinners who earned having awful punishment meted out to us.

Let us likewise not overlook the fact that Asaph repeats: "Cause thy face to shine; and we shall be saved." We cannot turn God's wrath away; and our conversion is not a work that earns salvation for us. Our conversion is God's work whereby he turned us, and it is the evidence that he turned us, because he looks down upon us as those whose sins his Son has blotted out by his blood.

What a brilliant light in the darkness of the night it was when Jesus was born and the glory of God shone down upon the shepherds! How bright the night became when Moses and Elijah appeared to Jesus on the Mount of Transfiguration! God's face was shining on his church; and by the Spirit of his Son he turns us so that we can see and enjoy that salvation. We are saved by grace. God turns us because in Christ his face shines upon us.

Read: Lamentations 5
Psalter versification: 220:5

SEEING THE WONDERS OF GOD'S LAW

Open thou mine eyes, that I may behold wondrous things
out of thy law. —Psalm 119:18

There are in God's law some terrifying statements. He will visit "the iniquity of the fathers upon the children" who hate him and show this by worshiping images; and he will "not hold him guiltless that taketh his name in vain" (Ex. 20:5, 7). But would you agree with the psalmist when in Psalm 119:18 he writes: "Open thou mine eyes, that I may behold wondrous things out of thy law"? What is so wonderful about the ten commandments that limit us so severely as to what we may and may not do?

As the psalmist writes in verse 17, God must "deal bountifully with" us if we are to escape God's wrath and live in his word. Surely we can stand in awe when we see the terrible, everlasting punishment he metes out upon the sinner. But can we see something wonderful in the law itself?

Yes, there is something wonderful in God's law. It is, however, something that only one with whom God has dealt bountifully in his Son, who died for the violations of his word, and by his Spirit has received a new heavenly life, who sees this. That something is that with our spiritual eye we see God in all his divine majesty. If the law of God shows us anything, it is that he is God, yea, a holy God who will not wink at one sin! The law holds before our eyes the truth that he is a sovereign God, who owns every creature in heaven and on earth and has the right to demand perfect, unceasing obedience before him.

And do not forget that when God opens our eyes, we see with the psalmist that God must deal bountifully with us in his grace, if we are to keep his word and live. That law reveals to us that God must send his only begotten Son into hellish agonies to pay for our transgressions and earn for us a new life that can and will keep his word and bring us to a life of joy before his face in heavenly glory.

Sing it then with the psalmist in our versification:

Thy servant, blest by Thee, shall live
And keep Thy word with awe;
Lord, open Thou my eyes to see
The wonders of Thy law.

Read: Psalm 119:17–32
Psalter versification: 323:1

A SURE SIGN OF HEAVENLY CITIZENSHIP

I am a stranger in the earth: hide not thy commandments from me. My soul breaketh for the longing that it hath unto thy judgments at all times. —Psalm 119:19–20

In Psalm 119:19–20 the psalmist makes some very striking statements, and they all revolve around the truth which he states, namely, that he is "a stranger in the earth" (v. 19). That does not simply mean that others here below do not understand him. That is true. But basically, that he is a pilgrim and stranger here below means that his citizenship is in heaven and that he wants to be loyal to his heavenly King. Taking that into consideration, we can understand his striking statements such as: "Hide not thy commandments from me," and, "My soul breaketh for the longing that it hath unto thy judgments at all times" (Ps. 119:19, 20).

Can you honestly say that? In the measure that you can, you have assurance that your citizenship is in heaven. Those whose citizenship is only here below do not even want to read God's law, and they consider those who break the first table of it as pretty nice, decent, lovable people. Those who break the second table they try to defend. You will never hear them singing our versification—unless it is because they like the music—which solemnly declares:

A pilgrim in the earth am I,
Thy will to me reveal;
To know Thy truth my spirit yearns,
Consumed with ardent zeal.

The question is whether we can sincerely sing that. How often do you try to defend yourself in a violation of God's law? How many neighbors and people with whom you work see you as one with citizenship in heaven and as one whose soul breaks with a longing to be pleasing at all times to the king of that kingdom of heaven? Are you really a stranger in the earth, or do your speech and conduct mark you to all who see you as one who is not a spiritual stranger to them?

Get down on your knees, as the psalmist did, and pray that God will not hide his commandments from you, that is, that he will reveal to you each step of the way in what direction you should go to please him and what words to speak that his glory may shine forth through you. Do that the first thing in the morning, so you know how to walk. Before you retire at night, ask him to show you your sins that you may confess them.

Read: Matthew 5:1–20
Psalter versification: 323:2

A PRAYER FOR DIVINE ASSURANCE

Thou hast rebuked the proud that are cursed, which do err from thy
commandments. Remove from me reproach and contempt; for I
have kept thy testimonies. —Psalm 119:21–22

It makes no difference in what form sin comes, it is always an act of pride. It is pride because sin always is rebellion against God. Every time we sin, we say by our deed that we do not need to obey God and please the almighty Creator of heaven and earth. In effect we tell God to keep still and to mind his own business. That surely is an act of stinking pride.

No wonder then that God moved the psalmist to write in Psalm 119:21, "Thou hast rebuked the proud that are cursed, which do err from thy commandments." And these proud sinners are so ready to reproach and speak contemptuously of those who do keep God's law. For that reason the psalmist adds the prayer: "Remove from me reproach and contempt; for I have kept thy testimonies" (v. 22).

It is interesting to note that God's commandments are here called his testimonies. For each one of the ten commandments testifies that he is God and must be obeyed. It is also interesting that our versification rightly calls sin an act of hatred against God in these words:

Thou dost rebuke the proud, O Lord,
Who hate Thy holy Name;
But since I keep Thy righteous law,
Deliver me from shame.

Now, removing reproach and contempt means making it known that we are those who keep God's law and are children whom he loves. And the idea then is not that he prays that God will make these sinners change their minds and speak favorably of him. Conversion and repentance in them he surely desires; but what he prays for here is that he may be assured of God's love and have removed from his mind the idea that he is proud and foolish when he walks in a way which he considers keeping God's law.

We need that badly today. We who hold on to the truth of God's word, condemn evil practices, keep the Sabbath holy, and worship the God of the Scriptures are painted black, ridiculed, called narrow-minded, old-fashioned, conceited, and silly. And we, like the psalmist, need the assurance from God that we are redeemed by the blood of Christ and are walking in his footsteps and teaching.

Read: Psalm 39
Psalter versification: 323:3

CHOOSING WISE COUNSELORS

Princes also did sit and speak against me: but thy servant did meditate in thy statutes. Thy testimonies also are my delight and my counselors. —Psalm 119:23–24

If someone files a court case against you, it would be wise to get legal help from one who can give you good advice and represent you as unjust charges are hurled at you before the judge. And as a child of God in the midst of a world where Satan uses crafty, clever men to try to get you accused of holding on to false doctrines and of being guilty of walking in a sinful way, it is an act of wisdom to do as the psalmist writes in Psalm 119:23–24. He points out that "Princes also did sit and speak against me: but thy servant did meditate in thy statutes. Thy testimonies also are my delight and my counsellors."

Turn to the word of God. Meditate in his statutes. Let his testimonies be your counselors. The point is that we had better know and quote the Scriptures for our defense. God must be our counselor as he speaks through his word. When Jesus was tempted by the devil in the wilderness, he quoted God's word, and each time he not only shielded himself from Satan's arrows by it, but used it to pierce Satan.

There are two activities which the psalmist tells us to perform when we are attacked or tempted to leave God's word and law and to join those who err from God's commandments. We should meditate in God's statutes so that we know fully what they say to us. And we should seek the counsel that God has provided for us in his word. Then we have weapons of defense but also of offense to drive our attackers away.

The day is soon coming when princes, that is, government officials, are going to sit and speak against us. Yea, even princes who are church officials will speak against us because we delight in God's statutes, laws, and testimonies. Satan is working hard to destroy the church of Christ and to produce the false Christ which Scripture calls the "man of sin" (2 Thess. 2:3).

Let God's word counsel you as to how to resist Satan and drive him away. Find comfort and hope in God's word and sing with the psalmist:

> I on Thy statutes meditate,
> Tho' evil men deride;
> Thy faithful word is my delight,
> My counselor and guide.

Read: Romans 7
Psalter versification: 323:4

POWERFUL HELP FOR THE HELPLESS

I will lift up mine eyes unto the hills, from whence cometh my help. My help cometh from the LORD, which made heaven and earth. —Psalm 121:1–2

Could you find a better place for one to be when injured severely than in a fully equipped and well-staffed hospital? Consider then what the psalmist says in Psalm 121:1–2. There we read: "I will lift up mine eyes unto the hills, from whence cometh my help. My help cometh from the LORD, which made heaven and earth."

Imagine that! The almighty God, he who made this vast creation, this large earth upon which we live, the starry hosts, these bodies millions of miles away from us, and the spiritual realm we also call heaven, is our help. What power! What wisdom! Therefore, what help there is then for us in all our sins and miseries!

And when the psalmist speaks of looking to the hills, he calls our attention to the fact that we have almighty, certain help for all our spiritual as well as physical needs, for all the needs of our souls as well as of our bodies. For these hills are Mount Moriah on which God's house was built by Solomon and Mount Zion where God's throne stood and where the kings from David onward reigned as types of Christ.

The significance of it all is that we can look for help to Christ, who now is at God's right hand with power over every creature in heaven and on earth and who died for our sins on the altar of the cross, which was pictured in that temple on Mount Moriah. Thus to God through Christ we may go with all our guilt and all the miseries upon us because of our guilt in Adam. We have protection from all our enemies and have bodies promised us that will be glorious and free from sin. About what then do we have to worry? We are in the hands of a powerful Savior who is driven by a love that moved him to die for our sins and to bring us to that glory.

Look up then to those hills no matter what your problem is, and let this daily be your song:

Unto the hills around do I lift up
My longing eyes;
O whence for me shall my salvation come,
From whence arise?
From God the Lord doth come my certain aid,
From God the Lord Who heav'n and earth hath made.

Read: Psalm 121
Psalter versification: 347:1

SAFE EVERY STEP OF THE WAY

He will not suffer thy foot to be moved: he that keepeth thee will not slumber.
Behold, he that keepeth Israel shall neither slumber nor sleep. —Psalm 121:3–4

The almighty, all-wise God watches over his universal church, which in Psalm 121:4 is called Israel—a name that means Prince of God. And he protects us so fully that each individual believer can say with the psalmist in Psalm 121:3–4, "He will not suffer thy foot to be moved: he that keepeth thee will not slumber. Behold, he that keepeth Israel shall neither slumber nor sleep." That means that he cares for each member of the body of Christ, the church he loved and for which he gave his life. Each child of God then may say: "He will not suffer *my* foot to be moved."

To appreciate this, consider that we are traveling on a mountain path that is narrow, and that either on the right or left side of that path, and sometimes on both sides, the ground drops off steeply, so that one who steps off will fall to certain death. That is why it is so very important that we have one to watch over us who does not sleep but looks down upon us every step of our way.

When we do with one foot step off that narrow path by sin of one kind or another, one must be there to lift that foot up and back upon the path, or catch us as we fall lest we plunge into the lake of fire. If our guardian sleeps for just a moment, and one of us has stepped off that pathway, that one enters everlasting perdition.

But no, here is the truth for our comfort:

He will not suffer that thy foot be moved,
Safe shalt thou be;
No careless slumber shall His eyelids close
Who keepeth thee;
Behold He sleepeth not, He slumbereth ne'er,
Who keepeth Israel in His holy care.

This versification expresses the beautiful truth that he cares for us in wondrous love. "No careless slumber shall His eyelids close." Of that you can be sure. He is the almighty God who is never tired or sleepy. We are safe day and night. We have a Savior who indeed saves us in a wonderful way and in unchangeable love. We are safe every step of our way to his house of many mansions, where places are prepared for us.

Read: Psalm 91
Psalter versification: 347:2

KEPT ON THE WAY TO GLORY

The LORD is thy keeper: the LORD is thy shade upon thy right hand. The sun shall not smite thee by day, nor the moon by night. —Psalm 121:5–6

The name of your pilot as you fly high above the earth really does not mean much, for it tells you that he is a human being; and as the saying goes: "To err is human." But because of what we read in Psalm 121:5–6, "The LORD is thy keeper: the LORD is thy shade upon thy right hand. The sun shall not smite thee by day, nor the moon by night," you can rely upon your Pilot with unwavering confidence. For the psalmist here uses the name Jehovah, and that name tells us that our keeper is unchangeable, not dependent upon any creature, has power over every creature, and is everywhere present.

As we saw yesterday, he will never allow our feet to move off that narrow pathway to heavenly glory. We will never fall away into everlasting destruction. And now he emphasizes this by stating that not for one fraction of a second, during the daytime or during the night, will he take his eye off us or remove his hand from holding us on that pathway to glory. As we sing:

> Jehovah is Himself thy keeper true;
> Thy changeless shade
> Jehovah, evermore on thy right hand,
> Himself hath made;
> And thee no sun by day shall ever smite,
> No moon shall harm thee in the silent night.

God is our shade, and this we need. For while we walk on that narrow path to glory, we are still in the vale of tears and sorrow, so that we have miseries in the daytime but also all through the night. Not for one fraction of a moment are we out from under the curse that came upon us because of Adam's sin, as far as our flesh is concerned. And we deserve in ourselves that flaming fire of God's holy wrath. But God is our shade. In Christ he is the umbrella that is between us and God's just and holy wrath.

Therefore, no matter how sick we are, how painful our life is, and even when the darkness of death covers us in our graves, we are safe and will pass safely through all of it and at God's appointed time will be lifted up above it all. Our keeper will keep us on the way to tasting his love everlastingly in glory.

Read: 1 Samuel 2:1–10
Psalter versification: 347:3

SAFE AT ALL TIMES

The LORD shall preserve thee from all evil: he shall preserve thy soul. The LORD shall preserve thy going out and thy coming in from this time forth, and even for evermore. —Psalm 121:7–8

It is understandable that at times we wonder why God sends us this or that affliction. We are not always ready to say with the psalmist in Psalm 119:71, "It is good for me that I have been afflicted; that I might learn thy statutes." Aches and pains in our flesh, sorrows and bereavements, losses and ridicule are not pleasant, and we can easily think along the lines of Asaph in Psalm 77:9, "Hath God forgotten to be gracious? hath he in anger shut up his tender mercies?" We do judge what happens to our flesh as evidence of God's grace and mercy or look for evidence in earthly things.

We do well, therefore, to be reminded of what God himself declares to us in Psalm 121:7–8, namely: "The LORD shall preserve thee from all evil: he shall preserve thy soul. The LORD shall preserve thy going out and thy coming in from this time forth, and even for evermore." Look first, we are here taught, at what God has done for your soul, and let what you find teach you that what he does with your flesh in no way denies that he is preserving you for the glory he promised in Christ.

Your soul he washed from all its guilt through the blood of his Son; and that soul by a rebirth through his Spirit he has renewed. Be assured then that no evil, that is, nothing that can keep you from the heavenly glory that he promised, will in any way and at any time interfere with your advance to heavenly glory.

Your going out of health and into sickness, your going out of your home and into the hospital, yea, your going out of this life and into death and the grave will in no sense keep you from everlasting blessedness. Be sure that all is well, for you are preserved by the almighty God, whom no one or nothing can prevent from fulfilling his promises.

Sing it then with enthusiasm and to his praise:

> From ev'ry evil shall He keep thy soul,
> From ev'ry sin;
> Jehovah shall preserve thy going out,
> Thy coming in;
> Above thee watching, He Whom we adore
> Shall keep thee henceforth, yea, for evermore.

Read: Psalm 119:65–72
Psalter versification: 347:4

A CRY FROM OUT OF THE DEPTHS

Out of the depths have I cried unto thee, O LORD. LORD, hear my voice: let thine ears be attentive to the voice of my supplications. —Psalm 130:1–2

Do you realize where you are? Financially you may consider yourself in difficult circumstances or in a position wherein you can add to the earthly goods you already have. Physically you may be suffering a lingering illness or be full of life, energy, and ambition, with enviable health. Socially you may be shunned and avoided, or you may be honored and highly respected. But my question is, Do you realize where you are spiritually, ethically, morally? Where are you in God's judgment?

How often is it not that we assume the position of the Pharisee in Jesus' parable (Luke 18:9–14) and are "thankful" that we are not like so and so in our city, or even in our congregation? How seldom is it that we say as the publican did: "God be merciful to me [the] sinner" (v. 13)? Yes, that is what he said according to the Greek. He called himself *the* sinner, for he could not read the hearts of others but saw his own sinful heart.

How often and how sincerely can we say the words of Psalm 130:1–2, namely: "Out of the depths have I cried unto thee, O LORD. LORD, hear my voice: let thine ears be attentive to the voice of my supplications."

Consider that one sin of Adam, which brought no bodily harm to anyone, did not consist in nasty, unclean words, and did not take God's name in vain, yet brought death to him and the whole human race. Bear in mind also that a sinful thought or desire deserves the punishment of being cast into the depths of hell.

Yes, that is where we are in ourselves: in the depths of hell as guilty in Adam. And no wonder then that the psalmist calls upon God to hear his voice. He is so very, very far away from God in those depths of sin and guilt and really does not deserve to be heard. There is salvation for those who with the psalmist say:

> From out the depths I cry to Thee;
> O let Thy ear attentive be,
> Hear Thou my supplicating plea,
> Have mercy, Lord.

Read: Psalm 130
Psalter versification: 364:1

SALVATION'S DEEPEST REASON

If thou, LORD, shouldest mark iniquities, O LORD, who shall stand? But there is forgiveness with thee, that thou mayest be feared. —Psalm 130:3–4

Would you be afraid of one who always showered good things upon you? Are we not rather afraid of the terrorists, murderers, and gangsters who exercise violence and make our streets and buildings dangerous? Yet the psalmist in Psalm 130:3–4 writes: "If thou, LORD, shouldest mark iniquities, O LORD, who shall stand? But there is forgiveness with thee, that thou mayest be feared." And our versification has it thus:

> If marked by Thee our sin appeared,
> Who, Lord, could stand in judgment cleared?
> Forgiveness, that Thou mayst be feared,
> There is with Thee.

Now, the psalmist had in verse 3 told us that we have every reason to be afraid of God, for marking our transgressions means marking us as rebels who deserve everlasting punishment. Why then does he tell us that God ought to be feared because he forgives sin? Does God not forgive us our sins so that we may live before his face with perfect peace and with all fear removed from our souls? Did not the angels, at Jesus' birth, say that now there was peace on earth? And, "Fear not: for, behold, I bring you good tidings of great joy" (Luke 2:10)?

Yes, but what the psalmist means here by fear is the awe and reverence of faith. God sent his Son to die for our sins, so that a legal basis might be laid for us to receive a new life of love and awe before God. What an amazing truth that is! God marks our sins, and no one so marked has the right to escape or way of escape by man's works. What a wonderful, awe-inspiring way it is, however, that God follows to save us! He sends his own Son to suffer all our punishment. And that ought to fill us with awe and reverence before him. God did this for sinners, rebels, enemies!

And here we have the deep reason for our salvation, namely, that we as believers may stand in awe before the God of our salvation and in his house of many mansions may everlastingly cry out: "O God, how great and good thou art." Yes, the deepest reason for our salvation is the glory of God.

Read: Jeremiah 33:1–16
Psalter versification: 364:2

WAITING IN HOPE

I wait for the LORD, my soul doth wait, and in his word do I hope. My soul waiteth for the LORD more than they that watch for the morning: I say, more than they that watch for the morning. —Psalm 130:5–6

Through the years words obtain new meaning. Speak today of a train and those who hear you think of a mechanical means of transportation that is confined to two steel tracks. But the Queen of Sheba had a train that followed her on her visit to Solomon, and it consisted in servants and dignitaries as well as the gifts she brought for Solomon.

A word with a different meaning today than as used in Scripture is the word *hope*. Today it means to most men merely desire or wish. "I hope so" means "I would like to see it happen." But in Scripture the word hope means "I expect and am confident it will happen."

Bear that in mind when you read the words of the psalmist in Psalm 130:5–6, "I wait for the LORD, my soul doth wait, and in his word do I hope. My soul waiteth for the Lord more than they that watch for the morning: I say, more than they that watch for the morning." Here the psalmist voices his great desire but also his absolute confidence that God will bless him and bring him out of the depths of guilt and sin into which he has fallen and that makes him worthy of everlasting punishment in hell.

For the psalmist is waiting, and doing so even more than those who wait for the morning, because it has come so consistently every day of his life. And what the psalmist is waiting for, plainly, is to be brought not simply out of his sin's guilt and punishment, but into that awe and reverence for God for which man was created.

And note that he says that he waits for the Lord. Applied to us today, that means that we with expectancy wait for Christ to come back and usher in that day when with body and soul God's people fully receive that reverence and awe of faith that glorified God.

Do you look eagerly for that day, and do you sing:

I wait for Thee, my soul doth wait,
Thy word my hope in ev'ry strait;
None watch, O Lord, at morning's gate
As I for Thee.

Read: Psalm 27
Psalter versification: 364:3

PLENTEOUS REDEMPTION

Let Israel hope in the LORD: for with the LORD there is mercy, and
with him is plenteous redemption. And he shall redeem Israel
from all his iniquities. —Psalm 130:7–8

In verse 3 of Psalm 130 the psalmist had stated that he whose sins are marked cannot stand. It simply is a hopeless case, because sin is rebellion against God, who is almighty and everywhere present. But we must note the fact that the psalmist speaks in Psalm 130:7–8 of a "plenteous redemption" and a redemption from all our iniquities. His words are these: "Let Israel hope in the LORD: for with the LORD there is mercy, and with him is plenteous redemption. And he shall redeem Israel from all his iniquities."

Now, our word *redeem* means to buy back, and surely by the cross of Christ our salvation was purchased; but the word the psalmist uses means to set free, to set loose from sin. And we do well to remember today and every day that we must also be set free from the love of sin and from the power of sin wherein Satan holds us. A full salvation is much more than saving us from our guilt and punishment which we deserve. The "plenteous redemption" that Jesus bought for us by his blood includes being set free from our love of sin, our sinful thoughts and desires, and includes a removal of all acts of sin in the new Jerusalem.

Listen to the versification as it sings:

> O Israel, hope thou in the Lord,
> His mercy will thy faith reward,
> He full redemption will accord
> From all thy sin.

Did you notice here mentioning of a full redemption from all sin? The idea is redemption from sin from every possible point of view. From it all we must be and will be freed.

Give this truth some serious consideration. God's mercy will realize such full redemption in the day of Christ. There we shall not be able to sin anymore. But we must also hope, that is, expect that in this life such deliverance begins, and the rest of our pilgrimage here below must more and more reveal deliverance from the love and power of sin. Pray for it, and in his mercy he will reward us with a full and blessed removal of both our guilt and sinful walk of life. He will deliver us from out of the depths into heavenly, spiritual heights.

Read: Psalm 103
Psalter versification: 364:4

ABLE TO PRAISE OUR CREATOR

Let Israel hope in the LORD: for with the LORD there is mercy, and
with him is plenteous redemption. And he shall redeem Israel
from all his iniquities. —Psalm 148:7–8

What wisdom our covenant God reveals even in the colors which he chose for his earthly creatures! How soothing for the eye is the green grass, when the bright summer sunshine comes down upon it on a cloudless summer day! How much does the pure white snow lighten up the earth on those cloudy winter days, when the sun strikes the earth from a greater angle and does not have the brilliancy and warmth it has on a summer's day!

But try to realize what life would be like had God chosen to have pure white grass with the summer's bright light falling upon it. Even now we find it necessary to wear sunglasses. What if the snowflakes on a cloudy day were green instead of white?

All this reminds us of what we read in Psalm 148:7–8, "Praise the LORD from the earth, ye dragons, and all deeps: fire, and hail; snow, and vapour; stormy wind fulfilling his word." Or as versified:

> Ye creatures in the sea
> And creatures on the earth,
> Your mighty Maker praise
> And tell His matchless worth;
> Praise Him, ye stormy winds that blow,
> Ye fire and hail, ye rain and snow.

Now, these creatures, of course, have no tongues with which to praise God. They do not even know that he exists. But God made man in his own image as a thinking, willing creature with a tongue and voice so he could praise God, that is, extol him for his virtues; and the point is that only those who can praise him for his love, mercy, and grace in Christ can and will praise him as their creator. God must in Christ be our savior if we are going to praise him as our creator. We must see him in the wisdom and power of our salvation if we are going to praise him for these in all his works in creation. We who see and know him as our savior in Christ are by him made able to praise him as our creator.

Do not then find fault with him for rain, snow, and stormy winds, but praise him as the God of wisdom and power.

Read: Psalm 148
Psalter versification: 404:3

BLEST WITH THE UPWARD LOOK

He watereth the hills from his chambers: the earth is satisfied with the fruit of thy works. He causeth the grass to grow for the cattle, and herb for the service of man: that he may bring forth food out of the earth. —Psalm 104:13–14

For us at this time of the year things are beginning to turn green, and seed has been sown so that we may have food. For others the more intense heat is returning, so that the hillsides burn and irrigation becomes very necessary. Still others are experiencing the chills of coming winter. Yet, except in the regions of the polar caps, there is a time when the soil begins to bring forth the plants we need for food. And of this we sing, as our versification of Psalm 104:13–14 does with these words:

> He waters the hills with rain from the skies,
> And plentiful grass and herbs He supplies,
> Supplying the cattle, and blessing man's toil
> With bread in abundance, with wine and with oil.

The Scriptures read thus: "He watereth the hills from his chambers: the earth is satisfied with the fruit of thy works. He causeth the grass to grow for the cattle, and herb for the service of man: that he may bring forth food out of the earth" (Ps. 104:13–14).

Even though this is true, how often do we, while we eat that food, think of God and his hand that supplies this food? How often can it not be said of us that, although we are labeled as confessing children of God, he is not in all our thoughts?

How much then do we not need God's grace to give us the upward look! We came into this world with eyes that look at earthly things; and so often we are cast down in dissatisfaction and gloom. And we are badly in need of a savior who will bless us with an upward look that is the result of knowing God as our provider, and that consists in sending praise and thanksgiving to him. Thank him for salvation as a free gift of his grace; but thank him also for food and drink. See him in all the material gifts which you receive, for they all come from him. He waters the hills and he gives us our food. Thank him, and then use the strength you derive from that food to serve and praise him.

Read: Psalm 104
Psalter versification: 286:1

A GIFT SO THAT WE MAY GIVE

Thou hast ascended on high, thou hast led captivity captive: thou hast received gifts for men; yea, for the rebellious also, that the LORD God might dwell among them. —Psalm 68:18

Yesterday we were reminded of our calling to look up to our Creator who supplies us with all our daily needs, and who saves us by his Son's blood and Spirit. It is well for us also to consider the fact that our Savior ascended up on high and has dominion over all things in heaven and on earth for our good.

For thirty years he dwelt with us and then died for our sins. For three days he was in his grave and then arose with a new, glorious life. For forty days he remained here below showing us his victory over death. And then he ascended up into heaven, fulfilling the prophecy which we find in Psalm 68:18. There we read: "Thou hast ascended on high, thou hast led captivity captive: thou hast received gifts for men; yea, for the rebellious also, that the LORD God might dwell among them."

We cannot appreciate that truth too much. His cross is of infinite value, and we must preach Christ crucified. But if you want to know what he earned for us by that cross, you must look up into heaven and see him there at God's right hand. Then you see what he is now preparing for us and what power he has to bring us there into all that glory. See that and you have a well-founded reason to sing:

O Lord, Thou hast ascended
On high in might to reign;
Captivity Thou leadest
A captive in Thy train.
Rich gifts to Thee are offered
By men who did rebel,
Who pray that now Jehovah
Their God with them may dwell.

Did you notice the change here? Psalm 68:18 has: "Thou hast received gifts *for men.*" The versification has: "Rich gifts *to Thee* are offered." Both are true. Christ received gifts for those for whom he died. But one of those gifts is to enable them to give the gifts of praise and thanks to God by turning them away from their rebellion and giving them a life of love to God. What a victory then did he win for us! Praise and thank him for it.

Read: Ephesians 4
Psalter versification: 183:1

A SOLID FOUNDATION

His foundation is in the holy mountains. The LORD loveth the gates of Zion more than all the dwellings of Jacob. Glorious things are spoken of thee, O city of God. Selah. —Psalm 87:1–3

Yes, there are holy mountains. There were holy mountains in the Old Testament times, and there are holy mountains today. In the Old Testament days, two of the hills on which Jerusalem was built were called holy: Mount Moriah, where the temple, God's dwelling place, was built, and Mount Zion, where the kings of the kingdom of Judah had their throne. That is why we read in Psalm 87:1–3, "His foundation is in the holy mountains. The LORD loveth the gates of Zion more than all the dwellings of Jacob. Glorious things are spoken of thee, O city of God."

Indeed, glorious things were spoken of Jerusalem, often called Zion because of that one hill. For God surely had his foundation there on Mount Moriah, where Christ was typically in the high priest and in the bloody sacrifices. And on Mount Zion the kings ruled as types of Christ now sitting at God's right hand and ruling all creation, in order to bring in the new Jerusalem, the glorious city of God.

There in that coming city of God, the new Jerusalem, we will find our merciful high priest, God's only begotten Son, who in his cross laid the foundation of that city where we will live with God in covenant fellowship unceasingly and in a glorious life.

This foundation, the basis for all our salvation, is in Christ whose work was pictured on Mount Moriah and on Mount Zion. No wonder glorious things are spoken of that new Jerusalem. We should speak it also as in our versification:

Zion, founded on the mountains,
God, thy Maker, loves thee well;
He has chosen thee, most precious,
He delights in thee to dwell;
God's own city, God's own city,
Who can all thy glory tell?

We will do that, and we will be glorious in that city, because Christ is there and is the foundation of that city.

Read: Psalm 67
Psalter versification: 238:1

A SOVEREIGNLY CHOSEN CHURCH

I will make mention of Rahab and Babylon to them that know me: behold Philistia, and Tyre, with Ethiopia; this man was born there. —Psalm 87:4

The glorious city of God called Zion in Psalm 87 verses 2 and 5, and declared in verse 3 to be a city of which "glorious things are spoken," has in it people who might seem to belong outside of it and far from it. Psalm 87:4 states: "I will make mention of Rahab and Babylon to them that know me: behold Philistia, and Tyre, with Ethiopia; this man was born there." Another name for Rahab is Egypt. Thus here we have listed some of the nations that were the fiercest enemies of the kingdom of Israel, the unbelieving nations round about the land of Canaan, where the church stood until the day of Pentecost. Yet we read that many from these Gentile nations were born in Zion.

Egypt was to the west and south of Canaan, Babylon was to the east, Tyre to the north, and Ethiopia to the far south, while the inhabitants of Philistia lived right there in Canaan, and Israel had to take their land away. Yet in the wonder of God's grace—and we can see that clearly today—God brought into the church people from other nations than the seed of Abraham. He has a universal church with people from every nation, tongue, and tribe. In fact, today there are more members in Christ's church from people outside of the Jewish race than in it.

Sovereignly, that is, with a perfect right and a power that cannot be challenged, God eternally chose who would be citizens in Zion. As our versification has it:

> Heathen lands and hostile peoples
> Soon shall come the Lord to know;
> Nations born again in Zion
> Shall the Lord's salvation show,
> God Almighty, God Almighty
> Shall on Zion strength bestow.

Did you note that the text ascribes it all to God? In every sense the church from Adam onward is the city of God, the city he brought forth. The city is glorious because glorious things are spoken of God who designed it and brought it into being in his Son.

Read: Revelation 5
Psalter versification: 238:2

THE FOUNTAIN OF LIFE

As well the singers as the players on instruments shall be there: all my springs are in thee. —Psalm 87:7

There is a fountain of life. No, it is not the one the world seeks and wants. But in Psalm 87:7 we read of it. The psalmist declares: "As well the singers as the players on instruments shall be there: all my springs are in thee." The word here translated as *springs* is often translated as *fountains*. And "shall be there" refers to Zion, the city of God, where there shall be these people from all those outside of Israel. In Zion shall be people from all nations, tongues, and tribes.

But what we ought to note today is that all in that city of God, both the singers and players on instruments, have their fountain of life in God. Our versification expresses it thus:

When the Lord shall count the nations,
Sons and daughters He shall see,
Born to endless life in Zion,
And their joyful song shall be,
"Blessed Zion, Blessed Zion,
All our fountains are in thee."

Out of Christ flows all our spiritual life. From him, as from a deep well that will never run dry, comes a life that will cause us to praise God, some of us with singing and others to enrich the music with instruments. What we saw two days ago is true, namely, glorious things are spoken of that city. But we must not overlook the fact that these glorious things are spoken by the citizens of the new Jerusalem.

What we begin to sing now, and will sing perfectly when Christ brings us with body and soul into this city of God, is that all our blessedness comes from God. He, in Christ, is the fountain, and therefore our song shall be everlasting praise to God. There in that new Jerusalem will Isaiah 43:21 be fulfilled: "This people have I formed for myself; they shall shew forth my praise."

What a beautiful, everlasting day it is of harmonious singing of such a beautiful melody of praise to God by a holy choir and holy players on instruments and composed of people out of every nation, tongue, and tribe, selected by God, so that glorious things are spoken of him and to him. For it is the city of God, the city he built through his Son.

Read: Revelation 4
Psalter versification: 238:3

A BLESSED EYE OPENER

Deal bountifully with thy servant, that I may live, and keep thy word. Open thou mine eyes, that I may behold wondrous things out of thy law. —Psalm 119:17–18

It is a good thing that we have traffic laws and that they must be kept. If each one could drive on whatever side of the road he wanted, and at the speed he preferred, the death rate would far exceed what it is today. There is something good about laws.

There is something even more wonderful that the psalmist tells us in Psalm 119:17–18 about God's law; and he prays that God will enable him to see those wonderful things in that law. He writes: "Deal bountifully with thy servant, that I may live, and keep thy word. Open thou mine eyes, that I may behold wondrous things out of thy law."

What is so wonderful about that law is first of all that it teaches us why we were created, namely to love God and live for his glory. Another wonderful thing is that we learn why the curse is upon this earth. It shows us why the death penalty rests upon the human race and how we must behave if we are going to live. It shows the folly of thinking that medicine, chemotherapy, and the like are going to remove the curse from mankind. It teaches us the need for the cross of Christ, if we are going to be delivered from God's holy wrath.

That is why the psalmist prays that God will deal bountifully with him so that he may be weaned away from breaking God's law. That our versification states in these words:

Thy servant, blest by Thee, shall live
And keep Thy word with awe;
Lord, open Thou my eyes to see
The wonders of Thy law.

By nature we do not see that in God's law. It does not look wonderful to us, but looks horrible. When we see that law fulfilled by Christ for us, we see the wonder of wonders. We see that the God against whom we sinned has in his Son suffered our punishment. And now we live for him in a love unto him that enables us and moves us to keep his law with awe and gladness.

Read: Psalm 119:17–32
Psalter versification: 323:1

CONSUMED WITH ARDENT ZEAL

I am a stranger in the earth: hide not thy commandments from me. My soul breaketh for the longing that it hath unto thy judgments at all times. —Psalm 119:19–20

Travel to a foreign land whose language you do not understand, and whose people do not understand one word of your language, and you will find yourself in great difficulty. Try to order a meal in a restaurant whose menu you cannot read and whose waiter or waitress cannot understand one word you say. Leave your hotel to go sightseeing and get lost on a cloudy day, when you cannot tell what is east or west, north or south, because there are no shadows. All the signs say nothing to you, and not a person can tell you your way back to the hotel. You are a stranger to the natives of that land.

We who are born again and thus have our citizenship in heaven are strangers here below to the unbelievers among whom we live. Their philosophers, educators, and psychiatrists cannot understand and help us. They cannot understand why we are so eager to know God's law and judgments. To them the psalmist is silly when in Psalm 119:19–20 he writes: "I am a stranger in the earth: hide not thy commandments from me. My soul breaketh for the longing that it hath unto thy judgments at all times." Never, no never, would they sing:

> A pilgrim in the earth am I,
> Thy will to me reveal;
> To know Thy truth my spirit yearns,
> Consumed with ardent zeal.

But God, who in Christ is our king, can set us straight. That is why the psalmist had prayed in verse 19, "Hide not thy commandments from me," and in verse 18, "Open thou mine eyes, that I may behold wondrous things out of thy law." And if your soul "breaketh for the longing that it hath" unto God's judgments (v. 20), you will be a stranger and make that your prayer.

Come, let us examine ourselves and ask whether our unbelieving neighbor and fellow worker see us as strangers. Let us pray for more of that enthusiasm to know what pleases God and what he judges to be good. Let us pray for "ardent zeal" to serve him as our glorious King.

Read: Hebrews 11:1–16
Psalter versification: 323:2

CONTEMPT WE CAN EXPECT

Thou hast rebuked the proud that are cursed, which do err from thy
commandments. Remove from me reproach and contempt; for I
have kept thy testimonies. —Psalm 119:21–22

Since spiritually we belong to another kingdom than the unbelievers do, they reproach us and show contempt. We will be despised and scorned. Upon that we can depend. In the measure that we reveal our citizenship to be in heaven, the unbelievers will hate us, despise us, and in the days of the antichrist persecute us sorely.

As citizens of a nation that conquered another land are despised and held in contempt by those conquered, so we are by those who belong to the kingdom over whose prince, Satan, Christ triumphed. That is why the psalmist writes in Psalm 119:21–22, "Thou hast rebuked the proud that are cursed, which do err from thy commandments. Remove from me reproach and contempt; for I have kept thy testimonies." He is not speaking of reproach and contempt that God hurls at him. In the next verse he says: "Princes also did sit and speak against me" (v. 23). He means rulers besides the citizens who reproached and showed contempt. Those under Satan hate those who are citizens of Christ's kingdom. Even those who should protect them, the princes, however, sit in judgment against them and speak against them, though their calling is to defend them.

This gives us a warning of what is ahead as we approach the end of time. Already we begin to see the world defending as well as protecting those who break God's law. Cursing and swearing are now considered cultured and refined language. Murder, adultery, Sabbath desecration are lauded and defended by authorities! Satan uses churches to ridicule and write scornfully of those that hold to the truth.

But note that God rebukes the proud; and in due time he will punish them. Sing then and get your children to sing:

> Thou dost rebuke the proud, O Lord,
> Who hate Thy holy Name;
> But since I keep Thy righteous law,
> Deliver me from shame.

Read: Matthew 24:1–22
Psalter versification: 323:3

MEDITATING IN GOD'S STATUTES

Princes also did sit and speak against me: but thy servant did meditate in thy statutes. Thy testimonies also are my delight and my counselors. —Psalm 119:23–24

To listen to what one has to say, and to do as you are told, is one thing. It is quite another thing to meditate on what someone else said. To meditate is to give serious thought. It is to turn over in your mind, seriously to strive to understand as fully as possible, the implications.

Of this the psalmist speaks when in Psalm 119:23–24 he states: "Princes also did sit and speak against me: but thy servant did meditate in thy statutes. Thy testimonies also are my delight and my counsellors." Here he tells us that the fruit of meditating in God's statutes is to find delight in them as God's testimony to us, and to listen to them as good counselors. We may be sure that through serious study, delving into God's testimonies, we are not going to hate those laws but let them counsel us as to how we can walk as citizens of Christ's kingdom. We will find delight in those statutes. As he said before, we will behold wondrous things out of his law.

All this is true because when a born-again child of God meditates in God's statutes, he meets God. These statutes are not merely his testimony that he is the sovereign God to whom all creation belongs and who dwells in majestic holiness. If that is all, your old nature will make you hate him and his law. But no, meditating as a believer, you by God's grace behold wondrous things out of his law and what his Son has done for you. You will see that he did not come to destroy that law but to fulfill it as our head and redeemer. You will see a law fulfilled, and your soul will sing:

> I on Thy statutes meditate,
> Tho' evil men deride;
> Thy faithful word is my delight,
> My counselor and guide.

Do not let the derision of men and their ridicule make you despise that law. Let it show you what a holy, righteous God we have and what a loving, powerful Savior he gave us, who blotted out all our sins, makes us desire to walk in love before God, and delivers us from all lawlessness, to walk as God counsels us.

Read: Psalm 19
Psalter versification: 323:4

REVIVED WITH GREATER LOVE TO GOD

My soul cleaveth unto the dust: quicken thou me according to thy word. I have declared my ways, and thou heardest me: teach me thy statutes. —Psalm 119:25–26

Quite plainly the psalmist who wrote Psalm 119 had a rough life. Because he kept God's law, he, according to verses 22–23, was reproached and held in contempt. In verses 25–26 he writes: "My soul cleaveth unto the dust: quicken thou me according to thy word. I have declared my ways, and thou heardest me: teach me thy statues." Now, that his soul cleaves to the dust means that he lies prostrate in the dust, so full of grief is he. Our versification expresses it thus:

My grieving soul revive, O Lord,
According to Thy word;
To Thee my ways I have declared,
And Thou my prayer hast heard.

Therefore, he prays that God will quicken, that is, revive him. But we are so apt at once to call down God's wrath upon the enemy, and it takes a long time before we pray that God will teach us his statutes so that we have peace and comfort.

How spiritual then is the psalmist! He had gone with his troubles to the right person and with the request for that which would help him. He wanted to know God's statutes more fully and does not want to hide his love for God in order to have a pleasant life for his flesh. He wants to serve God more fully. God comes first, not his flesh.

Looking to the future, when the antichrist is here and we cannot buy or sell, when things will really get rough for us, shall we withdraw and hide our love to God? Or shall we, as the psalmist does, pray for a clearer insight as to what pleases God? Shall we seek to please our flesh, or our God who is our creator and savior?

The answer is plain in these verses. Ridicule, contempt, persecution must never slow us down in works of love to God. They should spur us on to walk more fully as those redeemed by the blood of Christ and born with his life. Antichristian ridicule and persecution should move us to a more Christian witness, not to more fleshly comfort.

Read: Psalm 119:25–40
Psalter versification: 324:1

AN URGENT NEED

Make me to understand the way of thy precepts: so shall I talk of thy wondrous works. My soul melteth for heaviness: strengthen thou me according unto thy word. —Psalm 119:27–28

If the psalmist who wrote Psalm 119 saw the need that is recorded in verses 27–28, "Make me to understand the way of thy precepts: so shall I talk of thy wondrous works. My soul melteth for heaviness: strengthen thou me according to thy word," is it not plain that we should do likewise?

We have more revelation than he did, for we have God come in our flesh and with victory over death and the grave. We have a much richer insight into God's precepts than he did. That very revelation makes it plain that we constantly need to be strengthened according to God's word and to understand his precepts in this day and age.

The point is that sin has developed tremendously since the day of the psalmist. Satan with added years of experience comes with far craftier temptations and makes it much harder to determine what is really Christian, what we must believe, what is false and what is true doctrine. In this day when inventions such as television, radio, and the printed page can dangle so much deviltry before our eyes, we need to know what to accept and what to reject, what to seek and from what to flee. It is very urgent that our prayer is:

> Teach me to know Thy holy way
> And think upon Thy deeds;
> In grief I ask for promised grace
> According to my needs.

So quickly and easily our souls melt, and we are ready to yield to sinful practices and cravings of the flesh. We need to see clearly whether we are following Christ or the antichrist. Do we really talk properly about God's wondrous works? Or are we so ready to talk about worldly things? How many times yesterday did we talk about God and his wondrous works in Christ?

The heat of the battle so often makes our souls melt, and we cease to fight. We do need to pray daily to be strengthened according to God's word and to understand what his precepts declare is our calling at every step of our earthly way.

Read: Ephesians 6:10–24
Psalter versification: 324:2

DESIGNED AND EMPOWERED TO GLORIFY GOD

All the ends of the world shall remember and turn unto the LORD: and all the kindreds of the nations shall worship before thee. —Psalm 22:27

Our bodies were designed to have a definite number of members and organs, each having its own place, work, color, and shape. Divine wisdom designed our bodies, and God's power brought them into being.

So it is also with his church, which is often in Scripture called the body of Christ. It, too, was divinely designed to have a definite number of members, each having its own nature, place, and work to perform.

This was so clearly shown on the day of Pentecost, when the Son of God sent down his Spirit with a powerful sound, with light from divided tongues as of fire, and with unexpected speech in tongues the speakers did not know before that day. On that day the truth of Psalm 22:27 was displayed. There David wrote: "All the ends of the world shall remember and turn unto the LORD: and all the kindreds of the nations shall worship before thee." From that day of Pentecost onward the church, Christ's body, began to be gathered out of every nation, tongue, and tribe. The believers from the fleshly seed of David were powerfully moved, enlightened, and set on fire with holy zeal to speak in languages of other nations about their risen and exalted Lord, the head of the body, his church.

That sound as of a mighty rushing wind revealed the irresistible power of God that enlightens and sets on fire with holy zeal all the eternally designed members of that body, so that they will speak his praises. Indeed, we belong to a beautiful, divinely designed body. Let us then sing:

> The ends of all the earth shall hear
> And turn unto the Lord in fear;
> All kindreds of the earth shall own
> And worship Him as God alone.
> All earth to Him her homage brings,
> The Lord of lords, the King of kings.

We are many, but we are one in Christ. We are all different, but we have the Spirit of Christ and with Christ will glorify God.

Read: Acts 2:1–21
Psalter versification: 49:1

CHOOSING THE WAY OF TRUTH

Remove from me the way of lying: and grant me thy law graciously. I have chosen the way of truth: thy judgments have I laid before me. —Psalm 119:29–30

The psalmist writes in Psalm 119:29–30, "Remove from me the way of lying: and grant me thy law graciously. I have chosen the way of truth: thy judgments have I laid before me." This must not surprise us, even though he had from verse 1 onward revealed himself as a very spiritual child of God. Will such men walk in the lie and have to pray to be delivered from the way of lying?

Yes, they will. For no sin of any kind is very far away from the most faithful child of God. Here below we still have only a small beginning of the new obedience. With Paul we all must say: "O wretched man that I am! who shall deliver me from the body of this death?" (Rom. 7:24). And if we do not lie with our lips, we do by our deeds.

Think that over today. We go by the name Christian; but can Christ always be seen in our lives? Are we bearing a true or a false witness by our conduct? Do we clearly reveal that we are disciples of Christ? When we say that we were lucky or unlucky, or bet this or bet that, are we manifesting faith in God and the conviction that all comes out of his counsel? When we gamble with goods he gave us, are we using these things in the fear of his name? Are we glorifying him with these items which really belong to him and which we have only so we may serve and glorify him?

Well may we pray and learn to sing:

> Keep me from falsehood, let Thy law
> With me in grace abide;
> The way of faithfulness I choose,
> Thy precepts are my guide.

All through the day there is reason to pray for that law to be in our hearts as our guide and to be kept from falsehood. We need God's grace to keep us in the way of his law. Salvation is in every sense a gift; and we earn not the smallest blessing it contains. In fact, that we receive anything from God in his grace means that we deserve the opposite. God's grace is God giving blessings for nothing to those who deserve visitation in his wrath. It is for Christ's sake, not ours, that we are rewarded for the good works he enabled us to perform.

Read: Proverbs 6:1–19
Psalter versification: 324:3

RUNNING WITH AN ENLARGED HEART

I have stuck unto thy testimonies: O LORD, put me not to shame. I will run the way of thy commandments, when thou shalt enlarge my heart. —Psalm 119:31–32

Let us be honest and speak the truth. We are so frail spiritually and have a sinful flesh that troubles us every step of our way. So often we are proud of our sins rather than ashamed and sorry. By God's grace we have not fallen into unbelief and hatred against God; but we still are prone to stumble into sins which we ought to hate.

Is there ever going to be a change? Will we ever love God with all our heart? Yes, but it will not be because we in our strength put off all our love of sin and get full control of all our members. Listen to the psalmist in Psalm 119:31–32, "I have stuck unto thy testimonies: O LORD, put me not to shame. I will run the way of thy commandments, when thou shalt enlarge my heart." Get that! When God enlarges our hearts, we will run in his commandments.

As the newborn babe grows, its heart becomes larger. So it must be with us as children of God. Our hearts must become larger than they now are if we are going to run in God's commandments. That is, our hearts must be able to hold more spiritual blood to send to every fiber of our being if we are to run in holiness. That spiritual blood is love to God. A large heart full of it will walk as Christ walked.

But note that God must enlarge that heart; and then we will not walk but run in love to God. We sing that in our versification:

I cleave unto Thy truth, O Lord;
From shame deliver me;
In glad obedience I will live
Thro' strength bestowed by Thee.

There you have it. Strength bestowed by God will enable us to run the way of his commandments. Boast of doing so in your own strength, and you show yourself in Satan's clutches and that your heart is large with hatred against God. Love to God will praise him and make us strive to run faster in service to him than in the past. We will not be satisfied with walking but will want to serve him fully with every fiber of our being. Pray then that you may be kept from the shameful way of sin and of boasting. Run in the confession of God's love and grace.

Read: Psalm 119:97–112
Psalter versification: 324:4

WHOLEHEARTED PRAISE

I will praise thee, O LORD, with my whole heart; I will shew forth all thy
marvellous works. I will be glad and rejoice in thee: I will sing praise to thy name,
O thou most High. —Psalm 9:1–2

Many years ago, when our country was at war, a soldier wrote and said that the chaplain had preached on the subject of heaven and said that his first fifty years there, he was going to fish and hunt. Plainly he knew nothing about heaven. And we ourselves often entertain foolish notions about life in the new Jerusalem.

But listen to David as in Psalm 9:1–2 he writes: "I will praise thee, O LORD, with my whole heart; I will shew forth all thy marvellous works. I will be glad and rejoice in thee: I will sing praise to thy name, O thou most High."

Do you want that kind of heaven? Then you will now want to praise him, show his marvelous works, and rejoice in him. Or as we sing it:

O Lord Most High, with all my heart
Thy wondrous works I will proclaim;
I will be glad and give Thee thanks
And sing the praises of Thy Name.

Now, if it is true that we look forward to such a life, it is true that we purpose the remainder of our lives here below to praise God's name, because we rejoice in him who wrought such marvelous works through his Son, with whom we will live in the glory of his kingdom.

What a marvelous work he wrought in that Son! We are still under the curse that rests upon us in this vale of tears. Our bodies also are not yet glorified. But what a huge load of sin has he removed. It may be threescore years, and thus 25,550 days of sin which we committed. Multiply that by an innumerable host of saints, whose sins have been paid in full, and what a marvelous work that is! All accomplished by pouring out his holy wrath on that Son.

What a reason we have to be glad and rejoice in our God with such love for us! What a reason to praise him and thank him. We need an everlasting life to do that. And it is promised us. What is more, there it will indeed be a wholehearted praise of people who are spiritually glad.

Read: Psalm 9
Psalter versification: 17:1

OUR CAUSE MAINTAINED

When mine enemies are turned back, they shall fall and perish at thy presence. For thou hast maintained my right and my cause; thou satest in the throne judging right. —Psalm 9:3–4

A truth that we are so inclined to doubt is that God loves us and watches mercifully over us. It takes only a little misery, while the ungodly increase in their wealth and pleasures of the flesh, and we are ready to stop praising God and talking of his marvelous works. With Rebekah we are so quick to ask, "Why am I thus?" or, "Why does this have to happen to me?" (Gen. 25:22).

We do well therefore to listen to David, who indeed had a rough life with enemies within and outside of his kingdom. In Psalm 9:3–4 he wrote: "When mine enemies are turned back, they shall fall and perish at thy presence. For thou hast maintained my right and my cause; thou satest in the throne judging right."

Take careful note of that last statement. God is ruler over all things, sitting on a throne that is over all creation, and he judges righteously. Never doubt any one of these elements, no matter how miserable your life becomes, and regardless of how many and fierce your enemies become. God is never on vacation and never sleeps. He is on his throne with perfect control over every creature from Satan down to every speck of dust.

That he judges righteously means that he will not let anything happen to those whose sins his Son blotted out that will keep them from the particular place and degree of glory he eternally planned for them and promised them. In fact, all their griefs and sorrows, miseries and enemies he will use to bring them there at the right time and in the right way.

What a comfort as we approach the days of the antichrist, when the devil will raise up his "man of sin" (2 Thess. 2:3) to abuse us, our children, and our grandchildren. Signs of this are all around us today already, both outside of and inside of the church world. But let us sing:

The Lord, the everlasting King,
Is seated on His judgmentthrone;
The righteous judge of all the world
Will make His perfect justice known.

Read: 2 Thessalonians 2
Psalter versification: 17:2

KNOWING GOD IN HIS FAITHFULNESS

And they that know thy name will put their trust in thee: for thou, LORD, hast not forsaken them that seek thee. —Psalm 9:10

Although it may not look that way because we closed our eyes, yet God is always faithful and can be trusted to do fully all that which he promised us. Even though on a cloudy night we cannot see the moon or the stars, they are there above us in the sky; and it is folly to say that they are not there, just because we cannot see them. Yet so often we go by what our fleshly eyes see or cannot see and behave as though what the eye of faith sees does not exist. For we have closed our eye of faith and judge all things by what our fleshly eye sees.

David warns us against this when in Psalm 9:10 he writes: "And they that know thy name will put their trust in thee: for thou, LORD, hast not forsaken them that seek thee." David here uses the name Elohim, the Almighty One, and that name says that all the creatures have strength only when and in the measure that God gives it to them. And therefore, knowing God's name means that we know and see him with the eye of faith as the one who has every creature, large or small, animate or inanimate, in the angel world or in the world of men, completely under his control. They can only do what he eternally decreed that they would do and what he gives them the strength to do.

No wonder then that David says that those who know God's name can trust him and see that he never forsakes one of his children. And with David we can sing:

All they, O Lord, that know Thy Name
Their confidence in Thee will place,
For Thou hast ne'er forsaken them
Who earnestly have sought Thy face.

Consider then that, since our God is almighty, no one can prevent him from doing what he promised us, and no one has the strength to make him change his mind. See him then in that name, with your eye of faith, as an unchangeably faithful God who will destroy all your enemies and bring you to glory. And when things look bad, as far as the eye of flesh is concerned, look at him with the eye of faith.

Read: Revelation 20
Psalter versification: 17:4

SINGING GOD'S PRAISES PROPERLY

Sing praises to the LORD, which dwelleth in Zion: declare among the people his doings. —Psalm 9:11

David began Psalm 9 by declaring that he would praise God with his whole heart. But now in verse 11 he writes: "Sing praises to the LORD, which dwelleth in Zion: declare among the people his doings." Plainly he is calling others to do what he had been given grace to do. And the truth behind this is that if we truly are singing God's praises wholeheartedly, we will want others to do so as well.

A question we must answer, therefore, is whether we do sing God's praises with our whole heart. The question is not whether we sing his praises with our voices and tongues. There are many who hate God and never enter into his house of prayer to worship him who will sing certain hymns or oratorios because they like the music or are seeking the praise of men. And a pointed and important question is, What are your favorite songs? Are they the songs of men, or songs of praise to God? And is this one your favorite song because of the words, the truth expressed in it that praises God, or is it because of the smooth-flowing melody and rich harmony?

Another question is whether we are singing to men or to God. Do we have God in our thoughts when we sing? Are we perhaps singing so rapidly that we cannot even give thought to the truth we express with our lips? Notice the versification of this psalm:

Sing praises to the Lord Most High,
To Him Who doth in Zion dwell,
Declare His mighty deeds abroad,
His deeds among the nations tell.

Here is a call to sing praises unto God as well as of God. We must declare his mighty deeds abroad, but in a way that we direct our praise to God. We must do it in a way that teaches others to praise him. We must want others to know what he did for us in his Son, but our deepest concern must be that others confess him and with us praise him as the one of whom, through whom, and unto whom are all things. We must be interested in their salvation, but chiefly because we want God to have all the praise that is due unto his name. Then we will sing only that which is based on true biblical doctrine.

Read: Psalm 107:1–31
Psalter versification: 17:5

BLESSED MEEKNESS

LORD, my heart is not haughty, nor mine eyes lofty: neither do I exercise myself in great matters, or in things too high for me. —Psalm 131:1

Psalm 131 is another brief psalm, being only one verse more than Psalm 117, which is the shortest chapter in the Bible. And in verse 1 the psalmist declares: "LORD, my heart is not haughty, nor mine eyes lofty: neither do I exercise myself in great matters, or in things too high for me." Our versification helps us understand this when it says:

> Not haughty is my heart,
> Not lofty is my pride;
> I do not seek to know the things
> God's wisdom has denied.

The things "too high for me" are things God's wisdom had denied him knowledge of in this life. And to be haughty and proud is to act and think that we know better than God what ought to happen.

How about it? Were you fully satisfied with what God did yesterday? Are you willing to leave all things up to him today? We must bow before his will. We do, without much thought, often pray, "Thy will be done," but only a few minutes later we are so apt to pray that he will change things to satisfy our plans and ambitions.

Yet when God performs works which we do not understand, we should go in our thoughts to the cross of Christ. Many devout children of God stood around that cross wondering why it had to happen and wishing it had not taken place. But after the day of Pentecost they understood; and so do we.

There are those events that we call accidents. There are works of God that touch our families and lives and seem to deny his love and make us question his wisdom. But by all means do not in haughtiness and pride think for one moment that you could have run the world better or ordered in greater wisdom the things in your life. Be sure that all God's works are wrought in inscrutable wisdom. Never did he make a mistake. Never did things slip out of his control.

There are things too high for us. But in childlike meekness leave all things in God's hands. He knows the best means and the best way to fulfill all his promises to us. "Blessed are the meek; for they shall inherit the earth" (Matt. 5:5).

Read: Romans 8:28–39
Psalter versification: 366:1

CHILDLIKE TRUST IN GOD

Surely I have behaved and quieted myself, as a child that is weaned of his mother: my soul is even as a weaned child. —Psalm 131:2

When in Psalm 131:1 David confessed that he is not haughty and his eyes were not lofty, one might be inclined to say that his very words reveal pride and conceit. If you please, he says to *God* that he is not haughty. He says this to one who reads the heart and from whom nothing can be hid. Do not such words then show both pride and ignorance?

His words in the next verse seem to reveal even more pride. For there he states: "Surely I have behaved and quieted myself, as a child that is weaned of his mother: my soul is even as a weaned child" (Ps. 131:2). Is that not boasting of what he did, and that before the face of God?

No, David's reference to a mother reveals his humility. For he is speaking of what state a mother brought her child unto, not what he achieved by his own strength or ingenuity. Rightly understood, he confesses here that unto which God brought him. He trusts in God and calmly rests in the assurance that God will take care of him. He has a childlike contentment given to him and worked in him by God. As our versification sings it:

> With childlike trust, O Lord,
> In Thee I calmly rest,
> Contented as a little child
> Upon its mother's breast.

David is therefore confessing what God did to him. The fact that he begins the psalm with the word *LORD* reveals that. The psalm speaks of a divinely wrought humility, a childlike faith in God. And his use of the pronouns *my, mine, myself, me,* and *I* do not reveal pride but are used that he may express what God did to him.

Can you say that with David? Can you humbly say this is true of you as well as it was of David? Are you weaned from your fleshly desires so that you are content with whatever God sends you, assured it works together for your good? And, if you please, David could confess that long before the cross of Christ. Do we not have more reason than he to walk in childlike trust in God? If you cannot walk that way, then pray for the grace to do so.

Read: Psalm 130
Psalter versification: 366:2

HOPE THAT MAKETH NOT ASHAMED

Let Israel hope in the LORD from henceforth and for ever. —Psalm 131:3

If there is one word that is abused and wrongly taken upon the lips of a child of God very often in this day and age, it is the word *hope*. Much of the time we say, "I hope so," and all that we mean thereby is, "I would like to see it happen." However, the word *hope* means "to desire with expectancy and believe that it is attainable." And the hope of the child of God, as presented in Scripture, always has both of those elements in it, namely, desire or longing and expectation or assurance that the object hoped for will come.

Thus when in Psalm 131:3 David writes: "Let Israel hope in the LORD from henceforth and for ever," he means that we should desire salvation and its blessings, which God promises us, and live in the confidence that he will fulfill all of his promises in the minutest detail. Thus our versification has:

Ye people of the Lord,
In Him alone confide;
From this time forth and evermore
His wisdom be your guide.

All this fits in so beautifully with David's previous words that his heart is not haughty, and that he has behaved and quieted his soul (the Hebrew word is *soul* rather than *myself*). He is now like a child weaned, weaned away from his former silly and haughty notions that he knew better than God what was good for him.

What about you and me? Do we hope in God? When it comes down to it, you and I cannot hope in God's promises without conviction that they will be fulfilled. We hope, do we not, that Christ will return? We hope that he will lift us up above the curse which now rests upon this earth. But we also hope that he will deliver us completely from the power of sin, so that in the new Jerusalem it will be impossible for us to sin. We will awake with Christ's likeness and forever be satisfied (Ps. 17:15). But we hope for all this in the expectation of its coming. We hope because we are confident that it will take place.

Use the word *hope* that way. And live in that hope, which in Romans 5:5 Paul says "maketh not ashamed."

Read: Romans 5
Psalter versification: 366:3

WHERE OUR BLESSEDNESS BEGINS

Blessed is he whose transgression is forgiven, whose sin is covered. Blessed is the man unto whom the LORD imputeth not iniquity, and in whose spirit there is no guile. —Psalm 32:1–2

What do you consider to be a blessing? What above all would you like to have happen to you in this life? What do you consider very, very necessary and have before your consciousness as that for which by all means you should pray?

In Psalm 32:1–2 David writes: "Blessed is he whose transgression is forgiven, whose sin is covered. Blessed is the man unto whom the LORD imputeth not iniquity, and in whose spirit there is no guile." Do you agree? How many of your prayers contain an urgent plea for this blessing of having your sins covered and of not having your iniquity imputed to you?

It is easy to count material goods, life, and health as blessings, and then only way back in the mind to consider forgiveness of sin a blessing. We may be called upon in our worship service in God's house to sing the words below, but their seriousness and significance may not be before our minds. The versification has it thus:

How blest is he whose trespass
Hath freely been forgiv'n,
Whose sin is wholly covered
Before the sight of heav'n.
Blest he to whom Jehovah
Imputeth not his sin,
Who hath a guileless spirit,
Whose heart is true within.

Many, if not most, of the prayers that are heard in broadcasts, in public meetings, and even from pulpits of churches omit this important item in prayer and reveal that social, political, and material advantages for the flesh are much more important and are given much more time in prayer.

Do you feel pressing down upon your soul your awful load of guilt? Are you one of those of whom Jesus spoke, when he called those laboring to get rid of their load of sin and still finding themselves with the heavy load and as not having reached one bit of rest? If so, agree with David that he whose sin is forgiven has a rich blessing.

Be sure that here is where our blessings begin. If we do not have that blessing, we have no blessings at all.

Read: Psalm 32
Psalter versification: 83:1

THE WAY TO KNOWING GOD'S LOVE

I acknowledge my sin unto thee, and mine iniquity have I not hid. I said, I will confess my transgressions unto the Lord; and thou forgavest the iniquity of my sin. Selah. —Psalm 32:5

Having written in Psalm 32:2 that the man is blessed whose spirit has no guile, that is, no insincerity, David states in verse 5: "I acknowledged my sin unto thee, and mine iniquity have I not hid. I said, I will confess my transgressions unto the Lord; and thou forgavest the iniquity of my sin." This presents us with an awesome truth. If we fail to confess our sins, we are trying to hide them. And if we try to hide them, we are rightly branded as those whose spirit is full of guile.

Let us, every step of our way, from today onward, take with us the truth that defending ourselves in our sins is adding to our sins. We cannot cover our sins, but trying to do so only reveals how sinful we are. We are not deceiving God but deceiving ourselves.

Therefore, the call comes to us to confess every sin and not try to cover one either by silence or by untrue words. Instead, we must run to God with our sins, seeking salvation in his grace. Sing this truth:

> While I kept guilty silence
> My strength was spent with grief,
> Thy hand was heavy on me,
> My soul found no relief;
> But when I owned my trespass,
> My sin hid not from Thee,
> When I confessed transgression,
> Then Thou forgavest me.

The way to the assurance that Christ's blood blotted out all our sins is to confess that they are sins. It is to run to God and not merely admit to men that we sinned. It is running with a heart that expresses its hatred of that sin. Doing this, we confess our love to God against whom we sinned. Finding this love to God in our souls, we find a work in us that reveals God's love to us. Then, instead of feeling the heavy hand of God upon us in holy anger, we enjoy his heavy hand of mercy upon us as manifested in Christ.

Then we will enjoy the blessedness of forgiveness and live in the assurance of God's love for us.

Read: Luke 15:1–24
Psalter versification: 83:2

ENCOMPASSED WITH GOD'S MERCY

Many sorrows shall be to the wicked: but he that trusteth in the LORD, mercy shall compass him about. —Psalm 32:10

God is everywhere, and every creature exists only because God is there upholding it in his providence. But God is not everywhere with his mercy. As David wrote in Psalm 32:10, "Many sorrows shall be to the wicked: but he that trusteth in the LORD, mercy shall compass him about."

And that the wicked shall know many sorrows is because God encompasses them with his holy wrath. The wicked come up against God in their hatred toward him, and he comes up against them and gives them sorrows for their hatred toward him; and he comes up against them and gives them sorrows for their sins. A foolish man who runs into a bush that is full of sharp thorns will have many sorrows. How much more painful shall it be to run up against the almighty and holy God?

Remember that each time we sin, we are opposing God. It makes no difference whether it is a sinful thought, desire, word, or physical deed, sinning is going against the God who created us so that we might serve him in love.

But there is forgiveness for those who look to God in hatred of their sins. For trust in God—and David calls those who seek forgiveness those who trust in God—is first of all conviction that he is God and has the right to order our steps and decide what our conduct and behavior in his creation must be. Trusting him, we shall be surrounded and encircled by and with his mercy, as we sing:

> So let the godly seek Thee
> In times when Thou art near;
> No whelming floods shall reach them,
> Nor cause their hearts to fear.
> In Thee, O Lord, I hide me,
> Thou savest me from ill,
> And songs of Thy salvation
> My heart with rapture thrill.

The point is that those who trust in God are protected from the fiery darts of God's holy wrath. For they are encompassed, that is, encircled by Christ, who is our merciful savior. In him God treats us tenderly and in his time will bring us to his house of many mansions, where there is no sorrow but only joy and gladness.

Are you trusting him to do this to you?

Read: Psalm 37:1–29
Psalter versification: 83:3

NEEDED: AN UNDERSTANDING HEART

Teach me, O LORD, the way of thy statutes; and I shall keep it unto the end.
Give me understanding, and I shall keep thy law; yea, I shall observe it
with my whole heart. —Psalm 119:33–34

A way can be a pathway leading to a particular place or object. It may also be a manner of conducting oneself. Thus sometimes we say: "If you continue to live that way, you will be sorry." What the psalmist wrote in Psalm 119:33–34 means both. He writes: "Teach me, O LORD, the way of thy statutes; and I shall keep it unto the end. Give me understanding, and I shall keep thy law; yea, I shall observe it with my whole heart."

Quite plainly that way here is a pathway, for he will keep it to the end. However, understanding that way and doing so with his whole heart speaks of his conduct. And if the saints in the Old Testament times needed to be taught where to walk and how, we surely also do, and need to pray for understanding.

We have so many temptations that are far more subtle than those of the saints in the day when this psalm was written. Our lives are so crowded with the things of this world, which are so close to us. Satan has so many new devices to use to try to make us leave that path of God's law.

What we need is an understanding heart. We must not only know the path on which we must walk but also whether this deed or that is walking on that path. We can go to church on the Sabbath, but in our conduct are we worshiping God with our whole heart? Are our works there those of pure love to God? We may sing it there, but is this our sincere prayer?

Teach me, O Lord, Thy way of truth,
And from it I will not depart;
That I may steadfastly obey,
Give me an understanding heart.

Now, to get an understanding heart, we must live close to God's word and pray that he will teach us that way of his statutes. By nature our hearts do not like walking in that law of God. We love our own flesh too much. Therefore, make this your prayer. There is so much that we still need to learn.

Read: Psalm 119:33–48
Psalter versification: 325:1

CLEANSED FROM COVETOUSNESS

Make me to go in the path of thy commandments; for therein do I delight. Incline my heart unto thy testimonies, and not to covetousness. —Psalm 119:35–36

Do you realize that Satan's approach to Adam and Eve was to get them to fall into covetousness? His end was to get them to turn away from God and to live in hatred toward him. But his means was to get them to covet God's wisdom and sovereignty. Therefore, he told them that eating of the forbidden fruit would make them to be like God. And all our sin today is due to the fact that we covet God's unique position as our lawgiver, lord, and master, who may tell us what we must do and how to live.

It is also for that reason that the psalmist in Psalm 119:35–36 writes: "Make me to go in the path of thy commandments; for therein do I delight. Incline my heart unto thy testimonies, and not to covetousness."

Or as we sing it:

> In Thy commandments make me walk,
> For in Thy law my joy shall be;
> Give me a heart that loves Thy will,
> From discontent and envy free.

Did you notice that the psalmist speaks again of the path of God's commandments and prays that he may walk therein with a heart that is not covetous? It is the discontent of covetousness that makes us walk in sin. Walking in God's law demands complete self-denial. That is why the psalmist prays that his heart may be inclined to God's testimonies. Our hearts go out to the thing that pleases our flesh, not to what pleases God. When it comes down to it, we want to be God. Satan said that we could be like him, and our old nature wants us to tell God to obey us and be our servant.

Our lips may not say that. Adam's did not either. But our walk does, and often our idea of heaven is that it is a place where all will serve us. Serving God there is not in our thoughts of heaven's blessedness.

How necessary then that we pray earnestly and fervently that God will make us go in the path of righteousness. He must do it, and he sent his Son to earn the right for us to have it and to incline our hearts to loving submission to him. Make it your prayer today.

Read: Luke 12:13–31
Psalter versification: 325:2

QUICKENED IN GOD'S WAY

Turn away mine eyes from beholding vanity; and quicken thou me in thy way.
Stablish thy word unto thy servant, who is devoted to thy fear. —Psalm 119:37–38

In the wisdom that God gave Solomon, he wrote: "Vanity of vanities; all is vanity" (Ecc. 1:2). And in his grace God gave the psalmist in Psalm 119:37–38 to write: "Turn away mine eyes from beholding vanity; and quicken thou me in thy way. Stablish thy word unto thy servant, who is devoted to thy fear."

Two truths may be noted here. Beholding vanity is the opposite of walking in God's way, that is, serving God. And in order to be turned from vanity, we must be established in God's word.

Now, vanity is emptiness; and man's life by nature is vanity because it is completely void or empty of the service of God for which he was created.

The point to consider today is that because our lives are so full of sin, they are empty of service to God with our whole being and with all our earthly possessions. The psalmist does not merely mean that we must want to see that there is vanity in our lives, such as lack of worship of God, but that we must be kept from being attracted by all the vanity that is all around us. Our versification sings:

> Turn Thou my eyes from vanity,
> And cause me in Thy ways to tread;
> O let Thy servant prove Thy word
> And thus to godly fear be led.

Plainly he wants to be stopped from being attracted by that which keeps him from serving God and wants to serve him more fully.

How about it? A bottle cannot be full of water and of air at the same time. One's life cannot be empty of the service of God and at the same time be full of love toward God. We with the psalmist must want to have our hearts completely full of love to God and not be satisfied until that is the case with us.

Being turned from vanity means that we are quickened, that is, given zeal to do only what God calls us to do, namely, love him and serve him always every step of our way.

Is that your desire, or are you satisfied with your sinful walk?

Read: Isaiah 33
Psalter versification: 325:3

SAVED THAT WE MAY SERVE

Turn away my reproach which I fear: for thy judgments are good. Behold, I have longed after thy precepts: quicken me in thy righteousness. —Psalm 119:39–40

A murderer scheduled to die tomorrow in an electric chair will have some serious thoughts and mixed emotions. He should be filled with fear and be moved to plead for his life. If he is a child of God, as David who murdered Bathsheba's husband was, he will by God's grace confess that he deserves that punishment. That is what the psalmist also confesses in Psalm 119:39–40 in these words: "Turn away my reproach which I fear: for thy judgments are good. Behold, I have longed after thy precepts: quicken me in thy righteousness."

His reproach is his blame, his discredit, or if you will, his guilt, which calls for punishment in the terrors of hell. Because he believes that God's judgments are good and that he deserves this punishment, and because, being born again, he desires to walk in God's precepts, he does pray that his life may be spared in a righteous way. As we sing:

Turn Thou away reproach and fear;
Thy righteous judgments I confess;
To know Thy precepts I desire,
Revive me in Thy righteousness.

But we must not put too much stress on this escape from punishment and on a life of joy in its place. Take a good look at the psalmist's confession and his prayer that he be saved in a righteous way.

If we want relief and life in an unrighteous way, we add to our sins. For then we want nothing to do with Christ and his cross and are not longing to keep God's precepts. We are not revealing a love for God and to have him glorified but are manifesting a love for self. If we want to be quickened, or revived, we must want a life of love to God with a desire or longing to walk in his law and to say that his judgments are good.

The debt must be paid in full; but we must also long to be able to serve God fully with every fiber of our being. We may desire life; but we must want to live a life that says that God's ordinances are good and that we long to be able to keep his precepts perfectly. We must desire the removal of our guilt by Christ's cross; but we must also long for the work of his Spirit to fill us with love for God.

Read: Psalm 51
Psalter versification: 325:4

June 8

COMPLETELY AND PERFECTLY SAFE

God is our refuge and strength, a very present help in trouble. Therefore will not we fear, though the earth be removed, and though the mountains be carried into the midst of the sea; Though the waters thereof roar and be troubled, though the mountains shake with the swelling thereof. Selah. —Psalm 46:1–3

Who is there that can stop a violent earthquake? Who can put a cork on the mouth of a volcano and stop the flow of destructive and killing lava? Who can protect his house when a tornado is headed toward it? Who can ward off the attack of an overwhelming number of fully armed murderous thieves?

The answer we will find in Psalm 46:1–3, where we read: "God is our refuge and strength, a very present help in trouble. Therefore will not we fear, though the earth be removed, and though the mountains be carried into the midst of the sea; though the waters thereof roar and be troubled, though the mountains shake with the swelling thereof."

The almighty God is our hope. He has all things completely under his control. Threatening political, social, and economic situations are not due to temporary loss of control. With God there are no accidents. Every creature large and small, with life and without life, depends every split second upon God for its existence and does only what he is pleased to do through it. We have, therefore, a powerful Father who does not simply keep every creature from working against our good, but in working what is for the good he promised us. He is our refuge but also our strength. In him we hide, and his strength will surely keep us safe and bring us to everlasting blessedness.

A song we do well to learn and sing is our Psalter versification:

God is our refuge and our strength,
Our ever present aid,
And, therefore, though the earth remove,
We will not be afraid;
Though hills amidst the seas be cast,
Though foaming waters roar,
Yea, though the mighty billows shake
The mountains on the shore.

We are headed for "wars and rumors of wars," nation rising up against nation, "famines, and pestilences, and earthquakes in divers places (Matt. 24:6–7). But we are not only safe; all these will serve the purpose of preparing the way for Christ's return and will bring us to the city of God and its everlasting blessedness.

Read: Psalm 46
Psalter versification: 126:1

CERTAIN BLESSEDNESS IN THE CITY OF GOD

There is a river, the streams whereof shall make glad the city of God, the holy place of the tabernacles of the most High. God is in the midst of her; she shall not be moved: God shall help her, and that right early. —Psalm 46:4–5

There is a place where all misery and tears will forever be behind us. It is a place where we will dwell in the sunshine of God's presence and where nothing and no one can ever drive us out and away from heavenly blessedness. Of that place the psalmist sings in Psalm 46:4–5. He writes: "There is a river, the streams whereof shall make glad the city of God, the holy place of the tabernacles of the most High. God is in the midst of her; she shall not be moved: God shall help her, and that right early."

Satan succeeded in getting Adam and Eve out of the place that pictured this realm of everlasting bliss. But he is not going to keep us from entering and living forever in that city of which the garden of Eden was only a picture. And of all this we can be sure because God dwells in that city, and he is our refuge (v. 7). We ought to see this truth much more clearly than the psalmist, for by faith we have seen God's Son come into our flesh, blot out our sins, rise from the dead again the third day, and ascend to God's right hand with power over all things in heaven and on earth (Matt. 28:18).

Who can prevent that King from bringing us to this city and from keeping us there? His enemies God used to bring him to his cross for our salvation. The grave and death could not hold him; and now he has power over all our enemies. Satan and his host, the heathen, that is, all the unbelievers, are unable to lift one finger against us. We will reach that city.

If there ever was a safe place, if there ever was refuge for the oppressed, it is in that city of God. Sing it then:

> A river flows whose streams make glad
> The city of our God,
> The holy place wherein the Lord
> Most High has His abode;
> Since God is in the midst of her,
> Unmoved her walls shall stand,
> For God will be her early help,
> When trouble is at hand.

Read: John 14:1–27
Psalter versification: 126:2

THE SILENCE OF FAITH

Be still, and know that I am God: I will be exalted among the heathen, I will be exalted in the earth. —Psalm 46:10

One reveals one's faith by what one says. However, that speaking is not only that which is produced by the lips and voice. As the saying goes: "Actions speak louder than words." By our behavior or conduct we with a silent mouth say whether we are children of God or of the devil. But there is also a silence wrought by mouth and heart which is produced by faith. And there are times when, as the psalmist says in Psalm 46:10, we must "Be still, and know that I am God: I will be exalted among the heathen, I will be exalted in the earth."

The word *still*, used here, is most often translated as "be feeble, be idle, weaken, let alone, let go," and "stay." Quite plainly then we are here exhorted to stop questioning God's strength and faithfulness to his promises. Positively it means that we have implicit trust in God as our refuge. Beautifully this truth is sung in our versification:

> Be still and know that I am God,
> O'er all exalted high;
> The subject nations of the earth
> My Name shall magnify.
> The Lord of Hosts is on our side,
> Our safety to secure;
> The God of Jacob is for us
> A refuge strong and sure.

That we may have unshaken trust in God and be absolutely sure that we will dwell with him, the psalmist had written in verse 8: "Come, behold the works of the Lord, what desolations he hath made in the earth." And for us that means that we study the Scriptures and behold how he saved Noah and his family, brought Israel up out of Egypt and safely through the Red Sea, and gave Israel the whole promised land of Canaan. It means that we look closely at Christ and his cross every time we have doubts and fears. That cross was not the failure it looked like to some at that time. It was God's way of making a place for us in the new Jerusalem, the city of God and place of everlasting blessedness.

Be still then. Be silent as far as doubts and fears are concerned. We have a refuge, an absolutely safe place, and an absolutely safe journey to that city of God.

Read: Psalm 4
Psalter versification: 126:5

ENCIRCLED BY THE LOVE OF GOD

Unto thee, O God, do we give thanks, unto thee do we give thanks: for that thy name is near thy wondrous works declare. —Psalm 75:1

To give thanks unto a person is to say that he is good and has performed a good deed. The Hebrew word for giving thanks is to throw out the hand, that is, to point to one, to point him out as one who has done something good. Therefore, if there is anyone who should be thanked, it is God. No matter what he does, he always does what is good. That is why the psalmist writes in Psalm 75:1, "Unto Thee, O God, do we give thanks, unto thee do we give thanks: for that thy name is near thy wondrous works declare." Here he is pointing to God and his wondrous works.

Now, that God's name is near means that God himself is near us, embracing us with his love. For us this ought certainly to be clear, for by faith we have seen his wondrous works of his Son's virgin birth, blotting out of our sins by his cross, rising from the dead and ascending to God's right hand, and obtaining power over all things in heaven and on earth, so that heavenly goodness is prepared for us in God's house. And that we are so different spiritually from the unbelievers ought to cause us to point to him and say: "O God, how good and great thou art!"

We have every reason to sing:

To Thee, O God, we render thanks,
To Thee give thanks sincere,
Because Thy wondrous works declare
That Thou art ever near.

You and I must point to God and tell others that he is good. But we must also go to him with our words in prayer, telling him that he is good and that his work of salvation in Christ is wonderful.

We must tell our families but also the unbelievers with whom we work. We must be faithful witnesses of him, the God of all good. And by all means, every night before we close our eyes in sleep, we must thank him for encircling us with his love all during the day. Yea, we must thank him for giving us thankful hearts. That, too, is a wondrous work and one that he wrought in us by his Spirit. No wonder that the psalmist in this verse says twice that we give thanks to this wonder-working God.

Read: Psalm 75
Psalter versification: 206:1

SAVED IN RIGHTEOUS JUDGMENT

When I shall receive the congregation I will judge uprightly. The earth and all the inhabitants thereof are dissolved: I bear up the pillars of it. Selah. —Psalm 75:2–3

God is near to his people, encircling them in his love. And when the time is ripe, he will judge the wicked and cast them into everlasting punishment. For his name is the Almighty One, and he can and does perform the wondrous work of saving his people. But his name is also the Holy God, and he can stand no sin before his eyes. That is why the psalmist writes in Psalm 75:2–3, "When I shall receive the congregation I will judge uprightly. The earth and all the inhabitants thereof are dissolved: I bear up the pillars of it."

To us it may not look that way at times. Surely in the days when the antichrist shall try to starve us to death, while the wicked have a life far better than man ever had since Adam and Eve were driven out of paradise, it will be hard to believe that God is good to his church and is near her in his love.

But God has set a definite day and minute when he will bring his whole church into glory and will judge the wicked rightly by putting them in everlasting punishment. Therefore, we have reason to sing:

> Thy righteous judgment, Thou hast said,
> Shall in due time appear,
> And Thou Who didst establish it
> Wilt fill the earth with fear.

Then we shall see the goodness of God as we never before saw it. God will bring his church, or as here called, the congregation, the multitude he gathered as the body of Christ, into heavenly glory. Then the earth will be filled with the fear of God.

No, we will not be afraid either of the wicked or of God. Satan and his kingdom shall be dissolved, that is, removed from this earth. And we will have fear in the sense of respect and awe. For that word *fear* is the one used in the Old Testament for faith in God.

In a righteous judgment God delivers us from all our enemies and brings us through Christ out of all our guilt and free from the power of sin that is now in our flesh. Surely we have every reason to say that he is good. We will do so when we reach that glory; but we have reason to thank him now and in every circumstance of life.

Read: Revelation 7
Psalter versification: 206:2

OUR SURE VICTORY

I said unto the fools, Deal not foolishly: and to the wicked, Lift not up the horn: Lift not up your horn on high: speak not with a stiff neck. —Psalm 75:4–5

Peter tells us that Satan goes about as a roaring lion (1 Peter 5:8). But there are times when his followers attack us as an angered bull that charges with its horns to try to gore the one that irritated it. And keep in mind that the unbelievers are irritated when we hold God, his law, and his Christ before them. Was not Cain angry when Abel called his attention to his sinful sacrifice? And did he not kill Abel in anger?

This bears out the truth written in Psalm 75:4–5, where we read: "I said unto the fools, Deal not foolishly: and to the wicked, Lift not up the horn: lift not up your horn on high: speak not with a stiff neck." And plainly the horn mentioned here is not a musical instrument but the hard, pointed weapon of defense upon the head of a bull. Just call the unbeliever's attention to his sin and warn him of God's wrath, and he will, as the bull, lift up his horn to injure and drive you away from him. Not having the grace of God in his heart, the unbeliever will stiffen himself in his sin, and as the text states, he will lift up his stiff neck to gore us.

Therefore, the psalmist continues with: "For promotion cometh neither from the east, nor from the west, nor from the south. But God is the judge: he putteth down one, and setteth up another" (vv. 6–7). And by promotion he plainly means lifting up to what is truly good. Thus we sing:

Thou teachest meekness to the proud,
And makest sinners know
That none is judge but God alone,
To honor or bring low.

Never mind then when the world tries to push you aside and humble you physically and materially. God is judge, and he shall in his own time put down the whole world of wicked and lift his faithful children up to heavenly glory.

Let nothing and no one make you for one moment question God's love for his church. He will, because he judges us in Christ, lift us above all our enemies and unto himself in his grace. The world's attack upon God's church is folly. We have a sure victory in Christ.

Read: Revelation 22
Psalter versification: 206:3

A CUP WITH DEATH IN IT

For in the hand of the LORD there is a cup, and the wine is red; it is full of mixture; and he poureth out of the same: but the dregs thereof, all the wicked of the earth shall wring them out, and drink them. —Psalm 75:8

In this vale of tears and sorrows, and especially as we approach the days when the antichrist will be here to persecute the true church of Christ, we do well to take hold of the comfort of God's word as Asaph wrote it in Psalm 75:8. There we read: "For in the hand of the LORD there is a cup, and the wine is red; it is full of mixture; and he poureth out of the same: but the dregs thereof, all the wicked of the earth shall wring them out, and drink them."

Our versification explains it thus:

> Jehovah holds a cup of wrath,
> And holds it not in vain,
> For all the wicked of the earth
> Its bitter dregs shell drain.

The idea here very plainly is that the ungodly are not going to get away with their evil which brought them so much fleshly pleasure. And surely all the attacks of the world upon the church are going to cost them much.

It reminds us of drugs that at first give the flesh a pleasant, delightful sensation but destroy the body and bring the dope addict to his grave. This is also so very true of sin, no matter in what form or size it comes. The mockers and persecutors of God's church may have fleshly pleasure in this life; but they are dealing with a cup of God's wrath and are opening the gates of hell and the lake of fire.

Solomon in his wisdom, and God through him, in Proverbs 20:1 wrote: "Wine is a mocker, strong drink is raging: and whosoever is deceived thereby is not wise." Be wise and apply this also to sin. It is a mocker and raging, and those deceived by it are fools. Sin is like wine. It is a mocker that brings untold woe.

Sin will give the flesh a good time for a few moments; but it calls for everlasting misery as its punishment. When the world attacks the church, it is not going to get away with it.

Wisdom will move God's children to flee to the cross of Christ for refuge from the seed of the serpent but also from their own sins into which they have fallen.

Read: Revelation 14
Psalter versification: 206:4

GOD'S PRAISES JOYFULLY SUNG

But I will declare for ever; I will sing praises to the God of Jacob. All the horns of the wicked also will I cut off; but the horns of the righteous shall be exalted. —Psalm 75:9–10

A thankful heart will sing praises, as we saw. For to give thanks is to declare that someone has done something good. Therefore, having thanked God for his wondrous work of salvation, Asaph in Psalm 75:9–10 writes: "But I will declare for ever; I will sing praises to the God of Jacob. All the horns of the wicked also will I cut off; but the horns of the righteous shall be exalted."

Because God, as the righteous judge, will punish all the enemies of his church and in Christ has blotted out the sins of all his people so that he can, in his righteous judgment, bring them to everlasting glory, Asaph will not question God's goodness but will praise him.

The child of God is not, however, going to be idle. He will cut off the horns of the wicked. He will not fight them with the arm of flesh, but he will fight the lie they foster and the sins in which they walk. This he will do in the assurance that God will exalt the horns of the righteous. In fact, that is the wondrous work of God for which he praises him. But note the change of subjects. He will cut off the horns of the enemies, but the horns of the righteous shall be exalted by God.

Our versification expresses this truth thus:

> The God of Israel I will praise
> And all His glory show;
> The righteous He will high exalt
> And bring the wicked low.

What a joyful praise that is! Asaph says that he will sing God's praises, and that means that it comes out of his heart. He began by saying that he would declare these praises, and now quickly explains that he will sing them, so full of joy is his heart.

Do that today and every day. In his church sing his praises, but also before those who never go to church. Sing before them of God's wondrous work of saving us through the blood and Spirit of his Son. Such praise is the fruit and evidence that salvation has been begun in us and that we will be exalted to the glory of his house of many mansions.

Read: Psalm 89:1–18
Psalter versification: 206:5

STRENGTHENED TO WITHSTAND MOCKERY

Let thy mercies come also unto me, O LORD, even thy salvation, according to thy word. So shall I have wherewith to answer him that reproacheth me: for I trust in thy word. —Psalm 119:41–42

If you are a child of God, you have to one degree or another, and at one time or another, suffered mockery and ridicule. The gift of salvation makes a night and day difference between us and the world. Jesus once said: "By their fruits ye shall know them" (Matt. 7:20). This means that we ourselves will know by our works, and by our reaction to the mockery of the world, whether we in God's mercy have salvation begun in us.

Now, mockery, ridicule, derision, and sneering are not pleasant. And the child of God knows that, because he has only a small beginning of that new obedience, he can easily fall into hiding his faith to have a more pleasant life or respond to the mockery in a sinful way. Therefore, the psalmist prays in Psalm 119:41–42, "Let thy mercies come also unto me, O LORD, even thy salvation, according to thy word. So shall I have wherewith to answer him that reproacheth me: for I trust in thy word." And we sing:

Thy promised mercies send to me,
Thy great salvation, Lord;
So shall I answer those who scoff;
My trust is in Thy word.

Now, that which the psalmist prays for is not that he may be kept from that mockery and derision. Notice that he prays first for God's mercy and calls it salvation. Plainly he wants to continue to walk publicly as a child of God before the unbelievers. And he wants to answer them, not for fleshly advantage, but in order that he may defend the truth and be a living witness of the God of his salvation.

Consider also that to watch our tongue and to be careful that we do not sin in our reaction to this ridicule and scoffing, we need the mercy of God. In fact, we need salvation. In his mercy God must give us that part of our salvation that is called sanctification. We need the Spirit of Christ not only to encourage us but to hold and keep us faithful no matter how fiercely we are ridiculed and mocked.

We do trust in God's word, but only because of his mercy. And we will continue to be faithful only as he in his mercy continues the work of salvation in us.

Read: Psalm 119:41–48
Psalter versification: 326:1

MOUTHS FULL OF THE TRUTH

And take not the word of truth utterly out of my mouth; for I have hoped in thy judgments. So shall I keep thy law continually for ever and ever. —Psalm 119:43–44

When the unbelievers heap ridicule and scorn upon us, it is so easy to respond with sarcasm and with other sinful deeds. For that reason the psalmist asks God in Psalm 119:43–44, "And take not the word of truth utterly out of my mouth; for I have hoped in thy judgments. So shall I keep thy law continually for ever and ever." This is in harmony with what we read in James 3:2, "If any man offend not in word, the same is a perfect man, and able also to bridle the whole body." If there is one member of our bodies wherewith we sin, it is our tongue. And it is not only what we say, but often also what we fail to say that is sin.

With our tongues we are ready to defend our own honor, rather than the honor of God. We come with our own words instead of coming, as Jesus did to the devil, with the written word of God. Or we remain silent instead of instructing the mocker in the truth of God's word. We all therefore do wisely when we pray these words of our versification:

> My hope is in Thy judgment, Lord;
> Take not Thy truth from me,
> And in Thy law for evermore
> My daily walk shall be.

God must hold in our mouths his truth. Even as he must keep our hearts beating after they began months before we were born, so he must keep spiritual life in us by keeping the truth in our hearts and mouths.

If God does this, we will walk in his commandments when we are ridiculed—and presently are persecuted by the world—no matter how severe that mockery may be. We will continue to hope, that is, wait in silence for him to come in judgment on the evildoers that deride us.

If, then, you are ridiculed, bring God's law to those who break that law. But be silent as far as trying to get even with them is concerned. Such trying to get even is not waiting for his judgment. And it is ceasing to walk in his law.

Instead of doing that, pray God that he keep his truth in your mouth as well as in your heart.

Read: James 3
Psalter versification: 326:2

BLESSED WITH THE BOLDNESS OF FAITH

And I will walk at liberty: for I seek thy precepts. I will speak of thy testimonies also before kings, and will not be ashamed. —Psalm 119:45–46

That a man is bold and fearless before other men does not necessarily mean that he has the boldness of faith. Boldly Korah, Dathan, and Abiram challenged Moses and Aaron. And Gehazi lied boldly before his master, Elisha. But God punished them for works of unbelief.

The boldness of faith is in us when God puts the truth of his word in our mouths. Then as the psalmist writes, after having written that he wanted God's word in his mouth: "And I will walk at liberty: for I seek thy precepts. I will speak of thy testimonies also before kings, and will not be ashamed" (Ps. 119:45–46).

Walking at liberty means that his flesh does not hold him back in fear of ridicule and mockery. But more than that, the child of God blessed with the boldness of faith, because he has a firm grip on God's word and can quote it freely, will be bold to witness to God's glory. As we sing:

And I will walk at liberty
Because Thy truth I seek;
Thy truth before the kings of earth
With boldness I will speak.

We do well to note that one must be well-versed in the Scriptures. We must have something to say. And when we have a firm grip on God's word and see him as our King, we will have no fear of earthly kings. They have power to imprison and kill, but the truth assures us that all is well. No worldly power can keep us from entering the kingdom of heaven with all its blessedness.

How necessary then that we every day get a firmer grip on God's word. How important it is not only that we teach our children to commit to memory specific passages of Holy Writ but that we also commit them to memory.

Search the Scriptures. Look closely and daily at Christ our King of kings. See him in his glory and with the salvation he has prepared for us, and you have every reason not to be ashamed but to be bold before all men, no matter what political and physical power they have.

Read: Matthew 10:16–33
Psalter versification: 326:3

DELIGHTING IN GOD'S COMMANDMENTS

And I will delight myself in thy commandments, which I have loved. My hands also will I lift up unto thy commandments, which I have loved; and I will meditate in thy statutes. —Psalm 119:47–48

It is one thing to keep a law. It is quite a different thing to do with joy what that law demands. In fact, then it does not even seem like a law. And the question is whether we keep God's law because we must or because we find delight in doing so.

Then, too, it is one thing to demand something of someone else and quite another thing to find pleasure in doing so yourself. If then we find joy in doing what God's law sets forth, all the ridicule and derision the world heaps upon us will not stop us from doing what pleases God. That was the case with the psalmist, and he expresses that in Psalm 119:47–48 in these words: "And I will delight myself in thy commandments, which I have loved. My hands also will I lift up unto thy commandments, which I have loved; and I will meditate in thy statutes."

This we can do when we love God. Then we will also love his law. We will do what it demands because in love to God we want to please and serve him. And note that the psalmist says twice that he loves God's law, which is impossible if we do not love God. Not only must we not be ashamed of doing that which brings us ridicule, but we must want to continue walking in God's law because we delight in his commandments.

In fact, if we love God, and therefore love his law, we will meditate in it to see how we can be more pleasing in his sight than we are at the moment. We will lift our hands, that is, stretch them out unto his commandments, even as we sing:

The Lord's commands, which I have loved,
Shall still new joy impart;
With rev'rence I will hear Thy laws
And keep them in my heart.

If ridicule and mockery make us stop keeping God's law, we may not say that we love God, but we show love for our flesh and seek to please ourselves rather than striving to please God.

Look then in the mirror of God's law. Do you see one interested in pleasing God? Do you find one who wants to pray: "Take not the word of truth utterly out of my mouth" (v. 43)?

Read: James 1:13–27
Psalter versification: 326:4

June 20

SAVED BY GOD'S NAME

Save me, O God, by thy name, and judge me by thy strength. Hear my prayer, O God; give ear to the words of my mouth. —Psalm 54:1–2

Well may we ask, What is there in a name? Our names seldom say what we truly are. Mr. Long may be far shorter than others in his age group and race. Mr. Brown may have white skin, and a man named Daniel—which name means "my judge is God"—may be a man who walks in a way that reveals anything but trust in God as his judge.

But when we consider God's name, we must insist that he is everything that his name declares. He is the Almighty One, the self-sufficient Jehovah who needs nothing and no one outside of himself. And he is Lord and must not simply be called such.

It is for that reason that David in Psalm 54:1–2 writes: "Save me, O God, by thy name, and judge me by thy strength. Hear my prayer, O God; give ear to the words of my mouth." For there is nothing and no one from whom he cannot save us. David uses God's name Elohim here, which means the Almighty One. That not only makes our prayer wise, but it gives us the confidence that God can save us.

Therefore, our versification has it thus:

O save me by Thy Name
And judge me in Thy might;
O God, now grant my urgent claim,
Acceptance in Thy sight.

And the salvation for which David prays is not merely from the enemies of flesh and blood, but also from Satan and his host, and thus also from the power and love of sin that holds us as we are by nature, and because of which we deserve to be judged worthy of the same punishment as that to be given to Satan, the fallen angels, and all unbelievers.

But consider that God's name also is Savior. And when we pray to him to save us and judge us by his name, we are asking for the benefits of the cross of Christ, namely, the full blotting out of our sins. Then we need not fear God's wrath, nor anything Satan and his host can do to us.

Never, then, no never forget in your prayers to ask for salvation from sin. And never, no never approach the almighty God in any other way than through his Son, who earned the right of salvation for us.

Read: Psalm 54
Psalter versification: 147:1

ATTACKED BY SPIRITUAL STRANGERS

For strangers are risen up against me, and oppressors seek after my soul: they have not set God before them. Selah. —Psalm 54:3

When you meet one from a foreign country who speaks a language that you do not understand, you will rightly judge him to be a stranger. And when the child of God, who speaks the language of faith, which is the language of the kingdom of heaven, meets those who are citizens in the kingdom of darkness, they will appear to him to be strangers, even though they wear the same style of clothing and have the same color of skin.

What is more, because the child of God walks by faith, he wants no part in the sinful pleasures that the unbeliever enjoys. And if his godly walk threatens those sinful pleasures, those of the kingdom of darkness will come up against these believers and try to get them out of the way.

David had that experience and in Psalm 54:3 wrote: "For strangers are risen up against me, and oppressors seek after my soul: they have not set God before them." Our Psalter versification has it thus:

Strong foes against me rise,
Oppressors seek my soul,
Who set not God before their eyes,
Nor own His just control.

That is why in verse 1 he had written: "Save me, O God, by thy name, and judge me by thy strength." And for us today the question is whether there is that spiritual difference between us and the world. Do we go along with the world in their sinful pleasures of the flesh? Do they look strange to us, or are they our good friends? Are we strangers to them?

This is a serious matter today even more so than when David wrote these words. Not only is the world crowding into the church far more than in that day, but much in the church world today is joining with the forces of darkness. Even the language in the church sounds so often so much like that of the unbeliever. Satan with his six thousand years of experience and modern inventions has improved his tools and will soon produce an antichrist who will look so much like Christ that, were it not for the grace of God, many would be deceived and led astray. Then we shall see how strangers are risen up against us. They now seek our soul, but will also seek to take away our lives.

Read: Psalm 86
Psalter versification: 147:2

THE CERTAINTY OF OUR SALVATION

Behold, God is mine helper: the LORD is with them that uphold my soul. He shall reward evil unto mine enemies: cut them off in thy truth. —Psalm 54:4–5

Who would dare to deny that we, as citizens of the kingdom of heaven, have enemies? To deny that simply shows that the chief enemy, Satan, has a mighty grip upon us, and that our enemies are many more than we can count. A countless number there is of those who do not have God before them as the Lord whom they must serve every minute of their lives and with every creature they see, hear, smell, taste, and touch. And because we do love God and strive to serve him with all things at all times, we get in their way, and they hate us. They do not even want us to remind them of their calling before God.

But we are safe. As David wrote in Psalm 54:4–5, "Behold, God is mine helper: the Lord is with them that uphold my soul. He shall reward evil unto mine enemies: cut them off in thy truth." Once again David uses God's name Elohim, which means the Almighty One. And he calls us to look clearly and constantly at this truth. "Behold," he says, which means look with both eyes, and do not take them off for a fraction of a second from the fact that our Lord is the Almighty One, and he is our *helper*. He will save us, but he will also encourage us by his word and Spirit to put all our trust in him.

Not only will he save us completely from all our enemies, but he will through his Son, who has power over all things in heaven and on earth, give our enemies the reward of punishment which they deserve.

We may with confidence sing:

Lo, God my helper is,
The Lord, my mighty friend;
He shall requite my enemies,
Their just destruction send.

And you and I must encourage each other with that truth. We must take hold of that truth with both hands and hold on to it no matter what it is with which we are confronted. We must encourage each other in times of ridicule and in days of painful persecution. As we fight the good fight of faith, our banner must be: "The Almighty One is our helper."

Read: Psalm 118
Psalter versification: 147:3

STIMULATED UNTO PRAISING GOD

I will freely sacrifice unto thee: I will praise thy name, O LORD;
for it is good. —Psalm 54:6

Life will always manifest itself, and today men measure life not merely by the beating of the heart but also by brain waves. If brain waves can still be found, there is the possibility that the heart can be induced to begin beating again. Otherwise it is hopeless to try. And in our spiritual life, there are both of these signs of life.

We find this truth in Psalm 54:6, where David writes: "I will freely sacrifice unto thee: I will praise thy name, O LORD; for it is good." Or as our versification has it:

My sacrifice of praise
To Thee I freely bring;
My thanks, O Lord, to Thee I raise
And of Thy goodness sing.

Take note of the fact that David speaks of deeds that surely reveal that his heart is beating and enables him to bring a sacrifice of thanksgiving. He does not mean a sacrifice necessary for obtaining salvation, but one of thanks because he has received this gift. It is not one of shedding of blood, but one of thankfulness for blood shed. And when we today sing praises to God as our savior in Christ, we reveal that we have the gift of salvation.

However, there are "brain waves" and not mechanical devices that make our hearts beat and enable us to bring a sacrifice of thanksgiving to God. David speaks of the truth in his *mind* that God is good. Here are spiritual "brain waves," mental activity that makes our hearts beat with thankfulness to God. The minute we doubt God's goodness and question what his name declares to us concerning him, we cease praising him. Our hearts will continue to beat, but not in love to God. We can be forced by church rules to go through the motions of singing his praises and of thanking him, but it does not come from the assurance in the mind that he is good. We are not revealing spiritual life.

How important then is the word of God to stimulate us and teach us how good he is in his Son. What reason then do we not have to sing his praises and to thank him for a salvation that is full and free?

Read: Psalm 52
Psalter versification: 147:4

DELIVERED OUT OF ALL TROUBLE

For he hath delivered me out of all trouble: and mine eye hath seen his desire upon mine enemies. —Psalm 54:7

Would you ever dare to say that all your troubles are over? Death lies ahead for each of us. Would you then agree with David when he in Psalm 54:7 wrote: "For he hath delivered me out of all trouble: and mine eye hath seen his desire upon my enemies"?

It is true that David had been speaking of his enemies, the strangers who had risen up against him. But even then David still faces death. And Paul correctly states in 1 Corinthians 15:26, "The last enemy that shall be destroyed is death." When then we sing in our versification:

> From troubles and from woes
> Thou hast delivered me,
> The overthrow of all my foes
> Hast given me to see,

Death is included in those woes and foes. Yes, you and I can say with clearer insight than David that we are delivered out of all trouble, including death. For we see Christ, the head of the church, risen from the dead, lifted above all the things that trouble the members of his body, the church. And we can sing that our eye of faith has seen also this enemy destroyed.

We are going to die, and then our bodies are going to be destroyed. The church is going to have that trouble. But let it never be forgotten that, because of the cross and resurrection of Christ, death is God's tool—his instrument to bring our souls to the covenant blessedness of the trouble-free house of many mansions. And when Christ returns, that tool will be destroyed because we will be with body and soul in that blessed realm forever. There is then no need for that tool.

In our bereavements and upon our deathbeds, our eye should be fixed on Christ and his cross, resurrection, and ascension into heaven. Look at Christ, and you will see that he was delivered out of all trouble as head of his church. It is an established fact; and therefore the members of his church can look forward in all their troubles, and with David say that in principle they are, in Christ, conquerors and that death is one of the things that works together for our good.

Read: Psalm 59
Psalter versification: 147:5

KNOWING GOD IN HIS LOVE

In Judah is God known: his name is great in Israel. In Salem also is his tabernacle, and his dwelling place in Zion. —Psalm 76:1–2

There is a vast difference between knowing about a person and knowing that person. We all know much about Abraham, Isaac, and Jacob, but were they to appear before us today, we would not even be able to distinguish between them, if we saw them as they were at a specific and identical age.

When then in Psalm 76:1–2 Asaph writes: "In Judah is God known: his name is great in Israel. In Salem also is his tabernacle, and his dwelling place in Zion," he means much more than that in Israel men know about God. In fact, if anyone knows a great deal about God, it is the devil. But he does not know God. For to know him means to enjoy his fellowship and love and to experience all the blessedness that his name expresses. Did you notice? Asaph explains knowing God by stating that "his name is great in Israel." Our versification also expresses it that way:

> God is known among His people,
> Ev'ry mouth His praises fill;
> From of old He hath established
> His abode on Zion's hill;
> There He broke the sword and arrow,
> Bade the noise of war be still.

Singing his praises, then, is the sign that we do know him as our God and savior. For dwelling in Zion and having his tabernacle in Salem, that is, in Jerusalem, means that he lives in covenant fellowship with his people, and they taste the blessedness he has prepared for them in Christ. For Christ is pictured in that tabernacle and its priest, and the kings ruling on Mount Zion also represented him. They knew God in that they tasted his work on the cross and in the exaltation of Christ with power over all things in heaven and on earth.

Whether you and I know him that way, and to what degree we do, is to be seen in whether and to what degree we praise his name. If we have tasted the peace that he wrought in Christ, we know him in his love. We know him in his name Savior.

How much then, and how sincere, is your praise to God? And do you enjoy his nearness and love that upholds you in your spiritual life?

Read: Psalm 76
Psalter versification: 207:1

THE CHURCH'S CERTAIN SAFETY

Thou art more glorious and excellent than the mountains of prey. The stouthearted are spoiled, they have slept their sleep: and none of the men of might have found their hands. At thy rebuke, O God of Jacob, both the chariot and horse are cast into a dead sleep. Thou, even thou, art to be feared: and who may stand in thy sight when once thou art angry? —Psalm 76:4–7

Good questions are very important, for finding their answers reveals to us important truths. And in Psalm 76:4, 7 Asaph, having made two powerful statements, asks a very important question. He writes: "Thou art more glorious and excellent than the mountains of prey…Thou, even thou, art to be feared: and who may stand in thy sight when once thou art angry?" Or as our versification expresses it:

> Excellent and glorious art Thou,
> With Thy trophies from the fray;
> Thou hast slain the valianthearted,
> Wrapt in sleep of death are they;
> When Thy anger once is risen,
> Who can stand in that dread day?

He had written in verses 1–2 that God is known in Judah, and that "his name is great in Israel." Here, then, the church of our Lord Jesus Christ finds a tremendous comfort. For she is the Judah and Israel of today. No enemies of that church can stand before her Lord. Let them try to touch her, and he will be angry and come to punish in a way that they cannot withstand. They will be cast into the sleep of death.

Although the believers know God in all his covenant blessings of salvation, the enemies of his church will know him in his awful wrath and in everlasting punishment, which they will taste fully.

What a comfort for us today, in these days when the enemies of the church and of the truth are becoming bolder and bolder, and Satan tries through them to snatch our children away by craftiness, but also by bodily persecution. It may look at times as though the church cannot stand, and as though God has lost control.

Do not for one minute think that! He is using the wicked even as he used them to realize the cross of Christ: for our salvation. It looked then as though things had slipped out of his hands, but Christ's resurrection and ascension to God's right hand reveal his glory and exaltation. And he will in due time break the bow and shield and sword of the enemy. Not one of his children will be snatched away. No enemy can stand before him. All will fall into the lake of fire, when their work here below is finished.

Read: Exodus 15:20–26
Psalter versification: 207:2

WRATH THAT PRAISES GOD

Surely the wrath of man shall praise thee: the remainder of
wrath shalt thou restrain. —Psalm 76:10

Because their hearts were filled with sinful hatred, the Jews got the Roman soldiers to nail Jesus to his cross. Would you dare to say that God was praised by this dastardly deed? Asaph did, when in Psalm 76:10 he wrote: "Surely the wrath of man shall praise thee: the remainder of wrath shalt thou restrain." No, Asaph did not say that these wicked Jews praised God, but their work did. As our versification explains it:

> When from heav'n Thy sentence sounded,
> All the earth in fear was still,
> While to save the meek and lowly
> God in judgment wrought His will;
> E'en the wrath of man shall praise Thee,
> Thy designs it shall fulfill.

There you have it! The devil and his host do not hurt God's cause. What God designed, for the realization of the day when Christ returns to usher in a creation free from sin and the curse, will happen. And when that takes place, God's power, wisdom, and love will be manifested. That which in any way and to any degree would harm his cause God will restrain. Then also his power, wisdom, and love are displayed; and he is praised by it.

Consider the truth that God has the devil and all unbelievers completely under his control in the most absolute sense of the word. No one ever has or ever will keep him from doing, at the precise moment and in the exact way, what he wants done.

When the wicked strive to do something that would hurt the church, he will keep them from it. This work of God will say: "He is the Almighty One, the All-wise One, the God of love." That which they set out to do that will serve his church—as did the cross of Christ—will take place and also say: "He is the Almighty One, the All-wise One, the God of love." Behind every event is God using all his creatures to execute what he in his wisdom and love designed for his church. Nothing ever says anything else, but we must read all things correctly, as Asaph did in this psalm.

Shall we for one moment doubt that God's people shall know him in the way of tasting his greatness, wisdom, and love for his church? Nothing today will to any degree slow down or prevent Christ's return, and with it the church's glorification.

Read: Daniel 3
Psalter versification: 207:3

CALLED TO BRING THANKS TO GOD

Vow, and pay unto the LORD your God: let all that be round about him bring presents unto him that ought to be feared. He shall cut off the spirit of princes: he is terrible to the kings of the earth. —Psalm 76:11–12

Since every breath of life and every crumb of bread comes from God, and we cannot see or touch a creature that is not his, it might seem strange that Asaph concludes Psalm 76 with these words in verses 11–12: "Vow, and pay unto the LORD your God: let all that be round about him bring presents unto him that ought to be feared. He shall cut off the spirit of princes: he is terrible to the kings of the earth." That we should fear God is one thing, but that we can bring presents to him who owns all things is quite another thing.

Yet bear in mind that he also gives us the blessing of salvation, enabling us to praise him because we know him in his great name, in that we have tasted what he has done for us in his Son. Our gift to him then is not trying to enrich him, or trying to buy something from him. It is a gift of thanksgiving, a gift of praise of his name. It is not giving him something he did not have, but sending back to him, reflecting his glory that is in that great name. Created in the image of God, we are with heart and mouth displaying his glory by our words and works.

And because we have only a small beginning of that new obedience, we do need to be exhorted to make and keep a vow to bring to him the gift of thanks and praise. That is why our versification has these words:

> Vow and pay ye to Jehovah,
> Him your God forever own;
> All men, bring your gifts before Him,
> Worship Him, and Him alone;
> Mighty kings obey and fear Him,
> Princes bow before His throne.

Notice that there is no exception here. Kings and princes, men who have the right to demand obedience from those under their authority, are also exhorted to bring to God the gift of praise and thanksgiving. There is not one exception. The versification does not mean that they do fear and bow before him, but that they must do so.

You will have the evidence that you belong to those who know God when you find yourself bringing to God this gift of praise and thanksgiving. By that fruit you will know that you belong to Christ, the true vine.

Read: Revelation 4
Psalter versification: 207:4

CALLED TO BLESS GOD

Behold, bless ye the LORD, all ye servants of the LORD, which by night stand in the house of the LORD. —Psalm 134:1

A word that falls easily and often off our lips is the word *bless*. That word is used in two different ways in Scripture. We pray that God will bless us; and often in Scripture we are exhorted to bless God. Thus in Psalm 134:1 we read: "Behold, bless ye the LORD, all ye servants of the LORD, which by night stand in the house of the LORD."

But can we bless God? That he blesses us, we can understand; but can we bring a blessing upon him who is the fountain of all blessings? Can the creature bless the creator? Yes, man, as the only earthly creature created in God's image, can bless God. And he must bless God.

There is, however, a tremendous difference in that, when we bless God, we speak well of him. But when he blesses us, he calls down a good upon us. The word *bless* means to call good. When we bless God, we call him good, that is, praise him. When he blesses us, he commands and sends a good upon us. We speak as creatures. He speaks creatively. Thus in our versification we sing:

> Come, all ye servants of the Lord,
> Lift up your voice with one accord
> Jehovah's Name to bless;
> Ye that are standing night by night
> Within the house of His delight,
> His glorious Name confess.

There you have it. When we bless God, we confess that he is good. We bless his name, that is, we bless him for that wherein he is known. We say that he is good. When he blesses us, he makes us become good. He changes us from depraved sinners to become saints and gives us the joys of sinless creatures in his house of many mansions and that which brings us there. It is with the cross and by the Spirit of Christ that he blesses us.

What a reason we have then for blessing him. All the good of the forgiveness of our sins and the riches of Christ's kingdom he calls down upon us. Night by night we have reason to call him good. For eternally he is the fount of all good; and not a day must go by that we do not confess his goodness toward us in Christ.

Read: Psalm 134
Psalter versification: 372:1

COMING TO THE FOUNTAIN OF ALL BLESSEDNESS

Lift up your hands in the sanctuary, and bless the LORD. The LORD that made heaven and earth bless thee out of Zion. —Psalm 134:2–3

In Psalm 134:2–3 we read: "Lift up your hands in the sanctuary, and bless the LORD. The LORD that made heaven and earth bless thee out of Zion." That sanctuary is the temple, God's house, and lifting up the hands is pointing the soul unto God who is the fountain of all blessedness.

The hands only symbolize what the soul does. The mere closing of our eyes, folding of our hands, and bowing of our heads means nothing if the soul is not pointed to God. In our prayers we lift not only our desires but also our thoughts concerning God. Our thoughts while we pray will reveal whether we are blessing God or elevating ourselves above him and trying to make him our servant.

Then, too, lifting our souls to the sanctuary is pointing to Christ and his cross, which was so clearly pictured in the temple in its bloody sacrifices. That cross must be a basic reason for blessing God. Nothing he has done brings true goodness to us apart from that cross. As we in our versification sing:

> Yea, in His place of holiness
> Lift up your hands the Lord to bless;
> And unto you be giv'n,
> The joys that Zion doth afford,
> The richest blessing of the Lord
> Who made the earth and heav'n.

Here mention is made of "the joys that Zion doth afford." These are the blessings which we receive through God's Son as our heavenly King, because of what he did for us as our high priest and through his cross.

We do well also to note that he who blesses us is the maker of heaven and earth, and thus has all things completely under his control. Therefore, no matter what your problem is, go to him. He has the solution and the power to make all things well with you. Bless him as the one who knows what is good for you and can bring it to pass.

If you approach him that way, he will bless you. Not because a blessing upon you depends upon you blessing him, but because you are coming to the fount of all blessing. Question his goodness, and you are coming to an idol that cannot bless you.

Read: Psalm 124
Psalter versification: 372:2

QUICKENED UNTO STRONGER HOPE

Remember the word unto thy servant, upon which thou hast caused me to hope. This is my comfort in my affliction: for thy word hath quickened me. —Psalm 119:49–50

One of the comforting elements in the book of Psalms is that the psalms were written by fellow citizens of the kingdom of heaven. Our experiences were theirs, even though theirs occurred in a different nation and period of time. Somewhere in the psalms we find a situation similar to the one we are in. They had enemies, and so do we. They had weaknesses, and we have plenty of them. They had moments of grief and disappointment, and this is never far from us.

One thing we do have in common, however, is that God has spoken to all of us and given us rich promises, through which he gives us hope of a day when all fear, problems, and miseries are over, and our enemies are gone forever. Instead, we look forward to a life of spiritual perfection and heavenly blessedness.

There are times, though, when it seems as if God has forgotten his promises, and our spiritual life of hope and faith becomes weak. There are times when we forget that we are God's servants and think that he ought to be our servant and do things our way. Then we need to run to him and with the psalmist pray, as we find it in Psalm 119:49–50, "Remember the word unto thy servant, upon which thou hast caused me to hope. This is my comfort in my affliction: for thy word hath quickened me." Our versification has it this way:

> Lord, Thy word to me remember,
> Thou hast made me hope in Thee;
> This my comfort in affliction
> That Thy word hath quickened me.

Now, surely God never forgets for a split second, and the psalmist is not accusing him of doing so. The idea is that he asks God to do as he promised, even though it looks as though he had forgotten. And the psalmist's reason for his request is that God's word quickens him, that is, revives his spiritual life, so that he takes a firmer grip upon that word.

The significance for us plainly is that no matter what our problem is, we must go to God's word become flesh. Look at Christ and what he did for us. God will through this quicken us to stronger hope.

Read: Psalm 119:49–64
Psalter versification: 327:1

COMFORTED BY GOD'S JUDGMENTS

The proud have had me greatly in derision: yet have I not declined
from thy law. I remembered thy judgments of old, O LORD;
and have comforted myself. —Psalm 119:51–52

It is very easy and natural for us, as we are by nature, to hide our faith when there is danger of being ridiculed. We do not have to be in danger of being imprisoned or of bodily injury. Being laughed at is enough to tempt us to hide the fact that we are children of God who want to serve him. And it is only by the grace of God that we do keep his law and will not go along with the world in its sinful entertainment, Sabbath desecration, and other violations of his law. Surely we ought to say with the psalmist what he says in Psalm 119:51–52 in these words: "The proud have had me greatly in derision: yet have I not declined from thy law. I remembered thy judgments of old, O LORD; and have comforted myself."

Take note of the fact that it is because of God's judgments in days gone by that he found comfort during derision. Having those judgments, we also have the same comfort if we keep them in mind. Remember the flood, the destruction of Pharaoh and his host in the Red Sea, judgment upon Korah, Dathan, and Abiram, and many other visitations.

But by all means remember the judgment of God upon his Son in the three hours of darkness wherein he cried out of being forsaken of God. Then the judgment was upon him as our head who suffered the judgment against our sins. Remember that when you are ridiculed, and be sure that your proud enemies will also be forsaken by God and cast into the lake of fire. Then sing our versification, which declares:

Mocked by those who are unrighteous,
Still to Thy commands I cleave;
Thinking on Thy former judgments,
Help and comfort I receive.

A sure sign that God's judgment upon our sins was suffered by Christ we find when we continue to cling to God's law and are not turned away by mockery. For this shows that we have been born again because Christ earned a new life for us. We also have comfort because of the humility that he has given us. For breaking God's law is an act of pride, while walking in that law is humility before him as our Lord and master.

Read: Psalm 119:153–168
Psalter versification: 327:2

THE SINGING PILGRIM

Horror hath taken hold upon me because of the wicked that forsake thy law. Thy statutes have been my songs in the house of my pilgrimage. —Psalm 119:53–54

A coin has two sides but is by no means two-faced. The two sides do not contradict each other but give us the full picture. Both sides say the same thing, only in different ways.

So the child of God is not two-faced when with the psalmist he says: "Horror hath taken hold upon me because of the wicked that forsake thy law. Thy statutes have been my songs in the house of my pilgrimage" (Ps. 119:53–54). Here we have the reaction of the child of God to two contrasting realities. He is horrified when he sees the wicked break God's law. His heart breaks, and he is filled with sadness and indignation. But at the same time he is singing, and his heart is full of joy, because of God's commandments.

What a mirror before which to stand! If sin gives us pleasure, we will not sing God's praises. We will sing about sin and let the radios and tape recorders blare out the sins of the world. Then God's law will fill us with horror and make us sad.

How about it? Stand before that mirror. Do you see yourself as a child of God on his pilgrimage to God's house? Or do you see a person established firmly in this world and its horrible sins? Can you sing this:

> Wicked men Thy law forsaking
> Stirred my indignation strong,
> For in all my pilgrim journey
> Thy commandments are my song.

What songs did you sing today? And did you enjoy the world enacting sin in the theater or on the TV screen? In church, is your soul in it when you sing the songs of Zion that extol God and his law?

The answer to these questions will reveal whether we really are pilgrims here below, who are looking for the new Jerusalem when Christ returns, where no sin can ever be found. When men see you horrified by sin and joyfully singing God's praises and the beauty of his law, you are like a coin revealing one truth with a positive and negative side. You hate sin, but you love God. You cry because of sin but sing with joy when the love toward God is manifested before you.

Read: Psalm 119:129–136
Psalter versification: 327:3

REMEMBERING GOD'S NAME

I have remembered thy name, O LORD, in the night, and have kept thy law. This I had, because I kept thy precepts. —Psalm 119:55–56

A thing gets its name because of what it is made of, the purpose it serves, and to distinguish it from other objects. A day gets its name from what happened or will happen: thus birthday and Thanksgiving Day. A person gets his name by what he did or is doing. Thus he is called a carpenter or, in tragic circumstances, a murderer.

God's name tells us not only what he does but who he eternally and unchangeably is. A man first becomes a babe, and later a father. God eternally is unchangeably God. That is why the psalmist in Psalm 119:55–56 writes: "I have remembered thy name, O LORD, in the night, and have kept thy law. This I had, because I kept thy precepts." Thus the Hebrew has it; and Jehovah means I AM.

In the night of sin and death the psalmist keeps that truth before him. When the enemy comes, he remembers God's complete control over every creature, and he has no fear. In temptations he remembers who it is that he must love and serve. For us it is also to remember our sins and that his Son saved us by his blood. Then we remember to give God thanks.

We do well, however, to bear in mind that we remember God's name only in the way of keeping his law. Break God's law, and you say that he is not God. By sin we say that he has no right to demand this or that of us. Sin is not merely foolishness but is an act of hatred toward God. It is saying that his laws are not good, and therefore that he is not the *all*-wise God; and that we should give him another name than Lord and holy Law-Giver.

Flee from sin and sing with our versification:

> Thou hast been my meditation
> And Thy law hath been my guide;
> I have kept Thy righteous precepts,
> And have found them true and tried.

If you remember God's name, you will agree that his law is true, and you will sing of the trustworthiness of his commandments. Upon them you can depend as the way of life and as pointing out the way of love to him who is the one and only God, the God of our salvation.

Read: Psalm 63
Psalter versification: 327:4

July 5

THE CHURCH'S PERFECT SAFETY

They that trust in the LORD shall be as mount Zion, which cannot be removed, but abideth for ever. As the mountains are round about Jerusalem, so the LORD is round about his people from henceforth even for ever. —Psalm 125:1–2

Today man has some powerful explosives and earth-moving equipment, and one might be inclined then to question the words of the psalmist when in Psalm 125:1–2 he writes: "They that trust in the LORD shall be as mount Zion, which cannot be removed, but abideth forever. As the mountains are about Jerusalem, so the LORD is round about his people from henceforth even for ever."

It might seem as though man today can level that city of Jerusalem. But be sure that he cannot, for even though he has such powerful equipment, God is there and need but stop the beating of man's heart if he wants his sinful deeds stopped.

God is where his church is, and we today may freely sing:

All who with heart confiding
Depend on God alone,
Like Zion's mount abiding,
Shall ne'er be overthrown.
Like Zion's city bounded
By guarding mountains broad,
His people are surrounded
Forever by their God.

The question then for us to ask ourselves today is whether we are looking at man and his explosives and earth-moving equipment, or at the almighty God who loves his church. Is our eye of faith upon God or on our enemies?

We do well to go to another elevated place or hill called Golgotha. Yes, there the enemy killed God's Son and seemed to have the victory. The cause of the church seemed lost. But those very enemies who killed the King of the church were God's tools to bring us salvation and bring his Son to his right hand with power over all things in heaven and on earth, to bring forth the new Jerusalem and all its glory. They did not hurt the church but served it. And that is always the case. God is round about his church. It will reach the perfection and beauty that he has promised it.

Put your trust then in him, and you will never be put to shame. You just cannot find a better or more complete protection. The crafty devil, the coming antichrist, the whole innumerable host of unbelievers cannot keep the believers from reaching the blessed life of the new Jerusalem.

Read: Psalm 125
Psalter versification: 356:1

THE SAFETY OF UPRIGHT HEARTS

For the rod of the wicked shall not rest upon the lot of the righteous; lest the righteous put forth their hands unto iniquity. Do good, O LORD, unto those that be good, and to them that are upright in their hearts. —Psalm 125:3–4

Are you concerned about the well-being of your church? What is it that concerns you? Would the leveling of your church building by a fire disturb you more than the introduction of a false doctrine in the preaching? Would the loss of a goodly number of members bother you more than the loss of a cardinal truth of Scripture? Would the introduction of a worldly practice irk you less than the wearing out of the carpeting or the peeling of the paint upon the walls?

We do well to look at the psalmist's words, written after he had said that the church was safe because God was round about her. He continues in Psalm 125:3–4 with these words: "For the rod of the wicked shall not rest upon the lot of the righteous; lest the righteous put forth their hands unto iniquity. Do good, O LORD, unto those that be good, and to them that are upright in their hearts."

Did you notice that he is not merely speaking of enemies but of the wicked? And he speaks of those that are good in the sense that their hearts are upright. We have no promise of God that no material danger will come to our church buildings, and no loss of church membership. There were only eight souls saved from the flood, and far less than ten saved from the destruction of Sodom before the fire came down.

Spiritually, and as the body of Christ, the church is absolutely safe. In the coming days of the antichrist, church services will be denied to those who hold to the truth. The number of believers alive will dwindle to only a few because of the famine of not being allowed to buy or sell and by death through persecution. Yet confidently the church may sing:

> No scepter of oppression
> Shall hold unbroken sway,
> Lest unto base transgression
> The righteous turn away.
> Thy favor be imparted
> To godly men, O Lord;
> Bless all that are purehearted,
> The good with good reward.

Yes, God will bless his church with unchanging, upright hearts. The faith of his church shall not be taken away. As Mount Zion abides till Christ returns, the church shall hold on to the truth and fight iniquity.

Read: Psalm 46

Psalter versification: 356:2

PEACE UPON ISRAEL

As for such as turn aside unto their crooked ways, the LORD shall lead them forth with the workers of iniquity: but peace shall be upon Israel. —Psalm 125:5

"They are not all Israel, which are of Israel," is what Paul wrote in Romans 9:6. And it is likewise true that not all who call themselves Christians are Christians. Therefore, in Psalm 125:5 we read: "As for such as turn aside unto their crooked ways, the LORD shall lead them forth with the workers of iniquity: but peace shall be upon Israel." They who "turn aside" are the wicked of verse 3. This will never happen to the true Christian. But there are in the church here below those who will leave when the world to which they belong tempts them or comes with violent persecution.

The psalmist expresses a truth that we must not overlook. God will lead them aside into their crooked way. Notice that it is in *their* crooked way. God does not drive them into sin, but he drives them out of his church and into the sinful world of their liking. They had been hiding this love from the true Christians. And God does this to preserve his church. For he is around her like the mountains around Jerusalem, protecting her and keeping her safe. But he also does this so the church may have peace.

No, that does not mean that she will not be assaulted by the world. Were that the case, the psalmist would not reassure the church that God keeps her unmoved like Mount Zion. The closer we get to the end of time, the more enemies we will have, and the harder our life will be. But we will have peace in a twofold sense. As we sing, so is it:

> The men who falsehood cherish,
> Forsaking truth and right,
> With wicked men shall perish,
> God will their sin requite.
> From sin Thy saints defending,
> Their joy, O Lord, increase
> With mercy never ending
> And everlasting peace.

The point is that we will have peace with God. His love, mercy, and grace will surround us. His thoughts of peace we shall enjoy. And that, come what may, will give us peace of mind. We will be sure his church shall not be moved but stand and soon inherit the new earth, and live with God in peace that passes understanding.

Read: John 14
Psalter versification: 356:3

A BLESSED UNITY

Behold, how good and how pleasant it is for brethren to dwell together in unity! It is like the precious ointment upon the head, that ran down upon the beard, even Aaron's beard: that went down to the skirts of his garments. —Psalm 133:1–2

There are things that cannot go together and must be kept separate. By all means keep a flame of fire from the open can of gasoline that you are carrying! Light and darkness cannot be mixed. In the measure that the one comes, the other goes. But there are things that go well together.

There is a situation, to which the psalmist calls attention in Psalm 133:1–2, where a most blessed union is to be seen. There David writes: "Behold, how good and how pleasant it is for brethren to dwell together in unity! It is like the precious ointment upon the head, that ran down upon the beard, even Aaron's beard: that went down to the skirts of his garments." And we are called to look closely at that blessed unity.

The truth of these verses will be seen in the new Jerusalem, when the redeemed out of every nation, tongue, and tribe will be united as one holy nation, one glorious body of Christ with one life, one love, and one work to which they are consecrated.

But there is and must be a manifestation and exercise of this unity also in our lives today. We must live as well as sing David's words thus:

> How good and pleasant is the sight
> When brethren make it their delight
> To dwell in blest accord;
> Such love is like anointing oil
> That consecrates for holy toil
> The servants of the Lord.

Indeed, what a sight that is! And that unity is possible only between brethren, that is, those born again of the same Father, whose Son is the head of the church, who have the unction of his Spirit poured on them. They think alike, have the same love, and work together to glorify God. And from the head to their feet we see a beautiful picture of what brings goodness and pleasure.

But is this true in your life? Can you put aside fleshly cravings, forgive your brother or sister, and jointly seek the perfect harmony of serving and glorifying God? Does he come first in your life?

Look for that in your life and strive to walk with your brother in Christ, so that you see in your life what is good and truly pleasant.

Read: Psalm 133 and Romans 12
Psalter versification: 370:1

UNITED IN A BLESSED LIFE

As the dew of Hermon, and as the dew that descended upon the mountains of Zion: for there the LORD commanded the blessing, even life for evermore. —Psalm 133:3

It is during the darkness of the night that dew forms and refreshes the earth. And so it is that in the darkness of the night of sin, which fell upon the earth when man rebelled against God and broke the bond of unity wherein he was created, that the dew of the Spirit of Christ fell upon the church, and God's people were refreshed to a good and pleasant work by that anointing.

David spoke of this when in Psalm 133:3 he wrote: "As the dew of Hermon, and as the dew that descended upon the mountains of Zion: for there the LORD commanded the blessing, even life for evermore."

Do you really call it a blessing to receive Christ's Spirit, so that you can work with all the fellow saints in your church and locality? Do you call it good and pleasant? Or must you go your own separate way to find pleasure and do what you think is good?

The answer to that question will reveal whether you want to go to heaven. No one wants to go to hell; but not everyone wants to go to heaven. Not everyone calls a united front of serving God and of glorifying him a good and pleasant experience. Not all can honestly sing:

> Such love in peace and joy distils,
> As o'er the slopes of Hermon's hills
> Refreshing dew descends;
> The Lord commands His blessing there,
> And they that walk in love shall share
> In life that never ends.

So often we like to bring a united service of God to an end and go our own way and do our own thing. We will separate from those who call our attention to our sin, have anger and resentment against those who show us that we broke that unity of the body of Christ in God's service.

But get it straight! Everlasting life, the gift God prepared for us in Christ, is that we as members of one body, in the communion of the saints, work together for God's glory. Do you want that?

The "precious ointment" of the Spirit flows down from Christ, the head, to all members below, so that the whole body together glorifies God. That is life everlasting. Behold how good and pleasant it is!

Read: 1 Corinthians 12
Psalter versification: 370:2

A CRY FOR GOD'S GRACE

Thou art my portion, O LORD: I have said that I would keep thy words.
I intreated thy favour with my whole heart: be merciful unto me
according to thy word. —Psalm 119:57–58

You cannot give God anything that is not already his; and you cannot buy anything from him. No matter how faithful you have been, even if you can say with the psalmist, "Thou art my portion, O LORD: I have said that I would keep thy words" (Ps. 119:57), you have not earned anything. The strength and desire to serve God comes from God. He kept your heart beating and worked that desire in your heart. You owe him thanks, and he owes you nothing. In fact, you owe him for the opportunity to walk on his earth, to breathe his air, drink his water, and eat his food. Do then what the psalmist says in verse 58: "I entreated thy favour with my whole heart: be merciful unto me according to thy word."

Our versification has it thus:

> Thou art my portion, Lord;
> Thy words I ever heed;
> With all my heart Thy grace I seek,
> Thy promises I plead.

Notice that though the King James Version (KJV) has "be merciful," the versification has "Thy grace I seek." There is no conflict here. In God's grace we receive his mercy. His mercy displays his grace. Yet the word *grace* is closer to the meaning of the Hebrew word. In fact, in the text we read, "I entreated Thy favor," and grace is favor.

You cannot keep God's word perfectly, but you will need to pray for a blessing that Christ earned for you. Notice that the psalmist pleads for mercy that is according to God's word. That means according to Christ, God's Word become flesh. We must ask for blessings that are a pure, unmerited gift which Christ bought for us by his blood.

Our portion of the blessings that are in Christ are free gifts of God. And with our whole heart we must say that, not simply with our lips. For to ask for anything on any other basis is to add to our sins and would be a reason for us not to get the gift. A sure sign that we keep God's word is that we seek salvation as a pure, free, unmerited gift, confessing that in ourselves we do not deserve it, but deserve the opposite. Even our desire for salvation is a gift of God's grace. Praise him for it.

Read: Psalm 119:57–72
Psalter versification: 328:1

SANCTIFIED HASTE

I thought on my ways, and turned my feet unto thy testimonies. I made haste, and delayed not to keep thy commandments. —Psalm 119:59–60

As the saying goes, "Haste makes waste." But there is one way in which haste reveals grace. The psalmist spoke of this in Psalm 119:59–60 when he said: "I thought on my ways, and turned my feet unto thy testimonies. I made haste, and delayed not to keep thy commandments."

Or as our versification has it:

I thought upon my ways,
Thy testimonies learned;
With earnest haste, and waiting not,
To Thy commands I turned.

When you find yourself walking in sin—and how often is that not the case?—delay not but with all haste get back into the law of God. You just cannot get back too quickly! Take your time about it, and you are adding to your sin. For you are still saying that walking in sin is good, and that leaving it behind is losing something you deem precious.

What is more, we cannot think upon our ways in the light of God's law too quickly. We may be quick to look into a mirror to see if our hair is combed, whether it is turning gray, or whether our face is clean; but why are we so slow in looking into God's law?

The psalmist did so quickly because of the temptations that surrounded him. He had enemies that ridiculed him, taunted him, and made a fool of him. And he was eager, because of his old sinful nature, to stop this derision by hiding his faith. And we have the same problem, so that we do not think on the way God wants us to walk, but on the way that pleases our sinful flesh. And we, too, need to be reminded to give serious thought every hour of the day to God's law and to seek to find out whether we are walking in God's way or in our own fleshly way.

When we find any violation of God's law, we must not hesitate to turn from it and go back to the way God would have us walk.

How about it? Are you carrying a sin with you, thinking that when you get older, you will drop it? Do not think so for a moment! The longer you walk in it, the harder it will become to break from it. Be quick to turn from it, and your spiritual muscles will be strengthened so you can walk more firmly in a way that pleases God.

Read: Luke 15:11–24
Psalter versification: 328:2

MIDNIGHT THANKSGIVING

The bands of the wicked have robbed me: but I have not forgotten
thy law. At midnight I will rise to give thanks unto thee because
of thy righteous judgments. —Psalm 119:61–62

Out of custom and habit we often say "Thank you" when someone gives something to us. But in all sincerity could you say "Thank you" to God for giving us his law with all its strict requirements? It is interesting to note that in Psalm 119:61–62 the psalmist does that. He writes: "The bands of the wicked have robbed me: but I have not forgotten thy law. At midnight I will rise to give thanks unto thee because of thy righteous judgments."

Now, God's righteous judgments are that which God judges to be the right thing for man to do. It is easy to say that it is good that there are laws for the neighbor to keep. That makes our life safer and provides more pleasure for our flesh. But can you sincerely sing:

> While snares beset my path,
> Thy law I keep in view;
> At midnight I will give Thee praise
> For all Thy judgments true.

Since sleep is so sweet, why should we rise up at midnight or stay awake till midnight to thank God for his law? Does not that law deny us so much pleasure and threaten us with so much misery? Especially when our enemies oppress us, there is such an urge to do to them what God's law forbids us. We want to get revenge. We want to do to them what they did to us, or even to do more harm to them. Shall we rise up at midnight to give God thanks for that law that denies getting even with them?

Yes, the day is not long enough to thank God for his law. It teaches us how to live in love toward him, but also his great love for us. We on this side of the cross surely have reason for midnight thanksgiving. Only in the way of knowing that law can we understand and appreciate the cross of his Son. God's law demanded that cross as the way to our salvation. Knowing that law, we can understand what his Son suffered for us and how he fulfilled the demands of that law for us.

And seeing this by his grace, the day is not long enough to praise and thank him. In fact, God has promised an endless day that has no night, so that we can in the new Jerusalem praise and thank him for the salvation which he wrought through his Son.

Read: Psalm 19
Psalter versification: 328:3

A BLESSED COMPANIONSHIP

I am a companion of all them that fear thee, and of them
that keep thy precepts. —Psalm 119:63

Who are your friends? In whose company do you delight? Can you sincerely say with the psalmist what he wrote in Psalm 119:63? He wrote: "I am a companion of all them that fear thee, and of them that keep thy precepts." Or is there more enjoyment for you to be with those who trample God's law underfoot, show no fear of God, and glory in sin?

We do well to note that the fear of God reveals itself in keeping his precepts. Then, too, having the ungodly as your companions does not merely mean literal fellowship with them. It also includes bringing them into your home through your radio and television set to sing their sinful songs and enact sin for your entertainment. How many hours a day are they your companions?

But notice that the psalmist says that he is a companion of those who fear God. This we are, not only when we meet with them in God's house on the Sabbath, but also when we visit them in their afflictions and help them in every way we can to fight the good fight of faith.

That is why in verse 64 the psalmist writes: "The earth, O LORD, is full of thy mercy: teach me thy statutes." Not only is it God's mercy that enables us to become companions of those that fear him, but we must be taught his statutes. And in his mercy, that is, in Christ, who in mercy was sent to make it all possible, God teaches us his statutes. As we sing:

All those who fear Thy Name
Shall my companions be;
Thy mercy fills the earth, O Lord;
Thy statutes teach Thou me.

Did you ever think of it that way? God's *mercy* teaches us his law and thus makes us companions with those that fear him. When the policeman looks the other way when we break a traffic law, we call that a merciful act. No, in his mercy God shows us the exactness of his law. For only in God's law is there life. And only through God's law do we see our sins and sinfulness. That makes us see the need of Christ's cross. Without knowing that law, the cross means nothing. Without knowing that law, we cannot have the blessed companionship with Christ which is life everlasting.

Read: John 17
Psalter versification: 328:4

A NECESSARY PRAYER

Judge me, O God, and plead my cause against an ungodly nation: O deliver me from the deceitful and unjust man. —Psalm 43:1

It is obvious that man has come a long way since the day of David. All our labor-saving devices, medical advances, means of transportation, bodily comforts, and conveniences make life in the Old Testament look dull and monotonous. But we must not overlook the fact that man has also come a long way *in sin!* And that includes attacks upon the truth of God's word. Therefore, when in Psalm 43:1 David wrote, "Judge me, O God, and plead my cause against an ungodly nation: O deliver me from the deceitful and unjust man," we have a prayer that we ourselves are in great need of presenting to God.

Although we do not have "an ungodly nation" from which we need physical and bodily deliverance, we are surrounded by deceitful and unjust men who twist the Scriptures and attack us with heretical teachings. We are attacked and also our children, as far as our spiritual lives are concerned, and are assaulted with sharp arrows of the lie and with crafty approaches that appeal to our flesh. We, too, should pray:

Judge me, God of my salvation,
Plead my cause, for Thee I trust;
Hear my earnest supplication,
Save me from my foes unjust.

The sad and alarming fact today is that men do not take as seriously the attack of Satan and the men he uses to attack us with false doctrines as they do the fear of a nuclear war that will bring material loss and painful death. Men fear other men far more than they fear Satan and his innumerable host that tries to turn us away from Christ and to seek the things below rather than the things above in Christ's kingdom.

But remember that not only is the antichrist coming soon to have control of the whole earth and all men upon it, but as we read in 1 John 2:18, there are already many antichrists who are working hard to deceive us and our children, seeking to get us to seek the world and look for the antichrist rather than seek the things above and look for Christ to come.

We have very much need to pray that God will save his church from the antichrists which try to turn us away from Christ and the salvation from sin and from the lie which the antichrist will bring.

Read: Psalm 43
Psalter versification: 120:1

CORRECT ANSWERS TO OUR QUESTIONS

For thou art the God of my strength: why dost thou cast me off? why go I mourning because of the oppression of the enemy? —Psalm 43:2

May we ask God why he has done this or that? Is this not lifting ourselves in pride above him and making him our servant? Well, it makes a difference why you ask your question. Did not Jesus on the cross ask the Father why he had forsaken him? And when David in Psalm 43:2 asks, "For thou art the God of my strength: why dost thou cast me off? why go I mourning because of the oppression of the enemy?" we do not have a sinful prayer. He is not questioning God's justice or his mercy or grace.

God is his strength, and in this confession David reveals that he believes that God is able to deliver him. And because we with David believe this, we do not necessarily sin when we sing:

> On Thy strength alone relying,
> Why am I cast off by Thee,
> In my helpless sorrow sighing,
> While the foe oppresses me?

Neither with David nor with us is it fault-finding. We question neither God's justice nor his love. In fact, we clearly confess his ability to save us. For indeed every heartbeat and breath of life comes from him. He is our strength in every sense, for our enemy also gets every heartbeat and breath only from God.

But why then does David ask God why he has cast him off so that unbelievers oppress him? The answer is that we can get the correct answer to all our questions only from God. And further, what we must always remember is that we must go to God with all our problems. David sets a good example here for us.

The one difference between David and us is that we have the complete word of God in the sixty-six books of Scripture. We live on this side of the cross of Christ and have a richer picture of what God has in his counsel. That word of God has the answer to all our questions. We must search it, study it, as well as read it and hear it preached. And we must and may in prayer ask God to open the Scriptures to us. But if we do not read and study his word, we are not sincere in our request for light. God spoke and preserved his speech for us, so that we would have correct answers to all our questions.

Read: Psalm 42
Psalter versification: 120:2

THE LIGHT OF GOD'S TRUTH

O send out thy light and thy truth: let them lead me; let them bring me unto thy holy hill, and to thy tabernacles. —Psalm 43:3

The light of the sun which God gives us enables us to see and enjoy the things in creation round about us. But there is also a mental, intellectual, spiritual light that he gives us. When we do not understand a certain matter, someone may offer to help us and say: "Let me give you some light on the subject." And it is in that sense that David in Psalm 43:3 writes: "O send out thy light and thy truth: let them lead me; let them bring me unto thy holy hill, and to thy tabernacles." Or as we sing it in our versification:

> Light and truth, my way attending,
> Send Thou forth to be my guide,
> Till Thy holy mount ascending,
> I within Thy house abide.

You see, David's way had become dark. For he had been driven from Jerusalem, had to flee from Absalom, and was eager to get back where God's dwelling place was. He did not see why God separated him from his holy hill. His question in verse 2 was: "Why dost thou cast me off? why go I mourning because of the oppression of the enemy?"

Plainly he wanted light in that dark hour. And that means that he wanted God's grace to rest upon him, but also that he wanted to be enlightened in his mind as to why God brought him into this situation. He wants light, but also truth.

Now, truth is what gives us light on our dark pathway. Remember that Jesus said in John 14:6, "I am the way, the truth, and the life." And if we see Christ, we have light upon our pathway no matter how dark it is around us. Go to his cross. There God used Satan, Judas, and the wicked Jews as tools to bring us the victory which a few days later we saw in his resurrection from the dead as our head. We were not defeated there at his cross but victorious over sin, the curse, death, and the grave!

So it is today. All the wicked in all their evils are tools in God's hand whereby he is preparing the way for Christ to return and bring us to his holy hill in heaven where he dwells. And all our sicknesses and pains are also his means to bring us home to a life without sin and completely free from the curse.

Read: Psalm 3
Psalter versification: 120:3

A REVEALING THANKFULNESS AND PRAISE

Then will I go unto the altar of God, unto God my exceeding joy: yea, upon the harp will I praise thee, O God my God. —Psalm 43:4

One way to determine whether an unconscious person hurt in an accident is alive is to find out whether his heart is beating. One way to become aware that one's spiritual heart is beating is to look for what David writes in Psalm 43:4. He had cried out of being cast off and driven from God's house, which was a symbol of his love for his church. And he had prayed for light and truth to assure him that God's love would bring him back. That is why he wrote: "Then will I go unto the altar of God, unto God my exceeding joy: yea, upon the harp will I praise thee, O God my God." If God would bring him back, he would do this.

There are two spiritual activities mentioned here, two deeds that are clearly related to each other and yet distinct from each other. Going to God's altar is bringing to him a sacrifice of thanksgiving and declaring how good he is. The other is singing his praises, which includes thanksgiving but also speaks of his wisdom, power, faithfulness, love, mercy, and grace. Praise includes thanksgiving, but it is much more. And so we sing:

> At Thy sacred altar bending,
> God, my God, my boundless joy,
> Harp and voice, in worship blending,
> For Thy praise will I employ.

For us today, after the veil of the temple was rent in twain and the whole temple, as a type of God's fellowship with us in Christ, faded away, we still show our spiritual life by singing his praises and bringing an offering of thanksgiving to help the poor and needy and to support the preaching of God's great goodness unto his church.

David said that he will thank God and praise him. So will we when the light goes up in our souls and we see what he did for us in Christ. Search your soul today to see how strongly your spiritual heart beats and how thankful you are for the salvation God gave you through the altar of the cross of Christ. It is a good idea to feel your pulse; and if your heart is skipping some beats, go to the Great Physician and ask him to restore you to a life that is truly thankful and considers God to be your exceeding great joy.

Read: Psalm 138
Psalter versification: 120:4

July 18

A BLESSED HOPE

Why art thou cast down, O my soul? and why art thou disquieted within me? hope in God: for I shall yet praise him, who is the health of my countenance, and my God. —Psalm 43:5

So far in considering David's words in Psalm 43, the chorus of our versification was not given. The time has now come for us to sing:

O my soul, why art thou grieving?
What disquiets and dismays?
Hope in God; His help receiving,
I shall yet my Saviour praise.

That is the way David ends his psalm. He pleaded for help and was in deep need of spiritual light. And he wanted badly to go back to God's house where his joy was full, because there God revealed his boundless love in the forgiveness of our sins through the shed blood of Christ.

But now, when God enlightened him, he wrote: "Why art thou cast down, O my soul? and why art thou disquieted within me? hope in God: for I shall yet praise him, who is the health of my countenance, and my God" (Ps. 43:5).

You see, when we remember what God did for us through the cross of Christ, and typically displayed in the tabernacle, we are by God's grace given hope. And remember, that hope is confident expectancy. To hope is to desire with the expectation that it will come. And because God enlightened him by causing him to think of what went on in the tabernacle, David had hope worked in him, and he was sure he would go back to it.

Are you grieving? Is your soul disquieted and dismayed because of something that happened to your earthly life? Is your soul cast down and you fail to look up to the health of your countenance and your God?

Then take note of the fact that with all his troubles David went to God. Eight times in this brief psalm he speaks of God and calls him his God. With David go to him as we can now meet him in his word and as we now have light shed upon that altar in his earthly house. For now we see the Lamb of God sacrificed for our sins and the veil of the temple rent in twain, because a way has been prepared for us to live with God. In hope look for that day, and your present sorrows will fade away, and you will with joy look for that day when you will dwell with him in his glory. What a blessed hope that is!

Read: 1 Peter 1
Psalter versification: Chorus of 120

DEALT WITH AS GOD PROMISED

Thou hast dealt well with thy servant, O LORD, according unto
thy word. Teach me good judgment and knowledge: for I
have believed thy commandments. —Psalm 119:65–66

There are a few times when we are ready to agree that God has dealt well with us. Most of the time, however, things do not go our way, and we complain that he is not treating us well. The basic reason for this complaining is that we do not see things as the psalmist does when in Psalm 119:65–66 he writes: "Thou hast dealt well with thy servant, O LORD, according unto thy word. Teach me good judgment and knowledge: for I have believed thy commandments."

Did you notice that he says that God deals well with us *according to his word?* Our versification explains this for us when it states:

> Thou, Lord, hast dealt well with Thy servant,
> Thy promise is faithful and just;
> Instruct me in judgment and knowledge,
> For in Thy commandments I trust.

God's word here is his word of promise. Always and constantly God is dealing well with us in that he is giving us what he promised in Christ. That which he promised us is a new sinless life with him in the new creation. And all that he sends us works together to bring us there. Even as the plans of a house call for pieces of wood to be cut at a certain length and nails to be driven here and there, so our glory calls for affliction and pain, death and the grave through which we go unto heavenly glory.

No wonder is it then that the psalmist prays that he may be taught good judgment and knowledge. The more knowledge we have of God's promises, the more we will be able to judge that he is dealing well with us and bringing us to what he promised. Look at this present life under the curse and at the fleshly pleasures which God has not promised, and we will complain and say that he is not dealing well with us. But believing, as the psalmist confesses, that we are his servants, we will look for the day when we can serve him perfectly. And we will be interested in everything that helps us get there and now reminds us of our calling.

Do you want that kind of heavenly life hereafter? Then you will see that God is dealing with you as he promised and that all is well. Pray that you may have *good* judgment and knowledge.

Read: Psalm 119:65–80
Psalter versification: 329:1

THE BLESSEDNESS OF AFFLICTIONS

Before I was afflicted I went astray: but now have I kept thy word. Thou art good, and doest good; teach me thy statutes. —Psalm 119:67–68

Before we turn on the light in the middle of the night, the darkness keeps us from seeing the objects that are around us. But after the light is turned on, we can see them. And we do well to bear in mind that we are in the night of sin and death, and that in that darkness we cannot see our sins as sins and realize the awfulness of their punishment.

A truth we do well to bear in mind, therefore, is that God must, and in his grace does, turn on the light by sending afflictions. That is right! By means of afflictions God opens our eyes to the fact that there is a curse upon this earth because of sin, and that "the wages of sin is death" (Rom. 6:23). That is why the psalmist writes in Psalm 119:67–68, "Before I was afflicted I went astray: but now have I kept thy word. Thou art good, and doest good; teach me thy statutes."

That he went astray means that he went into ways of sin and death. And when God afflicted him, God also in his grace, and by his Spirit, made him see his waywardness as sin and that he deserved God's wrath upon him. In that way God brought him back to keep his word.

After God turned on the light for him, he also caused the psalmist to write: "Thou art good, and doest good." Indeed, by all our sicknesses and diseases, sorrows, and bereavements, God opens our eyes to the fact of sin and guilt and to bring us to pray, as the psalmist does, that he will teach us his statutes.

No, these afflictions do not deny the fact that Christ suffered all our punishment and blotted out all our guilt. But while we are still in this sinful flesh we need afflictions, and to see afflictions upon the world around us, to make us aware of our sins and to appreciate the cross of Christ and thereby taste God's goodness. We cannot do that if we do not see ourselves as sinners.

Let us therefore with the psalmist sing:

Before my affliction I wandered,
But now Thy good word I obey;
O Thou, Who art holy and gracious,
Now teach me Thy statutes, I pray.

Read: 2 Corinthians 4
Psalter versification: 329:2

DELIGHT IN GOD'S LAW

The proud have forged a lie against me: but I will keep thy precepts with my whole heart. Their heart is as fat as grease; but I delight in thy law. —Psalm 119:69–70

There are man-made laws which we must keep or be punished. We are not by man commanded to love these laws but to keep them to the letter. With God's laws it is different. We must keep them but also love them. And the psalmist teaches us this in Psalm 119:69–70 when he writes: "The proud have forged a lie against me: but I will keep thy precepts with my whole heart. Their heart is as fat as grease; but I delight in thy law."

Surely keeping God's law with the *whole heart* is hard to find because there is so little *delight* in God's law. When one forges a lie against us, we do not merely want to get even, but want to do more harm to him than he did to us.

Delighting in God's law and keeping it with our whole heart means that we show nothing but love to our neighbor, even when he hurts us. It means that we find joy in treating our enemies in love. Our versification presents it thus:

> The proud have assailed me with slander;
> Thy precepts shall still be my guide;
> Thy law is my joy and my treasure,
> Though sinners may boast in their pride.

This means then that our sin hurts us. We do not simply say that we did wrong. We say, when we hurt our neighbor with tongue or hand, that we hurt our own hearts. And the same thing is true about God's law in the first table of it. To delight in God's law means that it hurts us in our hearts when we displease God in any way and to any degree.

How important then it is that every night before we go to sleep, we examine our hearts. Do they ache because we did not obtain the same measure of earthly joy that those did whose "heart is as fat as grease"? Or do they ache because we love to walk in love to God, but find that we did very little that day in keeping his law? In the measure that we return blow for blow, word for word, to those who hurt us, we are as sinfully proud as they are, and we cannot then say that we delight in God's law.

Read: Psalm 119:25–40
Psalter versification: 329:3

THE RIGHT CHOICE

It is good for me that I have been afflicted; that I might learn thy statutes. The law of thy mouth is better unto me than thousands of gold and silver. —Psalm 119:71–72

If you had to choose between becoming a millionaire tomorrow, or continuing the rest of your life as you are and then when you die enter at once into heavenly glory, what would you choose? If you chose the latter, why did you do so? What do you consider heavenly glory to be, that makes you turn down a million dollars of silver and gold? Is it because you say with the psalmist what we read in Psalm 119:71–72? He wrote: "It is good for me that I have been afflicted; that I might learn thy statutes. The law of thy mouth is better unto me than thousands of gold and silver."

The point is that in heaven we will know the law of God's mouth, the statutes which he designed and decreed for us to keep. So the question is: Do you consider it heavenly to be so completely freed from sin that a sinful thought and desire never arises in your heart and mind? Or is heaven your desire first and only because you want to get rid of all the afflictions and miseries of your flesh?

The psalmist had already confessed that God is good and does good, and that God had dealt well with him in sending him afflictions. Can you sincerely sing these words of our versification?

> Affliction has been for my profit,
> That I to Thy statutes might hold;
> Thy law to my soul is more precious
> Than thousands of silver and gold.

This expresses a basic truth which we must have in mind before we think of or speak of heaven. It also makes the cross of Christ so meaningful and valuable. Christ died not merely to remove the curse from off us, but to bring us out from under the power of sin. He loves us, but he also loves God. And he came and died for us that he might make us love God as completely as he does.

Look deeply then into your soul to see whether that is the kind of heaven that you want to enter. And pray to God that he will already in this life teach you how to live in that law, so that you may walk in love to him no matter what an afflicted life you may have here on this earth.

Read: Hebrews 12:1–13
Psalter versification: 329:4

A FIXED HEART

O God, my heart is fixed; I will sing and give praise, even with my glory. Awake, psaltery and harp: I myself will awake early. —Psalm 108:1–2

One may ultimately come to the decision that a loved one should undergo very serious surgery and make up his mind to arrange for it. That does not, however, mean that he looks forward to it and will be singing during it. Singing requires more than a decision. It calls for a joy in the heart. In moments of sadness we cannot sing but are leaning toward weeping. Happiness must be there if we are going to sing.

David had such happiness in his heart when he in Psalm 108:1–2 wrote: "O God, my heart is fixed; I will sing and give praise, even with my glory. Awake, psaltery and harp: I myself will awake early." Our versification explains it this way:

My steadfast heart, O God,
Will sound Thy praise abroad
With tuneful string;
The dawn shall hear my song,
Thy praise I will prolong,
And where Thy people throng
Thanksgiving bring.

What we have here is a decision of David, but also an eagerness to sing God's praises. For his heart is fixed, or as the versification explains it, it is steadfast. He intends to sing God's praises and eagerly looks forward to doing so with joy. In fact, he will awake early in the morning to begin the day with such singing. And the word *awake* that is used here has the related idea of being set on fire. He is enthusiastic about such praise to God.

If you have already tasted the salvation that Christ realized for you, you also will be eager to praise God for the amazing work of grace which is upon you; and you will want to sing.

The question is then, how enthusiastically do you sing God's praises in the worship services on the Sabbath? And what about the days and hours between the Sabbath evening service and the morning service the next Sabbath? What did you sing during that period of time? On what was your heart fixed?

Oh that we might fill our days here below already with praise to God and turn from those carnal songs of the world.

Read: Psalm 108
Psalter versification: 298:1

IN PRAISE EXALTING GOD

I will praise thee, O Lord, among the people: and I will sing praises unto thee among the nations. For thy mercy is great above the heavens: and thy truth reacheth unto the clouds. —Psalm 108:3–4

In the measure that we appreciate the good someone has done for us, we respond with the praise of thanksgiving. And who is there that has done more good for us than God? Not only has he given us life and a wide and rich creation in which to live, but he has given us a new, spiritual life and is preparing for us a new world of blessedness and glory when Christ returns upon the clouds of heaven.

That is why David in Psalm 108:3–4 declares: "I will praise thee, O Lord, among the people: and I will sing praises unto thee among the nations. For thy mercy is great above the heavens: and thy truth reacheth unto the clouds."

For us today this means that we praise God for what he does for us in his Son. And nowhere will you find greater, more wonderful mercy and truth than what God showed in the cross of Christ. When David in the next two verses speaks of deliverance and salvation by God's right hand, he is speaking about Christ who is now at God's right hand as our king and head.

Therefore, we must never doubt that God is merciful to us, or that he is true to his word. We just cannot find a higher mercy and truth than that which is in God. And David tells us that he desires to have men praise God and in their speech exalt him for his mercy and truth.

The idea is not that we exalt God, but in our praise we declare how high he is as the merciful and true God. David means: "Let men exalt God in their speech." We cannot make God higher than he eternally is.

Now, remember that to praise someone is to make mention of that one's goodness. It is to say that this one is good to us, as we also sing in our versification:

Thy truth and tender love
Are high as heav'n above;
Thy help we crave.
Be Thou exalted high
Above the lofty sky;
Lest Thy beloved die,
O hear and save.

In our aches and pains we must not complain, but instead run to God in prayers of praise. For by faith we see Christ at God's right hand for our good, and coming again to lift us up to heavenly glory.

Read: Psalm 103
Psalter versification: 298:2

A SURE VICTORY

Through God we shall do valiantly: for he it is that shall
tread down our enemies. —Psalm 108:13

Here is a versification of David's words in Psalm 108 that we do well to commit to memory and take with us all through life:

God's word shall surely stand;
His Name through ev'ry land
Shall be adored;
Lord, who shall lead our host?
Thy aid we covet most,
In Thee is all our boast,
Strong in the Lord.

David had spoken of the loftiness of God's mercy and truth and had declared that his heart was fixed to praise God for them. But then to his mind came all the enemies from which he needed deliverance and salvation. And if David needed deliverance and salvation, we surely do also.

The devil hated the Old Testament church and tried in every way he could to destroy it. And you can be sure that, when he learned how he failed at the cross and knew of Christ's resurrection, he became furious. Now, as the church is spread all over the world, he is full of anger, and is trying to destroy all faith in Christ. He is working hard to produce the kingdom of the antichrist.

Yet all that David confessed in Psalm 108 is true. Though he spoke of the land of Canaan as a picture of the new creation God promises us, it is true that God's mercy and truth "reacheth unto the clouds" (v. 4), that is, are very sure and exalted things.

That being the case, we can and must take hold of his words in verse 13, namely: "Through God we shall do valiantly: for he it is that shall tread down our enemies." In a spiritual and very joyful way we may say: "We shall conquer!"

Because it does not depend upon us but upon God to tread down our enemies, namely, Satan, his host, the wicked world, and also sin and death, we may say: "We shall overcome!" God is for us, and he has complete control over every creature in heaven and on earth and in hell. And as we approach the days of the antichrist with his cruelty, teach your children to say that through God we shall do valiantly. He is true to his word and powerful to make it all come to pass.

Read: Romans 8:28–39
Psalter versification: 298:3

A BLESSED STATE AND CONDITION

Blessed is he whose transgression is forgiven, whose sin is covered. Blessed is the man unto whom the LORD imputeth not iniquity, and in whose spirit there is no guile. —Psalm 32:1–2

The fruit of a tree may be delicious, and the flower of a vine may have exquisite beauty. But remember that the tree brought forth that fruit, and the vine made that flower possible. And when it comes to our salvation, we may say that it is blessed to be freed from the curse and to have glory in the new Jerusalem. But keep clearly before your mind the fact that we must first have the blessings of forgiveness of our sins and of receiving a new, sinless life. Without these we will not receive a curse-free life, nor will we be able to enjoy it.

David teaches us this when he writes in Psalm 32:1–2, "Blessed is he whose transgression is forgiven, whose sin is covered. Blessed is the man unto whom the LORD imputeth not iniquity, and in whose spirit there is no guile." Being without guile means being without deceit. It means that one has been born again with a life that loves God. That state of righteousness is the legal basis for the blessing of enjoying heavenly glory. But the only way that we can enjoy it is that our spiritual condition is changed. Instead of being totally depraved sinners who hate God, we must be given a life that finds delight in serving God before his face. A fish in polluted water that is hot, many degrees above comfort for it, does not want to be on the dry land. Much less does one with a spirit of guile want to live with God, even though here below he has pains that are unbearable.

The psalmist says in Psalm 17:15, "I shall be satisfied, when I awake, with thy likeness." But our guilt will have to be removed, and our souls must be given love for God in order to get that joy. Commit to memory and sing then these words of David as versified in our Psalter:

How blest is he whose trespass
Hath freely been forgiv'n,
Whose sin is wholly covered
Before the sight of heav'n.
Blest he to whom Jehovah
Imputeth not his sin,
Who hath a guileless spirit,
Whose heart is true within.

Read: Psalm 32
Psalter versification: 83:1

CONFESSION AND FORGIVENESS

I acknowledge my sin unto thee, and mine iniquity have I not hid. I said, I will confess my transgressions unto the LORD; and thou forgavest the iniquity of my sin. Selah. —Psalm 32:5

You cannot buy anything from God. The gold and silver you might try to use is already his. And surely the price of salvation is too high for man to buy the smallest part of it. Yet David in Psalm 32 wrote that when he kept silent, God's hand was heavy upon him. He did not confess his sins, and he enjoyed no forgiveness. But then he writes: "I acknowledged my sin unto thee, and mine iniquity have I not hid. I said, I will confess my transgressions unto the LORD; and thou forgavest the iniquity of my sin" (v. 5). But be sure of it that David did not buy forgiveness by confessing his sins.

What is meant here is that God does not give the enjoyment of the truth of forgiveness to those who do not desire it. And the desire is made known in the confession. Confessing our sins means not only that we seek forgiveness, but also that we hate that sin and want to be separated from it. Covering our sins means that we do not have interest in Christ's blood covering them. Covering them means that we do not hate them but only want to escape their punishment. Confessing our sins means that we hate them and want to be pleasing in God's sight.

Such a desire is God's gift to us and not that whereby we buy forgiveness. God gives us a guileless spirit, and then we confess our sins.

There is much we can learn from our versification that sings:

> While I kept guilty silence
> My strength was spent with grief,
> Thy hand was heavy on me,
> My soul found no relief;
> But when I owned my trespass,
> My sin hid not from Thee,
> When I confessed transgression,
> Then Thou forgavest me.

Do that then before you close your eyes in sleep tonight. Confess your sins every hour of the day, when you stumble and fall into sin. You cannot know any blessing of God when you keep silent. Confess your sin to the one you sinned against, but always confess it to God. That is the way that he brings to his people the joy of their forgiveness.

Read: Proverbs 28:1–14
Psalter versification: 83:2

THE BLESSED THRILL OF FORGIVENESS

For this shall every one that is godly pray unto thee in a time when thou mayest be found: surely in the floods of great waters they shall not come nigh unto him. Thou art my hiding place; thou shalt preserve me from trouble; thou shalt compass me about with songs of deliverance. Selah. —Psalm 32:6–7

Did you ever stop to think that if you lived, or have lived, for 70 years and sinned only once a day, you would have 25,550 sins that needed forgiveness? That does not even count the years when there are 29 days in February. But who dares to commit the sin today of saying that he does not sin every hour of every day? How often is it not that we carry a sin with us every minute for days at a time before we confess it?

Surely then you understand why David in Psalm 32:6 speaks of a flood of waters that threatens us. But find comfort in his words when he writes: "For this shall every one that is godly pray unto thee in a time when thou mayest be found: surely in the floods of great waters they shall not come nigh unto him." Those floods of waters are God's holy wrath against sin.

He also adds in verse 7: "Thou art my hiding place; thou shalt preserve me from trouble; thou shalt compass me about with songs of deliverance." Or as we can and should sing it:

So let the godly seek Thee
In times when Thou art near;
No whelming floods shall reach them,
Nor cause their hearts to fear.
In Thee, O Lord, I hide me,
Thou savest me from ill,
And songs of Thy salvation
My heart with rapture thrill.

What assurance we have here, when we confess our sins! God will give us assurance that they are forgiven. The flood of millions of our sins, and the humanly innumerable number of sins of the whole church from Adam onward, were placed upon Christ. No wonder that he in the garden of Gethsemane cried in such agony when he saw what was coming, and then on the cross cried: "My God, my God, why hast thou forsaken me?" (Matt. 27:46).

Not only is God our hiding place who preserves us from all trouble, but he causes songs of salvation to thrill our hearts with rapture. Listen then to David when he tells us to come to God with a prayer of confession of sin. You will be encompassed with joyful songs of deliverance. That flood of sin and guilt will never touch you. God says so through David.

Read: Psalm 27
Psalter versification: 83:3

CORRECTIVE LOVE AND BOUNDLESS GRACE

I will instruct thee and teach thee in the way which thou shalt go: I will guide thee with mine eye. —Psalm 32:8

If you have been caught stealing someone's possessions, spreading lies about him, have slapped him in the face and called him some filthy, vile names, and then apologize, he might forgive you and treat you as before those sins. But should you a few days later do all this evil over again, would he trust you, forgive you, and treat you as his best friend?

Bring then to mind how many times you have sinned against God, confessed these sins, but went right back to them. Have you ever found a more patient, forgiving, and merciful person than the sovereign, almighty God who sent his Son to earn heavenly glory for us? Not only has he forgiven every sin and given us that precious gift of the beginning of a life that cannot sin (1 John 3:9), but listen to what David wrote in Psalm 32:8, "I will instruct thee and teach thee in the way which thou shalt go: I will guide thee with mine eye."

He will not turn from us and leave us alone, but turn unto us and be very close to us. For that he will guide us with his eye means that he will keep his eye upon us and see to it that we never fall into everlasting torment and hell fire, but will keep us on the way to his house of many mansions where we cannot sin, and where we will enjoy his covenant fellowship forever.

Add up all the sins you committed and into which you fell back time and time again. Can you then think of a greater love? God does not forsake us or ever come to say: "That is enough! I am through with you!" No, he continues to instruct us and make us spiritually wise and warns us not to behave as dumb beasts of the field, "which have no understanding, whose mouth must be held in with bit and bridle" (v. 9).

Come then and let us sing these words:

I graciously will teach thee
The way that thou shalt go,
And with My eye upon thee
My counsel make thee know.
But be ye not unruly,
Or slow to understand,
Be not perverse, but willing
To heed My wise command.

What corrective love and boundless grace! Take then his warnings as works of his love and grace to you.

Read: Psalm 33
Psalter versification: 84:1

A CALL TO REJOICE

Be ye not as the horse, or as the mule, which have no understanding: whose mouth must be held in with bit and bridle, lest they come near unto thee. Many sorrows shall be to the wicked: but he that trusteth in the Lᴏʀᴅ, mercy shall compass him about. Be glad in the Lᴏʀᴅ, and rejoice, ye righteous: and shout for joy, all ye that are upright in heart. —Psalm 32:9–11

Place some precious gold coins in the feeding trough of a horse or mule. But do not be surprised when it pushes these aside with its mouth and, having eaten all the food, walks away from them. It sees no value in them but rather considers them to be in its way. It is because we do not appreciate God's mercy as we ought that we are in Psalm 32:9 taught: "Be ye not as the horse, or as the mule, which have no understanding: whose mouth must be held in with bit and bridle, lest they come near unto thee."

The sad fact but undeniable truth is that we do not appreciate God's mercy as we ought, and God through David instructs us in verse 11: "Be glad in the Lᴏʀᴅ, and rejoice, ye righteous: and shout for joy, all ye that are upright in heart." We have been made righteous through the forgiveness of our sins and upright in heart by having been given a guileless spirit (v. 2); but we do not appreciate this as we ought, because we still have our sinful flesh and do not see the value of God's mercy of which David speaks in verse 10 in these words: "Many sorrows shall be to the wicked: but he that trusteth in the Lᴏʀᴅ, mercy shall compass him about." The truth of these two verses is expressed thus in our versification:

> The sorrows of the wicked
> In number shall abound,
> But those that trust Jehovah,
> His mercy shall surround;
> Then in the Lord be joyful,
> In song lift up your voice;
> Be glad in God, ye righteous,
> Rejoice, ye saints, rejoice.

Yes, we know the sorrows that come to the wicked. We, too, have sickness and disease. Death takes our loved ones away from us as well as theirs from them. But remember what David said: "Blessed is he whose transgression is forgiven, whose sin is covered" (v. 1). Sickness, disease, and death are God's wrath upon the wicked and his means to bring them to everlasting punishment. For us these are works of his mercy, for they are his means to prepare us for and bring us to the heavenly glory he prepared in Christ.

Be glad then and rejoice. Shout for joy! His mercy surrounds us; and no punishment can keep us from that glory, or touch us.

Read: Psalm 98
Psalter versification: 84:2

THE BELIEVER'S HOPE

Thy hands have made me and fashioned me: give me understanding, that I may
learn thy commandments. They that fear thee will be glad when they see me;
because I have hoped in thy word. —Psalm 119:73–74

To hope for something is to long for it, but also to expect it to come. In his wisdom Solomon wrote in Proverbs 10:28, "The hope of the righteous shall be gladness: but the expectation of the wicked shall perish." Hoping is expecting that for which one longs. Idol worshipers have hope, for they long to be set free from pain and suffering, and they expect their idol to bring them there. The righteous long and expect to be delivered from the *act* of sin as well as from the punishment of sin.

The psalmist makes that very plain when in Psalm 119:73–74 he writes: "Thy hands have made me and fashioned me: give me understanding, that I may learn thy commandments. They that fear thee will be glad when they see me; because I have hoped in thy word." Or as our versification has it:

> Thou, Who didst make and fashion me,
> O make me wise, Thy law to learn;
> Then they that fear Thee shall be glad
> When they my hope in God discern.

Notice that he does not pray that God will tell him what his commandments are, but that he may have understanding through learning these commandments. He prays that God, who "made and fashioned" him, will cause him to understand what it means that man was made and fashioned in the image of God, as his friend-servant. He is concerned with understanding and learning to know how to live in love toward God. He longs and yearns for the day when he will be able to think, will, and do only that which man was made and fashioned to do as God's image-bearer.

How about it? Is that your longing and expectation? Or is your idea of heaven merely an escape from suffering the curse, the punishment of sin? Do you want to be as sinless as Christ was during his sojourn among us?

If we only want escape from the punishment of sin, we do not understand God's commandments. And we do not understand what Christ did for us by going to his cross. That cross was God's way of lifting us up to holiness. For only those who are freed from the act of sin will be in that place where there is no punishment of sin.

Read: Psalm 119:73–88
Psalter versification: 330:1

A PRAYER FOR COMFORT

I know, O LORD, that thy judgments are right, and that thou in faithfulness hast afflicted me. Let, I pray thee, thy merciful kindness be for my comfort, according to thy word unto thy servant. —Psalm 119:75–76

The tenth section of Psalm 119 is full of prayers. In verse 73 the psalmist had prayed that God would give him understanding. Then follows in this section of the psalm five petitions that God will let this and that happen. In verses 75–76 he prays: "I know, O LORD, that thy judgments are right, and that thou in faithfulness hast afflicted me. Let, I pray thee, thy merciful kindness be for my comfort, according to thy word unto thy servant."

Here he prays for comfort in the midst of his afflictions. And because God has given him understanding, he judged God's judgment to be right. He had sinned and deserved those afflictions. Now, he wants the comfort of assurance that in God's merciful kindness he is forgiven.

Never can we get comfort apart from that merciful kindness. Never can we by anything we do get our guilt removed and be freed from the power of sin that holds us. We cannot open our hearts to let Christ come in. We cannot push aside our sinful natures by asking for it. We earn nothing by our prayers and never change God by them. If we think that we can open our hearts and can influence God by what we do, we had better pray for understanding as the psalmist did in verse 73.

No, God must remove our guilt and put spiritual life in us before we can do anything pleasing in his sight. He must do that before we can even want and then pray for salvation from sin and its punishment. His merciful kindness does this for us and in us.

God is the Alpha and Omega, the first and the last (Rev. 22:13). He opens our hearts before we can even want them to be opened. Every bit of our salvation is because of his merciful kindness. For it was in that kindness that he sent his own Son into our flesh to suffer our punishment so that he could earn for us the right to be delivered from the power of sin in which Satan holds us.

In that truth we can find comfort. God makes the first move always. A child is not born because it wanted it. And we are not born again because we wanted it. God's merciful kindness saves us. So also we sing:

Thou, Lord, art just in all Thy ways,
And faithful Thou chastenest me;
I pray Thee, let Thy promised grace
Thy servant's help and comfort be.

Read: Revelation 22
Psalter versification: 330:2

LIVING IN LOVE TOWARD GOD

Let thy tender mercies come unto me, that I may live: for thy law is my delight. Let the proud be ashamed; for they dealt perversely with me without a cause: but I will meditate in thy precepts. —Psalm 119:77–78

There are sicknesses and diseases which come upon us that are not man's attack upon us. But there are also afflictions which enemies bring upon us. Of such troubles the psalmist spoke in Psalm 119:77–78, where he wrote: "Let thy tender mercies come unto me, that I may live: for thy law is my delight. Let the proud be ashamed; for they dealt perversely with me without a cause: but I will meditate in thy precepts."

What we find here and must learn is that because God made and fashioned us in his own image to walk in love toward him, we sinners do not deserve to live on this earth, even as God told Adam: "In the day that thou eatest thereof thou shalt surely die" (Gen. 2:17). And as Paul states in Romans 6:23, "The wages of sin is death."

The psalmist had confessed that he deserved the affliction which men had brought upon him; but now he prays that in the mercy of God he may be given life wherein he will walk in God's commandments. The unbelievers will be punished with the shame of being cast into the lake of fire. The psalmist, however, wants to live, not to enjoy feasting, worldly pleasures, and amusements, but to serve God as man was made and fashioned to do.

What an example we have here to follow. Let us examine our souls as to why we want to live here on this earth. The psalmist does not pray for God's mercy because he keeps God's law. That earns us absolutely nothing. But he wants to live so that he may serve God as is his calling on God's earth with God's creatures. We sing these words, but let us also make them our prayer:

Show mercy, Lord, that I may live,
For in Thy law is all my joy;
While those who wrong me are rebuked,
Thy precepts shall my thought employ.

In his mercy God makes us want to live a life of love toward him. In that mercy Christ died that we might live. In that mercy Christ was taken to heaven that we might be lifted up to live with him in perfect sinlessness. The wages of sin is death, but God's mercy gives us life.

Read: Romans 6
Psalter versification: 330:3

PRAYING FOR A SOUND HEART

"Let those that fear thee turn unto me, and those that have known thy testimonies.
Let my heart be sound in thy statutes; that I be not ashamed." —Psalm 119:79–80

All the members of our bodies are important. God, who made and fashioned them, knew what he was doing when he made us as we are. And although some of the members of our bodies can be removed surgically without threat to our lives, and sometimes have to be removed because of cancer or some other disease, we cannot get along without a heart. And the healthier the heart is, the more active one can be, while an impaired heart will limit one's activity.

It is no wonder then that the psalmist wrote in Psalm 119:80, "Let my heart be sound in thy statutes; that I be not ashamed."

If we are going to live as we were made and fashioned to be, namely, to be image-bearers, that is, reflectors of God's glory, we must have a spiritual heart that is sound. The healthier that heart is, the more perfectly we will walk in love toward God, and therefore love his statutes. The more we hate sin and love God, the sounder our hearts are. The psalmist makes a very important petition here.

But there is another request of his that goes hand in hand with that request for a sound heart. He prays that others with sound hearts may turn to him. Because he had fallen into great sin, those with sound hearts had separated from him, finding no pleasure in having fellowship with one who walks in sin. And now he desires greatly that they see the change in his life and again become his friends. In verse 79 he writes: "Let those that fear thee turn unto me, and those that have known thy testimonies." These are those whose hearts are sound. And our versification has it thus:

> Let those that fear Thee turn to me,
> Thy truth to them will I proclaim;
> Instruct my heart to keep Thy law,
> That I may not be put to shame.

Who are your friends? With whom do you feel at home? It reveals how sound your heart is, and how earnestly we should pray for a sound heart. For a sound heart is a perfect heart; and only with a perfect heart will our walk of life be perfect, as our Savior's was perfect and fulfilled God's law for us.

Read: 1 John 2:1–17
Psalter versification: 330:4

A VERY INSTRUCTIVE QUESTION

The Lord is my light and my salvation; whom shall I fear? the Lord is the strength of my life; of whom shall I be afraid? —Psalm 27:1

Children learn by asking questions. At a very early age they ask what this and that is, why this happened and that happened, why we must do this and why we must do that. And parents give them answers to teach them. But parents also have questions and want answers so that light is brought on a particular subject. And they also ask questions in order to teach.

David did that so beautifully in Psalm 27:1, where he asks: "The Lord is my light and my salvation; whom shall I fear? the Lord is the strength of my life; of whom shall I be afraid?" Actually, of course, it is God who is asking us that question through David, so that we may be freed from fear. And a stronger reason for not being afraid there is not.

We will get a more literal translation of David's words in our versification that calls us to sing:

Jehovah is my light,
And my salvation near;
Who shall my soul affright,
Or cause my heart to fear?
While God my strength, my life sustains,
Secure from fear my soul remains.

For in that name Jehovah is all the light and confidence that we need. That name, which literally means I AM, presents God to us as a defender and protector who depends on no one and upon whom every creature depends.

We can have doubts about men who set out to protect and save us. They do not make their own hearts beat. How can we be sure they will succeed?

But Jehovah is our light because he is our strength. No matter how dark the situation may be and how powerful the enemy looks to be, Jehovah, who is the I AM and never says, "I will be if...," is our salvation in Christ. Our enemies can do only what he gives them the strength to do. We have absolutely no reason to fear what men will do to us. If it will not serve to bring us to the glory God promised us, he will not give them the strength to do so. If it will serve that goal, he will raise them up and give them the life and strength. The cross was no accident. God brought Judas, Caiaphas, Pilate, and the Roman soldiers into being and gave them life, because in Christ he is our salvation.

Read: Psalm 27
Psalter versification: 71:1

WELL-FOUNDED CONFIDENCE

When the wicked, even mine enemies and my foes, came upon me to eat up my flesh, they stumbled and fell. —Psalm 27:2

Having enemies is one thing. Being afraid of them is another. We have enemies; but we should not be afraid of them. In fact, if we have no enemies, we should be afraid. If Satan and the ungodly world are our friends, God is our enemy, and we have reason for terrible fear. But if he is our light and our salvation, we have no reason to be afraid, no matter how big a host of enemies is against us.

The first promise God gave his church, the mother promise of Genesis 3:15, assures us that our enemies' heads will be crushed! David speaks of this in Psalm 27:2 in these words: "When the wicked, even mine enemies and my foes, came upon me to eat up my flesh, they stumbled and fell." Doing so, he does not mean that God's people are going to escape all bodily harm. We may be injured severely or even be killed. The Scriptures give us many examples of this from Abel onward. But there are two facts that we should keep in mind.

All the church's enemies are going to be cast into the lake of fire. Satan and his innumerable host will enter into everlasting punishment. And every child of God shall enter into the glories of heaven because Jehovah is his light and salvation.

The only thing unbelievers can be sure of is that God will visit them with endless punishment. They may for a time seem to succeed; but they will stumble and fall into the torments of hell! For Jehovah, who has all things under his perfect control, will keep his promise to us. And that he is the I AM means that he can truthfully say, "I AM in charge! And I AM faithful!"

No matter then what happens, sing these words of our versification:

When evildoers came
To make my life their prey,
They stumbled in their shame
And fell in sore dismay;
Though hosts make war on ev'ry side,
Still fearless I in God confide.

Read: Revelation 20
Psalter versification: 71:2

A VERY REVEALING DESIRE

One thing have I desired of the LORD, that will I seek after; that I may dwell in the house of the LORD all the days of my life, to behold the beauty of the LORD, and to enquire in his temple. —Psalm 27:4

It cannot be denied that we all face death, and in 1 Corinthians 15:26 Paul calls death the last enemy to be destroyed. That makes us wonder how David could say in Psalm 27:1 that he has nothing to fear and that he is afraid of nothing and no one. For although we understand that his reason for this is that God is his light and his salvation, the question arises for us as to how we can be sure that God is *our* light and salvation.

We cannot find that out by looking into a mirror. Looking at our family tree and tracing our genealogical background will not give us the assurance that our names are in the Lamb's book of life, and that therefore we can be sure that God is our light and our salvation. But we can be sure, if we can find in our souls and with David sincerely say what he wrote in Psalm 27:4, namely: "One thing have I desired of the LORD, that will I seek after; that I may dwell in the house of the LORD all the days of my life, to behold the beauty of the LORD, and to enquire in his temple."

The reason why this confession reveals that we have nothing to fear is the fact that this makes it plain that God *is* our light and our salvation and has already begun to lift us out of the clutches of Satan, our worst enemy. He has already caused us to desire the full salvation from sin and death and made us want to taste and enjoy the beauty of his love, mercy, and grace.

Adam turned away from God and died spiritually; and we did with him. The desire to dwell in God's house means that we want to be brought back to him and to serve him in love again. This reveals that God has already begun to give us the victory over Satan, our worst enemy, and that he will most assuredly give us the full victory in the day of Christ. Victory over spiritual death is sure! And enjoying the full salvation prepared in Christ is undeniably ahead of us.

Sing it then with David:

My one request has been,
And still this prayer I raise,
That I may dwell within
God's house through all my days,
Jehovah's beauty to admire,
And in His temple to inquire.

Read: Psalm 91
Psalter versification: 71:3

OUR CERTAIN SAFETY

For in the time of trouble he shall hide me in his pavilion: in the secret of his tabernacle shall he hide me; he shall set me up upon a rock. —Psalm 27:5

A man with a so-called life insurance policy gets nothing out of it himself. The policy does not assure him that he will not die and promises nothing that will restore life to him. But the child of God has a life *assurance* policy that is based on the word of *the* almighty, unchangeable, ever faithful God of our salvation. That policy not only assures us that we will never lose the new life we got when born again, but it also promises us that we will get our bodies back, and this time in a far more glorious, heavenly form.

Of this David wrote after stating that he had no reason to be afraid of anyone and of anything. In Psalm 27:5 he wrote: "For in the time of trouble he shall hide me in his pavilion: in the secret of his tabernacle shall he hide me; he shall set me up upon a rock." This he states as the reason why his one desire is to dwell in the house of God all the days of his life. In that house he is safe. And believing this, with David we can sing:

When troubles round me swell,
When fears and dangers throng,
Securely I will dwell
In His pavilion strong;
Within the covert of His tent
He hides me till the storm is spent.

If David could say that, surely we can today. David had in mind the blood sprinkled upon the mercy seat of the ark behind the veil. We see not only the blood of the cross but also the risen, glorified Christ at God's right hand. There he has power over all things in heaven and on earth.

And though we do have troubles, they cannot hurt us and keep us from dwelling in God's house of heavenly glory. We are set up upon Christ, the solid rock, and cannot be injured by the fiercest storms.

Our safety is absolutely sure. That Christ is there as our head reveals that we can and will reach that glory. The waters of these storms, the troubles in this life, are all in the hand of Christ to use to prepare us for that glory. He who loved us so fully that he gave his life, and suffered hellish agonies for us, will keep us safe. We are safe, for we are upon him, the rock of our salvation.

Read: 2 Corinthians 4
Psalter versification: 71:4

LIFTED TO EVERLASTING PRAISE

And now shall mine head be lifted up above mine enemies round about me: therefore will I offer in his tabernacle sacrifices of joy; I will sing, yea, I will sing praises unto the LORD. —Psalm 27:6

In a fierce storm the wind whips up huge waves that dash against the rocks. But always the rock splits the waves and scatters the water left and right. Every time this happens, we have a picture of how safe the child of God is in the storms of life.

In Psalm 27:5 David had written that God had set him up upon a rock, which is Christ. Below are his enemies as powerful waves driven by Satan in an attempt to destroy the church. But the waves are dashed into pieces, while the rock is unharmed, and those set upon him are not touched. No wonder then that David and we can sing:

> Uplifted on a rock
> Above my foes around,
> Amid the battle shock
> My song shall still resound;
> Then joyful off'rings I will bring,
> Jehovah's praise my heart shall sing.

David stated it in these words in Psalm 27:6, "And now shall mine head be lifted up above mine enemies round about me: therefore will I offer in his tabernacle sacrifices of joy; I will sing, yea, I will sing praises unto the LORD."

Here we find David stating in other words what he had stated in verse 1, namely, that God is his light and his salvation. As his salvation, God lifted him up to safety above all his enemies, and, as his light, God had made him see that he had nothing to fear, no matter how dark his way seemed.

Therefore, being safe in God's house with its protection, he will offer to God sacrifices of joy and sing his praises. And we do well to consider that singing such praises is evidence that we have been lifted up upon Christ, the solid rock. In him and his cross God is our salvation; and by his Spirit who opens our spiritual eyes he is our light.

Lifted up upon Christ the rock means that we in God's counsel are lifted up to heaven where God's house of many mansions is. There the everlasting day will be full of songs of praise to God as our light and our salvation.

How often do you praise God as your light and salvation?

Read: Psalm 61
Psalter versification: 71:5

KEPT IN CHRIST

Hear, O LORD, when I cry with my voice: have mercy also upon me, and answer me. When thou saidst, Seek ye my face; my heart said unto thee, Thy face, LORD, will I seek. —Psalm 27:7–8

There are times when a child of God is upon the mountaintop of faith. There are also times when weakness of faith manifests itself. These two are in our lives because we still have the old man of sin until the day of our death. The new man in Christ will reveal himself; but the old man of sin will also at times be in control of our thinking, willing, and doing.

When David cried out in Psalm 27: "Whom shall I fear…Of whom shall I be afraid?" (v. 1), he was on the mountaintop of faith. But weakness of faith revealed itself when he stated in verses 7–8: "Hear, O LORD, when I cry with my voice: have mercy also upon me, and answer me. When thou saidst, Seek ye my face; my heart said unto thee, Thy face, LORD, will I seek." Our versification has it thus:

> Lord, hear me when I pray,
> And answer me in grace;
> Oft as I hear Thee say,
> Come ye and seek My face,
> My heart and lips their answer speak,
> Thy face, Jehovah, will I seek.

Here David still reveals faith in God. But he is not revealing the confidence he expressed in verse 1 of this psalm. Now, he is crying for help and voicing a measure of fear.

Nevertheless, there is an important truth here, namely, what David had stated in verse 5 in these words: "In the time of trouble he shall hide me in his pavilion: in the secret of his tabernacle shall he hide me." No, he was not now on the mountaintop of faith; but he does still reveal faith in God. For he prays to God, seeks his mercy, and expresses a desire to seek God's face. When Satan sent powerful waves in an attempt to wash him away into unbelief, he did not succeed. God was David's and is our light and salvation. In his unfailing grace and mercy God will keep us from losing our faith.

Once engrafted into Christ by faith, we will never be plucked out and be cast into unbelief. As for our salvation which is in Christ, God will keep us safe from falling away into unbelief and everlasting punishment. We do not need to be afraid that God will change and cast us into darkness.

Read: Psalm 37:1–24
Psalter versification: 72:1

WONDROUS LOVE

Hide not thy face far from me; put not thy servant away in anger: thou hast been my help; leave me not, neither forsake me, O God of my salvation. When my father and my mother forsake me, then the LORD will take me up. —Psalm 27:9–10

Although there are fathers and mothers who have forsaken their children and committed child abuse, the natural attitude to their own flesh and blood is that of tender, loving care. But there is one who loves his children more deeply than human words can express it. He is God.

God's love is perfect, unwavering, and so great that he gave his only begotten Son for our everlasting good. He knows our needs and sees us wherever we are. As the infinite, everywhere present God, he is not only next to us every minute but in us with his power, love, and mercy.

It might seem strange then that David wrote in Psalm 27:9–10, "Hide not thy face far from me; put not thy servant away in anger: thou hast been my help; leave me not, neither forsake me, O God of my salvation. When my father and my mother forsake me, then the LORD will take me up."

This may seem to be a great weakness of faith. Yet here is something very wonderful that ought to be also in us. It is something that we can experience only because God is our light and our salvation. David reveals very clearly here that he knows his unworthiness, knows that by nature he is a child of darkness and needs salvation, and sees no reason in himself why God should be his salvation, why he should not be forsaken and have God's face hidden from him.

Pretty soon we, having been exposed before the judgment seat of God (2 Cor. 5:10), and now fully saved and dwelling in God's house, are going to wonder more than now that God is our salvation with his face upon us, in Christ bestowing closer covenant fellowship than now. We will then know how unworthy we are in ourselves and understand fully what it means that he is our light and our salvation.

We, too, may and should with David sing:

> Hide not Thy face from me,
> In wrath turn not away,
> My help and Saviour be,
> Forsake me not, I pray;
> Should father, mother, both forsake,
> The Lord on me will pity take.

What wondrous love! There surely will be abundant reason in the new Jerusalem to sing God's praises.

Read: Psalm 103
Psalter versification: 72:2

WALKING ON A LEVEL PATHWAY

Teach me thy way, O LORD, and lead me in a plain path,
because of mine enemies. —Psalm 27:11

In this vale of tears and sorrows where we live, our lives are characterized by ups and downs. We can, as children of God, be one minute on the mountaintop of faith, and with David confess that God is our light and our salvation. The next minute we can slip down into doubts and perplexities. Then with David we cry out that God hide not his face from us and put us not away in anger. The reason for this is not that God has changed. It is due to the fact that we still have a sinful nature, and that there is so much in our lives that reveals that in us there is no reason why God should be our light and our salvation. Looking at ourselves, we see that there is no reason for us not to be afraid, not of men, but of God's holy wrath. When we fall into sin, we fall down from the mountaintop of faith. We read in Psalm 15 that only "he that walketh uprightly, and worketh righteousness" (v. 2) shall dwell in God's house.

Therefore, it is so necessary that we with David pray: "Teach me thy way, O LORD, and lead me in a plain path, because of mine enemies" (Ps. 27:11). For God's way is the way of his commandments. The plain path is better translated as the level path, one without ups and downs, but instead one with a steady faith and righteous walk. A plain is a level piece of ground. Mountains may be in the distance, but there are no chasms and canyons on it. And it is when we walk on God's way, which is prescribed in his law, and we know what he demands of us in every circumstance of life, that we will enjoy the truth that he is our light and our salvation. When we walk on the level and do not fall into sin, we will have that assurance that God is our light and salvation. We will know how to please him and find in our walk that he has begun salvation in us.

And we need to be taught his way because of the temptations of deceitful Satan and his followers. Well may we then pray and sing:

Teach me, O Lord, Thy way,
Make plain to me my path;
Because of foes, I pray,
Protect me from their wrath;
To false accusers, cruel foes,
O Lord, do not my soul expose.

Read: Psalm 1
Psalter versification: 72:3

WAITING COURAGEOUSLY

Wait on the LORD: be of good courage, and he shall strengthen thine heart: wait, I say, on the LORD. —Psalm 27:14

Because God is our light and our salvation, our desire to dwell in his house, and therein behold his beauty, will most assuredly be fulfilled. There are times when it does not look that way. We have enemies exactly because he is our light and our salvation. Those who hate God will hate us and treat us as they treated his Son who came into our flesh. Using false witnesses, breathing cruelty, they nailed him to his cross. And in the measure that we reveal him by walking in God's way, they will mock, torment, yea even kill us, if we do not fall into the temptations wherewith Satan tries to lead us away from a walk of love toward God.

That is why God himself through David calls us to "Wait on the LORD: be of good courage, and he shall strengthen thine heart: wait, I say, on the LORD" (Ps. 27:14). Or as we sing it from our versification:

> Faint-hearted would I be,
> Didst Thou not promise, Lord,
> I shall Thy goodness see
> While Thou dost life accord.
> Wait on the Lord, nor faint, nor fear,
> Yea, trust and wait, the Lord is near.

The truth here is that God will at his own appointed time make us experience fully that he is our light and our salvation. All the attacks of Satan and of the unbelievers only prove this to be true. But we must courageously wait until God sends his Son to resurrect our bodies that for a time lie in the grave and gives us the fullness of salvation.

Now, to wait on the Lord is not being idle, doing nothing. Those about to run in a race wait with their minds alert and their ears cocked so that they hear the signal that starts the race. So our minds must be fixed on that full salvation in the day of Christ when we shall fully know God as our light and our salvation.

Waiting courageously, then, means that we live in God's word. It is not a closed book for us but an open book. We wait with souls that are reaching out for that full salvation. We fear no disappointment or unfaithfulness on God's part. We know he is our light and salvation.

Read: John 14:1–21
Psalter versification: 72:4

THE HUMBLE UPWARD LOOK

Unto thee lift I up mine eyes, O thou that dwellest in the heavens. Behold, as the eyes of servants look unto the hand of their masters, and as the eyes of a maiden unto the hand of her mistress; so our eyes wait upon the LORD our God, until that he have mercy upon us. —Psalm 123:1–2

One of the most precious powers God implanted in the human body is the gift of sight. How rich does not the gift of sight make life! How much would we not miss, if it were taken from us? But spiritual sight is far more precious and important than seeing with the fleshly eye. What the psalmist lifts his eyes to see, and of what he speaks in Psalm 123:1–2, is of utmost importance. He writes: "Unto thee lift I up mine eyes, O thou that dwellest in the heavens. Behold, as the eyes of servants look unto the hand of their masters, and as the eyes of a maiden unto the hand of her mistress; so our eyes wait upon the LORD our God, until that he have mercy upon us."

It makes a world of difference, however, as to how we look unto God. The servants and the maids look to their masters and mistresses as their superiors. They look up to them, realizing that the hands of their masters and mistresses give them what they need. Our versification has it thus:

To Thee, O Lord, I lift my eyes,
O Thou enthroned above the skies;
As servants watch their master's hand,
Or maidens by their mistress stand,
So to the Lord our eyes we raise,
Until His mercy He displays.

The question is whether in our prayers we look to God as the exalted, almighty, sovereign God. If he is not above all creatures, what good is it for us to pray to him? If we approach him as though he is our servant rather than our master, we get no blessing, but only add to the reason why we ought to receive more punishment. In fact, then we are not praying to God but to an idol, a mental image we manufactured in our minds.

Our prayers must always be humble requests. We must look *up* to him and not down upon him. Surely then this means that we look to him through Christ who is at his right hand and has the universe in his hand. In profound and sincere humility we must bow before him. We must look up to him as one enthroned *above* the skies. Prayer requires a humble upward look.

Read: Psalms 121, 123
Psalter versification: 351:1

AN URGENT PRAYER FOR MERCY

Have mercy upon us, O LORD, have mercy upon us: for we are exceedingly filled with contempt. Our soul is exceedingly filled with the scorning of those that are at ease, and with the contempt of the proud. —Psalm 123:3–4

In Psalm 123:2 the psalmist had said that his eye waits upon God until he has mercy upon him. Now in verses 3–4 he writes: "Have mercy upon us, O LORD, have mercy upon us: for we are exceedingly filled with contempt. Our soul is exceedingly filled with the scorning of those that are at ease, and with the contempt of the proud."

Now, we are not told just what he suffered; but we do know that if we look to God in prayer, and before men confess that he is in the highest heavens, we are going to be scorned and filled with contempt. The world will ridicule us and deny that he created the world and has every bit of it in his hands. In their schools they will not allow prayers to be raised to him. Soon in the days of the coming antichrist we will be forbidden to pray to him in our homes and churches.

Then, but also today, there is need for us to pray to God for his mercy to bear that scorn and mockery and pain; we need his mercy to keep us faithful and continuously looking up to him, never taking our eyes from him as the God of our salvation, the almighty, sovereign, exalted God who is high above all creation.

And when the psalmist prays to God *until* his mercy is upon us, he does not mean that he is trying to wear God out by constant praying till he gets his way. Rather the idea is that when we experience that mercy upon us, our prayers are going to be changed to those of praise and thanksgiving.

Sing then this versification of the psalmist's words:

> O Lord, our God, Thy mercy show,
> For man's contempt and scorn we know;
> Reproach and shame Thy saints endure
> From wicked men who dwell secure;
> Man's proud contempt and scorn we know;
> O Lord, our God, Thy mercy show.

In all the ridicule and scorn that we suffer, we need to have God assure us that his own Son was "despised and rejected of men, a man of sorrows, and acquainted with grief" (Isa. 53:3), in order that he might bring us to heavenly glory and everlasting blessedness.

Read: Psalm 136
Psalter versification: 351:2

AN AWESOME TRUTH

O LORD, thou hast searched me, and known me. Thou knowest my downsitting and mine uprising, thou understandest my thought afar off. —Psalm 139:1–2

A truth which we often brush aside and forget is expressed powerfully in Psalm 139:1–2, where David writes: "O LORD, thou hast searched me, and known me. Thou knowest my downsitting and mine uprising, thou understandest my thought afar off." Our lives, according to these words of God given through David, are an open book. We can look in only one direction at a time and must often close our eyes in sleep. But God never sleeps and is ever watchful over all his creation. He sees it all in every detail without one moment of ceasing from doing so.

God not only sees our outward deeds but reads the thoughts of our hearts, and he knows what is in our minds. He understands our thought afar off. No one ever has or ever can hide one word, one thought or desire, or one action from the everywhere present God. We sing that this way in our versification of these words of David:

Lord, Thou hast searched me, and dost know
Where'er I rest, where'er I go;
Thou knowest all that I have planned,
And all my ways are in Thy hand.

Realize then what this means for us sinful creatures whose best works even are polluted with sin. Not only does God know everything that we think, will, and do, but he knows how filthy, how sinful all that we do is.

The name David uses here strengthens the awesomeness of this truth. The name Jehovah, which he uses, means I AM! This not only means that we depend upon him, for we can only say, "I will be, if I am given life;" but it also means that I must constantly serve him every moment of my life. And it also means that we cannot escape his judgment.

What an awesome truth! What an undeniable evidence it is then that we need his Son and his cross! For only as God sees us in him, and what he did for us, is there any hope of salvation. His name, therefore, tells us not only that he can and does say, "I am God!" but he also can and does say, "I am your Savior." He sees all our sins, but he also sees us in his righteous and holy Son.

Read: Psalm 139
Psalter versification: 382:1

THE FEAR OF REVERENCE AND AWE

Thou compassest my path and my lying down, and art acquainted with all my ways. For there is not a word in my tongue, but, lo, O Lord, thou knowest it altogether. —Psalm 139:3–4

Not only does the name Jehovah literally mean I AM and express the truth "I am God," but it also means: "I am the self-sufficient God, I need no one and have in myself all that I need." Further, it means: "I am the everywhere present God." You and I are here or there, but God is everywhere.

That is why David in Psalm 139:3–4 writes: "Thou compassest my path and my lying down, and art acquainted with all my ways. For there is not a word in my tongue, but, lo, O Lord, thou knowest it altogether." Using the name Jehovah here again, David writes what ought to fill us with the fear of reverence and awe.

So often we behave as though God is miles and miles away from us. We can do this and do that and need have no fear, because God is out of our thoughts, as though he were too far away to see or hear what we do and say. How seldom is it that we can sincerely sing:

> My words from Thee I cannot hide,
> I feel Thy pow'r on every side;
> O wondrous knowledge, awful might,
> Unfathomed depth, unmeasured height!

There should be more of that in our lives. And as those redeemed by the blood of God's Son, we should have a fear of reverence and awe before the God of our salvation. Fear of punishment, because of all the sins he sees in us, must not be the end of our reaction to the truth that he is everywhere present and knows every word in our mouths which expresses the filthy thoughts and desires of our hearts and minds. We must have a deep reverence and awe coupled with a sincere thankfulness. Yes, we should be thankful that his name is Jehovah, and that he is all that which this name declares. For it also means: "I AM your Savior in Christ My Son."

We cannot get away from his searching eyes. Neither can we get away from his infinite love, mercy, and grace. These our everywhere present God has, and these he makes us taste and enjoy. Surely they are of unfathomed depths and unmeasured height. For they are the virtues of the I AM that I AM.

Read: Psalm 103
Psalter versification: 382:2

NO PLACE TO HIDE

Whither shall I go from thy spirit? or whither shall I flee from thy presence?
If I ascend up into heaven, thou art there: if I make my bed in hell,
behold, thou art there. —Psalm 139:7–8

Bearing in mind that God, whom we were created to serve and called to walk before in love, punishes every sin committed, the first thing that enters our minds when we become aware of our sins is to try, as Adam and Eve did, to flee from that awful wrath. But, since he is the everywhere present God, this we can never do. David expresses that so emphatically when in Psalm 139:7–8 he writes: "Whither shall I go from thy spirit? or whither shall I flee from thy presence? If I ascend up into heaven, thou art there: if I make my bed in hell, behold, thou art there." And our Psalter versification has it thus:

> Where can I go apart from Thee,
> Or whither from Thy presence flee?
> In heav'n? it is Thy dwelling fair;
> In death's abode? lo, Thou art there.

You will notice that our versification speaks of death's abode rather than of hell. The Hebrew word is often translated that way, or as in Psalm 141:7, it is translated as *grave* in these words: "Our bones are scattered at the grave's mouth." It really makes no difference, for in death and the grave we are not hidden from God's eyes and have not escaped his awful wrath, and in hell as the lake of fire one is in that awful wrath.

If we keep the word *death* or *grave* instead of *hellfire*, we still have the word of God condemning the idea that death is the end for man. Never, no never, get the idea that death takes the sinner away from the everlasting punishment which he deserves. One cannot hide from God in his grave. Death does not mean that this is the end of his existence and thus of his suffering the wrath of God. If one makes one's bed in the grave or in physical death, one does not hide from God's Spirit and presence. There just is no way of escape, no possibility of fleeing from God's holy wrath other than through the cross of his Son and in his sovereign grace.

There is no place where man can hide from God's holy wrath. But there is a person, God's Son, in whom God hides us, and whom he punished as our covenant head and representative so that our sins are paid for in full. God's grace does not hide our sins but removes them from us, placing the iniquity of them upon his own Son.

Read: Isaiah 53
Psalter versification: 382:3

DIVINELY LED AND UPHELD

If I take the wings of the morning, and dwell in the uttermost parts of the sea; Even there shall thy hand lead me, and thy right hand shall hold me. —Psalm 139:9–10

In jet aircraft, man can travel faster than the speed of sound. But he can never in any way do anything faster than the speed of light. The sun comes up in the morning, and the rays of light swiftly race westward over the face of the earth. Over the sea, that light races unhindered by hills or mountains to a very distant point at tremendous speed.

Way back in the days of David men knew of this speed of light. David spoke of it in Psalm 139:9–10 in these words: "If I take the wings of the morning, and dwell in the uttermost parts of the sea; even there shall thy hand lead me, and thy right hand shall hold me."

Here David emphasizes the truth that man cannot hide from God or flee from his holy wrath against sin. Wherever we go, we will find that God is already there before we arrive. He does not catch up with us, but he is there waiting for us. We may flee far out into the sea where no people dwell; but God is there dwelling in all his power.

Now, however, David presents another facet of the truth as well. God is not only in all things, but he gives life to all living creatures and existence to the rest. He makes it possible for man to travel from one point to another. Man gets where he arrives because God led him and upheld him. Man depends upon God and continues to live there only as God gives him everything he needs. Our versification has it thus:

> If I the wings of morning take,
> And far away my dwelling make,
> The hand that leadeth me is Thine,
> And my support Thy pow'r divine.

The truth we ought to take hold of here is that "in him we live, and move, and have our being" (Acts 17:28). We cannot flee from him; but we cannot live apart from him either.

We therefore owe him everlasting thanks for every heartbeat and breath of life. We also ought to see more clearly how worthy of punishment we are, for we have used very few heartbeats and breaths of life to serve him. What grace then does he bestow upon us that blots out all these millions upon millions of sins through the blood of his own Son!

Read: Acts 17:16–31
Psalter versification: 382:4

BLESSED LIGHT IN DEEPEST DARKNESS

If I say, Surely the darkness shall cover me; even the night shall be light about me. Yea, the darkness hideth not from thee; but the night shineth as the day: the darkness and the light are both alike to thee. —Psalm 139:11–12

In the first ten verses of Psalm 139 David makes some true and very profound statements. God not only sees every move we make, but hears every word we speak. Yea, he reads our thoughts and is right next to us no matter where we go. Our lives are an open book to him, and we just cannot hide from him. We can do nothing behind his back. We cannot cover our sins nor hide to get away from the punishment we deserve.

And now in Psalm 139:11–12 David presents another reason why we cannot hide from God. There he states: "If I say, Surely the darkness shall cover me; even the night shall be light about me. Yea, the darkness hideth not from thee; but the night shineth as the day: the darkness and the light are both alike to thee." And we sing that truth thus:

> If deepest darkness cover me,
> The darkness hideth not from Thee;
> To Thee both night and day are bright,
> The darkness shineth as the light.

How hopeless then escape from punishment seems to us! Yet even in this awesome truth there is tremendous comfort for the believer. Remember that God's Son came into our flesh and for three hours hung in darkness that could be felt. During those hours and that darkness he suffered the hellish agonies that we deserve, while he in flawless obedience and unwavering love to God brought to God the perfect obedience we failed even to begin to do since the day Adam fell into sin. But God *saw* it all! The darkness did not hide this marvelous work of our Savior. No, the night shines as the day. That night did not hide from God's eyes what his Son was doing for us! And it did not escape him that his Son suffered all this as our head and representative. He saw his Son bring our everlasting punishment to its end and the perfect works of love demanded of us brought in full measure.

We cannot hide from God or cover our sins from his view. To try to do so is to add to our guilt and to the punishment we deserve. But God covered them and made a day of light for us, a day when we shall see fully his love and mercy unto us in his Son.

Read: Isaiah 60
Psalter versification: 382:5

FORMED FOR GOD'S PRAISE

For thou hast possessed my reins: thou hast covered me in my mother's womb. I will praise thee; for I am fearfully and wonderfully made: marvellous are thy works; and that my soul knoweth right well. —Psalm 139:13–14

What an awesome truth David now presents to us! He had, as we already saw, made plain in Psalm 139 that we cannot hide ourselves, or even our inmost thoughts, from God who is everywhere present. He hears every word we speak, is before us and behind us, is in heaven but also in hell, and sees very clearly in the deepest darkness we can imagine. Now, in verses 13–14 David adds the truth that not only is God all around us but also in us! He writes: "For thou hast possessed my reins: thou hast covered me in my mother's womb. I will praise thee; for I am fearfully and wonderfully made: marvellous are thy works; and that my soul knoweth right well."

David confesses here that God was in his mother as he was being formed. And God was also in that body that was being formed, causing all the organs to come into being in the right place, with the right cell structure for the right capabilities. We were, indeed, fearfully and wonderfully wrought by God's hand!

What a truth is it then to commit to memory and to sing as we do in our versification of David's words! They are these:

> All that I am I owe to Thee,
> Thy wisdom, Lord, hath fashioned me;
> I give my Maker thankful praise,
> Whose wondrous works my soul amaze.

God does not only know all things that man does, but he made man to be exactly what he is. This presents to us another awesome truth, namely, that we are in debt to God for all the powers and abilities we possess. We are wonderfully but also fearfully made. That means that we were made to live in the fear of reverence and awe before God. We are to be one hundred percent, and in every sense, his possession with an unavoidable calling to serve him always with all that we have.

Surely there is no room for boasting on our part. Never for a fraction of a moment should we think that he owes us anything. As far as our salvation is concerned, we bring him nothing; but it and its faith are God's gifts to us. As our versification stated it, we owe him everlasting praise. He formed us to "shew forth his praise" (Isa. 43:21).

Read: Isaiah 43:1–21
Psalter versification: 383:1

DIVINELY DESIGNED

My substance was not hid from thee, when I was made in secret, and curiously wrought in the lowest parts of the earth. Thine eyes did see my substance, yet being unperfect; and in thy book all my members were written, which in continuance were fashioned, when as yet there was none of them. —Psalm 139:15–16

How a physician, and especially a surgeon, can believe that man came into being by a process of evolution is hard to understand. When we realize how marvelous the human body is with all its organs so properly positioned, working together so harmoniously, capable of such synchronous functions, it is hard to figure out how they, who know so much about the human body, can believe that it came into being without planning by the all-wise God. Did the intricate and powerful gasoline engine come into being without planning? Did one piece bring forth an entirely different kind of part made of another kind of material? Did the jet-propelled airplane and the computer come into being apart from the human mind? And did a dead object ever bring forth life?

How true are the words of David in Psalm 139:15–16! He wrote: "My substance was not hid from thee, when I was made in secret, and curiously wrought in the lowest parts of the earth. Thine eyes did see my substance, yet being unperfect; and in thy book all my members were written, which in continuance were fashioned, when as yet there was none of them."

God's book here is his eternal counsel, his living plan which he had with him before a creature existed and according to which all that happened from the first day of creation onward took place. And all this brings us to another aspect of the truth that our lives are an open book before God. We cannot hide anything from him anywhere, or in the darkest night. But even before we came into existence, he saw us in that book, and saw us exactly as we are at the moment. Our versification has it thus:

Ere into being I was bro't,
Thy eye did see, and in Thy tho't
My life in all its perfect plan
Was ordered ere my days began.

We then, as David did in verse 14, should say: "I will praise thee; for I am fearfully and wonderfully made: marvellous are thy works; and that my soul knoweth right well." Rather than foolishly try to hide from God, we should praise him for his wisdom, power, and sovereignty. His eye saw us before we had eyes. He knows about us all that there is to know. Being divinely designed, our calling is to render him divine praise.

Read: Psalm 148
Psalter versification: 383:2

GOD'S PRECIOUS THOUGHTS UNTO US

How precious also are thy thoughts unto me, O God! how great is the sum of them! If I should count them, they are more in number than the sand: when I awake, I am still with thee. —Psalm 139:17–18

In Psalm 139 David clearly and definitely established the truth that God sees us and that our life is unto him an open book that reveals in the smallest detail what we are and do. But most wonderful and important is *how* he looks upon us. What are his thoughts when he looks upon us? Does he look at us or upon us? In awesome language David expresses the truth of how God looks upon us in love. He writes in verses 17–18: "How precious also are thy thoughts unto me, O God! how great is the sum of them! If I should count them, they are more in number than the sand: when I awake, I am still with thee."

Because God designed not only the human body with its amazing members and faculties, but also the body of Christ, the church, and sees us as members thereof, it certainly is true what David writes. God has precious thoughts toward us! For all the blessings of salvation tell us how much he loves us. What love of God it is that sent his only begotten Son to the torments of hell that we might have the precious blessings of heaven! That Son is his most precious possession. And yet he sent him to hellish agonies that we might have a more glorious life than Adam had, and one which has everlasting blessings that cannot come to an end.

So precious are these thoughts of God toward us that we cannot count them any more than we can count the grains of sand on a given beach. Still more, David tells us, and correctly so, that after we have begun trying to count them, we will become weary and fall asleep. And when we awake from sleep, we will still be busy, if we are going to count and evaluate them all. For they are everlasting blessings. And our versification states it beautifully in these words:

Thy tho'ts, O God, how manifold,
More precious unto me than gold!
I muse on their infinity,
Awaking I am still with Thee.

We cannot hide from God; but that, too, is a blessing. For his thoughts penetrate the night of sin and bring us blessings from the kingdom of light. How precious then God's thoughts toward us are in Christ!

Read: Psalm 40
Psalter versification: 383:3

HATRED THAT REVEALS LOVE

Surely thou wilt slay the wicked, O God: depart from me therefore, ye
bloody men. For they speak against thee wickedly, and thine enemies take
thy name in vain. —Psalm 139:19–20

What a contrast David makes in the last part of Psalm 139! He had spoken of the preciousness of God's thoughts unto him. Now in verses 19–20 he declares what God will do to the wicked. He writes: "Surely thou wilt slay the wicked, O God: depart from me therefore, ye bloody men. For they speak against thee wickedly, and thine enemies take thy name in vain." Or as our versification has it:

> The wicked Thou wilt surely slay,
> From me let sinners turn away;
> They speak against the Name divine,
> I count God's enemies as mine.

This clearly reveals that by God's precious thoughts David has in mind the salvation God has prepared in Christ. This David saw in the bloody sacrifices in the temple. He reveals no fear of punishment upon his own sins which the everywhere present God, who sees and hears all, knows. He knows himself as one whose sins are blotted out. And he wants nothing to do with those who speak wickedly against God and take his name in vain. He counts God's enemies his enemies. All this reveals that God has begun the work of salvation in him, for he has been born again with a new life that loves God.

What David reveals here is that gospel truth which God preached to Adam and Eve the day they became God's enemies. He promised them that he would bring forth a people that hated sin and those who walk in sin. He promised them in Genesis 3:15 that he would "slay the wicked" (Ps. 139:19), for Christ, the seed of the woman, would crush the serpent's head and the heads of those who are not delivered from his power.

The question is whether we can say that with David. Do we want sinners to depart from us? Or do we enjoy them in their sinful ways? Do we feel at home with them, like their company, seek them rather than say to them, "Depart from me"? If we do, then we consider their thoughts and actions more precious than God's. Hatred of the world reveals love of God. Love of the world reveals hatred of God. God's love makes us love him and hate the world and all its sins.

Read: Jude
Psalter versification: 383:4

August 24

A PRAYER FOR HOLINESS

Search me, O God, and know my heart: try me, and know my thoughts: And see if there be any wicked way in me, and lead me in the way everlasting. —Psalm 139:23–24

As the saying goes: "Talk is cheap." It is so easy to say with David: "Do not I hate them, O LORD, that hate thee? and am not I grieved with those that rise up against thee? I hate them with perfect hatred: I count them mine enemies" (Ps. 139:21–22). But we do well to ask ourselves how true this is of us, bearing in mind what David had written, namely, that God knows our thoughts afar off, and that there is not a word in our tongue that he does not know altogether.

If we give that serious thought, we will also with David pray, "Search me, O God, and know my heart: try me, and know my thoughts: and see if there be any wicked way in me, and lead me in the way everlasting" (Ps. 139:23–24).

But since David already wrote that his life was as an open book to God, must God *search* to see whether there is any wicked way in him? Yes, but we must understand this in light of his last words in this verse. He prays that God will lead him in the way everlasting. He wants to be delivered from the way of sin that still is deep in his soul. He wants to be made holy and to love God perfectly with all his being.

Our Psalter versification states it thus:

> Search me, O God, my heart discern,
> Try me, my inmost tho't to learn;
> And lead me, if in sin I stray,
> To choose the everlasting way.

We label sins as little sins and big sins, and often defend what we call little sins. This is wrong. For then Adam's eating of a piece of fruit hurt no man and was a little sin. Yet it was an act of hatred against God, and so great a sin that it brought death on the whole human race!

If we are sincere and want to be led in the way everlasting, we will want every sin in us to be rooted out completely. This is then a prayer we should bring to God every day. It reveals a sincere love of God and is not cheap talk. Sing these words of David, but sing them as a prayer that is sincere and from the bottom of your heart.

Read: Psalm 139
Psalter versification: 383:5

August 25

HOPE FOR A SURE SALVATION

My soul fainteth for thy salvation: but I hope in thy word. Mine eyes fail for thy word, saying, When wilt thou comfort me? —Psalm 119:81–82

Salvation always implies misery of one kind or another. Joyous moments and happy situations we want to keep. But out of discomforts and sufferings, whether light or severe, we want to be lifted. This explains the words of the psalmist in Psalm 119:81–82, where we read: "My soul fainteth for thy salvation: but I hope in thy word. Mine eyes fail for thy word, saying, When wilt thou comfort me?"

The exact situation of the psalmist we do not know, although in broad lines we do read that he had afflictions (v. 75) and that enemies "dealt perversely with" him (v. 78). But we do well to note from verse 75 that he acknowledges that God afflicted him through these enemies and that he did so in faithfulness. He is not finding fault with God. He reveals clearly that he is convinced that God will save him out of his afflictions.

Two truths we should note and make our own. The psalmist speaks of *God's* salvation, and he reveals implicit trust in God's promises to deliver him. This our versification also clearly states in these words:

> My soul for Thy salvation faints,
> But still I hope in Thee;
> I long to see Thy promised help,
> When Thou shalt comfort me.

All too often we rule God out, or at least forget to run to him with our problems. We forget that salvation, whether it be from a physical woe or a spiritual condition, always comes from God and comes only from him. He uses means and creatures; but *he* saves and comforts us. We forget that he promised in his word to work *all things* together for our good (Rom. 8:28). The cross of Christ and the amazing love of God displayed in it we so often brush aside.

When miseries seem about to crush us in losses of loved ones through the cold hand of death, when prolonged and painful illnesses besiege our bodies, and the world torments and ridicules us, we must hope in God's word of promise. We may with the psalmist wonder when God will save us; but we must never doubt that he will keep his promise to do so.

Our eyes may fail for God's word in the sense that they do not see the fulfillment. But never, no never, doubt, but hope with expectation.

Read: Psalm 119:73–88
Psalter versification: 331:1

HUMBLY WAITING FOR SALVATION

For I am become like a bottle in the smoke; yet do I not forget thy statutes.
How many are the days of thy servant? when wilt thou execute judgment on
them that persecute me? —Psalm 119:83–84

The suffering of the child of God who wrote Psalm 119 was intense. He expresses this in verses 83–84 in these words: "For I am become like a bottle in the smoke; yet do I not forget thy statutes. How many are the days of thy servant? when wilt thou execute judgment on them that persecute me?" Plainly it seemed to him that, if God did not come with salvation, his life would soon be ended. His life was in great peril.

He did not mean that he was like a glass bottle, but rather like a leather bottle, a wineskin. These when not used were hung up and not only shriveled and dried but cracked due to lack of moisture. They also became stained and coated by the smoke of an open fire in the house. No doubt he suffered in a way that caused him to lose weight so that wrinkles appeared on his face; and his suffering showed clearly on his face. Our versification expresses it this way:

Thy statutes I do not forget,
Tho' wasting grief I know;
Thy servant's days are few, O Lord;
When wilt Thou judge my foe?

The truth we should take hold of is that, even though he was in a sad physical condition and appeared to be ready to die, spiritually he was strong. He did not swerve from walking upon the pathway of God's law in order to escape this suffering. He rightfully calls himself God's servant.

What humility he shows here, but also what spirituality! So often in our afflictions we act as though God must be our servant; and if he does not relieve us soon, we, forgetting his statutes, worship and have before him another god. Yes, that is right. We break the first commandment of his law! That god is our flesh. God must serve us and must do it our way. We find it hard and often fail to pray: "Thy will be done on earth as it is in heaven." Not so with the psalmist, though he desires relief.

Follow this example of the psalmist. Let nothing turn you from serving him. Never humiliate him by treating him as though he is your servant. Wondering *when* he will execute judgment is not wondering *whether* he will do so. Hope in his word, and you will not be disappointed.

Read: Psalm 125
Psalter versification: 331:2

A JUST PRAYER FOR HELP

The proud have digged pits for me, which are not after thy law. All thy commandments are faithful: they persecute me wrongfully; help thou me. —Psalm 119:85–86

Although thus far they did not succeed, the enemies of the psalmist were trying to kill him. He states this in Psalm 119:85–86 in these words: "The proud have digged pits for me, which are not after thy law. All thy commandments are faithful: they persecute me wrongfully; help thou me." From these words we learn that the enemies attack him under the guise of punishing a sinner. Falsely they accuse him *of a sin worthy of death*. Nevertheless, the punishment is not called for by God's law, and they persecute him wrongfully. That law, the psalmist points out, is good. He calls it faithful. Our versification presents it this way:

The proud, disdainful of Thy law,
Entrap me wrongfully;
O Thou, Whose law is just and true,
Help and deliver me.

Here that law, and correctly so, is called just, for it rightfully calls for punishment upon sin. And the pits which the enemies digged were designed to entrap him, that is, make him seemingly to fall into sin. In that way they will seem to be innocent when they punish him with death.

All this is prophetic. For this exactly pictures the death of Christ. The wicked Jews caught him in the garden as though he were an evildoer, brought him to trial before the high priest, then before Pilate they accused him of threatening Caesar's throne. They called for a punishment God's law calls for upon those who obey not their authorities and intend to overthrow their king.

We can expect the same thing in the days ahead of us. The antichrist will demand on our right hand or forehead a sign of loyalty to him. That requirement will be our pit which he digs and will call for death, because we object to his reign of hatred against God and his Christ. We will be accused of breaking the fifth commandment. But that will be wrongful, sinful treatment. For it is to defend breaking the first commandment, namely, having a god before Jehovah the one, true God.

Pray then for help from God. His law is faithful because he is faithful, and through Christ's unjust crucifixion our sins are blotted out.

Read: John 19:1–18
Psalter versification: 331:3

QUICKENED IN GOD'S MERCY

Quicken me after thy lovingkindness; so shall I keep the
testimony of thy mouth. —Psalm 119:88

One truth that we should hold on to tightly is the teaching of Scripture that all our salvation comes from God. We do not earn the smallest part of it. We get not one blessing by fulfilling a condition. In fact, the very desire for salvation is God's gift to us, and we owe him thanks for that. As surely as physical birth does not come to us because we asked for it, so surely being born again is due to God's desire for it and not ours.

God himself through the psalmist states that clearly in Psalm 119:88, where we read: "Quicken me after thy lovingkindness; so shall I keep the testimony of thy mouth."

Notice that the psalmist, who had cruel and crafty foes that had "almost consumed" him (v. 87), prays God to quicken him so that he may remain faithful to God and not forsake God's law to get the enemies off his back. God must strengthen him and give him the desire to keep his testimonies. As he himself confesses, he will keep God's commandments *only* if God quickens him. For he has enemies inside himself as well as outside and all around him. He has his old man of sin and Satan inside, as well as Satan's servants outside and round about him. These strive to draw him away from God's law. Listen to the versification of his words:

Almost consumed, yet from Thy law
I have not turned away;
In lovingkindness give me strength,
That I may still obey.

Boast about what we did through our strength, and we reveal that we are not keeping God's precepts. For he forbids us to have a god besides him. And if we get blessings because we fulfilled conditions, we saved God from disappointment; and then he depends upon us. Only if he quickens us will we keep his commandments.

Let us be careful not to elevate ourselves above him, but rather thank him for giving us every bit of our salvation through his Son and his Spirit. We cannot even say sincerely that he quickened us, until he gives us the desire and strength to do so. It is his mercy in Christ and not our self-manufactured piety that saves us.

Read: Ephesians 2
Psalter versification: 331:4

PROMISES THAT WILL BE KEPT

For ever, O LORD, thy word is settled in heaven. Thy faithfulness is unto all generations: thou hast established the earth, and it abideth. —Psalm 119:89–90

The more serious the surgery is, the more serious the thought must be that is given to choosing one to perform it. When one's life is in danger, one cannot be too careful or demand too much care. And what is far more serious than physical death is our relationship with God. Both physical and spiritual enemies may make life dangerous for us. Financial losses may be hard to bear. But what God does to us, and what he promises us, is what counts. The punishment he metes out is everlasting and makes man as miserable as he possibly can be. We had better be very serious and concerned about our guilty state before God. We must be sure that his promise to save us will be kept in its smallest detail.

The psalmist was sure and wrote in Psalm 119:89–90, "For ever, O LORD, thy word is settled in heaven. Thy faithfulness is unto all generations: thou hast established the earth, and it abideth." Notice that he speaks of God's dealing both in heaven and on earth. He speaks of God's absolute control over all things in heaven and on earth and of God's absolute faithfulness. Not temporarily but forever, every split second of time, God's counsel is fulfilled. His will is executed unto all generations. He is faithful to his word and never goes back upon one word of that which he has promised.

To him we should look for help in our state of guilt and in our spiritually weak condition. Who can help us better than he? Who can help us if he does not? Our versification has it beautifully in these words:

> Forever settled in the heav'ns,
> Thy word, O Lord, shall firmly stand;
> Thy faithfulness shall never fail;
> The earth abides at Thy command.

Look to God in the confidence that he will keep his promise and that you are safe in his keeping. He has promised full salvation and will keep his word. He has perfect control of all creation, and nothing shall prevent him from giving us what he has promised in Christ. All your enemies are in his hand. Over them he has absolute control.

Read: Psalm 37
Psalter versification: 332:1

GOD-GIVEN DELIGHT IN HIS LAW

They continue this day according to thine ordinances: for all are thy servants. Unless thy law had been my delights, I should then have perished in mine affliction. —Psalm 119:91–92

In God's providence the moon continues in its orbit so marvelously that it is exactly on time month after month, so that our calendars for next year can tell us when it will be full moon and when it will be new moon. For thousands of years the earth has rotated on its axis at an unchanging speed, so that the rising of the sun and the setting thereof may be predicted day after day and year after year.

But man, made in God's image, by nature never keeps the law according to which God created him. And in Psalm 119:91–92 the psalmist had already in that day written: "They continue this day according to thine ordinances: for all are thy servants. Unless thy law had been my delights, I should then have perished in mine affliction."

Here he is referring to the inanimate creatures in the heavens, including this earth. They function according to the laws wherein God created them. But man, made in God's image, lives by nature as though he were god and need not keep God's commandments.

He also points out that by God's grace he does keep God's law, because God made him have delight in that law. He does not mean by "I should have perished" that he would have died at the hands of his enemies if he kept God's law. He was not in danger because he kept that law. He means that had he not been given delight in God's law, he would then not have continued to keep God's law. His spiritual life would have perished.

When we see the sun set tonight or rise tomorrow morning, shame should cover our faces. They keep God's law, and we do not. These indeed are dumb creatures but move in harmony with God's law. And it is only by God's grace that we can sing sincerely:

Thy word and works unmoved remain,
Thy ev'ry purpose to fulfill;
All things are Thine and Thee obey,
And all as servants wait Thy will.
I should have perished in my woe
Had not I loved Thy law divine;
That law I never can forget;
O save me, Lord, for I am Thine.

Yes, God makes us as Christ's sheep delight in his law and thereby enables us to walk in harmony with it.

Read: Psalm 119:81–96
Psalter versification: 332:2–3

THE COMING PERFECTION

I have seen an end of all perfection: but thy
commandment is exceeding broad. —Psalm 119:96

Can there be something better than what is perfect? What the psalmist wrote in Psalm 119:96 seems to teach that. He wrote: "I have seen an end of all perfection: but thy commandment is exceeding broad."

He had stated that all things are God's servants and created within certain laws. These laws they all keep perfectly. Man, however, was created also under the ten commandments, the moral law. And this law, he states, is broader than those laws wherein all creatures were created, the physical laws of their being. Our versification has it thus:

> The wicked would destroy my soul,
> But on Thy truth I muse with awe;
> Imperfect I have found all else,
> But boundless is Thy wondrous law.

Now, imperfection can be incompleteness. A building is not perfect until it is completed. That does not mean that the part already set up is imperfect, that is, not constructed properly or of poor material. It means that the completed form is not yet there. That the psalmist had in mind.

We live in a world wherein the laws of creation are never broken, even though God's holy law, the ten commandments given man, is not kept since man fell in Adam. But a more wonderful creation is coming in which man will keep God's law perfectly. A creation comes where there is a broader keeping of God's law, a creation in which the inanimate creatures act and react according to the physical laws, but one also wherein God's holy law is kept by all as perfectly as God's Son did so when he tabernacled with us.

What a broader picture then do we get here! The end of this present creation brings forth a kingdom of heaven wherein in no way does any creature fail to be a servant of God. What is more, this present creation, in which the laws of creation are flawlessly kept, serves as God's means to bring forth that broader end, namely, the kingdom of heaven.

We should look beyond the things necessary for our natural life, the laws we must keep to protect our physical life. Look to that law of God wherein he created man in his own image. Keep his holy law before you, looking forward to the day when you will keep it perfectly.

Read: Revelation 22:1–14
Psalter versification: 332:4

A CALL TO SING UNTO GOD

O sing unto the LORD a new song: sing unto the LORD, all the earth. Sing unto the LORD, bless his name; shew forth his salvation from day to day. —Psalm 96:1–2

There is an important difference between speaking and singing. In both of them we express what is in our souls; but singing is expressing thoughts that fill us with joy. And in Psalm 96:1–2 we are exhorted to do that. There we read: "O sing unto the LORD a new song: sing unto the LORD, all the earth. Sing unto the LORD, bless his name; shew forth his salvation from day to day."

Worth taking note of here is the fact that we are to sing unto the Lord. That certainly means that we have him in our thoughts when we sing at home, in the church services, or in the choral society. And it must not be the music that makes us happy and pleases our souls. It must be the truth we are expressing. And our singing must not simply be expressing the truth about God. It must be singing the truth unto him.

That we sing a new song unto him means that a change has come in our lives. Our old man of sin used to sing the songs of the world with the world. Now, as born-again children of God, we are thrilled by spiritual matters, the things of our salvation. We sing what the holy angels sing and the saints already in heaven sing. As the psalmist states it, we bless God in our singing.

Notice that the psalmist literally exhorts us to show forth in our singing his salvation from day to day. The singing of the child of God is characterized by that salvation. Christ is the center and heart of our singing. What God did for us in him makes us so happy that not only do we sing unto God, but we want others to do so as well. Here then is our versification of the psalmist's words:

Sing to the Lord, sing His praise, all ye peoples,
New be your song as new honors ye pay;
Sing of His majesty, bless Him forever,
Show His salvation from day to day.

Is that the kind of singing your mouth and vocal cords produce? Are your songs those of the old man of sin or of the new man in Christ? Drop, push aside those of the world and bless God in your singing.

Read: Psalm 96
Psalter versification: 259:1

JOYFUL SINGING WITNESSES

Declare his glory among the heathen, his wonders among all people. For the LORD is great, and greatly to be praised: he is to be feared above all gods. —Psalm 96:3–4

In this day and age, it is hard to escape the songs of the world. Radios blare in stores, offices, and factories. One cannot listen to the news without a product being advertised by means of singing to praise it.

The word of God, however, exhorts us otherwise. There we read: "Declare his glory among the heathen, his wonders among all people. For the LORD is great, and greatly to be praised: he is to be feared above all gods" (Ps. 96:3–4).

The wonders for which he is to be praised, as the psalmist pointed out in the preceding verses, are the works of salvation in Christ. Indeed, there is no more wonderful work, no miracle like the work of God when he saved us by a virgin birth, an accursed death, and a glorious resurrection of his own Son. What a miracle to make dead sinners alive with the glory of Christ—as holy as he is and with heavenly beauty and glory!

Do we really need to be exhorted then to praise him and to sing his praises before the world? The joy of that salvation ought to impel us to sing songs of his praise so that we just cannot keep still.

Our versification presents it that way in these words:

Tell of His wondrous works, tell of His glory,
Till through the nations His Name is revered;
Praise and exalt Him, for He is almighty,
God over all let the Lord be feared.

This brings to us an awesome calling and reason for soul-searching. What songs do the unbelievers hear you sing? Are they the songs of the world that deny that he is above all the gods of man's imagination? Are you a joyful witness of his power and wonder-working grace? Are you eager to have him praised by all men and want them all to confess that he alone is God?

Keep the songs of the devil out of your home, and let your lips sing God's praises before all men. Be a joyful witness in this vale of tears and sorrows. We have reason to sing and ought to give the world this reason and show them the folly and sin in their singing.

Read: Psalm 145
Psalter versification: 259:2

TRUST IN AND THANKS UNTO GOD

For all the gods of the nations are idols: but the LORD made the heavens. Honour and majesty are before him: strength and beauty are in his sanctuary. —Psalm 96:5–6

What man makes depends upon man. An engine can lift a heavier object than the man who made it can. But a man must put the fuel into the tank, turn the switch to start it, and place upon it the object to be lifted. And it came into being by the work of man's hand and mind.

How foolish it is then for man not to trust in and worship God who made him, rather than to trust in and worship the things that he thought up, made, and must carry about if they are going to be moved. And how wise it is to take heed to the words of the psalmist as in Psalm 96:5–6 he wrote these words: "For all the gods of the nations are idols: but the LORD made the heavens. Honour and majesty are before him: strength and beauty are in his sanctuary."

Our versification sings it thus:

Vain are the heathen gods, idols and helpless;
God made the heav'ns, and His glory they tell;
Honor and majesty shine out before Him,
Beauty and strength in His temple dwell.

This is presented by the psalmist because he had called us to sing praises to God and to tell the world that he is God alone. He made the heavens, which are the highest point in creation. Upon him all things depend; and he depends on no one and on nothing. If we do not trust in him and worship him, we trust in and worship that which has no majesty and honor, no strength and beauty. The unbeliever trusts in and worships that which does not exist and is an imaginary god.

In wisdom we sing praises to God and tell the world round about us that he is God alone. Man and his idol depend upon God. Unto him only should we look for blessings, and him we should thank for everything we receive.

Every morning when we awake, we should look to God for the needs of the day. Every night, thank him for what we received. And that does not simply mean our material, earthly needs. Strength and beauty are in his sanctuary. There typically men saw the strength and beauty of the cross that brings us all the heavenly blessings of our salvation.

Read: Psalm 115
Psalter versification: 259:3

THE BEAUTY OF GOD'S HOLINESS

O worship the LORD in the beauty of holiness: fear before
him, all the earth. —Psalm 96:9

There are beautiful musical compositions that we enjoy hearing over and over again. There are flowers that because of their beauty we use to beautify our yards and the rooms in our homes. And there are breathtaking scenes of mountains and waterfalls that we call scenic beauty spots.

But an important question is whether we consider holiness to be beautiful, as the psalmist does when in Psalm 96:9 he wrote: "O worship the LORD in the beauty of holiness: fear before him, all the earth." As we are by nature, it goes against the grain to see and call holiness beautiful. We find joy and pleasure in unholy things. For to be holy means to be cut off from sin. And we sin in order to get what we call a beautiful life. Did not Adam and Eve sin to become like God? They did not want Jehovah to be God alone and above them. His beauty they sinfully wanted.

You see, the root meaning of the word *holy* is to be cut off, to be separated. In the context the psalmist had presented the holiness of God, which consists in his being separated from all creatures as being God and God alone. The idols were made of materials which he created. And we must worship God in that beauty of being God alone.

Note that the psalmist, all through the psalm in the Hebrew, uses the name Jehovah, the I AM. Only God can rightfully say that he is God. And every time we sin, we say: "No, you are not! I can do as I please!" God's holiness is not beautiful to us.

Listen to our versification that urges us to flee from this pride:

Give unto God Most High glory and honor,
Come with your off'rings and humbly draw near;
In holy beauty now worship Jehovah,
Tremble before Him with godly fear.

To worship God in the beauty of holiness means that we must humble ourselves before him and approach him as well as serve him with the fear of reverence and awe.

Do you see God in the beauty of that holiness of being God alone? Do you consider it to be a beautiful life to flee from sin and to serve him?

Read: Revelation 4
Psalter versification: 259:4

CAREFUL, GOD-GLORIFYING SPEECH

Say among the heathen that the LORD reigneth: the world also shall be established that it shall not be moved: he shall judge the people righteously. —Psalm 96:10

Among the unbelievers living around us, the events of the day, or the desired events of tomorrow, are so often ascribed to "Mother Nature." And though those unbelievers have no graven image that they worship, they have an idol whom they honor and look up to for what they want. They rule out God and ascribe what happens to a nonexistent idol. Truly it is harder to smash in pieces a mental image than one made of wood, stone, or of the hardest kind of metal.

We have the calling, nevertheless, that the psalmist presents in Psalm 96:10 in these words: "Say among the heathen that the LORD reigneth: the world also shall be established that it shall not be moved: he shall judge the people righteously." Or as our versification sings it:

> Make all the nations know God reigns forever;
> Earth is established as He did decree;
> Righteous and just is the King of the nations,
> Judging the people with equity.

We do have that calling as surely as the saints did in the Old Testament times. And the sad truth is that so often we ourselves need to be rebuked and told to keep the psalmist's words. Every time we ascribe anything to luck, or speak of our good luck or bad luck, we reveal that we have a mental image, an idol in our heads, even though we have no graven image of wood or stone.

It is so easy to look down on those with graven images and fail to look into the mirror of God's word and see that we have a more subtle and crafty idol than those who have idols of gold, silver, brass.

The psalmist, yea, God through the psalmist, calls us to be very careful in our speech before the world and to speak in such a way that we positively say before the world that God reigns. And in these last days, when fear of a nuclear war that will wipe all life from this earth is expressed, we do well to tell the world that this earth will be established as it pleases God and shall not be moved in any way that he has not eternally decreed. A kingdom of glory is coming.

Read: Psalm 104
Psalter versification: 259:5

A JOYFUL NEW CREATION

Let the heavens rejoice, and let the earth be glad; let the sea roar, and the fulness thereof. Let the field be joyful, and all that is therein: then shall all the trees of the wood rejoice before the LORD: for he cometh, for he cometh to judge the earth: he shall judge the world with righteousness, and the people with his truth. —Psalm 96:11–13

If you love God, you will want all men to acknowledge him as God alone and to serve him with all their being. You will, as the psalmist did in Psalm 96:11–13, also declare:

Let the heavens rejoice, and let the earth be glad; let the sea roar, and the fulness thereof. Let the field be joyful, and all that is therein: then shall all the trees of the wood rejoice before the Lord: for he cometh, for he cometh to judge the earth: he shall judge the world with righteousness, and the people with his truth.

Of course only man can, as the psalmist wrote in verse 9, worship God "in the beauty of holiness." Fields and trees, seas, the sun, moon, and stars cannot rejoice. Consider, however, that in the day when Christ returns and brings forth a new creation, those whom God in his righteous judgment in Christ brings into that creation will use all that inanimate and irrational creation in the fear of reverence and awe before God in all his majesty and glory.

Today most men worship a nonexistent god and commit sins that irrational creation cannot commit. But that new creation will not, the psalmist says, be moved, and that means that it will not be misused or, if you will, be removed from the service of God, as man has done since he fell into sin. All men in that new creation will use it to glorify God.

This will happen through Christ, for only through him can there be a righteous judgment that brings man into this service and glory. No wonder is it then that the psalmist began this psalm with these words: "O sing unto the LORD a new song: sing unto the LORD, all the earth" (v. 1).

Shall we not then do this with the words of this versification?

Let heav'n and earth be glad; waves of the ocean,
Forest and field, exultation express;
For God is coming, the Judge of the nations,
Coming to judge in His righteousness.

We now live in a vale of tears and sorrow. But a day is coming when there shall be an earth with everlasting joy. For all creation shall through sinless men be directed to God and glorify him.

Read: Isaiah 65
Psalter versification: 259:6

POSSESSING TRUE WISDOM

O how love I thy law! it is my meditation all the day. Thou through thy
commandments hast made me wiser than mine enemies: for they are ever with me.
—Psalm 119:97–98

Would you call it wise for a couple to put their children to bed and then also themselves retire, even though they know that a tornado or earthquake is going to destroy their house in about an hour? Would you then call it an act of wisdom for one who knows that he is going to die to continue to walk in unbelief and sin, when death for such means entrance into an everlasting torment?

No, man does wisely when he with the psalmist declares: "O how love I thy law! it is my meditation all the day. Thou through thy commandments hast made me wiser than my enemies: for they are ever with me" (Ps. 119:97–98). Plainly, true wisdom comes through knowing and loving God's commandments.

Loving God's law means loving God, for that is what his law reveals is our calling. And loving God means that we are by him assured that death brings us closer to him, with a more blessed covenant life with treasures that are everlasting. The world may know how to gather earthly treasures and pleasures. In fact, in Daniel 12:4 we read that in the last days knowledge will increase. Surely man today knows much more than a couple of decades ago. And he will learn much more than computers, satellites, laser beams, and the like.

But the child of God knows about everlasting blessedness through Christ and is truly wise when he chooses to walk in God's law.

How important is it not that we sing:

How I love Thy law, O Lord!
Daily joy its truths afford;
In its constant light I go,
Wise to conquer ev'ry foe.

Yes, in the measure that we meditate in God's law, we are wise and we learn how to walk wisely and seek what has true, lasting value. Sin may bring fleshly pleasure, but it is the height of folly to walk in it.

The question is not whether we can amass earthly things, which are going to be taken from us when we die. The question is whether we love God and therefore love his law. Meditating in that law, we will see the need for Christ, and one who sees that need is truly wise. Him God will assure that in his love he sent Christ to bring us where we, in love of God's law, will walk perfectly in it in sweet communion with God.

Psalm 119:97–112
Psalter versification: 333

KEPT IN GOD'S LAW BY HIS GRACE

I have more understanding than all my teachers: for thy testimonies are my meditation. I understand more than the ancients, because I keep thy precepts. I have refrained my feet from every evil way, that I might keep thy word. I have not departed from thy judgments: for thou hast taught me. —Psalm 119:99–102

Do you know any people with "I" trouble? Their vision may be very good, and they may not need a magnifying glass for fine print. But the "I" trouble wherewith some are afflicted is their conceit and boasting. And it would almost seem as though the psalmist who wrote Psalm 119 had such "I" trouble.

In the third through sixth verses of the thirteenth section of the psalm, he writes: "I have more understanding than all my teachers…I understand more than the ancients…I have refrained my feet from every evil way…I have not departed from thy judgments" (Ps. 119:99–102). It is I, I, I, I!

However, by no means was he boasting. For in verse 102 he adds: "I have not departed from thy judgments: for thou hast taught me." And all these verses which begin with "I" follow his first verse in this section, where he wrote, "O how love I thy law," and also that God's commandments had made him wiser than his enemies. All this makes a big difference.

We may be personal and say, "I have this," or "I did this," if we plainly reveal that this is because of what God has done in us. Remember Jesus' parable. The Pharisee, instead of thanking God, boasted of what he had done, as though God owed him thanks for what he did. If we so speak, we have "I" trouble and also behave as though God owes us thanks.

Always for all things we owe God thanks. Surely we owe him thanks for teaching us his law. This means that he taught us that he loves us, chose us in Christ, and gave us a new life in Christ. Many there are in the church and out of the church to whom he has revealed his law. But only those whom he redeemed by the blood of Christ are taught that law by God himself.

We cannot thank God enough for all the blessings which he bestows upon us. And surely we owe him thanks for being able to sing:

> While my heart Thy word obeys,
> I am kept from evil ways;
> From Thy law, with Thee to guide,
> I have never turned aside.

Here all boasting is excluded and confession is made of what God in his grace has done. Surely every day should be filled with praise and thanks to him for keeping us and guiding us in a walk of love to him.

Read: Isaiah 40:28–41:10
Psalter versification: 333:3

RIGHTEOUS HATRED AND DELIGHT

How sweet are thy words unto my taste! yea, sweeter than honey to my mouth! Through thy precepts I get understanding: therefore I hate every false way. —Psalm 119:103–104

To commit a sin, no matter what kind of sin it is, always means that we are walking in a false way. Not only are we not walking in the right way, the way designed by and demanded by God, but we are saying something false. To ourselves we will be saying that this is a pleasant thing to do; but we are also saying to God that he is not God, may not tell us what to do, and has no right to intrude into our lives and tell us what to do.

That is why in Psalm 14:1 we read that the fool has said in his heart that there is no God. We say that there is no God every time we sin! But we ought to say what we read in Psalm 119:103–104, namely: "How sweet are thy words unto my taste! yea, sweeter than honey to my mouth! Through thy precepts I get understanding: therefore I hate every false way."

Did you notice that the psalmist stated that God's precepts give him understanding? That means that they give us the truth. God's law in no uncertain terms tells us the truth that he is God and that we are his servants. Through his precepts he causes us to understand that to sin is to walk in a false way, and that to obey him is the true way in which we should walk.

Think that over today. If you sincerely say that to sin is to walk in a false way, you say with the psalmist that God's commandments are sweet in your mouth and that you hate that false way. You will then sing:

Sweeter are Thy words to me
Than all other good can be;
Safe I walk, Thy truth my light,
Hating falsehood, loving right.

The false way will lead you away from and against Christ and into the lake of fire with a bitter taste in your mouth. Walking in God's law, you will be walking with Christ, who never left the way of love to God. Then you will come to God's house, where you will enjoy the sweetness of his mercy and love. Then you will hear it said unto you: "Well done, good and faithful servant; thou hast been faithful over a few things, I will make thee ruler over many things: enter thou into the joy of thy lord" (Matt. 25:23).

Read: Matthew 25:1–30
Psalter versification: 333:4

MEETING GOD IN HIS HOUSE

How amiable are thy tabernacles, O LORD of hosts! My soul longeth, yea,
even fainteth for the courts of the LORD: my heart and my flesh crieth out
for the living God. —Psalm 84:1–2

The question is not how beautiful your church building is. The important thing is not where do you meet, but whom do you meet? When the psalmist writes in Psalm 84:1–2, "How amiable are thy tabernacles, O LORD of hosts! My soul longeth, yea, even fainteth for the courts of the LORD: my heart and my flesh crieth out for the living God," he is not thinking of the earthly beauty of the temple with its gold, delicate carvings, and beautiful tapestry. Notice that he states: "My heart and my flesh crieth out for the living God." It is God whom he wants to meet.

He writes about God's courts and tabernacle because there the everywhere-present God meets man in a special way. There he meets man not simply in his providence but in his grace in Christ his Son.

All over in the tabernacle and temple were types and shadows of Christ, but especially in the holy of holies, that secret place behind the veil, where God dwelt symbolically between the cherubim on the mercy seat.

There was God's mercy, for there was Christ's blood that paid for all our sins, sprinkled on the mercy seat. In that tabernacle God said: "I love you; and my mercy is upon you." Therefore, that tabernacle was amiable, that is, lovely, because there God revealed his love in Christ.

That same truth we ought to see in the place where we worship God. Never mind the surroundings. Let not the earthly beauty or crudeness keep you from seeing God as in Christ he is preached. Now that Christ suffered, died, and is risen from the dead in victory over sin, we hear more clearly and powerfully of God's love and mercy than the Old Testament saints did in the temple. Hearing Christ preached, you can sing:

How lovely, Lord of Hosts, to me
The tabernacles of Thy grace;
O how I long, yea, faint to see
Thy hallowed courts, Thy dwellingplace;
For Thee my heart and spirit sigh,
For Thee, O living God, I cry.

Do you look forward to going to church on the sabbath day? God will be there in his love and mercy where Christ is preached. Go then, and meet him. The veil has been rent in twain. And he will reveal himself in Christ in the word preached.

Read: Psalm 84
Psalter versification: 229:1

September 11

BLESSED IN GOD'S HOUSE

Yea, the sparrow hath found an house, and the swallow a nest for herself, where she may lay her young, even thine altars, O LORD of hosts, my King, and my God. Blessed are they that dwell in thy house: they will be still praising thee. Selah. —Psalm 84:3–4

Although man is the only earthly creature created in the image of God and therefore is a thinking, willing creature, the creatures who were created below man often put him to shame after his fall into sin. Of that the psalmist speaks in Psalm 84:3–4, in these words: "Yea, the sparrow hath found an house, and the swallow a nest for herself, where she may lay her young, even thine altars, O LORD of hosts, my King, and my God. Blessed are they that dwell in thy house: they will be still praising thee. Selah."

These creatures knew their needs and sought a solution to their problems. They found protection, safety, comfort, and where they might bring forth their young and shield them. That place meant very much to them. But how lovely do we really consider God's house to be? Are there not so many other places where we would rather go? Is not the sermon too long? Do our sins really bother us, and do we know our need and want comfort? Are we not pretty callous about our guilt? Can we sincerely sing:

The sparrow has her place of rest;
The swallow, thro' Thy kindly care,
Has found where she may build her nest
And brood her young in safety there;
Thy altars as my rest I sing,
O Lord of Hosts, my God, my King.

Surely in God's house we obtain blessings and are moved to praise God for his mercy in Christ. In the measure that we go to his house and do listen to him in the preaching, we will be blessed and want to praise him. In the measure Christ is preached from our pulpit, we will cry out: "How lovely are thy tabernacles, O Lord of hosts!"

There you have the psalmist expressing his enjoyment in meeting God. There, too, you hear him praising God for his mercy in Christ.

His last word, namely, Selah, is also important. It means: pause and think this over! By all means do that. Do not rush away from the preaching and brush it aside. Give the truth sincere and profound thought. Listen to what God has to say to you in his house. More precious and valuable speech you will hear nowhere else. Is then his house a lovely place in your judgment?

Read: Hebrews 4
Psalter versification: 229:2

OUR ASSURANCE OF HEAVENLY GLORY

Blessed is the man whose strength is in thee; in whose heart are the ways of them. Who passing through the valley of Baca make it a well; the rain also filleth the pools. —Psalm 84:5–6

When Christ returns and "the tabernacle of God is with men," as we read in Revelation 21:3, man will have reached the highest point of bliss and glory that is possible for the creature to know and enjoy. It is that blessedness of which Psalm 84:1 speaks when it declares how amiable, that is, how lovely, God's tabernacles are.

However, those who reach that glory will never boast of having gotten there by their own strength. No, the psalmist states in verses 5–6: "Blessed is the man whose strength is in thee; in whose heart are the ways of them. Who passing through the valley of Baca make it a well; the rain also filleth the pools."

That valley of Baca is explained in our versification thus:

> Blest they who in Thy house abide,
> They still to Thee shall render praise;
> Blest they who in Thy strength confide,
> And in whose hearts are Zion's ways;
> Tho' passing thro' the vale of tears,
> Like springs of joy Thy grace appears.

The valley of Baca is a valley of tears. It is what David calls "the valley of the shadow of death" (Ps. 23:4). Significant is that statement in the psalm that our strength is in God. Only because of that fact can we want to be in God's house and can we walk on the way to it. We have absolutely no room to boast, not even for the desire to dwell with God. We have every reason always to thank God for every bit of our salvation and the desire for it. That the ways of those who reach that glory are in their hearts is because God put them there. Faith is God's gift to us, not our gift to him. We were "created in Christ Jesus unto good works" and do not create ourselves by good works (Eph. 2:8–10).

If reaching God's house depends upon one thing we must do, it is hopeless. Ephesians 2:1 tells us that we "were dead in trespasses and sins." Our assurance, all of it, rests upon the truth that our spiritual strength is in God and that he gives it to us in his grace in Christ.

Read: Ephesians 2
Psalter versification: 229:3

A VERY REVEALING PRAYER

They go from strength to strength, every one of them in Zion appeareth before God. O LORD God of hosts, hear my prayer: give ear, O God of Jacob. Selah. —Psalm 84:7–8

If you want something badly, you are not going where it cannot be given to you. Parents who want their out-of-state children to come and visit them are not going to leave town the day scheduled for that visit. And if we agree with the psalmist that God's tabernacles are lovely, and that to dwell with him there is most blessed, we are going to seek it and pray for strength to walk on the way unto it.

Therefore, the psalmist in Psalm 84:7–8 wrote: "They go from strength to strength, every one of them in Zion appeareth before God. O LORD God of hosts, hear my prayer: give ear, O God of Jacob. Selah." If you want to dwell with God in his house, you will pray for strength to seek it and for a strengthening of the desire for it in your heart.

Since this desire for a life of holiness—which is the only life that can be allowed in God's presence—and this strength to walk on the way unto it is ours, we will and must pray to God for the continuance of them and the strengthening of them.

Here is a measuring rod wherewith to determine how much we really do want to dwell in God's house of holiness. The question is not whether we want to get out of that valley of tears, that dry valley of Baca. Everyone, the devil and his fallen angels included, wants to escape the curse in this life and the lake of fire after death.

The question is whether you consider the place where you can live in love toward God and serve him with all your being to be a truly lovely, amiable place. And our prayers reveal how intensely we want to appear in Zion. Our versification presents it in these words:

> Advancing still from strength to strength,
> They onward go where saints have trod,
> Till ev'ry one appears at length
> In Zion's courts before his God;
> Jehovah, God of Hosts, give ear,
> Our fathers' God, in mercy hear.

Read: Psalm 138
Psalter versification: 229:4

TRANSCENDENT BLESSEDNESS

For a day in thy courts is better than a thousand. I had rather be a doorkeeper in the house of my God, than to dwell in the tents of wickedness. —Psalm 84:10

If the psalmist were living today, he would no doubt write that a day in God's house is better than a million, yea, even perhaps better than a trillion days in this world of sin. But when he did in Psalm 84:10 write, "For a day in thy courts is better than a thousand. I had rather be a doorkeeper in the house of my God, than to dwell in the tents of wickedness," he was speaking of what in that day was a great percentage. One day in a thousand is an overwhelming percentage. Even today, who would prefer to work for a dollar a day rather than one thousand, if he could get it? Who would want to live one more day, if he could be healed to live a thousand more days?

By his statement the psalmist underscores what he stated previously in the psalm, namely, that to him God's house is lovely, and that he would be happy if he could be just inside the door of that house. That is what he wrote. Indeed, he is willing to serve God there as the doorkeeper: but what he wrote is better translated as "sit at the threshold." Even then he makes an awesome contrast! So rich, so full of spiritual joy, and of such transcendent blessedness is that house that, if we are just inside the door, we are overwhelmed with blessedness.

Consider how far the sun is from us, yet it brings us precious light and warmth. How delightful it makes life for us even from such a distance! Much more is God's house filled with his love, mercy, grace, and covenant fellowship. Easy it is to understand our versification, which says:

> Upon us look, O God, our shield,
> The face of Thy anointed see;
> A thousand other days can yield
> No gladness like one day with Thee;
> Tho' only at Thy door I wait,
> No tents of sin give joy so great.

Do you agree? You want to see the sun arise again tomorrow; but do you, as the psalmist did, want to pray that God will look upon you and send down upon you the rays of his love in Christ? Transcendent blessedness awaits God's church. Do you want it?

Read: Revelation 21
Psalter versification: 229:5

A BLESSED, STEADFAST TRUST

For the LORD God is a sun and shield: the LORD will give grace and glory: no good thing will he withhold from them that walk uprightly. O LORD of hosts, blessed is the man that trusteth in thee. —Psalm 84:11–12

Life has its requirements, and because sin entered into the world, life also needs protection. That is why the psalmist concludes Psalm 84 by stating in verses 11–12: "For the LORD God is a sun and shield: the LORD will give grace and glory: no good thing will he withhold from them that walk uprightly. O LORD of hosts, blessed is the man that trusteth in thee."

Now if there is one thing our earthly life needs, it is the sun. No food will there be without it. No work will man be able to perform in the total darkness. Because the curse is on the earth, we need to be shielded from very many things.

Spiritually, God is that sun and shield. In Christ he supplies us with all our spiritual life needs. In Christ he protects us from falling away from the spiritual life that he gave us. His grace is upon us and will bring us to glory in Christ in the day that he returns to us.

The psalmist therefore had good reason for stating: "Blessed is the man that trusteth in thee." That trust manifests itself in an upright walk. And all this fits in so beautifully with the psalmist's opening statement that God's tabernacles are amiable, that is, lovely. Longing for entrance into God's house of many mansions, the child of God walks uprightly in the sight of God with whom he longs to live. In God he trusts in the strength that God has given him already in this valley of tears. God our sun gives us faith and preserves us in it. Thus in this life already we receive blessings out of God's house and are sure we will reach that house; for God, our sun and shield, is the ever faithful, almighty God.

Enthusiastically we can sing this from our versification:

> Jehovah, God our Shield and Sun,
> Will grace and glory surely give;
> No good will He withhold from one
> Who in His sight shall rightly live;
> O Lord of Hosts, most blest is he
> Who puts his steadfast trust in Thee.

Read: Psalm 31
Psalter versification: 229:6

OUR GUIDING LIGHT

Thy word is a lamp unto my feet, and a light unto my path. I have sworn, and I will perform it, that I will keep thy righteous judgments. —Psalm 119:105–106

Not only is it foolish but also dishonest to promise that which you know you cannot do. And therefore one might wonder why the psalmist wrote in Psalm 119:106, "I have sworn, and I will perform it, that I will keep thy righteous judgments." How does he dare to do that?

Well, for one thing, he reveals in the preceding verse what enables him to do what he swore he would do. He stated: "Thy word is a lamp unto my feet, and a light unto my path" (v. 105). And although these words do not directly state how he would be able to do these works demanded by God in his righteous judgment, this does explain why he knows the requirements, that is, where he must walk and how he must conduct himself. God's word makes that clear. In this night of sin, wherein we all are since the fall of Adam through Satan's lie, God's word shows us what we were created to do, namely, walk in love before God and bring all of creation unto God in praise and thanksgiving. Satan deceived us into believing that we are here for our fleshly pleasures. Therefore, we think, by nature, that we can decide what is good and evil for us.

The word of God, our Bible, gives us light and shows us not only exactly where to walk, but also that we can walk because of God's grace in Christ. So that now we may sing:

> Thy word sheds light upon my path;
> A shining light, it guides my feet;
> Thy righteous judgments to observe
> My solemn vow I now repeat.

Your bankbook and checkbook are not your most valuable books. Scripture is our richest book, a treasure in our hearts. By all means do not leave it closed and on the shelf. Read it every day so that you may keep this vow.

God's word reveals Christ to us as his Word became flesh. Christ makes it possible for us to keep God's righteous judgments. Meet him in God's word. He will guide you and lighten your way so that your feet are walking in righteousness before God.

Read: Psalm 119:105–112
Psalter versification: 334:1

AN URGENT PRAYER FOR INSTRUCTION

I am afflicted very much: quicken me, O LORD, according unto thy word.
Accept, I beseech thee, the freewill offerings of my mouth, O LORD, and
teach me thy judgments. —Psalm 119:107–108

A musical instrument played properly can produce pleasing music and, if obtained as a gift, calls for words of thanks unto the giver. But that gift will serve no good purpose until the one who receives it is taught how to play it. Likewise, God's word, which is a lamp unto our feet and a light unto our path (Ps. 119:105), is a rich gift; but God must teach us what that which we read therein means and what it calls us to do.

Therefore, we find the psalmist praying in Psalm 119:108, "Accept, I beseech Thee, the freewill offerings of my mouth, O LORD, and teach me thy judgments." He had already in the preceding verse written: "I am afflicted very much: quicken me, O LORD, according unto thy word" (v. 107). Plainly his prayer is urgent because he was finding it difficult to keep his vow of walking in God's righteous judgments. He speaks of being greatly afflicted by unbelievers. And the temptation is always there to cease keeping God's statutes in order to escape this affliction.

We need to be quickened, that is, revived to more earnest and open keeping of God's judgments. These we need to be taught more fully. We may know and even be able to quote from memory God's law. We may even, as the psalmist did, praise and thank God for giving us his word. We may know many warnings and exhortations in the Bible. But we need to be taught in trying circumstances how to walk. We must by our deeds, not simply our mouths, say that his statutes are good. Make this your prayer and sing these words:

In my distress I plead with Thee,
Send help according to Thy word;
Accept my sacrifice of praise
And make me know Thy judgments, Lord.

Read God's word, but study it as well. And by all means pray God that he will teach you how to walk in love to him no matter what the circumstances in which you find yourself are. Especially when you are being ridiculed and mocked by the world, pray for grace to know how to continue walking in love to God.

Read: Psalm 25
Psalter versification: 334:2

FAITHFUL IN ADVERSITY

My soul is continually in my hand: yet do I not forget thy law. The wicked have laid a snare for me: yet I erred not from thy precepts. —Psalm 119:109–110

From God, on whose earth we walk, whose plants provide us with all our food, who gives us every heartbeat and breath of life, we cannot earn or buy the smallest part of this earthly creation. Yea, instead, every minute we become more and more indebted to him. Much less can we earn or buy or talk him into giving us the smallest blessing of the kingdom of heaven. Although it may look as though the psalmist is in Psalm 119:109–110 seeking to move God into blessing him for what he did, this is not so at all.

The psalmist was in a difficult position. In verse 109 he stated that his soul was continually in his hand, and in verse 110 that the enemy had laid a snare for him to fall into; and then he wrote, "Yet do I not forget thy law," and "Yet I erred not from thy precepts." In this he was not trying to persuade God to bless him because he had done so well thus far. He is not boasting here, even though it may look that way.

Our versification states it this way:

> In danger oft and nigh to death,
> Thy law remembered is my aid;
> The wicked seek my overthrow,
> Yet from Thy truth I have not strayed.

Notice that he confesses that he must keep God's law. God made that known to him, and for this he owes God thanks. And his statement that he erred not underscores his sincerity when he wrote that he loved God's law and considered it to be a lamp unto his feet (v. 105).

We do well to remember these words of the psalmist. God owes us nothing; but we owe him thanks for sending his Son who took not one step outside God's law and died for all our missteps. In him his people will be kept faithful even in adversity, not because they deserve it, but because of God's grace in Christ. When we pray for faithfulness, God will give it to us. Through Christ he will "make you perfect in every good work to do his will, working in you that which is wellpleasing in his sight" (Heb. 13:21).

Read: Hebrews 13
Psalter versification: 334:3

A WONDERFUL INHERITANCE

Thy testimonies have I taken as an heritage for ever: for they are the rejoicing
of my heart. I have inclined mine heart to perform thy statutes alway,
even unto the end. —Psalm 119:111–112

If you could choose that which you are going to inherit, what would you choose? What would make you really happy? Would you say with the psalmist: "Thy testimonies have I taken as an heritage for ever: for they are the rejoicing of my heart. I have inclined my heart to perform thy statutes alway, even unto the end" (Ps. 119:111–112)?

Do these testimonies of God give you so much joy that what you want to obtain is entrance into the kingdom of heaven, where all the citizens keep God's law perfectly, and where you will be able to do nothing but walk in perfect love before God?

God's testimonies and statutes are the laws according to which we were created and which God designed for our life in the new Jerusalem. There we will have strict, exacting laws in which the citizens of that kingdom find great joy. They are the rejoicing of their hearts, and they will want to be keeping them continuously, everlastingly (v. 112).

Now, an inheritance is obtained only through the death of one who decreed to have you receive it. Here Christ is the one who died, in order that those given him by the Father might enter that kingdom of righteousness and be given a life that cannot sin but rejoices in those statutes. These by his Spirit will sing:

> Thy precepts are my heritage,
> For daily they my heart rejoice;
> To keep Thy statutes faithfully
> Shall ever be my willing choice.

We are surrounded by a host that does not want that kind of future. For them it is a case of seeking this world and the lust thereof. They are interested only in what they can inherit in this life and of this world's deceptive treasures.

Are you like the psalmist or like the world that surrounds us? Desire that wonderful inheritance that is coming in the day of Christ, and you may be sure that in God's grace you will receive it. A kingdom of perfect love is coming. In it, because of the perfect love of God, there will be a perfect love of all the citizens of that kingdom for each other.

Read: 1 Corinthians 13
Psalter versification: 334:4

BLESSING THE GOD WHO BLESSES US

Bless the LORD, O my soul: and all that is within me, bless his holy name. —Psalm 103:1

What goes against our flesh, but we are often exhorted to do in Scripture, is to bless God. We like the idea that he blesses us. Even those who never worship him on the sabbath day in his house will say to each other: "God bless you!" We do, however, have a calling to bless him; and therefore in Psalm 103:1 we read: "Bless the LORD, O my soul: and all that is within me, bless his holy name."

Now, to bless God means something quite different from God blessing us, for God is no creature, and to bless means basically to call well or good. When we bless God, we say that he is good. We praise and honor him. Therefore, our versification has it this way:

> O praise and bless the Lord, my soul,
> His wondrous love proclaim;
> Join heart and voice and all my pow'rs
> To bless His holy Name.

But when God blesses us, he calls that which is good to come upon us. We cannot add anything to God; but we can say that he is good. He calls in the sense of commanding goodness upon us.

Now, we are called to speak well of him with our lips before others; but we must also say this by our deeds and say it unto God in our prayers. In them we must tell him: "O God, how great and good thou art!"

Our calling is to bless his holy name, and that means that, even more than we call the judge "Your Honor," we must address God in a reverent way as one high above us and all creation. We must speak to him as the Holy One who is exalted above all persons. He is our friend and loves us; but with God we cannot get "chummy." He must be worshiped, not brought down to the level of the creature.

This blessing of him we must do with our whole being. It must begin in our soul, that is, in the innermost recesses of our being; but then by it through our whole being we must reveal love and respect for him.

Surely then we must bow our heads before him and must use the most respect- and honor-expressing words that we can. Call him your Father, but be sure that you address him as your heavenly Father. Jesus taught us to begin our prayers with "Hallowed be thy name."

Read: Psalm 103
Psalter versification: 277:1

THANKFUL FOR EVERY BENEFIT

Bless the LORD, O my soul, and forget not all his benefits. —Psalm 103:2

An athlete makes a name for himself by the records he breaks and the amazing statistics his activities produce. The Lord our God, however, does not make a name for himself. He does reveal his name to us in wonderful works; but he competes with no one, does not develop in skills and abilities. He is today what he eternally is. His name, therefore, is eternal and eternally the same. That name is holy because it is set apart from all other names of creatures, since of him, through him, and unto him are all things. He is high above all creation.

David, in Psalm 103:1, tells us to bless his name, and then in verse 2 continues: "Bless the LORD, O my soul, and forget not all his benefits." Here he brings us another amazing truth, namely, God's name declares him to be the one from whom all that we are and have came. Name something you have that pleases you—it came from God, and you have a reason to bless and thank him. You just cannot mention an earthly object that you have that did not come from him. Every day and every minute of your life came from him and calls for you to bless him.

We avoid this and fail to do so. We have joyful experiences. We have much that we call benefits. But we fail to see God in them. Sometimes we will utter a few hasty words of thanks, but the moments wherein we have this joyful experience are hundreds of times more than those in which we blessed God for giving them to us. Or the experience itself is so delightful that God, the giver, never enters into our thoughts. Well then may we listen to the psalmist as he writes and we sing:

> O praise and bless the Lord, my soul,
> And ever thankful be;
> Forget not all the benefits
> He has bestowed on thee.

Learn these words. Commit them to memory and put them into practice. There is a reason why David begins the first two verses with the call to bless the Lord, and then ends the psalm with the last three verses also exhorting not only angels but all his works to bless the Lord. There is so much for which to bless God and so much that reveals that his name is holy as our great benefactor.

Read: Psalm 104
Psalter versification: 277:2

BLESSED WITH THE BASIC BENEFIT

Who forgiveth all thine iniquities; who healeth all thy diseases. —Psalm 103:3

As the saying goes: "First things come first." We can err in that respect and often fail to mention or list first what ought to be brought to the attention of our hearers. But God never slips or makes mistakes. Having been told that, we should bless him for all the benefits which he bestowed upon us. He now in verse 3 of Psalm 103, through David, lists first of all the benefit of the forgiveness of our sins.

There just is no benefit as important as that one. If we do not receive it, we cannot be given the healing of our diseases; we cannot be redeemed from destruction, be crowned with loving-kindness and tender mercy, have our mouths satisfied with good things and our youth renewed like the eagle's (vv. 3–5). We sing correctly:

> He freely pardons all thy sins,
> And He is strong to save;
> He heals thy sickness, soothes thy pain,
> And ransoms from the grave.

In the forgiving of our sins our salvation is begun. If God does not give us this benefit, we have no right to any benefit of any kind. God may and does give men food and drink, life and talents, joyful experiences and the like. He gives life and talents also to the devil and his host. But these are not blessings to them and therefore are not benefits. They are that which they must receive to do what God decreed in his counsel that they should do; but we err if we think that these are works of his loving-kindness and tender mercies. Unless he forgives our sins, what he gives us is not a work of his grace. His grace falls only on those whose sins are blotted out by the blood of Christ. There just is no legal basis for the righteous God to bestow his grace on those whose sins are not blotted out.

Since he does forgive our sins, giving us that very important benefit, we surely should bless his name. Forget not all his benefits; but by all means, do not forget that tremendous gift of forgiveness. You just cannot bless him too much for that!

Read: Romans 5
Psalter versification: 277:3

ADDED REASONS FOR BLESSING GOD'S NAME

Who forgiveth all thine iniquities; who healeth all thy diseases; Who redeemeth thy life from destruction; who crowneth thee with lovingkindness and tender mercies; Who satisfieth thy mouth with good things; so that thy youth is renewed like the eagle's. —Psalm 103:3–5

With our iniquities forgiven, because Christ suffered the punishment which we deserve and performed the works of love we failed to bring to God, we may and must bless God "who healeth all thy diseases; who redeemeth thy life from destruction; who crowneth thee with lovingkindness and tender mercies; who satisfieth thy mouth with good things; so that thy youth is renewed like the eagle's" (Ps. 103:3–5).

And we can sing:

> He heals thy sickness, soothes thy pain,
> And ransoms from the grave.
> He crowns thee with His grace and love,
> And, with His strength endued,
> Thou mountest up with eagle's wings,
> Thy joyous youth renewed.

Add it all up! Let the fact of it all sink deeply into your soul, and you will understand David's words in verse 2, namely: "Bless the LORD, O my soul, and forget not all his benefits."

Do we really have to be exhorted to do this? Do we forget these benefits? Yes, that is the sad truth of the matter. We so often fail to see God's holy name. His name Savior is far out of our minds so often. We look rather upon him as our servant. We are so eager to have him serve us in healing our diseases, keeping our lives from destruction, making us taste his tender mercy, and in the twilight of our lives to have our youth renewed. That matter of the forgiveness of our sins is so often so far removed from our thoughts. The truth that he is our savior in Christ and forgives our sins fails to make us bless his name.

Urgent and important then it is that we be exhorted to bless his name in our prayers and not simply in them to ask for benefits. Did Jesus not teach us to begin our prayers with, "Hallowed be Thy name"? Is this not to control our prayers for bread?

Examine your prayers, and if they lack blessing his name and contain only requests for things of this life, by all means change them! Make it an important element in your prayers that you request the ability and desire to bless his name and that your spiritual life be renewed so that you may soar high in blessing his name.

Read: Exodus 15
Psalter versification: 277:3–4

A PARTICULAR BLESSEDNESS

"The LORD executeth righteousness and judgment for all that are oppressed. He made known his ways unto Moses, his acts unto the children of Israel." —Psalm 103:6–7

The day is coming when the antichrist will rule the whole world. Then those that believe in Christ will be oppressed with starvation, not being able to buy or sell (Rev. 13:15–17). They will, however, have every reason in that day to sing:

> The Lord will judge in righteousness
> For all that are oppressed;
> To all His saints His gracious acts
> And ways are manifest.

God himself through David wrote this in Psalm 103:6–7 in these words: "The LORD executeth righteousness and judgment for all that are oppressed. He made known his ways unto Moses, his acts unto the children of Israel."

We may note, however, how particular God's love and grace are. Israel was oppressed by Egypt. Therefore "all that are oppressed" does not include those that oppress, namely the Egyptians. God's love and grace come not to all men. He does not love everybody; and his grace is only upon those that belong to Christ. Christ is the Israel. That name means Prince of God, and Christ is the Prince of Peace. The "children of Israel" then are the children of Christ, the believers.

What is more, "the LORD executeth righteousness and judgment." That means that those who are not judged to be righteous in Christ are guilty and worthy of everlasting punishment. They may not have God's love and grace for even one minute.

It is true that all men are oppressed, being under the curse because of Adam's sin. But here is a special oppression. Israel was oppressed by Egypt, and Egypt was not under this oppression. So it is that, as Jesus said: "I lay down my life for the sheep" (John 10:15). He died for the oppression of a particular group of people. God's love and grace are only for them.

Let us then bless God for that cross of Christ. Because of it, God judges us to be righteous; and then the first benefit, namely the forgiveness of our sins, is realized. Now, out of it all the blessings of salvation flow. Do not forget to bless God for this particular blessing of being made righteous in Christ.

Read: John 10:1–30
Psalter versification: 277:5

THE MEETING OF MERCY AND TRUTH

The LORD is merciful and gracious, slow to anger,
and plenteous in mercy. —Psalm 103:8

The judge may be full of pity for a man whom he must sentence; but he may not in any way and to any degree minimize the sentence that the law of the land requires. If he does, he is breaking the law and deserves to be punished. There is then only one explanation for the seeming contradiction which David wrote in Psalm 103:6–8. He wrote that God executes righteousness and judgment for all that are oppressed. And now in verse 8 he adds: "The LORD is merciful and gracious, slow to anger, and plenteous in mercy."

Bear in mind that although the Israelites were taken from underneath the bondage and oppression of the Egyptians, these Israelites soon showed all manner of sins and deserved to be cast into the greater oppression of hell fire. How then could the psalmist speak of the God of righteousness and judgment being gracious and plenteous in his mercy toward them?

Really there is no contradiction here. The cross of Christ stands between those two facts and truths. Yea, the cross stands between God and these sinners of Israel who are dealt with in tender mercy and in abundant grace.

Because Christ was our covenant head, God poured out upon him all the punishment that we deserve. Seeing us in him, God, in strictest righteousness and judgment, declared that all the punishment which we deserve was fully suffered. Not the slightest fraction of the punishment the law required was withheld. Because of this, God can in righteous judgment deal with us graciously and mercifully. It is so very true that:

The Lord is ever merciful,
And unto anger slow;
His lovingkindness and His grace
In rich abundance flow.

We can and must say that God's mercy and grace are upon us, not in spite of his righteousness and judgment, or contrary to them, but due to that righteousness and judgment.

Bless his name then for that cross of Christ, in whom mercy and truth are met together and righteousness and peace have kissed each other.

Read: Psalm 85
Psalter versification: 277:6

GOD'S ABIDING LOVE AND GRACE

He will not always chide: neither will he keep his anger for ever. He hath not dealt with us after our sins; nor rewarded us according to our iniquities. —Psalm 103:9–10

The child of God may be thankful and bless God's name when God is angry with him and chides him in his anger. Anger does not always mean hatred. Parents who love their children become angry when the children walk in sin, exactly because they love them. Anger can very well mean that you love the person whom you chide. Listen to what David wrote in Psalm 103:9, "He will not always chide: neither will he keep his anger forever." Take note also of our versification that sings:

> Yea, the Lord is full of mercy
> And compassion for distress,
> Slow to anger and abundant
> In His grace and tenderness.
> He will not be angry alway,
> Nor will He forever chide;
> Tho' we oft have sinned against Him
> Still His love and grace abide.

You see, to chide is to reprove, rebuke, or admonish, and it is that work of God's mercy whereby he corrects us and improves our spiritual lives. He is angry when we sin. He is displeased. But because of what Christ did for us, "he hath not dealt with us after our sins; nor rewarded us according to our iniquities" (v. 10). He does not chide us because he hates us. His love for us moves him to chide and correct us.

But get this and let it comfort you when he rebukes you in your sins: the day is coming when he will no longer chide us, for he will have brought us, with a body completely delivered from the power of sin, before his face in glory. Now already he has blotted out all our sins; but he will also take from us our old man of sin, with which we fall so easily into sin. That makes rebukes necessary. But the moment we die, all need for chiding is gone. Then we will never see his anger again and instead will see the smile on his face. And fully we will experience all this in a resurrected, spiritual body that has no sin. He will not always chide. We will be sinless and pleasing in his sight.

Our sins were blotted out in his love. Bless him for that! But bless him also for rebuking you when you fall into sin. It means that he intends to bring you to sinlessness and a richer taste of his love in a sin-free creation.

Read: Psalm 145
Psalter versification: 280:3

IMMEASURABLE MERCY

For as the heaven is high above the earth, so great is his mercy toward them that fear him. As far as the east is from the west, so far hath he removed our transgressions from us. —Psalm 103:11–12

Man has gone far into outer space and found ways to measure the distance from the earth to heavenly bodies that are far, far away. But man cannot tell us how far space extends beyond the farthest star that he has measured. Much less can he measure God's mercy. It is as big as God is, and he is infinite. Never is it possible that the church will run out of mercy from God. Nowhere can we go and be cut off from it. As David states it in Psalm 103:11, "For as the heaven is high above the earth, so great is his mercy toward them that fear him."

This mercy is so great because "As far as the east is from the west, so far hath he removed our transgressions from us" (v. 12). Consider the fact that you can go eastward as far as you want, but you will not get one step closer to the west. The earth is a globe, so that if you travel eastward, you will always be facing eastward no matter how far you go. So it is also that you will never reach a point where you will again come in contact with your sins that God took away by the blood of his Son, Christ our savior.

Well may we daily sing these words of our versification:

As heaven is high above the earth,
So great His mercy proves;
As far from us as east from west
He all our sin removes.

It is for that reason that we can be so sure that we are redeemed from destruction, and that all the benefits David listed in the first part of this psalm are everlastingly ours in Christ. Because we can never reach these sins, which he took off our backs, and no one else can find them and attach them to us once again, we can be sure of the immeasurable mercy of God being upon us everlastingly.

Remember that truth when you get aches and pains, bereavements and persecutions, losses and disappointments. God's mercy is still there. These do not come as punishment upon your sins. That lofty mercy is polishing you, working all things together for your good so that you may be lifted to a glory you can never measure. Bless God's name for that truth and comfort.

Read: 2 Corinthians 4
Psalter versification: 277:8

FEARING BUT NOT AFRAID

Like as a father pitieth his children, so the LORD pitieth
them that fear him. —Psalm 103:13

It might seem strange that in Psalm 103 David mentions all the benefits that God's loving-kindness and mercy bestow upon us, and then states in verse 13: "Like as a father pitieth his children, so the LORD pitieth them that fear him."

Why should we fear the God whose mercy is as high as the heavens and who has removed our transgressions from us as far as the east is from the west? Is our versification right when it sings thus?

The tender love a father has
For all his children dear,
Such love the Lord bestows on them
Who worship Him in fear.

That word *worship* seems to modify things a bit. But we still have that word *fear*. Why fear God when he does all this for us? Well, we are not afraid of God with Christ and his cross standing between us and God. Our guilt is all gone! And he loves us in him. But the fear that is here meant is the fear of reverence and awe. In the Old Testament Scriptures, the word *fear* is used so very often as faith. Only twice—in Habakkuk 2:4 and in Deuteronomy 32:20—will you find the word *faith*. Amazing, is it not? It is those who believe in him whom God pities as a father pities his children.

While we are still in this vale of tears, God pities us because our sins are blotted out by his Son. But we still live where the curse rests since Adam's sin. We have sicknesses and pain, bereavements and losses, enemies and persecution. In all this God pities us, and our faith in him is a sign to us that he pities us and that in that pity he is going to remove the curse completely from us. That faith or fear means that we have already been born again, begotten unto a lively hope.

Being the holy, unchangeable God, his pity far outshines that of a human father. We have, therefore, no reason to be afraid that he will cast us into the lake of fire, but we can be sure that he will bring us into the curse-free, curseless new Jerusalem. We need not be one whit afraid of the day when Christ returns. That is the day of our glory, the day when all fear of his wrath is forever behind us.

Read: Revelation 22
Psalter versification: 278:1

MERCY AMID MISERIES

As for man, his days are as grass: as a flower of the field, so he flourisheth.
For the wind passeth over it, and it is gone; and the place thereof shall
know it no more. —Psalm 103:15–16

One thing in life that is sure is death. We do not know what day we are going to die. A particular disease may tell us that it will be soon. But death is not only all around us. It is in us. In Psalm 103:15–16 we read: "As for man, his days are as grass: as a flower of the field, so he flourisheth. For the wind passeth over it, and it is gone; and the place thereof shall know it no more."

This David wrote after stating that God knows our frame and remembers that we are dust (v. 4). All this we sing beautifully in this versification:

> The Lord remembers we are dust,
> And all our frailty knows;
> Man's days are like the tender grass,
> And as the flow'r he grows.
> The flow'r is withered by the wind
> That smites with blighting breath;
> So man is quickly swept away
> Before the blast of death.

All this stands in connection with the truth that we are to bless God and remember all his benefits. But in that connection comes the comforting assurance, that rich truth, that like as a father pities his children, so God pities us (v. 13).

Before us then is the blessed truth that our fading and withering does not hurt us but serves us. God knows our frame and that we are dust. Our afflictions do not surprise him. He sends them, and at the right time sends us death. And he sent his Son into our death in order to bore a hole through it and the grave, so that we can be lifted up from this sin-cursed world and into his glorious kingdom. All this comes in loving-kindness and tender mercies.

Until the day we arrive in that glory, God does have compassion on us. He does not forget us. He sends no misery that is not necessary for our particular place in glory. "Our light affliction, which is but for a moment, worketh for us a far more exceeding and eternal weight of glory" (2 Cor. 4:17).

Read: 2 Corinthians 4
Psalter versification: 278:2–3

September 30

EVERLASTING MERCY AND RIGHTEOUSNESS

But the mercy of the LORD is from everlasting to everlasting upon them that fear him, and his righteousness unto children's children. —Psalm 103:17

There can be no thunder without lightning, and no rainbow in the sky without sunlight. Similarly, there can be no mercy for God to show us without a righteousness which he gave us in Christ. And both of these David mentioned in Psalm 103:17. He wrote, "But the mercy of the LORD is from everlasting to everlasting upon them that fear him, and his righteousness unto children's children."

David had said the same thing in Psalm 85:10, where he spoke prophetically of the cross of Christ. There he stated: "Mercy and truth are met together; righteousness and peace have kissed each other." Now righteousness is truth, and peace comes only in God's mercy, so that we may state it this way: "Mercy and righteousness are met together; at the cross of Christ they have kissed each other."

We do well to note that in Psalm 103:17 David made a contrast between the truth of God's mercy and righteousness and the fact that God knows that we are like grass that is here today and gone tomorrow. Our stay here is brief, while God's mercy is "from everlasting to everlasting." And though we will soon be gone, God's righteousness will be on our children and grandchildren.

Beautifully we sing this truth as follows:

Unchanging is the love of God,
From age to age the same,
Displayed to all who do His will
And reverence His Name.
Those who His gracious covenant keep
The Lord will ever bless;
Their children's children shall rejoice
To see His righteousness.

We will die sooner or later; but we will die in God's mercy. For that mercy is from everlasting to everlasting upon us. And in that mercy our children will be in the place we left behind and receive God's righteousness that is in Christ, and therefore also will be dealt with in God's mercy.

Be assured from God's word that his mercy will bring you to the everlasting blessedness that he has prepared for you. And that he will keep his covenant promises and also bring our children there.

Read: Genesis 17:1–8
Psalter versification: 278:4–5

276

BLESSING GOD AS KING OVER ALL

Bless the Lord, ye his angels, that excel in strength, that do his commandments, hearkening unto the voice of his word. Bless ye the Lord, all ye his hosts; ye ministers of his, that do his pleasure. Bless the Lord, all his works in all places of his dominion: bless the Lord, O my soul. —Psalm 103:20–22

It is easy to tell others what to do. It is much harder to tell your own tongue what to say, your eyes what to turn from, and your feet not to go on a specific path. Yet David speaks directly to his soul with these words: "Bless the Lord, O my soul" (Ps. 103:22).

With these words he began this psalm, and with these same words he brings this psalm to its close. In between he tells us why God must be blessed. Actually, he tells all creation to bless God. He writes: "Bless the Lord, ye his angels, that excel...Bless ye the Lord, all ye his hosts; ye ministers of his, that do his pleasure. Bless the Lord, all his works in all places of his dominion" (Ps. 103:20–22).

In verse 19 he told us why all creatures must bless him. He wrote: "His kingdom ruleth over all." Here also we have the reason why he already in verse 1 had said: "Bless his holy name." His name is God Over All! He rules and owns all things. Not only does he deserve to be blessed, but he must be blessed by all creation. The thinking, willing creatures, men and angels, must do so; and through them and their use of the other creatures which he gives to them, God must be blessed.

Take hold of that truth today and put it into practice more fully every day the rest of your life. Bless his name by saying in your actions as well as with your mouth that he is the one who "ruleth over all" and is above all creation. Bless him as God and as God alone.

Sing our versification, but live that way as well:

Established in the highest heav'ns
The Lord has set His throne,
And over all His kingdom rules,
For He is God alone.
Bless ye the Lord, all ye His works
In His dominion broad,
And, never ceasing, O my soul,
Bless thou the Lord, thy God.

Created in the image of God, man stands between God and the whole earthly creation and is able to speak to God. He must use it all in the consciousness that it is God's and is given so that through man's soul it may return to God. Every morning, tell your soul to bless him through the whole day that is before you.

Read: Psalm 148
Psalter versification: 279:1, 4

HOPE FOR SPIRITUAL SAFETY

I hate vain thoughts: but thy law do I love. Thou art my hiding place and my shield: I hope in thy word. —Psalm 119:113–114

Have you ever said, and do you dare to say, that you know more than God does? Did you ever think that he was wrong and you were right? Well, take hold of this truth before you say no! Every time that you sin, you say by that deed that you know better than God does what is good and what is evil for you. You say that you are right and God is wrong in forbidding this and demanding that. Just look at Psalm 119:113–114. We read: "I hate vain thoughts: but thy law do I love. Thou art my hiding place and my shield: I hope in thy word."

Plainly, anything contrary to God's law springs from vain thoughts. And our versification puts it this way:

> Deceit and falsehood I abhor,
> But love Thy law, Thy truth revealed;
> My steadfast hope is in Thy word;
> Thou art my refuge and my shield;
> The paths of sin I have not trod,
> But kept the precepts of my God.

Whenever we sin, we are guilty of deceit and falsehood. We were created in the image of God. But it may reverently be said that when we sin, we look like the devil! We were created to walk in love to God; but when we sin, we manifest hatred toward him.

Bear in mind that it was the devil's vain thoughts that led us into sin. He made us believe that we could decide what is good and what is evil. And because of that fact we need a hiding place and shield, not merely from God's holy wrath, but from Satan's devilish power.

As the psalmist did, put your hope in God's word for such protection. Adam tried to find safety by fig leaves instead of running unto God. We, who know the Word of God made flesh, Christ our savior, must trust in him. In him we can safely hide; and he is a shield that will keep us safe from God's wrath and Satan's power.

By all means, see Satan as your chief enemy and realize how important it is to be shielded from his vain thoughts which he wants to implant and keep in your mind. Hope in God's word that presents Christ and his cross but also a new life of love to God by a rebirth.

Read: Psalm 119:113–120
Psalter versification: 335:1

SAFE IN THE ARMS OF JESUS

Depart from me, ye evildoers: for I will keep the commandments of my God. Uphold me according unto thy word, that I may live: and let me not be ashamed of my hope. Hold thou me up, and I shall be safe: and I will have respect unto thy statutes continually. —Psalm 119:115–117

A desire does not mean that one has the ability to do that which will fulfill it. One with a malignant tumor will want it removed, but he surely cannot do that himself. So the child of God, because of his new spiritual life, will want to be freed from Satan's power and to be able to keep God's law perfectly, and will say to the world: "Depart from me, ye evildoers: for I will keep the commandments of my God" (Ps. 119:115). But because he cannot make them depart, he prays to God: "Uphold me according unto thy word, that I may live: and let me not be ashamed of my hope. Hold thou me up, and I shall be safe: and I will have respect unto thy statutes continually" (vv. 116–117).

What we say then to the world, and to Satan the prince of this world, must be in perfect harmony with our prayer to God. If we really want to walk in love to God, we must tell the world to depart from us. We cannot have fellowship with God and those who hate God.

Join the world in its carnal entertainment and glorification of sin, and you do not mean it when you pray: "Let me not be ashamed of my hope."

In Romans 1:32 Paul exposes the evil of having pleasure in them that have pleasure in sin. And the psalmist reveals a very important truth here. We must realize our complete dependency upon God for a righteous walk. Think that you can do that alone, and you do not really want to walk in love to God. And you do not really see how much Satan has you in his power. No, the child of God prays that God will hold him up. He sings, and in his song he prays:

> According to Thy gracious word
> Uphold me, Lord, deliver me;
> O do not let me be ashamed
> Of patient hope and trust in Thee;
> O hold Thou me, and I shall stand
> And ever follow Thy command.

We are safe because we are upheld according to God's word. And that word assures us that we are safe in the arms of Jesus, who blotted out our sins and now has all power in heaven and on earth to bring forth presently, and now keep, a perfect church to God's glory.

Read: Psalm 118
Psalter versification: 335:2

AWESOME JUDGMENT AND SURE COMFORT

Thou hast trodden down all them that err from thy statutes: for their deceit is falsehood. Thou puttest away all the wicked of the earth like dross: therefore I love thy testimonies. My flesh trembleth for fear of thee; and I am afraid of thy judgments.
—Psalm 119:118–120

The child of God is safe. The wicked of the earth are not only in great danger, but shall most assuredly be punished everlastingly for their sins. Children of God sing that, too, in this versification:

> The froward Thou hast set at nought
> Who vainly wander from the right;
> The wicked Thou dost count as dross;
> Thy just decrees are my delight;
> For fear of Thee I stand in awe
> And rev'rence Thy most holy law.

These words express the truth of Psalm 119:118–120, where we read: "Thou hast trodden down all them that err from thy statutes: for their deceit is falsehood. Thou puttest away all the wicked of the earth like dross: therefore I love thy testimonies. My flesh trembleth for fear of thee; and I am afraid of thy judgments."

History is full of that truth. The wicked are trodden underfoot by God. Think of the destruction of the whole human race, with the exception of eight souls, at the time of the flood in Noah's day. Recall what happened to Egypt when ten plagues were sent, and at the Red Sea. But in due time every wicked man dies. How true: "Thou puttest away all the wicked of the earth like dross."

Is it any wonder then that the psalmist says that his flesh trembles for fear of God and that he is afraid of God's judgments? But remember that in verse 117 he had prayed: "Hold thou me up, and I shall be safe." It is understandable that he is afraid of God's judgments and that his flesh trembles for fear of God. However, there is no contradiction here.

When the believer sees himself, he has reason to fear God for what he does to those whose sins were not blotted out by the blood of Christ. The torment of hell is enough to make our flesh tremble when we think of it and when we realize how often we fall into sin.

But those who love God's testimonies, according to the new man in Christ implanted in them, can be sure that God will uphold them according to his word. Hold on to that word for its blessed comfort.

God's judgment is awesome; but he gives us a sure comfort.

Read: Psalm 1
Psalter versification: 335:3

A HUMBLE AND NECESSARY CONFESSION

I have done judgment and justice: leave me not to mine oppressors. Be surety for thy servant for good: let not the proud oppress me. Mine eyes fail for thy salvation, and for the word of thy righteousness. Deal with thy servant according unto thy mercy, and teach me thy statutes. —Psalm 119:121–124

It might seem as though the psalmist began the sixteenth section of Psalm 119 in a proud, boastful way. In verse 121 he begins: "I have done judgment and justice." Is this not a boast of what he did? And then in verse 123 he writes: "Mine eyes fail for thy salvation, and for the word of thy righteousness." Have we not here a proud boast of how pious and spiritual he is?

Well, look carefully at verses 121–124. You will find in them five things that he wrote, which reveal that he speaks not in pride but in childlike humility before God. He writes: "Leave me not to mine oppressors. Be surety for thy servant for good: let not the proud oppress me…Deal with thy servant according unto thy mercy, and teach me thy statutes." Or as our versification presents this passage:

I have followed truth and justice;
Leave me not in deep distress;
Be my help and my protection,
Let the proud no more oppress.
For Thy word and Thy salvation,
Lord, my eyes with longing fail;
Teach Thy statutes to Thy servants,
Let Thy mercy now prevail.

When he speaks of what he did, and how he longs for salvation and God's word of righteousness, he is confessing what God wrought in him and not what he brought to God. Then, too, twice he humbly confesses himself to be God's servant and expresses the desire to be taught by God.

And what we ought to be taught here by God, who used the psalmist to speak to us, is that we must confess unto God in song and prayer what he has done for us in his grace. Yes, when we sing, we should be singing to God. He wants to hear us confess what we have by his grace. He created us so that we could and would. And we must pray to God for protection not only from pain and persecution, but also from falling into sin. We must pray to God that he will teach us how in every circumstance of our lives we can walk in judgment and in justice.

Not to be overlooked is also our calling to pray for our salvation and God's word of righteousness. We must long and pray for the day of salvation when Christ completes it and we walk in perfect righteousness.

Read: Psalm 119:121–136
Psalter versification: 336:1

LOVE FOR GOD'S LAW

Therefore I love thy commandments above gold; yea, above fine gold. Therefore I
esteem all thy precepts concerning all things to be right; and I hate every false way.
—Psalm 119:127–128

The humility of the psalmist manifests itself again in the last four verses of the sixteenth section of Psalm 119. For the third time in this section, he calls himself God's servant. This time emphatically he confesses: "I am thy servant" (v. 125). This truth he underscores when in verses 127–128 he writes: "Therefore I love thy commandments above gold; yea, above fine gold. Therefore I esteem all thy precepts concerning all things to be right; and I hate every false way."

That is strong language! It is language of a faithful servant. And it is the reason why he prays: "Give me understanding, that I may know thy testimonies" (v. 125). It also explains why he says that it is time for God to work (v. 126). Seeing men all around him breaking God's law, which he loves, he is eager to have God put an end to all the evil he sees.

Two questions arise here. Does it hurt you when you see men working on the Sabbath or pursuing their sports? Or do you find pleasure listening to and watching them desecrate the Sabbath? Another question: Is God's law more precious to you than earthly treasures? When a new job or an increase in salary brings you more gold, are you happy that you have greater means to support the preaching of God's word, to finance mission projects, to relieve the poor, and to help spread the gospel by the printed page and airwaves to a greater degree?

What a gift of God's grace it is when we can sincerely sing:

> I am Thine, O give me wisdom,
> Make me know Thy truth, I pray;
> Sinners have despised Thy statutes;
> Now, O Lord, Thy power display.
> Lord, I love Thy good commandments
> And esteem them more than gold;
> All Thy precepts are most righteous;
> Hating sin, to these I hold.

For all of us, no one excluded, this is a prayer we must present to God every day: "Give me understanding, that I may know thy testimonies." We all have only a small beginning of a new life. That work of God we must want executed upon us, namely, a richer measure of the life Christ earned for us, so that God's commandments are loved by us above the finest gold.

Read: Matthew 5:27–48
Psalter versification: 336:2

SAFE IN THE STORMS OF LIFE

Hear my cry, O God; attend unto my prayer. From the end of the earth will I cry unto thee, when my heart is overwhelmed: lead me to the rock that is higher than I. —Psalm 61:1–2

When we are in serious trouble, there is the possibility of help if we are near a phone by means of which we can contact one who is able to help us. And if the trouble is the rising waters of a flood that threaten to reach a level above our heads, we need to be lifted to a place where we can still breathe the oxygen we need for life.

The child of God, when he exercises his faith in God, is never, no matter where he is, afraid that he cannot reach God. He believes that there is a high point where God will lift him above all that threatens his well-being and life.

David, a child of God, expresses this in Psalm 61:1–2 in these words: "Hear my cry, O God; attend unto my prayer. From the end of the earth will I cry unto thee, when my heart is overwhelmed: lead me to the rock that is higher than I."

Here we have a prayer of confidence. Go where you will. Be at the end of the earth. God is very near you. And you do not need to run to a phone. You could lose precious time that way, and help might come too late. You need not cry loudly to God, or even open your mouth to call him. He knows your thoughts and the prayers in your soul.

God has a rock that keeps his sheep in absolute safety. That rock is his Son whom he lifted up upon his cross to blot out our guilt, and who is now lifted to God's right hand with power over all things in heaven and on earth. Surely then the child of God is safe no matter where he is and what threatens his well-being. Our powerful enemy, Satan, is completely under Christ's control. Our sins, which call for everlasting agony in hell, will not touch us because of what Christ, our rock of refuge, suffered in our stead. We are absolutely safe from all that which would keep us from reaching and enjoying everlasting bliss and blessedness with him in heavenly glory. We are safe in all the storms of life. Sing these words then:

O God, regard my humble plea;
I cannot be so far from Thee
But Thou wilt hear my cry;
When I by trouble am distressed,
Then lead me on the Rock to rest
That higher is than I.

Read: Psalm 61
Psalter versification: 159:1

A SURE REFUGE

For thou hast been a shelter for me, and a strong tower from the enemy. I will abide in thy tabernacle for ever: I will trust in the covert of thy wings. Selah. —Psalm 61:3–4

Even in times of peace we need shelter and protection. There is the cold and heat that make life miserable. There are diseases that make us want something to keep them away from us. And surely in times of war, bomb shelters today are urgently needed.

In Psalm 61:3–4 David speaks of troubles that call for help when he writes: "For thou hast been a shelter for me, and a strong tower from the enemy. I will abide in thy tabernacle for ever: I will trust in the covert of thy wings. Selah."

Plainly, past experiences have made it sure in David's mind that he is going to escape all that would harm him in the future. And he reveals a firm conviction that he will reach heavenly glory. Believing it was God who protected him in the past, he is sure of absolute protection in the future. Looking back, he is sure of what is ahead of him.

That is also true for us. We should never look forward without looking back at what God did in his Son long ago, and at what was written in his word before we were born. The whole history of his church from creation to the day of Pentecost reveals what we can expect in the remaining years of our lives and of this present creation. What God has done for his church also reveals what we are going to find, namely, that all is well; we are going to have refuge and safety, so that we can sing with confidence:

> In Thee my soul hath shelter found,
> And Thou hast been from foes around
> The tow'r to which I flee.
> Within Thy house will I abide;
> My refuge sure, whate'er betide,
> Thy shelt'ring wings shall be.

What comfort is there not in those words! God's faithfulness in the past assures us that the almighty, unchangeable God will take good care of us. When what lies ahead seems to threaten you, look back at what he did already for you. His Son he built as a high tower, a sure shelter for us. Even as he raised his Son, our exalted King, he will bring us there into his house and is preparing our place.

Read: Daniel 6
Psalter versification: 159:2

COMFORTING SIGNS

For thou, O God, hast heard my vows: thou hast given me the heritage
of those that fear thy name. Thou wilt prolong the king's life: and his
years as many generations. —Psalm 61:5–6

Signs are important in our lives. They are visible representations of invisible realities. Take the sign away, and those walking past the house will not know that it is for sale. Drive eastward on a one-way street whose sign, indicating that traffic may only go westward, has been taken away, and you may get into a serious accident.

So there are signs that we are safe in God's care on the Rock that is higher than we are. There are signs that we are going to dwell with God in a most blessed life, signs that we have been born again and that we most assuredly do have a new life given to us by God in his grace.

David speaks of such a sign in Psalm 61:5–6 when he writes: "For thou, O God, hast heard my vows: thou hast given me the heritage of those that fear thy name. Thou wilt prolong the king's life: and his years as many generations." Here David gives the reason for what he had said in the preceding verse, namely, that he would dwell in God's house forever, because he was safe under the shadow and shelter of God's wings. God is his tower and shelter from all his enemies. And according to verse 8, his vow is to praise God's name. That God has enabled him to make that vow, and that he has given him the heritage, or inheritance, which Christ earned for his elect children, are signs that we will abide in God's house with all its blessings.

We sing it thus:

> For Thou, O God, my vows hast heard,
> On me the heritage conferred
> Of those that fear Thy Name;
> A blest anointing Thou dost give,
> And Thou wilt ever make me live
> Thy praises to proclaim.

Yes, today we also have signs from God. He made us fear his name, that is, believe in him and his Son. This is a sign that we have been born again; and that in turn is a sign that we will inherit the kingdom the death of his Son realized for us.

Do you find those signs in your life? Do you find that new life that makes you desire to praise God? In it he is speaking to you and telling you that what he says in his word in all its promises are his word to you.

Read: 1 John 5
Psalter versification: 159:3

DIVINELY FORMED FOR DIVINE PRAISES

He shall abide before God for ever: O prepare mercy and truth, which may preserve him. So will I sing praise unto thy name for ever, that I may daily perform my vows. —Psalm 61:7–8

On Mars Hill the apostle Paul stated the profound truth that in God "we live and move and have our being" (Acts 17:28). That is true of every creature that lives and moves, but also of the inanimate creatures. They also have all their being in God.

Although there are those who deny that all our spiritual living, moving, and being is in God, so it surely is. We do nothing spiritually good unless God gives us a new life with its strength. God does not invite spiritually dead men to "accept" Christ. A dead tree cannot bring forth fruit, and a spiritually dead person cannot want salvation.

Listen to what David says in Psalm 61:7–8, "He shall abide before God for ever: O prepare mercy and truth, which may preserve him. So will I sing praise unto thy name for ever, that I may daily perform my vows."

David had prophetically spoken of Christ, who in the line of David's descendants would become the everlasting king. And it is in God's mercy and truth in Christ that we receive life, strength, and spiritual existence, so that we not only vow but keep the vows of praising God's name.

Praise is important. God said in Isaiah 43:21, "This people have I formed for myself; they shall shew forth my praise." We were made and saved so that God may be praised. And it all is God's work upon us. He does not foolishly wait for dead men to decide whether they want to be saved.

If there is anything about which we ought to praise God, it is that our salvation is one hundred percent his work in us. From the desire for it to the full enjoyment in the new Jerusalem, it is God's work that gives us all this. He makes us sing with joy in our souls:

> Before Thy face shall I abide;
> O God, Thy truth and grace provide
> To guard me in the way;
> So I will make Thy praises known,
> And, humbly bending at Thy throne,
> My vows will daily pay.

Praise him then as the one in whom you live and move and have all your spiritual being.

Read: Ephesians 2
Psalter versification: 159:4

AWESOME AND PROFOUND RESPECT

The LORD reigneth; let the people tremble: he sitteth between the cherubims; let the earth be moved. The LORD is great in Zion; and he is high above all the people. Let them praise thy great and terrible name; for it is holy. —Psalm 99:1–3

The tendency today is to bring God down from his exalted position as creator and king over all creatures and make him on a level with us. We show respect to our judges and address them as "Your Honor." The man appointed to preside over a meeting we call "Mr. Chairman," but the King over all kings, the supreme and glorious God, men want to address as though he were a human friend. Our English language has the pronouns *thee* and *thou*, which we can reserve for God as one far above us. But men want to address him as though he is on our level.

We do well to consider what he himself wrote through the psalmist in Psalm 99:1–3. Listen to this: "The LORD reigneth; let the people tremble: he sitteth between the cherubims; let the earth be moved. The LORD is great in Zion; and he is high above all the people. Let them praise thy great and terrible name; for it is holy." This ought to fill us with reverence and awe and warn us to speak of him and to him with profound respect and not as we do to each other.

Let us remember those cherubim that guarded the way to the tree of life after man fell, when he attempted to climb up to God and decide for himself what was good and evil for man. God dwelt behind the veil in the temple and might not be approached as a man in man's ways.

Yes, those cherubim stood on the mercy seat of the ark, and on it the blood of Christ was symbolically sprinkled. But should not that fact raise and not lower God in our estimation? What lofty love does that not display? Sing solemnly with profound respect:

God is King forever: let the nations tremble;
Throned above the cherubim, by all the earth adored;
He is great in Zion, high above all peoples;
Praise Him with fear, for holy is the Lord.

You cannot show the Holy One too much respect and love. The very way in which we approach him should be one of praise and acknowledgment of the fact that he is holy, that is, set apart and above all creatures. Bow your head in prayer but also your soul before the exalted God.

Read: Psalm 99
Psalter versification: 266:1

WORSHIPING GOD AT HIS FOOTSTOOL

The king's strength also loveth judgment; thou dost establish equity, thou executest judgment and righteousness in Jacob. Exalt ye the Lord our God, and worship at his footstool; for he is holy. —Psalm 99:4–5

Satan, the father of the lie, told Eve, and through her told Adam, that God is a liar. He told them that if they would disobey God, they would not die as God had said but would become like him, knowing that which is good for them and evil unto them. But how different is that which God says through the psalmist in Psalm 99:4–5, where we read: "The king's strength also loveth judgment; thou dost establish equity, thou executest judgment and righteousness in Jacob. Exalt ye the Lord our God, and worship at his footstool; for he is holy."

Instead of saying the truth about God, Satan made man believe that he can be God's equal. He denied the whole truth wherewith the psalmist began this psalm, namely, that God reigns and is high above us.

And do not ever forget that every time we sin, we say by that act that we know better than he does what is good and what is evil for us, that we are above God and need not bow before him and his will. We say that in every sin we commit.

How important it is that we listen to God and not to the devil and our flesh. How important that we sing:

Merciful as mighty, He delights in justice,
For He reigns in righteousness and rules in equity;
Worship and exalt Him, bowing down before Him,
Perfect in pow'r and holiness is He.

God reigns over all that which he made, and he judges all men and angels in strict justice. He does not waver to any degree at any time. We are going to have to take hold of that truth, if we are going to understand and appreciate what he did for us in his Son. Because he loves strict justice, he sent his Son to suffer our punishment and to fulfill the law for us.

What a calling we have then to humble ourselves at his feet and to worship him as one who is high above us. We must look up to him, for we are at his feet in his grace.

Read: Revelation 4
Psalter versification: 266:2

EXALTING THE LORD OUR GOD

Exalt the LORD our God, and worship at his holy hill; for the LORD
our God is holy. —Psalm 99:9

A word or phrase may be repeated for emphasis. That word or phrase may also be repeated in order to help us remember it. Both of these are true concerning the phrase in Psalm 99:3, namely, "for it is holy," referring to God's name; in verse 5 stating "for he is holy"; and in verse 9, where we read: "For the LORD our God is holy."

This last time the psalmist says this in connection with the truth that God answered the holy men of old, who called on him, and forgave their sins (vv. 6–8). Now, that he is holy means that he is set apart, he is in a class by himself. Not only is he cut off from all sin, but he and he only is God.

In what way does forgiving the sins of those that call upon him make him holy? In the sense that he is the only one who can do that, and that he did it in the holy way of sending his own Son to suffer our punishment and be raised as our head, and through him conquered death and the grave. In our salvation, as well as being the sovereign God who rules all things, and in righteous judgment establishes equity, he is in a class by himself, the highly exalted and only God.

Our versification sings it thus:

Holy men of old in Him alone confided;
He forgave their sins, although they felt His chast'ning rod;
In His holy temple worship and adore Him,
Faithful and holy is the Lord our God.

You may notice that in verse 9 we are called to worship him "at his holy hill." That means at his temple. And that temple was built on a hill in Jerusalem. This was not incidental or accidental but by the design of God. He is high above all creation. His typical dwelling place must also be a place to which we ascend. And when we are told to exalt him, the idea is that in our minds we are to see him as the sovereign God who is high above all things and worthy of the highest praise and worship. Look up then to him and worship him as God alone and our only hope of salvation.

Read: Exodus 15:1–19
Psalter versification: 266:3

ENLIGHTENED BY GOD'S WORD

Thy testimonies are wonderful: therefore doth my soul keep them. The entrance of thy words giveth light; it giveth understanding unto the simple. —Psalm 119:129–130

There is a great deal that we understand; and the older we get, the more we understand the things around us. But that which above all we should understand, we by nature do not even want to hear about, much less understand.

Man must not only know but understand why he was created and what his calling is before God, who made him and continues to give him every heartbeat. Man must know and understand that he was created for the glory of God (Isa. 43:21) and walk in love for him so that, with all he comes in contact with, he can praise and glorify God.

This explains the psalmist's words in Psalm 119:129–130, where we read: "Thy testimonies are wonderful: therefore doth my soul keep them. The entrance of thy words giveth light; it giveth understanding unto the simple."

Truly he who understands his calling will say with the psalmist that God's testimonies are wonderful. Satan led man to believe that they were bad for man. After man succumbed to that lie and fell into the darkness of sin, God's words bring light when these words enter not simply the fleshly mind but into the soul. If they do that, we will be very understanding people.

Listen to how our Psalter versification states it:

> Thy wondrous testimonies, Lord,
> My soul will keep and greatly praise;
> Thy word, by faithful lips proclaimed,
> To simplest minds the truth conveys.

Never mind college and university degrees and praise of men. Strive to be a man or woman of spiritual understanding, and go where by faithful lips God's word is proclaimed. Live very close to the word of God. Then you will understand not only what your calling is but also how desperately you are in need of Christ and his blood. Only in that way will you understand what he accomplished for you and what it is to which he will one day bring you.

How much of that word of God do you read every day? That will show how sincerely you, too, can call God's law wonderful.

Read: Psalm 119:129–144
Psalter versification: 337:1

October 15

LONGING FOR A SANCTIFIED WALK

I opened my mouth, and panted: for I longed for thy commandments. Look thou upon me, and be merciful unto me, as thou usest to do unto those that love thy name. —Psalm 119:131–132

One thing that we will learn when we understand God's law is how far short we come as far as keeping it is concerned. In fact, in the measure that we understand God's testimonies, we will with the psalmist say: "I opened my mouth, and panted: for I longed for thy commandments. Look thou upon me, and be merciful unto me, as thou usest to do unto those that love thy name" (Ps. 119:131–132). For to open one's mouth and pant is to strive to obtain an essential of life, namely, oxygen. It is feeling the serious need for it.

So the child of God, who loves God's name, that is, loves God as he truly is and is revealed in his word, will gasp for mercy when he understands what God's law requires. For that he longs for God's commandments means that he longs to be able to keep those commandments because he loves God and considers his testimonies to be wonderful.

Surely we need God's mercy, because we fall so far short of our calling. When we understand God's law, we understand the punishment which we deserve for not keeping it. We understand how much we walk in hatred toward God rather than in love to him. We understand that what we formerly called little sins, or perhaps mistakes rather than sins, were desperately wicked deeds in God's eyes, works of hatred. The more we understand God's law, the more the light of that law will expose the blackness of our souls and need for God's mercy to save us.

There is, however, more to remember. We need God's grace to supply us with strength to keep his law. In fact, the word the psalmist uses is better translated as *grace* instead of *mercy*. It takes God's grace, and it was in God's grace that he came to fallen Adam and Eve, who were trying to hide their sin by their own works, to assure them that he would put enmity in them against Satan and sin. In his grace he was going to make them love his name.

Let us with the psalmist then sing:

> I thirst for Thy commandments, Lord,
> And for Thy mercy press my claim;
> O look on me, and show the grace
> Displayed to all who love Thy Name.

Read: Psalm 42
Psalter versification: 337:2

A SMILE FOR THOSE IN TEARS

Make thy face to shine upon thy servant; and teach me thy statutes. Rivers of waters run down mine eyes, because they keep not thy law. —Psalm 119:135–136

Some years ago, signs were displayed in public places that read: "Smile—God Loves You." And indeed, there are times when we do not smile with the assurance that God is smiling down upon us. The psalmist in Psalm 119:135 expresses it this way: "Make thy face to shine upon thy servant; and teach me thy statutes." Now, the shining of God's face is the displaying of his love. And plainly the psalmist was eager to have an assurance of God's love upon him.

But surely we err if we say that God loves everybody who reads that sign. If that were the case, would he not save everybody? If someone you love is attempting to commit suicide, would you let him do so, if you had it in your power to stop him? Can the sinner prevent the almighty God from saving him from going to the lake of fire? Can the sinner change the unchangeable God and stop his love?

No, his love makes them so that, as we read in verse 136: "Rivers of waters run down mine eyes, because they keep not thy law." There you have the evidence that God's face shines on you. You know God loves you when he works such tears in your eyes. And did you notice that after the psalmist prayed for God's face to shine on him, he added: "And teach me thy statutes"? The reason for this is that God loves those only who keep his statutes. He does not love them because they keep his law, even though he loves them when and while they keep it. No, he loved them eternally in Christ.

In fact, we keep God's law because he loves us. His love makes rivers of water run down our eyes when we witness sin. Therefore, we pray that he will teach us his statutes. Having that knowledge, we know that his face is in Christ shining down upon us. Those to whose eyes tears come because they see sin, including their own sins, can smile, assured that God loves them.

Sing that truth then in this Psalter versification:

O make Thy face to shine on me,
And teach me all Thy laws to keep;
Because Thy statutes are despised,
With overwhelming grief I weep.

Read: Luke 18:1–14
Psalter versification: 337:4

OUR EVERLASTING DWELLING PLACE

Lord, thou hast been our dwelling place in all generations. Before the mountains were brought forth, or ever thou hadst formed the earth and the world, even from everlasting to everlasting, thou art God. —Psalm 90:1–2

What Moses wrote in Psalm 90:1–2 might seem strange to us. There he wrote: "Lord, thou hast been our dwelling place in all generations. Before the mountains were brought forth, or ever thou hadst formed the earth and the world, even from everlasting to everlasting, thou art God."

That last part we can understand, namely, that he is God. But that he is our dwelling place is something else. Had he written, as David did in Psalm 46:1, "God is our refuge and strength," we would say that he presents an important truth. But God is our dwelling place? Is that not an insult? Moses wrote these words when the Israelites were dwelling in tents. God is a tent? He is a dwelling place that wears out and cannot stand the winds and hail of the storms?

No, God himself inspired Moses to write this, and it is a praiseworthy statement. The idea is that in him we have our life and its comforts. As Paul said, according to Acts 17:28, "In him we live, and move, and have our being." Apart from him there is no life and no existence. As Moses writes in verse 2 of Psalm 90, God existed before any creature was brought forth. From everlasting he is God.

Take note of the fact that he is *God*. He is not a creature, but the creator of all things. Our dwelling places were made by men, whether they are tents or houses of wood and stone. But God as our dwelling place is eternal, living before there were any mountains or trees, and before there was an earth and a world.

This means that he needs nothing that is outside of himself, and that all that which we need comes from him. As his children we have an endless store of blessings. All our spiritual life as well as our physical existence comes from him and through his Son. The forgiveness of our sins and life everlasting comes from him.

With confidence we may sing:

Lord, Thou hast been our dwelling place
Through all the ages of our race;
Before the mountains had their birth,
Or ever Thou hadst formed the earth,
From everlasting Thou art God,
To everlasting our abode.

Read: Psalm 90
Psalter versification: 245:1

A RETURN TO THE DUST

Thou turnest man to destruction; and sayest, Return, ye children of men. —Psalm 90:3

Sooner or later we are going to die. This is so because it pleases God to reach down and cause it to happen. Through Moses he declares in Psalm 90:3, "Thou turnest man to destruction; and sayest, Return, ye children of men." And by *return* he means *return to the dust out of which man was created.*

A versification of Psalm 39:4–5 states that truth this way:

> My end, Lord, make me know,
> My days, how soon they fail;
> And to my thoughtful spirit show
> How weak I am and frail.
> To Thy eternal thought
> My days are but a span;
> To Thee my years appear as nought,
> A breath at best is man.

We do well to take note of the fact that God commands death to overtake us. Men will at times pray God to prevent death that threatens a loved one. But the correct view is that rather than overruling death, God sends it and commands it to come to us. Death is not something against which he must work. It is a tool with which he works. And as the sovereign God that he is, he has a right to send it to destroy our earthly bodies. He had that right before we fell. He surely has it now since we fell into sin. He told us that the day we sinned we would die. And as the holy, sovereign God, he may return us to the dust.

But always we should look at all God's works in the light of the death of his own Son, who died as our covenant head and representative. The souls of those not chosen in him are plunged into everlasting torment. What happens to their bodies at the moment of death is minor compared with what happens when Christ returns. But those for whose sins Christ died have, the moment that their bodies enter death, in their souls everlasting blessedness and joy with Christ.

They can expect their bodies to be raised and brought back to life. This time it will be a body more glorious than Adam's was. With that in mind God says to the believer's body: "Return to the dust!" For he intends to say to it pretty soon: "Be glorified with the glory of my Son!"

Read: Ecclesiastes 12
Psalter versification: 105:4–5

MAN'S MOMENTARY LIFE ON EARTH

For a thousand years in thy sight are but as yesterday when it is past, and as a watch in the night. —Psalm 90:4

All men are aware of the fact that one by one we all return to the dust from whence man came. Not all men, however, confess what Moses wrote concerning God in Psalm 90:4, namely: "For a thousand years in thy sight are but as yesterday when it is past, and as a watch in the night." Few there are who are with Moses ready to say of those who die: "Thou carriest them away as with a flood; they are as a sleep: in the morning they are like grass which groweth up. In the morning it flourisheth, and groweth up; in the evening it is cut down, and withereth" (vv. 5–6).

Yes, they will agree that life is short, and that the last years of life are not at all like the early or midlife years. But holding on to their foolish evolutionistic idea of how man came into being, they do not subscribe to the truth that there is a God who made man and carries him away as with a flood.

But here is a truth we had better believe and sing:

> Man soon yields up his fleeting breath
> Before the swelling tide of death;
> Like transient sleep his seasons pass,
> His life is like the tender grass,
> Luxuriant 'neath the morning sun,
> And withered ere the day is done.

Let us maintain that tremendous contrast made by Moses. Man's life is very short, while God's has no beginning or end. Man's life is like a drop of water in the vast Pacific Ocean of God's life. And that is true even of Methuselah, who almost reached a thousand years, dying when he was 969 years old. Appreciate then the fact that God's love for his people is as infinite as his being. It also has no beginning or end. And because Christ is the eternal Son in that triune God, he can and did give us victory over death and everlasting life and glory.

Read: 1 Corinthians 15:41–58
Psalter versification: 245:3

VISITED IN HOLY WRATH

For we are consumed by thine anger, and by thy wrath are we troubled. Thou
has set our iniquities before thee, our secret sins in the light of thy countenance.
For all our days are passed away in thy wrath: we spend our years as a
tale that is told. —Psalm 90:7–9

Some people die of cancer and others of heart attacks. Some are killed in an automobile accident or plane crash. Or it may be a fire or storm, to mention only a few possibilities. But we do well to remember that all these are secondary causes. They are the way in which God brings death because of the primary reason, namely sin, which moves God to anger and wrath. Listen to what he says through Moses in Psalm 90:7–9, "For we are consumed by thine anger, and by thy wrath are we troubled. Thou hast set our iniquities before thee, our secret sins in the light of thy countenance. For all our days are passed away in thy wrath; we spend our years as a tale that is told."

To help us commit this truth to memory, sing this versification:

Man in Thy anger is consumed,
And unto grief and sorrow doomed;
Before Thy clear and searching sight
Our secret sins are brought to light;
Beneath Thy wrath we pine and die,
Our life expiring like a sigh.

Let us bear that in mind. Not only death, but all our sicknesses and diseases, all our losses and tears, are here because of sin. Through them God is speaking to us.

Yes, he loves us, and his wrath and anger do not stem from hatred toward those whom he chose in Christ. Them he loves. We ought to keep two truths in mind. In his grace he uses these trials to bring us out from under the curse and into the new Jerusalem with all his blessings and glory.

What is more, in all these miseries and sorrows here below, he in love is teaching us. With death and all that leads up to it, he is chastening his people. He chastens us to bring us out of our sinful walk to a walk of righteousness (Heb. 12:9–11). What is more, this suffering and death, which is punishment in the sense of chastisement, make us aware not only of what we deserve, but also how undeserving we are of his blessings. All these underscore the truth that we are saved by grace and not by our works. They help to make us appreciate Christ's suffering and death in our stead.

Read: Hebrews 12:1–13
Psalter versification: 245:4

KNOWING THE POWER OF GOD'S WRATH

The days of our years are threescore years and ten; and if by reason of strength they be fourscore years, yet is their strength labour and sorrow; for it is soon cut off, and we fly away. Who knoweth the power of thine anger? even according to thy fear, so is thy wrath. —Psalm 90:10–11

There were times when men lived to be hundreds of years old. Adam was 930 years old when he died. Methuselah reached 969, and Noah died when he was 950 years old. But after the flood, things changed quickly. Abraham did live until he was 175 years old, and Moses, even though he lived to be 120 years old, spoke the truth when in Psalm 90 he said: "The days of our years are threescore years and ten; and if by reason of strength they be fourscore years, yet is their strength labour and sorrow; for it is soon cut off, and we fly away" (v. 10).

But the question Moses then asks is an important one. In verse 11 he asks: "Who knoweth the power of thine anger? even according to thy fear, so is thy wrath." We do well to note that the words *so is* are in italics, which means that they do not appear in the original Hebrew. A better translation is: "Who knoweth the fierceness of thy anger and thy wrath according to thy fear?" The idea is that those who fear God, that is, have faith in him, are aware of the fierceness of his wrath and can know the power of it and of God's anger.

The unbelievers die, and sometimes take their own lives, without fear because they do not believe that there is a God whom they will face, and to whom they must give answer for all their deeds. They think that death is relief and ends all their miseries, rather than that by the power of God they will have to face awful, unending misery in the lake of fire. Therefore, they continue in their sins and add to the punishment they are going to suffer.

No, we must know the power of God's wrath; and we ought to sing:

> For threescore years and ten we wait,
> Or fourscore years if strength be great;
> But grief and toil attend life's day,
> And soon our spirits fly away;
> O who with true and rev'rent thought
> Can fear Thy anger as he ought?

What folly the unbeliever displays! Stand in awe before that power.

Read: Psalm 39
Psalter versification: 245:5

October 22

A WISE PRAYER

So teach us to number our days, that we may apply
our hearts unto wisdom. —Psalm 90:12

In the eyes of the world we seem foolish, because we deny ourselves so many pleasures that they seek and enjoy. They shake their heads when on the Sabbath we go to God's house to sing his praises and to meet him in his word preached. To them life is way too short for man to cut himself off from worldly pleasures, and a good time here below should be gotten while we still can. Get out of life what you can!

However, we are not fools but wise; and they are fools. For it is God who through Moses teaches us in Psalm 90:12 to pray: "So teach us to number our days, that we may apply our hearts unto wisdom."

This is a very important prayer. We are desperately in need of being taught to number our days. No, we cannot count ahead to see how many we will still get. Nor do we need to count back to see how many we have had. But we should be taught to appreciate what a short time we have here below and be taught to live in the consciousness of the fact that this life's end means the beginning of another life. And that this one will be an everlasting life in heaven or in hell!

Our present afflictions and impending death must show us the seriousness of the end of our life. We must know and believe that our present woes point to what we deserve, and that if it were not for God's mercy in Christ, we now have a foretaste of what is coming after death. We must then also count how valuable that cross of Christ is, and how much we need it, if we are going to have the joy of life with God in heavenly glory.

Sing then this prayer as we have it versified in these words:

O teach Thou us to count our days
And set our hearts on wisdom's ways;
Turn, Lord, to us in our distress,
In pity now Thy servants bless;
Let mercy's dawn dispel our night,
And all our day with joy be bright.

In sanctified wisdom make that your daily prayer.

Read: Psalm 14
Psalter versification: 246:1

UNDERSTANDING OUR AFFLICTIONS

Let thy work appear unto thy servants, and thy
glory unto their children. —Psalm 90:16

It is not uplifting to watch men tear down an old decrepit building. It is far more interesting to see a new, well-constructed, and beautiful building rise up in its place. And Moses, having given us a picture of the house in which our souls dwell, and how God, step by step, is breaking it down, now writes this significant prayer in Psalm 90:16, "Let thy work appear unto thy servants, and thy glory unto their children." That work, according to verse 14, is the work of God in Christ. For there he wrote: "O satisfy us early with thy mercy." God's mercy is all in Christ. Apart from him there is no mercy or grace of God.

As Paul writes in 2 Corinthians 5:1, the earthly house in which we live, that is, our bodies, is being dissolved. For those outside of Christ this is in God's holy wrath. For those in Christ it is that work of God's mercy according to which he is building an everlasting and beautiful house for our souls, the new resurrected body.

Seeing that work of God during our pilgrimage here below, we still have aches and pains and ultimately death. But with the eye of faith we understand and have joy during these miseries of this life and sing:

O send the day of joy and light,
For long has been our sorrow's night;
Afflicted through the weary years,
We wait until Thy help appears;
With us and with our sons abide,
In us let God be glorified.

We can be sure that God will hear our prayers. We can be sure because he gave us the light of the face of Christ and his cross which blotted out our guilt. In his word which he moved men to write, and which all these years he preserved for us, we will see that when the "earthly house of this tabernacle" is dissolved, we will have a house not made with hands, eternal in the heavens.

And we will see the glory of God as he in Christ glorifies us. Those bodies will be made so that they can and do reflect the glory of God. That is the ultimate purpose of our salvation. Glory must be to God in the highest. Our glory must be a reflection of his glory.

Read: 2 Corinthians 5
Psalter versification: 246:2

IN GLORY ESTABLISHED

And let the beauty of the LORD our God be upon us: and establish thou the work of our hands upon us; yea, the work of our hands establish thou it. —Psalm 90:17

The temple that Solomon built was a picture of the house that God is building and wherein he will dwell. That house is his church of which Christ is the chief cornerstone (Eph. 2:20). That house will be finished the day that Christ returns. Today God is cutting, shaping, polishing, and assembling the material he is pleased to use in building this house.

This cutting, shaping, and polishing hurts. As Moses wrote in Psalm 90, we are filled with sorrow and fly away (v. 10). For to no degree are we fit to be stones in God's holy temple. By nature we are not fit even for the lowest place in that house. Our bodies with their old man of sin must therefore be returned to the dust in order to be changed. It is in his mercy that God is changing us to bring us the glad days of life with him in heavenly glory.

However, we must bear in mind that in this house we will be "lively stones," not dead, senseless, irrational beings (1 Pet. 2:5). The beauty of God is going to shine through our thinking, willing, and acting. Our speech will reflect God's glory. But our hands also will glorify God. All we do in the new Jerusalem will show forth God's glory and beauty. That is why what Moses wrote may be versified thus:

So let there be on us bestowed
The beauty of the Lord our God;
The work accomplished by our hand
Establish Thou, and make it stand;
Yea, let our hopeful labor be
Established evermore by Thee.

Moses wrote it thus: "And let the beauty of the LORD our God be upon us: and establish thou the work of our hands upon us; yea, the work of our hands establish thou it" (Ps. 90:17).

Our works are going to be made firm. All that we will do with our resurrected bodies will glorify God. All that which we will do in the new Jerusalem is going to glorify God consciously and willingly. How important it is that we make this our prayer as Moses made it his.

Read: 1 Peter 2
Psalter versification: 246:3

CALLING GOD'S COMMANDMENTS GOOD

Righteous art thou, O LORD, and upright are thy judgments. Thy testimonies that thou hast commanded are righteous and very faithful. —Psalm 119:137–138

When all goes well as far as our flesh is concerned, it is easy to say that God is good. When things go against our flesh, however, we find it difficult to thank and praise God for what has happened. There is a virtue of God that means that he is good that we find very difficult to confess, even when things go well with our flesh.

What the psalmist wrote in Psalm 119:137–138 reveals this truth. We read: "Righteous art thou, O LORD, and upright are thy judgments. Thy testimonies that thou hast commanded are righteous and very faithful."

That God is righteous means that he is good. He is ethically, morally good. There is no sin in him. And there is no sin either in his law. In fact, that law reveals how righteous he is and how faithful he is to himself. Our calling is to say by walking in his law that he is good. The minute we sin, we say that God has not given us a good law, and thus there is evil in him. When we sin, we disagree with God as to what is good for us. Then we cannot honestly sing:

O Lord, Thy perfect righteousness
Is in Thy judgments shown;
In Thy unchanging faithfulness
Thy truth Thou hast made known.

It is true that God's law is good for our neighbor. It keeps him from hurting or killing us, from stealing what is ours, and from putting us to shame. But that is not the whole picture. Our calling is to say that God's law is good for us to keep and that it serves our spiritual good.

In verse 140 the psalmist rightly called himself God's servant. That we are, and the good thing for a servant to do is to obey his master fully and always. And if the life of Christ is in us, we will see the good of God's law.

Jesus said that to the devil when he said: "Man shall not live by bread alone, but by every word that proceedeth out of the mouth of God" (Matt. 4:4). That is a good reply, and serving God is a good work.

Be careful then today so that you do not by sins say that God is not good and that you have a better idea of what is good.

Read: Psalm 119:137–152
Psalter versification: 338:1

GREATLY TROUBLED SOULS

My zeal hath consumed me, because mine enemies have forgotten thy words. Thy word is very pure: therefore thy servant loveth it. —Psalm 119:139–140

Are you jealous? Well, you should be. No, you may not be jealous of what your neighbor has. God's law, which is righteous, forbids us to covet anything the neighbor has. And the first table of the law forbids us to be jealous of God's glory.

Our calling is to want him to have all the glory. The word *zeal* in Psalm 119:139 in this sentence does mean to be jealous: "My zeal hath consumed me, because mine enemies have forgotten thy words." That the psalmist's jealousy consumed him means that the sins of the enemies destroyed his joy. And that explains why in the next verse he writes: "Thy word is very pure; therefore thy servant loveth it."

Now, jealousy is exacting, exclusive devotion, intolerant rivalry. In that sense God says in his law that he is a jealous God; and we had better not forget that. He is exclusively devoted to his own glory and has a perfect right to be so devoted, for he is God, and there is no God besides him. The psalmist's zeal or jealousy is his exclusive devotion to God's glorification. Therefore, seeing his enemies forgetting God's law takes from him all his joy. For he loves God. That he loves God is plain from the fact that he loves his word. You cannot love God and not love his law or word.

Whether we believe that God is righteous and that his law is upright will manifest itself in how much we are bothered, and our joy is taken away, when we see God's law broken. If we are greatly disturbed, we will sing these words:

Because Thy foes forget Thy law
My soul is greatly stirred;
Thy servant loves the purity
Of Thy most holy word.

Now, if the psalmist was touched that way in his day, what ought to be the case with us today? Sin has developed tremendously. And soon the "man of sin" will appear (2 Thess. 2:3).

Search your soul today. Do all the sins both of the first and second table of God's law bother you? Stand before the mirror of God's law to see whether you love him and sin troubles your soul.

Read: Romans 7
Psalter versification: 338:2

AN HONORABLE HUMILIATION

I am small and despised: yet do not I forget thy precepts. Thy righteousness is an everlasting righteousness, and thy law is the truth. —Psalm 119:141–142

Because we are inclined to forget that which does not interest us, we need to have certain things repeated. But even when we have not forgotten a truth, there are times when it needs to be stated again for emphasis. That is what the psalmist does in Psalm 119:142.

He had in verse 138 written that God's testimonies are righteous and faithful. In verse 140 he wrote that God's word is very pure. And now in verse 142 he states: "Thy righteousness is an everlasting righteousness, and thy law is the truth." To that we had better hold on with both hands. God's law is truth, is pure and ever faithful.

If by God's grace you believe this and live according to that law of God, you can depend upon it that what he wrote in verse 141 will be true of you. He wrote: "I am small and despised: yet do not I forget thy precepts."

That word *small* has the idea of being humiliated. If we keep that word, as we find in the KJV, we must understand it as meaning that in the eyes of the unbelievers he is insignificant, a man they look down upon and therefore despise. Our versification has it thus:

> Tho' I am humble and despised,
> I strive Thy will to do;
> Eternal is Thy righteousness,
> And all Thy law is true.

The question for us is whether that is the world's opinion of us. If we do not forget God's law and do walk in it before the world, we are going to be looked down upon as fools and despised as troublemakers. The question is whether we are eager to be extolled by the world or to be pleasing in God's sight. It is a case of either-or.

When humiliation and being despised because you walk in love before God is your lot, you have reason to rejoice. If this is not the case, you must in love be rebuked.

Our Savior was laughed at and hung in shame upon his cross because he loved God and his law. He was despised and spit upon, taunted and mocked. If you are born again with his life, you can expect ridicule and shame, but also when he returns, elevation and honor before God.

Read: Isaiah 53
Psalter versification: 338:3

October 28

UNDERSTANDING GOD'S TESTIMONIES

Trouble and anguish have taken hold on me: yet thy commandments are my delights. The righteousness of thy testimonies is everlasting: give me understanding, and I shall live. —Psalm 119:143–144

If the world looks down on you and despises you because you love God's commandments and show this before their eyes, you may be sure that you are going to be troubled and have anguish. The psalmist experienced this and wrote in Psalm 119:143, "Trouble and anguish have taken hold on me: yet thy commandments are my delights." One of the reasons why we have it so good for our flesh is that we do not show our faith in God as clearly as we should.

Ask yourself how often and clearly your light shone yesterday before the world. Can the world tell by your speech and by your dress, by your actions and by what you refuse to do, that God's commandments are your delight? It is not simply a question of what you do outwardly. But do you delight in God's law?

There surely is much room for us and great need that we pray with the psalmist: "Give me understanding, and I shall live" (Ps. 119:144). For we must understand what the law of God means and requires of us in every circumstance of life. There is no denying the fact that our lives today are so much more complicated than they were in the days of the psalmist. With magazines and books, radio and television, automobiles and airplanes we can do so much more, and the world is so much closer to us.

So much that is called Christian today is actually antichristian. So much is allowed by churches that was rightfully called sin in ages gone by and by those who did indeed delight in God's law. We do indeed need to pray for understanding. Well may we sing:

Delight amid distress and pain
Do Thy commandments give;
Thy word is righteous evermore,
Teach me that I may live.

The idea is that we live when we walk in God's holy law. Any works outside God's law are acts of spiritual death. And if we live in God's law now in this life, we have the assurance that we will have everlasting life in the kingdom of heaven when Christ returns. All our enemies will be far removed from us forever.

Read: 2 Corinthians 6
Psalter versification: 338:4

A CRY FOR HELP

I cried with my whole heart; hear me, O LORD: I will keep thy statutes. I cried unto thee; save me, and I shall keep thy testimonies. —Psalm 119:145–146

The truth we must hold on to with all our might is the teaching of Scripture that salvation from beginning to end, in every part, and from every point of view, is God's work. That we must be saved means that even the desire for salvation is God's gift to us. We do not save ourselves from the lack of desire. No man can make us change our minds about salvation. God will have to do that. If we desire it, that is because God wrought the desire in us and gave us the life to do so.

Scripture teaches us this in the words of the psalmist in Psalm 119:145–146, "I cried with my whole heart; hear me, O LORD: I will keep thy statutes. I cried unto thee; save me, and I shall keep thy testimonies." Or as we may sing this truth:

> O Lord, my earnest cry
> Thy list'ning ear has heard;
> With Thy salvation answer me,
> And I will keep Thy word.

Did you notice that the psalmist states that if God saves him, he will keep his testimonies? The reason for this is that God said to Adam that the day he sinned he would die. He did die spiritually that day, and every one of his descendants comes into this world spiritually dead (Eph. 2:1). God must begin salvation by implanting in us that seed of a new life, if there is going to be any salvation from the love of sin and the desire to serve God.

It is important that we keep this in mind. We are often ridiculed, looked down upon, and despised for teaching this truth. But that is what God teaches.

Always we need God's help for our salvation, as surely as we need his power to keep our hearts beating. Only God can make alive what has died.

Every morning then pray that God will save you from sinning against him in the day that lies ahead of you. Cry with your whole heart as the psalmist did. And when you do, be sure to thank him for working that desire for salvation and its holy walk in you. He gives you the strength and desire to make this your prayer.

Read: Psalm 119:145–160
Psalter versification: 339:1

TIME FOR THE THINGS SPIRITUAL

I prevented the dawning of the morning, and cried: I hoped in thy word. Mine eyes prevent the night watches, that I might meditate in thy word. —Psalm 119:147–148

As time passes by, words obtain new meanings. When the queen of Sheba came to visit Solomon, we read in 1 Kings 10:2, "And she came to Jerusalem with a very great train." Surely what we call a train today is quite different. So the word *prevent*, as used in Scripture, has a different meaning from what we have in mind when we use it today. To prevent, for us, is to keep from happening. In Scripture it has the meaning of the two words from which it comes, namely *before* and *come*.

Thus when in Psalm 119:147–148 we read, "I prevented the dawning of the morning, and cried: I hoped in thy word. Mine eyes prevent the night watches, that I might meditate in thy word," a better translation would be, "I came before the dawning of the morning and cried: I hoped in thy word. Mine eyes came before the night watches to meditate in thy word." The idea is that he filled the day as fully as he could in meditating in God's word and praying for understanding of God's law. Our versification has it thus:

> At early dawn I prayed,
> Thy promises my trust;
> At night I thought upon Thy word,
> Most holy and most just.

What an example he sets here for us! In serious illnesses and when dangers arise, we will pray. We may ask God to bless our food before we eat it and afterward give thanks to him for it. But how often do we pray for a clearer understanding of what his law requires of us and what our duty is in the particular present situation in which we find ourselves?

We think that physical exercises are important for our bodies. There are times when we are convinced that we should have a vacation so that we can get from under the strain. But do we consider reading and studying God's word important? Do we want to see Christ and his blessings more richly? Is our newspaper and are our newscasts more important than God's word? Do we spend as much time with God's word as with books and magazines?

Truly we have a great deal to learn from the psalmist.

Read: Matthew 6:19–34
Psalter versification: 339:2

A PRAYER FOR NEEDFUL QUICKENING

They draw nigh that follow after mischief: they are far from thy law. Thou art near, O LORD; and all thy commandments are truth. —Psalm 119:150–151

As the saying goes: "Forewarned is forearmed." If we know that the enemy is planning to attack us, we can get ready to defend ourselves and will not be caught by surprise. And the more we know about the enemy and his plans, the better we can prepare.

For us today, forewarned means that we are made aware of the fact that Satan intends to attack us through the antichrist. In fact, it means that we are aware that already there are "many antichrists" (1 John 2:18), even though he has not come yet in his last and most dreadful form. We do have a description of him in Psalm 119:150, where we read: "They draw nigh that follow after mischief: they are far from thy law."

The word *mischief* means crafty, deceitful. And much there is today that calls itself Christian but is antichristian and is against Christ and his church. They come with teachings that corrupt the truth about Christ and why he came. They are far from God's law.

We need to know the way to be protected against them. As the psalmist did, so must we cry out: "Hear my voice according unto thy lovingkindness: O LORD, quicken me according to thy judgment" (Ps. 119:149). For our only hope and only protection is God in his only begotten Son. We need to be quickened, that is, be kept spiritually alive and active. And God must perform this work upon us. He is our defense and our strength.

It is important that we remember that all our spiritual life comes from God in his loving-kindness, that is, in Christ and through his cross and Spirit. He implants a new life, but he must also keep it there and make it active. We must then pray for a needful quickening so that we continue to fight the good fight of faith.

Our flesh wants to stop to escape ridicule, hardships, and persecution. We like to lay down our spiritual life for the advantage of our natural life. But be wise and follow the psalmist's example.

Pray and sing these words:

> O hear me in Thy grace,
> In mercy quicken me;
> The wicked plan to do me harm,
> But they are far from Thee.

Read: Psalm 144
Psalter versification: 339:3

LIVING IN GOD'S LAW

Thou art near, O LORD; and all thy commandments are truth. —Psalm 119:151

How frustrating and frightening it would be if a loved one has been seriously injured, and we cannot contact a doctor, ambulance, or hospital because the phone has been made useless by the storm. How much more disappointing and frightening it would be if we try to call upon God for help, and he cannot hear us because we are too far away from him.

That, of course, can never happen, because he is the everywhere-present God who is in every atom of every creature, and in his mercy and grace is in every one of his born-again children.

Of this the psalmist speaks when in Psalm 119:151 he says: "Thou art near, O LORD; and all thy commandments are truth." This he had written after stating in this section of the psalm, "I cried with my whole heart…I cried unto thee; save me" (vv. 145–146), and, "Hear my voice according unto thy lovingkindness" (v. 149).

But he had also written about his enemies that they deny God and his law. They follow mischief and are far from his law (v. 150). Thus they maintain that God does not exist and that therefore his laws are nonsense. If there is no God, why keep the law which we claim he made? But the psalmist confesses in verse 152: "Concerning thy testimonies, I have known of old that thou hast founded them for ever."

That we do well to keep in mind. God not only hears our cries, but his commandments are very real. We were created in them. They were not added to us after we were made. As a fish cannot live outside of the water, so we cannot live outside of God's law wherein we were created. Outside of that law is death for man. God's commandments very really and assuredly are truth. Let no enemy of God ever make you believe otherwise. The enemies who follow after mischief, that is, after deceit, trickery, are fools. They are far from God's law; and God's law is the only place wherein man can live. Sing this truth:

Thou, Lord, art near to me,
And true are Thy commands;
Of old Thy testimonies show
Thy truth eternal stands.

Read: Psalm 19
Psalter versification: 339:4

PRAYERS OF PRAISE

Praise waiteth for thee, O God, in Sion: and unto thee shall the vow be performed. O thou that hearest prayer, unto thee shall all flesh come. —Psalm 65:1–2

One lesson we all learned from childhood onward is that there are so many things for which we have to wait. We have to wait for the sun to rise, for our meals to be prepared, for the water to boil, a friend to arrive, the rain to stop, to mention only a few of these things. And all this ought to teach us how great our God is. For he waits for nothing but realizes on time all things according to his eternal counsel or plan. Nothing stops him or delays what he wants.

When then in Psalm 65:1–2 we read: "Praise waiteth for thee, O God, in Sion: and…unto thee shall all flesh come," we should note that David speaks here of God's praise waiting, not God waiting for that praise. That word *waiteth* means literally "to be silent." And that praise is silent means it serves God. In that day the servant was silent waiting to hear the instructions from his master as to what he must do. He did this to serve his master fully. So God's praise serves him (Isa. 43:21).

Notice that God's praise waits in Zion. Zion here means God's church as that church is ruled by Christ its glorified head. For Zion was the hill in Jerusalem where David's throne was set. It was a picture of Christ at God's right hand ruling all things as head of his church, so that the praise of God flows forth constantly.

For us today that praise flows forth in our prayers as well as in our songs. We do well to examine our prayers to see how fully we do serve God with praise. Do we with our hearts sing?

> Praise waits in Zion, Lord, for Thee,
> And unto Thee shall vows be paid;
> O Thou that hearest those who cry,
> To Thee by all shall prayer be made.

Are your prayers merely requests for material advantages? Look at the prayer Jesus gave us and notice the literal and implied praise in it. Our praise to God must not wait until we arrive in heaven. If you belong to Zion, praise will be in your prayers today.

Read: Psalm 65
Psalter versification: 166:1

PRAISING GOD AS OUR REDEEMER

Iniquities prevail against me: as for our transgressions, thou
shalt purge them away. —Psalm 65:3

To praise someone is to proclaim his virtues. Therefore, to praise God is to confess that he is God. Higher praise to him than that, there is not. That lifts him above all creatures and explains Paul's words that "in him we live, and move, and have our being" (Acts 17:28). That praise man must render to God. And the day is coming when, as we read in Psalm 65:2, "Unto thee shall all flesh come"—that is, come with praise.

When Christ returns, Zion, the church, will praise God. But the ungodly in the lake of fire will also do so. They will then acknowledge that he is God and that they are in torment because they sinned against him. They are not going to deny him as they did in this life.

The difference between the praise of Zion and of those outside of Zion is that the believers can and do praise God for something for which the unbelievers cannot praise him. David writes in Psalm 65:3, "Iniquities prevail against me: as for our transgressions, thou shalt purge them away."

Or as we sing:

> Against us sin has battled hard;
> For help we look to Thee and pray;
> Thou our transgressions wilt forgive,
> Yea, Thou wilt take them all away.

That the ungodly can never sing. For forgiveness of their sins they can never pray or praise God from out of hell. But for those of Zion, this is a very basic work that calls for praise. Take the forgiveness of our sins away, and you take away all right to blessedness. The wages of sin is death! If those wages are not removed, death remains our lot.

We ought therefore to be Christ-minded in all our songs and prayers. Forget Christ in your prayers, and you have no reason for praising God as your savior. Forget the cross, and you forget the basic reason for Zion's praise to God. You forget what makes it possible for us to praise God in this life.

Forgiveness of our sins opens the door to all other blessings. Be sure then to praise God as your redeemer in his Son.

Read: Hebrews 7:1–22
Psalter versification: 166:2

CHOSEN UNTO HEAVENLY BLESSEDNESS

Blessed is the man whom thou choosest, and causest to approach unto thee, that he may dwell in thy courts: we shall be satisfied with the goodness of thy house, even of thy holy temple. —Psalm 65:4

Before you do a day's work, you have no right to the wages of such work. If you do the work before you were chosen as an employee in that office or factory, you have no right to ask for wages for the work which you performed.

So it is that the basic blessing we need is the forgiveness of our sins, and without it we have no right to any blessing. Christ had to do the work of suffering our punishment and of fulfilling God's law in our stead. And we had to be chosen in him.

That is why David, moved by God, wrote in Psalm 65:4, "Blessed is the man whom thou choosest, and causest to approach unto thee, that he may dwell in thy courts: we shall be satisfied with the goodness of thy house, even of thy holy temple."

It all depends on God's eternal, sovereign election. God is the one who chooses those for whom Christ will die. Christ must be the employee for this work; but we must belong to him, or his work is not for us. What David writes then means that only those are blessed whom God has chosen as the ones for whom Christ would die.

Iniquities and transgressions bring us into debt before God. When we sin we fail to perform a work of love that God demands of us. Such failure does not simply call for a withholding of a blessing, but also the suffering of an everlasting punishment to its end. Christ, the eternal Son of God, can give eternal value to a work he performs in a moment of time.

How blessed then are they who are chosen in Christ. Sing it thus:

> How blest are they whom Thou dost choose
> To come and in Thy courts abide;
> Communing in Thy holy house,
> With good we shall be satisfied.

What praise then is it not that we owe God! It all depended on him, and all the praise must be bestowed upon him.

Read: Ephesians 1
Psalter versification: 166:3

SAVED IN AWESOME RIGHTEOUSNESS

By terrible things in righteousness wilt thou answer us, O God of our salvation;
who art the confidence of all the ends of the earth, and of them that are afar
off upon the sea. —Psalm 65:5

By mighty deeds in righteousness
Prayer's answer surely comes from Thee,
O God our Saviour, God the trust
Of all Thy saints on land or sea.

Thus we sing the truth that David wrote in Psalm 65:5. He wrote: "By terrible things in righteousness wilt thou answer us, O God of our salvation; who art the confidence of all the ends of the earth, and of them that are afar off upon the sea."

Very plainly David in these words brings us to the cross of Christ. He did not see the cross itself with his fleshly eye, and neither have we done so. But with the eye of faith he saw that cross in these "terrible things in righteousness."

The word *terrible* could better be translated as terrifying. It suggests Jesus' own words: "My God, my God, why hast thou forsaken me?" (Matt. 27:46). There were at the cross three hours of terrifying darkness and awesome suffering of hellish agonies!

Through all this Jesus paid for our sins. In the righteous way of suffering our punishment and doing so in perfect love to God, Jesus earned for us the right to dwell with God in his house of glory. We can be saved only in a righteous way. Otherwise we add punishment.

Here we have another reason to praise God. He is the almighty, sovereign God and the God of love, mercy, and grace. But he is also the righteous God who will save only in the way of his justice being satisfied.

That being the case, he is the confidence of all the ends of the earth. Who could confide in one who does not meet all the requirements? God sends his Son to go all the way and completely satisfy his justice. And we can be confident that there is no suffering of punishment for our sins that we must still endure.

Praise God then for his righteousness and as the God of our salvation.

Read: Colossians 1
Psalter versification: 166:4

ALL IS WELL

Which by his strength setteth fast the mountains; being girded with power:
Which stilleth the noise of the seas, the noise of their waves, and the
tumult of the people. —Psalm 65:6–7

First things come first. Therefore, having spoken of the praise that waits for God in Zion, David mentioned the praise of God as our savior who purges away our transgressions. When our guilt is gone, we can have blessings. But woe to those whose guilt is not removed. Those things the flesh enjoys are not gifts of God's grace to them. They will misuse them and add to their guilt and punishment. They will not praise God for them, and from him will get condemnation.

But God has more virtues than his love and grace that through the cross of Christ blotted out our sins. He works in those who are made to be righteous in Christ a new spiritual life, which will also move them to praise him as the creator and sustainer of all that which he made. That is why David, having begun with the all-important work of our justification, now mentions in Psalm 65:6, "Which by his strength setteth fast the mountains; being girded with power." And then he adds in verse 7: "Which stilleth the noise of the seas, the noise of their waves, and the tumult of the people."

Here we have God praised for his strength; and our versification has it thus:

> Thy power has set the mountains firm,
> O God Almighty, girt with strength;
> At Thy command the waves are still,
> The nations cease from war at length.

God's power made these lofty peaks. His little finger stills the tempestuous sea and brings wars to their end. It all reveals so clearly that he has absolute control over all his creatures. All things serve his purpose.

Those whom he chose in Christ can rest assured that all is always well. "The Lord of hosts is with us; the God of Jacob is our refuge" (Ps. 46:7).

Praise him then as the almighty God who in love, for those whose sins he blotted out, will work all things together for their good.

Read: Psalm 46
Psalter versification: 166:5

REMEMBERING GOD'S PROVIDENTIAL CARE

Thou visitest the earth, and waterest it: thou greatly enrichest it with the
river of God, which is full of water: thou preparest them corn, when thou hast
so provided for it. —Psalm 65:9

Do you give any thought, when you sit down to eat, to what God has done to provide you with that food? We do go through the formality of thanking him for giving us our daily bread. But do you thank him for all the work he performed to get that bread and meat on your table?

The psalmist calls our attention to it in Psalm 65:9 in these words: "Thou visitest the earth, and waterest it: thou greatly enrichest it with the river of God, which is full of water: thou preparest them corn, when thou hast so provided for it."

We depend so completely and entirely upon God to bring the sun up every morning for the plants, and for the rain when it is needed. And the sad thing is that we can eat without giving any thought to God and his works of providence. We can walk through the supermarket with all its canned food, vegetable and fruit displays, bread and cakes, and fail completely to give one thought about God and to praise him as we ought. A good verse for us to commit to memory and take with us in the store, and unto the table before we eat, are these words of our versification:

Thou visitest the earth in love
And sendest showers from above,
Enriching all the land;
Thy streams exhaustless bless the field,
Preparing it the grain to yield
Provided by Thy hand.

Yes, in his love for his people God blesses the fields so that his church may have its daily bread for its physical needs.

And here is another work of God that calls for us to praise him. He is our savior and blotted out our guilt. With almighty power he upholds the whole creation which he made and rules it sovereignly. But he should be praised also for all his works of providence.

Surely praise waits for him in Zion. Those outside of Zion see trees and plants and food but have no praise for God. Those redeemed by the blood of his Son can praise him and must do so.

Praise God from whom all blessings flow,
Praise him all creatures here below.

Read: Psalm 104
Psalter versification: 169:1

CHOSEN TO PRAISE GOD

Thou waterest the ridges thereof abundantly: thou settlest the furrows thereof: thou makest it soft with showers: thou blessest the springing thereof. Thou crownest the year with thy goodness; and thy paths drop fatness. —Psalm 65:10–11

When children of God speak about spiritual matters, their faith will manifest itself. When they speak about natural things, they often sound no different from the world. They may not with the world call incidents the work of mother nature. They may not say with the unbeliever that they were "lucky" or "had bad luck." But because they do not have God in all their thoughts, they often speak in a way that renders no praise to God, even though that is our calling.

It is very revealing and instructive to notice what David wrote in Psalm 65:10–11. He wrote: "Thou waterest the ridges thereof abundantly: thou settlest the furrows thereof: thou makest it soft with showers: thou blessest the springing thereof. Thou crownest the year with thy goodness; and thy paths drop fatness."

Did you notice the emphasis upon the words *thou* and *thy*, ascribing what happens in natural life to God and his goodness? Read these verses again and put emphasis upon "thou" and "thy". The world will say: "It rains and pours outside." Or: "It is snowing again." Faith would say: "God is sending abundant rain." Or: "It pleases God to make the snow fall again." Faith will sing a versification like this:

> The furrows, sown with living grain,
> Are softened by Thy gentle rain
> The springing corn to bless;
> The year with goodness Thou dost crown,
> Rich gifts in mercy sending down
> To cheer the wilderness.

How different it all is going to be in the new Jerusalem, when all sin is rooted out of our bodies, and we are completely freed from the old man of sin. Then we are not all simply going to speak one language, regardless of what nation, tongue, or tribe we belonged to here below. But we are always in everything going to speak praises of God.

Read what Peter wrote for our instruction, but also for our comfort: "But ye are a chosen generation, a royal priesthood, an holy nation, a peculiar people; that ye should shew forth the praises of him who hath called you out of darkness into his marvellous light" (1 Pet. 2:9).

That should be manifested *now* in our life here below.

Read: 1 Peter 2
Psalter versification: 169:2

CREATION SINGS

They drop upon the pastures of the wilderness: and the little hills rejoice on every side. The pastures are clothed with flocks; the valleys also are covered over with corn; they shout for joy, they also sing. —Psalm 65:12–13

Did you ever hear little hills rejoice and valleys sing?

David did, and therefore after writing about the goodness of God wherewith he crowns the year, he wrote in Psalm 65:12–13, "They drop upon the pastures of the wilderness: and the little hills rejoice on every side. The pastures are clothed with flocks; the valleys also are covered over with corn; they shout for joy, they also sing."

Our versification explains this a bit in these words:

> The hills and vales, with verdure clad
> Are girt with joy, the earth is glad,
> New life is all abroad;
> With feeding flocks the pastures teem,
> With golden grain the valleys gleam;
> All nature praises God.

There you have it: all nature, that is, creation, praises God. Whether we hear it or not, all creation does praise God. And do we not often say that actions speak louder than words?

It does take a pair of spiritual ears to hear creation sing of God's power and wisdom. And even though this earthly creation lies under the curse, creation does sing of God's goodness. God is good. He is right in all that which he does. The way he treats every creature is good; and he never does anything that is evil. He never makes a mistake. And all creation sings, that is, manifests his goodness.

The question is whether we hear creation shout and sing God's praises. The unbeliever may hear the sound in the powerful waterfall, but he cannot distinguish the words. He does not hear it as God's power and wisdom. He sees the valleys gleam with grain but does not hear the song of God's power, wisdom, and faithfulness.

But what about you? Do you need a spiritual hearing aid? Do you see God's beauty in creation and the works of his hands? Remember that David began this psalm with the words: "Praise waiteth for thee, O God, in Sion." Are you in Zion? If you hear his praise in creation, you surely are yourself going to sing his praises loudly for salvation, as well as for all the works of his hands in creation.

Read: Psalm 148
Psalter versification: 169:3

REJOICING IN GOD'S WORD

Princes have persecuted me without a cause: but my heart standeth in awe of thy word. I rejoice at thy word, as one that findeth great spoil. —Psalm 119:161–162

To think that a thing is good is one thing. To rejoice in that thing is something else. There are times when surgery is good for us, because it will relieve a misery or even prevent death that threatens. But who rejoices in the surgery itself? The pain thereof may last for days and weeks.

The same thing is true, only in a more powerful way, when we think of God's word and his law therein. We are ready to agree that it is good that God forbids the neighbor to steal, bear false witness, and kill. But do we rejoice in that law? All our violations of both tables of the law show that we do not rejoice in that law.

The psalmist did rejoice in God's word and wrote in Psalm 119:161–162, "Princes have persecuted me without a cause: but my heart standeth in awe of thy word. I rejoice at thy word, as one that findeth great spoil." And our versification puts it this way:

> Though mighty foes assail me, Lord,
> I fear not them, but Thee;
> As boundless wealth and priceless spoil,
> Thy word rejoices me.

It is plain, is it not, that the psalmist writes this while he was in great trouble? Rulers, men in authority who had power to hurt him severely, were persecuting him. He could escape the pain and fear if he would turn from God's word. But no, he rejoices in it, and his heart stands in awe of God's word. That word he deemed valuable. His heart went out to it as a man's heart does when in a battle he obtains an abundance of gold and silver.

How much of that rejoicing in God's word do you find? Do you look forward to hearing it expounded on the sabbath day? Do you sing it with other children of God because of the words, rather than because of the music?

Do you read it thoughtfully, and does it taste better to you than the food you just ate? Do you study it and give deep thought to it? How many minutes in the day do you spend thinking about what God wrote in his word? Do you look for Christ in every chapter?

Read: Psalm 119:161–176
Psalter versification: 341:1

A LIFE THAT PRAISES GOD

I hate and abhor lying: but thy law do I love. Seven times a day do I praise thee because of thy righteous judgments. —Psalm 119:163–164

Did it ever occur to you that every time we break God's law, we tell a lie? We do. Whenever we sin, we say by that deed that we do not need to obey the God who made us in his own image with the calling to serve him with all his creation every minute of our lives.

In fact, every time we sin, we bear false witness against God. We not only tell a lie about him, but by our actions, which speak louder than words, we lie unto him, telling him that he is not God and has no right to tell us what to do.

That is why the psalmist wrote in Psalm 119:163–164, "I hate and abhor lying: but thy law do I love. Seven times a day do I praise thee because of thy righteous judgments."

Plainly, although our calling is to praise him as God, whenever we sin we say that he is not worthy of that praise. The psalmist then has a reason for linking up lying and praising God as two opposites. We are doing the one or the other and never both at the same time.

Since praising God is extolling him for his virtues, the psalmist also in these verses links up loving God's law and believing that his judgments are righteous. He praises God seven times a day because God is righteous. Whenever we sin, we by that deed say the opposite, namely, that God is not righteous, but we are. He has no right to tell us what to do. Did Adam not believe that God told a lie when he said that to sin would bring death? He found that Satan did the lying. But by his act Adam said that God was not righteous, and he did not praise him.

Strive then to keep that law of God. Pray that God may enable you to sing sincerely:

Deceit and falsehood I abhor,
But in Thy law delight;
Throughout the day I praise Thy name,
For all Thy ways are right.

The psalmist praises God seven times a day. As our versification has it, he praises God throughout the day. Our lives must be full of praise, for our lives must be full of walking in God's law even as his Son did when he came in our flesh.

Read: Psalm 147
Psalter versification: 341:2

SAFELY WALKING TO EVERLASTING PEACE

Great peace have they which love thy law: and nothing shall offend them. LORD, I have hoped for thy salvation, and done thy commandments. —Psalm 119:165-166

Picture before your mind a very, very narrow mountain path which on one side has a steep rocky wall of the mountain, and on the other side has a sharp drop-off that plunges down hundreds of feet into a pool of steaming water. How dangerous it would be to stumble while walking on that path!

The Lord assures us in Psalm 119:165–166 that he who loves God's law has no reason to fear falling into that deadly peril. Literally he wrote through the psalmist: "Great peace have they which love thy law: and nothing shall offend them. LORD, I have hoped in thy salvation, and done thy commandments."

The word *offend* here does not mean to hurt one's feelings. The Hebrew word means basically to stumble. Our versification explains it thus:

> Great peace has he who loves Thy law,
> Unmoved, he safely stands;
> For Thy salvation I have hoped
> And followed Thy commands.

Standing safely pictures the situation as the psalmist had it in mind. He was being persecuted because he loved God's law and his word. Satan was using men to try to destroy him because he loved God. They placed stones on his pathway to make him stumble to death.

But through the psalmist God assures us that he will take care of us, and we will have great peace. For we will have peace with God. Men will hate us and seek to destroy us, but God will uphold us in the battle.

It is hard to walk that narrow pathway which is also steep. God's law makes life very narrow for us as far as our flesh is concerned. But we can be absolutely sure that we will reach everlasting peace in the new Jerusalem, if we walk on that path in love to God.

God's Son was slain by the enemy because God decreed it that way to pay for our sins. When in love to God we walk our pathway, we will not stumble and fall into the lake of fire of God's holy wrath. We will be safe, because God will protect and uphold us.

Read: Daniel 2
Psalter versification: 341:3

SOULS FILLED WITH LOVE FOR GOD

My soul hath kept thy testimonies; and I love them exceedingly. I have kept thy precepts and thy testimonies: for all my ways are before thee. —Psalm 119:167–168

We walk upon a very narrow pathway and may not take one step off it to the left or right. Our hands may not take hold of everything in the world. Adam sinned when his hand reached out and took the forbidden fruit. Our eyes must turn away and our ears be stopped many times in regard to many things. David should have turned his eyes away from Bathsheba. Aaron should not have listened to the people when they called for a golden calf. James warns us against a multitude of sins committed by the tongue.

But there is something deeper than the sins we see round about us. The psalmist wrote in Psalm 119:167–168, "My soul hath kept thy testimonies; and I love them exceedingly. I have kept thy precepts and thy testimonies: for all my ways are before thee."

Notice that our souls must keep God's testimonies. For what the soul does will determine what the foot, hand, eye, ear, and tongue will do. Our souls must love God, or we will not walk in love and perform any deeds of love with our bodies. Therefore, our souls must love God's testimonies. No man can sincerely sing these words unless and until he loves God's law:

> Thy testimonies I have kept,
> They are my chief delight;
> Observant of Thy law and truth,
> I walk before Thy sight.

It does not please God for us to put up a pious front as a Pharisee. That fills him with anger. And God cannot be deceived. He knows what is in our souls. And he will judge us according to what he sees there.

What satisfies man's standards does not count. God is satisfied only when from the soul outward we have pure love for his law. Love for God must be in every atom of our being from the depth of our souls outward, to control us in all our activities.

Yea, all our ways must be before God. That means also that we perform them in the consciousness of the fact that God sees them and the soul that activates them.

Read: Matthew 6:1–18
Psalter versification: 341:4

THE WAY TO CRY FOR MERCY

Hear me when I call, O God of my righteousness: thou hast enlarged me when I was in distress; have mercy upon me, and hear my prayer. —Psalm 4:1

As the saying goes: "History repeats itself." However, this is true only in a general sense and because it pleases God to do what he did in the past. All is the execution of his eternal plan. Also in the history of the church and its members God repeats his work of mercy and grace. He is faithful and unchangeable and in his mercy and grace brings his people back from ways of sin and from ways of difficulty for their flesh to assurance of his love.

David spoke of this in Psalm 4:1 when he wrote: "Hear me when I call, O God of my righteousness: thou hast enlarged me when I was in distress; have mercy upon me, and hear my prayer." Plainly he is praying that God will repeat his work of bringing him out of difficulties, as he did in the past. He is praying that a bit of history in his life may be repeated.

What his problem was this time we are not told. But praying for enlargement reveals that he was in a tight situation. And if we live as children of God today, as we approach the days of the antichrist, we will be pressed into a corner and have a difficult time. In the measure we show our faith today, we will be ridiculed, shunned, and denied freedoms. More and more wickedness is pressing down upon the world, and there is reason for us today to sing:

> My righteous God, Who oft of old
> Hast saved from troubles manifold,
> Give answer when I call to Thee,
> Be gracious now and hear my plea.

But notice that the ground of David's prayer for mercy is the fact that he prays to the God of his righteousness. We can in our singing call him our righteous God. But our KJV brings out a truth which we must never overlook: he is the God of our righteousness. He made us righteous in Christ, and on the basis of that righteousness we may be dealt with in mercy. Remember that when you pray.

In Jesus' parable the proud Pharisee was not heard when he prayed. The publican was heard and went home justified.

Read: Luke 18:1–14
Psalter versification: 6:1

STANDING IN AWE

Stand in awe, and sin not: commune with your own heart upon your bed, and be still. Selah. —Psalm 4:4

In Psalm 4 David exhorts us to "Stand in awe, and sin not: commune with your own heart upon your bed, and be still. Selah" (v. 4). Our versification sings it thus:

Stand in awe, and sin not,
Bid your heart be still;
Thro' the silent watches
Think upon His will.

This he wrote because, as verse 1 reveals, he was in distress. And he is speaking to his own soul. This is so very necessary whenever we have troubles. We so quickly and continuously look at what is happening instead of looking to God, who has all things completely under his control and causes all things to work together for good to his people.

Now, what David means here is that we stand in awe before God, that is, that we have profound respect for him, fear him in the sense that we are fully conscious of who he is and what he is able to do. If we do that, and we tell our hearts that he is God, we will be silent as far as complaining about what happened to us is concerned.

How often is it not that we have to commune with our own hearts and tell them that he is God? We are so ready to question his works, and, as David had just done, we are quick to accuse him of not listening to our cries. We run to him and plead with him that he will hear us, while we fail to listen to him and what he says to us in his word.

Just tell your heart what a mighty God he is, who not only created all things, but also gives us such rich promises and revealed such tremendous faithfulness to Noah, Abraham, and the Israelites, and in due time sent his own Son for our salvation.

Stand in awe, that is, be filled with awe before our mighty and ever faithful God. Tell your soul what awesome things he has done. And if you do, you will with David say: "The LORD will hear when I call unto him" (Ps. 4:3).

Through the silent watches think upon his will. And be sure that he will work all things together for good to those that love him.

Read: Psalm 4
Psalter versification: 7:1

IMPLICIT TRUST IN GOD

Offer the sacrifices of righteousness, and put your trust in the LORD. —Psalm 4:5

There are times when we should not speak, and there are times when speaking is our undeniable calling. There are words which we should not utter, and words that must come out of our mouths. That is why David, having spoken to his soul and commanded it to be silent and not to question God's faithfulness, continued with: "Offer the sacrifices of righteousness, and put your trust in the LORD" (Ps. 4:5).

What David has in mind here is speaking by his actions. His mouth must bring a sacrifice of righteousness to God rather than complain because he has not been relieved of his troubles.

Our versification in these words tells us how we must speak:

> Lay upon God's altar
> Good and loving deeds,
> And in all things trust Him
> To supply your needs.
> Anxious and despairing,
> Many walk in night;
> But to those that fear Him
> God will send His light.

Here sacrifices of righteousness are called "good and loving deeds." This is certainly true, especially for us today when the temple and all its types and shadows are fulfilled in Christ. We are to walk as Christ walked, loving God and showing this with all our deeds. Then we bring God sacrifices of righteousness.

Our complaining but also our impatience, when God does not at once bring us out of our distress and disappointments, is not a work of righteousness. Therefore, our calling is to trust in God. Revealing that trust, we are bringing sacrifices of righteousness. We are doing that which is right. We are sacrificing our ideas and wishes and telling God that we submit to his way and will.

Therefore, whatever your situation is and your troubles are, be silent as far as complaints are concerned. But open your mouth wide and by your actions reveal unshaken trust in God.

David began this psalm by saying that God enlarged him when he was in distress. And we, having the cross, resurrection, and ascension of Christ into heaven as our head, have stronger words to express our trust in God for the wonders he has wrought in his Son.

Read: Psalm 62
Psalter versification: 7:2

SWEET AND PEACEFUL SLEEP

I will both lay me down in peace, and sleep: for thou, LORD, only makest
me dwell in safety. —Psalm 4:8

If you see the enemy coming toward you, you can rise up and flee. Or if you hear his threats, you can call on others to come to your aid to protect you. But if he comes while you are asleep, you are in mortal danger.

And yet David says in Psalm 4:8, "I will both lay me down in peace, and sleep: for thou, LORD, only makest me dwell in safety." Our sleep, with such an almighty, everywhere present, and faithful God, will be sure and absolutely safe. Not only is it true that he is more powerful than all our enemies, but his enemies depend upon him for every heartbeat. He knows to the smallest detail all their thoughts, plans, and desires.

Can you then not see why we should and can sing?

> In God's love abiding,
> I have joy and peace
> More than all the wicked,
> Tho' their wealth increase.
> In His care confiding,
> I will sweetly sleep,
> For the Lord, my Saviour,
> Will in safety keep.

Take hold of this truth that he will keep you safe. Not only is he the almighty God, who is always right next to us and in us. But he is our savior who, through the blood of his Son, blotted out all our guilt and is preparing a place for us in his house of many mansions.

Take hold of those words of the versification: "In God's love abiding, I have joy and peace." He loves us, as Christ's cross clearly shows. And because he loves us, we can be sure that he will not allow anything to happen to us that would keep us from reaching his house and from enjoying all its blessings.

Dreadful, painful days are coming. There is an enemy that is ready to strike us. Paul calls him the last enemy to be destroyed, namely, death (1 Cor. 15:26). And the antichrist is also scheduled to come soon.

But put your trust in God. In him and in his care confiding you can have joy and peace. What happens to you will serve bringing you to the glory of God's kingdom.

Read: Psalm 3
Psalter versification: 7:3

GREAT PRAISE FOR OUR GREAT GOD

Great is the Lord, and greatly to be praised in the city of our God, in the mountain of his holiness. —Psalm 48:1

The larger the diamond is, or the piece of solid gold, the more its value is. The greater one's talents are, the more spectacular will one's work be. What shall we say, then, when the psalmist writes in Psalm 48:1, "Great is the Lord, and greatly to be praised in the city of our God, in the mountain of his holiness"? That greatness is immeasurable! He is the God of infinite greatness.

It is worthy of our notice that the psalmist declares that he is greatly to be praised in his city and in the mountain of his holiness. For although he must be praised by all men, his greatness is praised in a special way in his church. His greatness is so obvious when we look at the universe which he created and at all its creatures. What a vast universe it is! What a great God he is who made it all, fills it all, upholds it all, controls all that is in it!

But look at the salvation that he wrought in his only begotten Son. Look, as the psalmist did, at the city and holy mountain that he made, namely, his church in which he is praised.

The psalmist has in mind Jerusalem, where Mount Moriah, God's holy mountain where the temple stood, speaks of his greatness of love, mercy, and grace. It all pointed to Christ and his cross, resurrection, and ascension into heaven.

Surely then we have the calling expressed thus in our versification:

> The Lord is great; with worthy praise
> Proclaim His pow'r, His name confess,
> Within the city of our God,
> Upon His mount of holiness.

We simply cannot praise him enough. Praising him too much is absolutely impossible. He has prepared everlasting life so that we can without ceasing continue to praise him with all the praise due unto his name.

We are not yet in the new Jerusalem. But every Sabbath we go to his house. There, but also wherever we are, we are called to give great praise to our great God.

Read: Psalm 48
Psalter versification: 131:1

THE CHURCH'S BEAUTY AND JOY

Beautiful for situation, the joy of the whole earth, is mount Zion, on the sides of the north, the city of the great King. —Psalm 48:2

Jerusalem was built on four hills, of which two were of special significance. On Mount Moriah the temple was built, and on Mount Zion the king's throne stood. Speaking in Psalm 48:1 of the mountain of his holiness, the psalmist refers to Mount Moriah and the temple with its holy place and holy of holies, where God dwelt symbolically between the cherubim on the altar in that holy of holies. That made Jerusalem the holy city. In verse 2, the psalmist speaks literally of Mount Zion. He writes: "Beautiful for situation, the joy of the whole earth, is mount Zion, on the sides of the north, the city of the great King."

Therefore, it was not a physical beauty the psalmist had in mind when he wrote these words. Its beauty consisted in this, that God was there. It was the city of the great King who was there in Christ, who was there typically in the blood sprinkled on that mercy seat and was upon the throne in all the kings who were types of Christ.

Christ made that temple and city beautiful. He brings joy, and any nation that does not have him as their king has no real beauty and joy. Outside and apart from Christ all lies under the curse, has shame, and is under God's holy wrath.

But the citizens of Christ's kingdom have blessedness because their beauty and joy is heavenly and everlasting. This they will never lose. In him they are securely blessed and can confidently sing:

> Mount Zion, glorious and fair,
> Gives joy to people in all lands;
> The city of the mighty King
> In majesty securely stands.

Apply that to your church. The question is not what a beautiful building you have, or what delightful music your organ can produce. Is God there in the pure preaching of his word? Is its refuge Christ and his cross? Are its members spiritually beautiful, because they have been born again and the Spirit clothes them with Christ's beauty?

The church's beauty is the beauty of Christ, and its joy is the salvation he has realized for all its members.

Read: Isaiah 61
Psalter versification: 131:2

THE CHURCH'S ABSOLUTE SAFETY

As we have heard, so have we seen in the city of the LORD of hosts, in the city of our God: God will establish it for ever. Selah. —Psalm 48:8

On every coin used in our country we read: "In God we trust." How wonderful it would be if that were true. We then would be saying with the psalmist: "As we have heard, so have we seen in the city of the LORD of hosts, in the city of our God: God will establish it for ever" (Ps. 48:8).

The psalmist is here referring to God's church, not the city of Jerusalem as such. And our versification has it thus:

> Within her dwellings for defense
> Our God has made His presence known,
> And hostile kings, in sudden fear,
> Have fled as ships by tempest blown.
> With our own eyes we have beheld
> What oft our fathers told before,
> That God Who in His Zion dwells
> Will keep her safely evermore.

Although this refers to the days when Israel dwelt in Canaan, and God dwelt in the temple in Jerusalem, this truth holds true for the church of all ages. God's church is safe, absolutely safe. As the psalmist wrote in verse 3: "God is known in her palaces for a refuge."

The church has, and from the dawn of history had, powerful and fierce enemies. Do not forget that the day man fell God told him that there would be enmity between him and his seed and between the devil and his evil kingdom. But do not forget also that God told the church then already that she has the victory. Her heel would be bruised. But the serpent's head would be crushed (Gen. 3:15)!

Remember also that Jesus said that "the gates of hell shall not prevail against" the church (Matt. 16:18). And take hold of the first verse in this psalm: "Great is the LORD, and greatly to be praised."

There will be some rough days ahead for the church. We who have heard of what God did to destroy Pharaoh's hold on Israel, and of how he performed amazing miracles in the wilderness and gave them the whole promised land, also know of the cross, resurrection, and ascension of Christ. He is our refuge and will establish his church and give her the new creation with all its blessedness. We are safe, absolutely safe. Our great God will take care of us.

Read: Revelation 21
Psalter versification: 131:3–4

PRAISING GOD FOR HIS RIGHTEOUSNESS

We have thought of thy lovingkindness, O God, in the midst of thy temple. According to thy name, O God, so is thy praise unto the ends of the earth: thy right hand is full of righteousness. —Psalm 48:9–10

A truth that ought to receive more emphasis today is the righteousness of God. There is so much talk about his love that completely ignores and even denies his righteousness. But the psalmist, being guided by God himself, does not do that. He had spoken of God's greatness and worthiness of great praise and had written about the safety of God's church. Then he wrote: "We have thought of thy lovingkindness, O God, in the midst of thy temple. According to thy name, O God, so is thy praise unto the ends of the earth: thy right hand is full of righteousness" (Ps. 48:9–10).

Speaking of God's loving-kindness, the psalmist does not ignore his righteousness. For God has no loving-kindness, no mercy, and no grace apart from his righteousness. It is all based on his righteousness. The temple in Jerusalem declared that in its altar and bloody sacrifices. And Christ, who is at God's right hand in heaven, manifests that righteousness.

God's righteousness demands full payment of the debt which we owe him. The everlasting punishment for our sins must be suffered fully; and all the work of love which we did not bring to him must still be brought in full measure. Until and unless that is done, there is no loving-kindness that God can show us. He is the righteous God.

All this Christ did for us. He is that right hand of God who saves us and because of whom God's love, mercy, and grace come down upon us. He made us to be righteous. This we ought to see more clearly than the Old Testament saints, who had the altar in the temple to show it.

Surely then we should sing meaningfully:

Within Thy temple, Lord,
In that most holy place,
We on Thy lovingkindness dwell,
The wonders of Thy grace.
Men sing Thy praise, O God,
Where'er Thy Name is known;
By ev'ry deed Thy hand hath wrought
Thy righteousness is shown.

Praise God for his righteousness. That belongs to his greatness. And that makes his grace, mercy, and love to us possible.

Read: Isaiah 53
Psalter versification: 134:1

JUDGMENT DAY JOY

Let mount Zion rejoice, let the daughters of Judah be glad,
because of thy judgments. —Psalm 48:11

When a judge announces his decision, it is always in one party's favor and against another party. Both sides await the judge's decision; but only one side will be glad and rejoice in the decision. When God in his righteousness announces his decision in the day of Christ, his whole church is going to rejoice and sing in gladness.

Of this we read in Psalm 48:11 in these words: "Let mount Zion rejoice, let the daughters of Judah be glad, because of thy judgments." Mount Zion here refers to the entire church of God, God's people everywhere. All the believers are going to and have reason to sing:

> Thy hand is full of righteousness;
> Let Zion's gladness then be great,
> And let her daughters sing for joy
> And all Thy judgments celebrate.

In the day when Christ returns, this will be realized in full. But in this life already we have reason to be glad and rejoice in God's judgments. The cross of Christ, his resurrection, and his ascension up into heaven announced God's judgment in our favor. That cross declared that he was forsaken of God because of our sins. His resurrection reveals that he succeeded in blotting them out. His ascension up into heaven tells us where we are going to go. We are not there yet, but God has clearly announced his judgment that we will be with him in glory.

Now, we do have fears and doubts, because we still have our old man of sin whose works God in righteous judgment condemns. When, however, we by faith look at Christ both as far as what he did and where he now is, we have reason to rejoice and be glad. We know that we can anticipate judgment day joy that will be forever and will be boundless.

Listen then to the words of the psalmist when he tells us to rejoice and be glad. Wipe away the tears from your eyes. See your sins, but look also to Christ. On the day you die, believe that also to you he will say: "To day shalt thou be with me in paradise" (Luke 23:43).

Read: Revelation 20
Psalter versification: 132:3

WALKING ABOUT ZION

Walk about Zion, and go round about her: tell the towers thereof.
Mark ye well her bulwarks, consider her palaces; that ye may tell it
to the generation following. —Psalm 48:12–13

So often shame should cover our faces when we read what the psalmist wrote as he brought Psalm 48 to its close. He wrote: "Walk about Zion, and go round about her: tell the towers thereof. Mark ye well her bulwarks, consider her palaces" (vv. 12–13).

Are you that interested in our great God's church? How much walking, telling, and marking of her strength and beauty do you do? Is God's church your main interest, or your earthly possessions?

In the measure that we rejoice and are glad because of God's judgments in Christ, we will walk about Zion and sing:

> About Mount Zion go,
> Her tow'rs and ramparts tell;
> That ye her strength may know,
> Mark her defenses well;
> Her royal palaces behold
> That ye her glories may unfold.

There will be a different form of walking for us than what the psalmist could do. He lived in a time of types and shadows that pointed to Christ and his kingdom of heaven, which he will usher in at his return. We have that cross, resurrection, and ascension of Christ and sitting at God's right hand that our souls can walk around. We can tell the towers of salvation which he built and take careful note of the bulwarks he has established and the beautiful dwelling place called God's house of many mansions, which he realized for us.

The question is, How often do you look at Christ? How often do the eyes of your soul go round about him and his kingdom as we can find them in Scripture? Was your Bible open yesterday, or today? Did you look into it to be comforted about its strength and certainty? Did your soul digest what you read?

Our God is a great God and is greatly to be praised. This we will understand and appreciate when we look into his word to see what he did for us in Christ. The safety and security of his church is all inseparably connected with Christ. He is its tower and bulwarks. He has already reached its palaces. Consider that fact and look for him to come and bring you there in God's grace.

Read: Revelation 22
Psalter versification: 133:2

CONCERN FOR TOMORROW'S CHURCH

Mark ye well her bulwarks, consider her palaces; that ye may tell it
to the generation following. —Psalm 48:13

If there ever was a man who was not selfish, and if there ever was one who looked out for the good of others and was willing to lose all that others might gain what man never had before, it was our Savior. He went to hell so that we might go to heaven. He never hesitated because of what it would cost him. He was concerned with what would bring us joy and blessedness. And as members of his body, we have a calling to follow his example.

The psalmist points this out when, having written that we should walk about Zion and tell her towers, mark her bulwarks, and consider her palaces, he writes: "That ye may tell it to the generation following" (Ps. 48:13). Our versification explains it this way:

To all the coming race
Repeat the message o'er:
This mighty God of grace
Is ours for evermore;
Yea, He our Saviour will abide,
And unto death will be our guide.

We must be concerned about the whole church of God and want those following us to enjoy spiritual blessedness. We must walk about Zion and go round about her, not as tourists who go for their own flesh's pleasure, but so that we can tell our children how great our righteous God is and teach them to put their trust in him and his Son through whom we have salvation and everlasting glory.

That does not simply mean our own flesh and blood. Surely we must do all we can to enrich their spiritual lives and knowledge. But the psalmist speaks of the whole coming generation. The exhortation then comes to the childless and unmarried as well as to parents.

It means that the church today must study and develop in the truth so that Satan and his host, coming with crafty, subtle, false doctrines, do not mislead them; but that they may see the wonderful work Christ performed for us, may see the greatness of our God, and may then lead the next generation into the rich truth as it is in Christ. Our great God must be greatly praised. And we should do all we can to bring the coming generation into a richer, not poorer, praise to God.

Read: Deuteronomy 6
Psalter versification: 133:3

OUR MIGHTY GOD AND FAITHFUL GUIDE

For this God is our God for ever and ever: he will be our
guide even unto death. —Psalm 48:14

Whether he will admit it or not, every unbeliever has a god. One may claim to be an atheist, but you will find him trusting in this or that object and revealing superstition. He will speak of lucky numbers and of good luck and bad luck. Doing so, he speaks of powers outside himself which determine his lot. And that is an admission of trusting in a god.

But the child of God believes in the one true God and makes a very rich and powerful confession. With the psalmist he says: "For this God is our God for ever and ever: he will be our guide even unto death" (Ps. 48:14).

This God is the great God who is greatly to be praised and who is mentioned in the preceding verses: the God who did so much for his people in his loving-kindness based on his righteousness. He is the God who has absolute power over all other so-called gods. He is called "the Lord of lords" in Psalm 136:3.

We ought to put the emphasis upon the word *our*. This God is *our* God. His loving-kindness and righteousness in Christ are our comfort and protection. Before the world we are going to cry out with confidence that *this* God is *our* God forever and ever! And we are going to tell the coming generation the truth concerning him. Before and with our children we are going to sing:

This mighty God forever lives
Our God and Saviour to abide,
And till our pilgrim days shall end
Will ever be our faithful guide.

Death is coming to all of us. No unbeliever has a god that can stop death from coming or give us victory over it. But our God guides us not simply until death but into death in order to deliver us from our sinful flesh; and because of his Son's sin-removing sacrificial death, he guides our souls through the door of death into heavenly glory. When Christ returns, he will raise the body with greater power and blessedness than Adam had in paradise.

Our God is an infallible guide and a powerful savior. Tell all the world in all your life that he is your God.

Read: Daniel 3
Psalter versification: 132:5

UNDERSTANDING OUR SALVATION

Let my cry come near before thee, O Lᴏʀᴅ: give me understanding
according to thy word. Let my supplication come before thee: deliver me
according to thy word. —Psalm 119:169–170

Salvation is a very wonderful gift which we surely ought to seek. Understanding our salvation and how we are and can be saved is also of extreme importance. That is why the psalmist wrote: "Let my cry come near before thee, O Lᴏʀᴅ: give me understanding according to thy word. Let my supplication come before thee: deliver me according to thy word" (Ps. 119:169–170). Our versification has it thus:

O let my supplicating cry
By Thee, my gracious Lord, be heard;
Give wisdom and deliver me
According to Thy faithful word.

In verse 166 he had written: "Lᴏʀᴅ, I have hoped for thy salvation." And that salvation he has here in mind. When he was persecuted by men, he certainly desired deliverance from it. But his cry for understanding and deliverance in verses 169–170 means that he is praying for salvation from sin, not from sinners.

We must keep in mind that salvation is far more than deliverance from guilt and punishment. Salvation is deliverance from the love and power of sin. Salvation delivers us from the act of sin and from a sinful nature. And if we do not want that, our cry for salvation only adds to our sin and increases the reason for its punishment.

We must therefore cry to God for the work of the Spirit of Christ that will make us hate sin and enable us to flee from it. Such deliverance that destroys the power of sin over us we must seek.

Further, we must understand how this salvation is wrought and how it is possible. The psalmist prays for understanding and deliverance according to God's word. We must understand that we are saved by grace and because God's Son, the Word become flesh, suffered our punishment and made us not guilty before God.

Then, too, "according to thy word" means according to his word of promise. He promised it to those whom he eternally chose in Christ. That, we must constantly keep in mind. Never may we cry to God as though salvation is coming to us because of what we did or because of what we are in ourselves.

Read: Psalm 119:165–176
Psalter versification: 342:1

SALVATION'S SURE RESPONSE

My lips shall utter praise, when thou hast taught me thy statutes. My tongue shall speak of thy word: for all thy commandments are righteousness. —Psalm 119:171–172

As we saw yesterday, salvation is a wonderful gift. It also has a wonderful response. Of this we read in Psalm 119:171–172 in these words: "My lips shall utter praise, when thou hast taught me thy statutes. My tongue shall speak of thy word: for all thy commandments are righteousness." Our versification explains it thus:

> Instructed in Thy holy law,
> To praise Thy word I lift my voice;
> O Lord, be Thou my present help,
> For Thy commandments are my choice.

We do well to note that here again salvation is presented as deliverance from the love of sin and not simply from its guilt and punishment. Being saved from that love of sin, we are going to praise God. Until we are saved from it by the Spirit of Christ, on the basis of his cross, we cannot praise God but will speak against him.

The praise of God the psalmist has in mind is that he is God and that we must bow before his sovereign will. For that God's commandments are righteousness means that God is righteous. For these commandments express his will. And when he teaches us his statutes, he teaches us that he is right in demanding perfect obedience by keeping his law every step of our way.

Every time we sin, we go against God and insult him rather than praise him. When we sin, we praise ourselves, presenting ourselves as those who may do as they please. When we by sins say that we do not love God's law, we say that we do not love God. We say that we find something wrong with God instead of praising him as the righteous God that he is.

Bearing this in mind, we can see why the psalmist prayed in verse 169 that God would give him understanding. We must be delivered from folly and cry to God to have our cry come near unto him. For we do not deserve to be heard.

Do your prayers contain this request? Are you sincerely desirous of praising God? A mere desire to be saved from punishment is not enough. The devil and all his followers want that. Love for God will produce a desire to serve and praise God as God almighty and sovereign.

Read: Psalm 19
Psalter versification: 342:2

A CRY FOR HELP

Let thine hand help me; for I have chosen thy precepts. I have longed for thy salvation, O LORD; and thy law is my delight. —Psalm 119:173–174

It was the pride that Satan worked into Adam's and Eve's hearts that moved them to commit man's first sin. Man was moved to desire to be like God and not remain a servant of God. And every sin that we commit is due to that sinful pride that is in us from the day of our birth.

Salvation, therefore, requires the removal of that pride. If we are going to be saved from breaking God's law, we must be humbled by the truth that he is God and that we were created to serve and praise him as God. That is why the psalmist wrote in Psalm 119:173–174, "Let thine hand help me; for I have chosen thy precepts. I have longed for thy salvation, O LORD; and thy law is my delight."

God's hand must reach down and save us. We are like a drowning man with nothing on which to stand and in need of a hand that will lift us up out of the water and certain death. A cry for this comes out of a humble heart that wants to be lifted out of the sea of sin. Born again, we long for salvation; for God's law is our delight. We do have the old sinful nature, the old man of sin, but also the principle of new life that wants to keep God's law and to praise him as God. And God, whose hand put that new life in us, must reach down and strengthen it.

We can see that hand of God more clearly than the psalmist did. For we can see Christ, God's right hand, and the pouring out of his Spirit that works in us this prayer as versified in our Psalter:

> For Thy salvation I have longed,
> And in Thy law is my delight;
> Enrich my soul with life divine,
> And help me by Thy judgments right.

We must have a divine life in the sense that we must be given the same sinless life that God's Son had when he came in our flesh.

Try to keep God's law in your own strength, and you will not only fail but will drown in added sins. Look instead to Christ, who is not only God's hand but also sits at God's right hand with power over everything in heaven and on earth. He will lift you completely out of sin into everlasting sinlessness in the day of his return. Cry to him for help. In God's grace he will give it to you.

Read: Psalm 130
Psalter versification: 342:3

OUR GREATEST NEED

Let my soul live, and it shall praise thee; and let thy judgments help
me. I have gone astray like a lost sheep; seek thy servant; for I do
not forget thy commandments. —Psalm 119:175–176

Are you more concerned about your body than about your soul? There can be no denying of the fact that man is deeply concerned about his body. All the physicians, hospitals, and establishments that manufacture medicines reveal how much man is concerned with the life of his body.

There is nothing wrong with this. Jesus healed many bodies and raised three of them from the dead. But the life and well-being of the soul is far more important and must be there, or our concern for the body is sinful. The psalmist writes: "Let my soul live, and it shall praise thee; and let thy judgments help me. I have gone astray like a lost sheep; seek thy servant; for I do not forget thy commandments" (Ps. 119:175–176). Our versification has it in these words:

Thy servant like a wand'ring sheep
Has lost the path and gone astray;
Restore my soul and lead me home,
For Thy commands I would obey.

The undeniable fact is that if our souls are not given the life of Christ, our bodies are going to suffer more misery in the lake of fire than we now know and medicine has temporarily relieved.

What becomes plain here in these last verses of this lengthy psalm is that the psalmist, and we with him, slip and slide and fall back into sin time and time again. We have only a small beginning of that new obedience. We are like sheep that go astray and cannot find their way back.

Neither by word nor deed do we praise God the way we ought. God must continue to make our souls live, if we are to praise him by our deeds and by our words.

How important then is it not that we live close to God's word. In it and out of it we learn what our calling is before him. From it we learn our calling to praise him and how to do so. That word will show us clearly that we have strayed and how vile and evil we are. We need God's word more than we need daily bread. The life of our souls, that is, the spiritual life of our souls, is far more important than the life of our bodies. With the psalmist we surely should pray, and pray earnestly, that God will let our souls live, that we may praise him.

Read: Luke 12:16–34
Psalter versification: 342:4

TRUSTING IN GOD

In the LORD put I my trust: how say ye to my soul, Flee as a bird to your mountain? For, lo, the wicked bend their bow, they make ready their arrow upon the string, that they may privily shoot at the upright in heart. —Psalm 11:1–2

In an effort to establish peace and to maintain it, a League of Nations was formed. When it failed and a more widespread war broke out, there was formed a United Nations which, instead of fostering peace, manifests increased friction between the nations. And today wars and rumors of war are great in number.

There is one war that has never ceased even for one day and will soon come to an awesome climax when the antichrist arises. This war began the day man fell into sin and God announced enmity which he would put between the seed of the woman and the seed of the serpent (Gen. 3:15). Because of that war, we do well to heed David's words in Psalm 11:1–2, namely: "In the LORD put I my trust: how say ye to my soul, Flee as a bird to your mountain? For, lo, the wicked bend their bow, they make ready their arrow upon the string, that they may privily shoot at the upright in heart."

Do not listen to those who tell you to flee as a bird, that is, trust in your own strength and ability to flee to some creature for safety. Tell your soul, your children's souls, and the souls of your fellow church members to put their trust in God. Tell them to sing:

> In God will I trust, tho' my counselors say,
> O flee as a bird to your mountain away;
> The wicked are strong and the righteous are weak,
> Foundations are shaken, yet God will I seek.

Even as the nations today have far more powerful weapons than bows and arrows as in David's day, so Satan has far more crafty and powerful means to try to destroy our faith and capture God's church.

Our only hope is in God. And we ought to see more clearly than David could that we should flee to Christ and his cross on which Satan's head was crushed. We ought to flee to Christ, who is at God's right hand and by his Spirit sustains and defends his church. We can look for him to save us and give complete victory when he returns on the clouds of heaven.

Read: Psalm 11
Psalter versification: 20:1

TRIED IN GOD'S GRACE

The LORD is in his holy temple, the LORD's throne is in heaven: his eyes behold, his eyelids try, the children of men. The LORD trieth the righteous: but the wicked and him that loveth violence his soul hateth. —Psalm 11:4–5

Although it is claimed that God loves everybody and has a grace that rests upon more than those whom he chose eternally in Christ, the Scriptures teach something quite different. In Psalm 11:4–5 we read: "The LORD is in his holy temple, the LORD's throne is in heaven: his eyes behold, his eyelids try, the children of men. The LORD trieth the righteous: but the wicked and him that loveth violence his soul hateth."

We find here a sharp contrast. The human race is divided into the righteous and the wicked. The righteous God tries, but the wicked he hates. That he tries the righteous does not mean that he tries to get them to accept Christ. It does not mean that he tries to find out what is in their hearts. No, his throne is in heaven, and from there he knows all that happens below him and has power to give Christ and his blessings to whomsoever he wills. He need not and does not try to get men to help him get men to believe in Christ.

That he tries the righteous means that they are already righteous in Christ and that he purifies them as silver is tried by fire. And those who trust in God will see that, when the wicked bend their bows to shoot their arrows, God is purifying his church and polishing her members so that they can reflect his glory more fully.

Our flesh does not like these trials; but through these afflictions God purifies and strengthens the faith of those who were chosen in Christ. Those outside of Christ, the wicked unbelievers whom he hates, he punishes; and the fire he sends upon them destroys them. Rather than building them up, he is casting them down to everlasting punishment. Listen to our versification:

> The Lord in His temple shall ever abide;
> His throne is eternal, whatever betide.
> The children of men He beholds from on high,
> The wicked to punish, the righteous to try.

These trials are a blessing to his church. The prosperity and wealth of the unbelievers will bring them to everlasting woe.

Read: 2 Corinthians 4:1–5:2
Psalter versification: 20:2

A REASON FOR WEEPING

By the rivers of Babylon, there we sat down, yea, we wept, when we remembered Zion. We hanged our harps upon the willows in the midst thereof. —Psalm 137:1–2

There were times when God's people in the Old Testament dispensation sang lustily and enthusiastically. Just read Exodus 15 and note how they sang after God brought them safely across the Red Sea and destroyed all of Egypt's army.

But there also were times when there was bitter weeping among these children of God. Listen to what we read in Psalm 137:1–2, "By the rivers of Babylon, there we sat down, yea, we wept, when we remembered Zion. We hanged our harps upon the willows in the midst thereof." They were no longer in the land God promised them. They were in the bondage of Babylon and remembered the blessings they enjoyed in Canaan and their ready access to God's temple, which now was in ruins.

Not for one minute should we find fault with them for this sorrow. In fact their sorrow ought to be ours today. We have every reason for singing today:

By Babel's streams we sat and wept,
For mem'ry still to Zion clung;
The winds alone our harpstrings swept,
That on the drooping willows hung.

If we only open our eyes and see the church's situation today, we have abundant reason to weep. Her bondage is not in the city of Babylon. She does not weep because her temple is in ruins and Jerusalem's walls are a pile of broken stones. But today so much of what is called the church of Christ is in the bondage of Satan. And although our church buildings are in good condition, the truth concerning Christ has been so greatly corrupted that we, remembering the truth God gave his church in ages gone by, have reason to weep bitterly. The faith once delivered to the saints is crumbling, the pillars of the truth are tumbling down in many churches.

Does this fill you with sadness? Is your harp hanging on the willows because of the doctrines boldly and widely proclaimed that militate against that faith once delivered to the saints?

Read: Psalm 137
Psalter versification: 379:1

SATAN'S CHANGE OF TACTICS

For there they that carried us away captive required of us a song; and they that wasted us required of us mirth, saying, Sing us one of the songs of Zion. —Psalm 137:3

A truth we ought never to forget is that Satan will change his tactics, and even reverse them, if it serves his devilish purpose of seeking to destroy the church of Christ.

When God gave the Israelites over to suffer the Babylonian captivity, Satan sought to ridicule the believers. We read in Psalm 137:3, "For there they that carried us away captive required of us a song; and they that wasted us required of us mirth, saying, Sing us one of the songs of Zion." Our versification presents it thus:

> There our rude captors, flushed with pride,
> A song required to mock our wrongs;
> Our spoilers called for mirth, and cried,
> Come, sing us one of Zion's songs.

Today Satan still tries to turn God's people away from him by ridicule and sarcasm. But today he also gets men in the church to produce songs that corrupt the truth and are not Zion's songs. This he does cleverly so that some words and phrases in the songs are the truth; but there are also words and phrases that destroy faith in Christ. And he appeals to the flesh by means of melodies, harmonies, and rhythms that also the unbelievers enjoy.

The question is whether we today respond as the believers did in Babylon and say: "How shall we sing the LORD's song in a strange land?" (v. 4). How shall we sing with words that are strange to the faith in Christ and that do not praise God? Does it hurt you and do you keep silent when others sing the songs of Satan as though they were the songs of Zion and of God?

Does it grieve you to hear those in churches sing of a Christ who is frustrated by those whom he wants to save, because they will not fulfill the conditions upon which their salvation depends?

We do well to examine our songs carefully to be sure that they are songs of God, songs that praise him. Satan wants us to believe that God depends upon us. As far as such songs are concerned: be silent!

Read: Romans 9
Psalter versification: 379:2

BLESSED WITH SALVATION

Salvation belongeth unto the LORD: thy blessing is
upon thy people. Selah. —Psalm 3:8

No child of God denies that the world and all that it contains belongs to God. The Scriptures begin by impressing upon our minds that God made it all and did so out of nothing. But every child of God should also say with David: "Salvation belongeth unto the LORD: thy blessing is upon thy people. Selah" (Ps. 3:8). We sing it thus:

Salvation to the Lord belongs,
In Him His saints are blest;
O let Thy blessing evermore
Upon Thy people rest.

Now, that salvation belongs to God certainly means that all the credit for it is his. He realized every part of it, and in no way and to no degree, and not for the slightest fraction of a moment, does man help God save him. God, the creator of all, in no way is ever saved from disappointment by the work of the creatures he made.

Our savior's name is Jesus. That name comes from the Hebrew words *Jehovah* and *salvation*. Did not the angel tell Joseph that the child that would be born to Mary must be called Jesus "for he shall save his people from their sins" (Matt. 1:21)?

The word *selah* means pause and think this over. Surely in this present day and age we ought to give serious thought to this truth. Salvation belongs to God. He realizes it in its smallest detail. Therefore, he should receive all the praise and thanksgiving for this tremendously important work.

So often we hear men deny this truth in their preaching and witnessing. Emphatically and correctly they say that he wants to save. But we must go a step further. He saves and does not simply try to save. Never does he fail to save even one of those he sets out to save. He is not dependent upon the will of the man he sets out to save. He commands faith and does not plead with man to believe in order that he may save him.

Let us reject any idea that God is ever frustrated by man. Salvation belongs to God. It is his gift to us, and we give him nothing for it. Man does not let God save him. God blesses us with full salvation.

Read: Psalm 3
Psalter versification: 5:5

SEEING THE FOUNTAIN OF ETERNAL LIFE

For with thee is the fountain of life: in thy light shall we see light. —Psalm 36:9

No child ever had anything to say as to whether he would or would not be conceived and born. No man or woman can decide that a child is going to be born to them. They may be very desirous of having a child, and there may seem to be no reason why they cannot have one. But whether they will or not depends upon God's will.

Concerning God, David writes in Psalm 36:9, "For with thee is the fountain of life: in thy light shall we see light." We therefore sing:

> The fountain of eternal life
> Is found alone with Thee,
> And in the brightness of Thy light
> We clearly light shall see.

This is so important for us to remember when we are considering being born again with the everlasting life of the kingdom of heaven. As surely as no child is born physically at its request, so surely no man is born again with spiritual life because he asked for it. He cannot ask for it, or even want it, until it has already been given to him. He was not here physically before his natural birth and therefore could not ask for it. There was likewise no spiritual life in him that could want to ask for a rebirth, until he had already been born again. Christ earned it for us, and God eternally decreed that we would have it.

Is it not God who speaks here through David and says that the fountain of life is with him? Yesterday we saw that salvation belongs to God. It is his work from beginning to end; and all the credit, the praise and thanksgiving for it must be given to God. Being born again is the beginning of that salvation in us. It is a free gift that we do not even want until it has been begun in us.

And since even the desire for it is God's gift to us, we owe him everlasting praise and thanksgiving. Not one drop of the water of everlasting life that comes out of this fountain of life comes from us. Before we receive life out of it, we cannot even see that Christ is that fountain of life. Did not those not born again crucify Christ, this fountain of life? Born again, we see Christ as that whole source of our new heavenly life.

Read: Psalm 36
Psalter versification: 94:4

LIGHT FOR OUR LIFE

For with thee is the fountain of life: in thy light shall we see light. —Psalm 36:9

So completely do we depend upon God for our salvation that we receive not one part of it that did not come from God and was given us because he wanted us to have it. As surely as every heartbeat comes from him, as surely as all our sunshine comes from him, so every aspect and phase of our salvation comes from God as a *free* gift.

In Psalm 36:9, which we considered briefly yesterday, David wrote: "For with thee is the fountain of life: in thy light shall we see light." That last clause surely presents an awesome and wonderful truth. In God's light we see light. If God does not turn on the light, we are not going to see any of the works of salvation which he performed for us in his Son, and in us by his Son's Spirit. The cross will mean nothing to us. We will not really know what a blessing is but will continue to call the things lying under the curse blessings. The works of darkness we will call beautiful. Worldly fools we will call wise.

Having caused us to be born again, God also enlightens us and makes us see his work for us in Christ, understand it, and call it beautiful. In God's light we shall see what spiritually is light and not darkness. We shall see Christ as the "light to lighten the Gentiles" (Luke 2:32). Then we will sing:

> Lord, to me Thy ways make known,
> Guide in truth and teach Thou me;
> Thou my Saviour art alone,
> All the day I wait for Thee.

We need life; but we also need instruction. We must be spiritually alive; but we must also receive spiritual enlightenment. We are saved by grace; but we are saved in order to be able to serve God and praise and magnify his name. It is good that we have been saved; but we are saved in order to do good and must be called away from our unbelief and evil works.

Therefore, we must see God as God, but also as our savior. We must see Christ and the truth that is in him. The new life we received must be activated. With spiritual light shining in our souls, we shall walk in the light and reveal ourselves as children of light.

Read: Psalm 25
Psalter versification: 67:1

TRUST AND THANKFULNESS

In thee, O LORD, do I put my trust: let me never be put to confusion. Deliver
me in thy righteousness, and cause me to escape: incline thine ear unto
me, and save me. —Psalm 71:1–2

That which has no life can be moved. Lofty mountain peaks have been moved by earthquakes and volcanoes. But only that which has life can either move itself or produce movement within itself. The living seed sends a shoot upward and roots downward. The tree sends nourishment from the roots to the tip of its leaves.

Applied spiritually, we can say that the child of God who has been born again with the new life of the kingdom of heaven, and has been enlightened by the call of the Spirit of Christ, is going to produce conscious, willing activity. We read of this in Psalm 71:1–2. David writes: "In thee, O LORD, do I put my trust: let me never be put to confusion. Deliver me in thy righteousness, and cause me to escape: incline thine ear unto me, and save me." Our versification states it thus:

In Thee, O Lord, I put my trust;
Shamed let me never be:
O save me in Thy righteousness,
Give ear, and rescue me.

Here plainly we have the activity of faith in God as our savior in Christ. Faith is trust, for it is not only a certain knowledge but also an assured confidence. God as our light gives us knowledge, and by the act of faith we declare it to be certain, true revelation of fact. And faith is absolutely sure and confident that what God promises will happen.

Faith moves us to pray to God, clinging tightly to his promises, running to him for the blessings of salvation which he promises us. God is the one who gave us a new spiritual life. He enlightened our minds with the truth as it is in Christ. But now also it is God who gives us faith. He works in us that trust and confidence.

How much thanks then do we not owe God! How powerful and full of love he is to do all this to those who, before they were born again, hated him and walked in rebellion against him! Surely we are saved by grace and are called to be thankful for such a blessed and sure salvation.

Read: Psalm 71
Psalter versification: 190:1

December 8

OUR INIQUITY FORGIVEN

Thou hast forgiven the iniquity of thy people, thou hast covered
all their sin. Selah. —Psalm 85:2

One truth that we must embrace and hold tightly is expressed beautifully by David in Psalm 85:2. There he wrote: "Thou hast forgiven the iniquity of thy people, thou hast covered all their sin. Selah." For here we have the legal basis for all the blessings of salvation.

We are guilty in Adam and have walked in a multitude of our own sins. The wages of sin is death, and it opens the doors of hell with all its woe. How then can we be born again? What right do we have to let the light of God's grace fall on us? On what basis can we trust God to bestow on us as much as one blessing?

The answer is beautifully stated in our versification:

> Lord, Thou hast favor shown Thy land,
> Restored again Thy captive band;
> Thy people's sins Thou pardoned hast;
> And all their guilt hast covered o'er,
> Removed from them Thy anger sore,
> All Thy fierce wrath behind Thee cast.

It is wonderful that God delivers us from the punishment of sin; but more important it is that he delivers us from the guilt that calls for this punishment. And note that God forgave our iniquity. He covered our sins. He covered us with the robes of righteousness of Christ.

He is the unchangeable, righteous judge who will keep his word to Adam that in the day man sins, he deserves death. That word he will keep, and therefore he sent his Son to suffer the punishment and blot out our guilt.

How thankful then we ought to be as we approach the day when we celebrate the birth of that Son.

Forgiven in the righteousness of the cross of Christ, we can be born again and, by the Spirit of Christ, enlightened in regard to this wonder of God's grace. And then faith in God and his Son may be and is given to us.

Read: Psalm 85
Psalter versification: 231:1

SALVATION'S INEVITABLE FRUIT

My voice shalt thou hear in the morning, O LORD; in the morning will I direct my prayer unto thee, and will look up. For thou art not a God that hath pleasure in wickedness: neither shall evil dwell with thee. —Psalm 5:3–4

Precious things cost a lot of money. That which is worthless you can pick up without giving as much as a penny. But this must not lead us to think that because salvation is a free gift, it has little or no value. It is the most precious gift that can be given to man. Although it costs us nothing, it cost God the extremely great price of the death of his only begotten Son.

The preciousness of that gift of salvation is to be seen in that which those whom God saves are made capable of doing. Of that we read in Psalm 5:3–4, "My voice shalt thou hear in the morning, O Lord; in the morning will I direct my prayer unto thee, and will look up. For thou art not a God that hath pleasure in wickedness: neither shall evil dwell with thee."

Note that David not only prays each day, but he begins every day with a prayer. He also reveals his own displeasure with sin and his love for God. That will always happen when God, on the basis of the cross of Christ, has caused one to be born again, made him to know the truth and to trust in God. In other words, sanctification, or making a man holy, will always follow a rebirth. That new life will always manifest itself in a holy walk. And even as the heartbeat reveals life of the body, walking in holiness reveals a new life in the soul.

Look then at your life. Can you sing with David?

In the fullness of Thy grace
To Thy house I will repair,
Bowing tow'rd Thy holy place,
In Thy fear will worship there.
Lead me in Thy righteousness,
Let my foes assail in vain;
Lest my feet be turned aside,
Make Thy way before me plain.

If you can find any of that in your life, you have assurance that you have been born again and have the inevitable fruit of a rebirth.

If you find only a little of that holiness, by all means do as David did. Each morning pray to God to keep you from all pleasure in sin. Pray the first thing each morning that God may make you appreciate that precious gift of salvation by his grace.

Read: Psalm 5
Psalter versification: 10:1

GLORY FOR THE NEWBORN CHILD OF GOD

But the king shall rejoice in God; every one that sweareth by him shall glory: but the mouth of them that speak lies shall be stopped. —Psalm 63:11

A beautiful truth that a born-again child of God can and will sing is stated in these words:

> My Saviour, 'neath Thy shelt'ring wings
> My soul delights to dwell;
> Still closer to Thy side I press,
> For near Thee all is well.
> My soul shall conquer ev'ry foe,
> Upholden by Thy hand;
> Thy people shall rejoice in God,
> Thy saints in glory stand.

This is the versification of Psalm 63:11. In this verse David wrote: "But the king shall rejoice in God; every one that sweareth by him shall glory: but the mouth of them that speak lies shall be stopped."

We should note two elements here. The born-again child of God will "rejoice in God" and "shall glory." For the last step in the work of salvation for the child of God is that God glorifies him and gives him the heavenly joy of a covenant life of fellowship with God.

Now, glory is the radiation, the shining forth of virtue. That lies ahead for every child of God. Not only will he receive a glorified body, like that of Christ, wherein his new man in Christ shall have a life of bliss, but he will rejoice in fellowship with God.

Glory makes us rejoice. The curse brings us tears and sorrow. That will all be behind us when we reach the glory promised us. Now already we have protection. As David wrote in verse 7: "Because thou hast been my help, therefore in the shadow of thy wings will I rejoice." Satan and his servants cannot keep the reborn child of God from reaching that heavenly glory. And reaching that glory with both body and soul, he will have an endless life of heavenly bliss.

Our new life wants that covenant fellowship with God. That is the blessedness that every reborn child of God hopes to obtain. That he will reach, and then he will rejoice in the Lord and shall have glory that never fades. What a work of salvation it is then that God wrought in Christ!

What a great praise and thanksgiving we owe him and will in that glory be able to bring to him!

Read: Psalm 63
Psalter versification: 163:3

SAVED FROM SPIRITUAL SHAME

Unto thee, O LORD, do I lift up my soul. O my God, I trust in thee: let me not be ashamed, let not mine enemies triumph over me. —Psalm 25:1–2

Ever since man fell into sin, man has had enemies. Performing that first act of sin against God, Adam introduced into the human race hatred also between man and man. If we do not keep the first table of the law, we will not keep the second table either. If we do not love God, we will not love the neighbor. As soon as God implants the new life of Christ in a man, that man will find the enmity of the seed of the serpent against him as seed of the woman (Gen. 3:15).

The question therefore is not whether we have enemies, but who they are. In Psalm 25:1–2 David prays: "Unto thee, O LORD, do I lift up my soul. O my God, I trust in thee: let me not be ashamed, let not mine enemies triumph over me." He has in mind enemies who are God's enemies, enemies who hate him because they hate God. Therefore, making David ashamed means treating God shamefully. And that should concern us.

We are ready to pray to God when enemies threaten our natural, physical life and we want it stopped. But what about our spiritual life? Are we concerned about spiritual shame? What about spiritual enemies?

Do they bother you as much as physical enemies? Satan is always trying to make the church look silly, to ridicule the believer, and to make faith in God and in his Christ look like nonsense. From that we need full protection. And that we had better bear in mind when we sing:

> To Thee I lift my soul,
> In Thee my trust repose;
> My God, O put me not to shame
> Before triumphant foes.

Do not forget this aspect of the many difficulties a child of God has in this life. Do not push into the background the enmity that the world has against God and his church. Bear in mind that this is all enmity against Christ, the seed of the woman.

In your prayer sincerely ask the God of our salvation that you may be kept from going along with the world in order to avoid shame to your name. Pray that you may not bring shame upon his church by your attitude toward those that hate God, his Christ, and the truth.

Read: Psalm 25
Psalter versification: 60:1

NECESSARY GUIDANCE

Shew me thy ways, O Lord; teach me thy paths. Lead me in thy truth, and teach me: for thou art the God of my salvation; on thee do I wait all the day. —Psalm 25:4–5

If you trust in your own strength, you are going to be put to shame. Man is like the flower of the grass that soon fades and dies. The child of God has the devil and his host lined up against him, making his cause hopeless if it depends upon him. Peter boasted that he would never forsake Christ. Only a few hours later he denied all connection with him, and even of knowledge concerning him. If in the battle of faith we are going to trust in self, we are going to be overcome. Then our flesh will be serving Satan instead of fighting him.

That is why David prayed that God would keep him from the shameful act of denying God and his faith in God. That is also why he wrote in Psalm 25:4–5, "Shew me thy ways, O Lord; teach me thy paths. Lead me in thy truth, and teach me: for thou art the God of my salvation; on thee do I wait all the day." What a powerful confession!

God must show us and teach us and lead us into the truth. Jehovah is the God of our salvation. What humility we have here! But also what profound, basic truth is here given us! In God we live, move, and have all our being in our spiritual as well as physical life. Our safety in our spiritual life depends completely upon God. Wisely then sing:

> Show me Thy paths, O Lord,
> Teach me Thy perfect way,
> O guide me in Thy truth divine,
> And lead me day by day.

Yes, we must wait upon God all the day. He must lead us after showing us the right path which he designed for our feet, the perfect way that will bring the church to glory rather than to shame. He must keep us from bringing shame to his church in this vale of tears.

Walk Satan's path; listen to him; let him teach you; and he will keep you in the shame into which he led Adam, and in Adam led the whole human race.

Pray to God that he will lead you step by step every day of your pilgrimage here below. Pray that he may cause your feet to walk in the footsteps of his Son. They led away from shame and unto glory.

Read: Psalm 119:33–48
Psalter versification: 60:3

REMEMBERED IN CHRIST

Remember not the sins of my youth, nor my transgressions: according to thy mercy remember thou me for thy goodness' sake, O LORD. —Psalm 25:7

There are members of our bodies that can be surgically removed for our health's sake. But without a heart man cannot live. And when we are speaking about our spiritual life, the heart of our salvation is Christ. Without him there just is no spiritual life for fallen man. That is why David wrote in Psalm 25:7, "Remember not the sins of my youth, nor my transgressions: according to thy mercy remember thou me for thy goodness' sake, O LORD."

In those two words, namely, mercy and goodness, David speaks of Christ. For all of God's mercy comes to us through Christ. Our sins can be forgotten only because Christ suffered all their punishment and because he performed all the works of love required of us. Apart from Christ man cannot taste and enjoy God's mercy. And is there any good thing, on earth or in heaven, for sinful man other than and apart from Christ who was sent into our flesh by God's grace? Is he not "the way, the truth, and the life" (John 14:6)?

If Satan then is not going to have the victory over us, and we are going to escape the shame of everlasting punishment in the lake of fire because of our sins from the day of our birth till the day of our death, we must have Christ and his cross. If God does not remember what Christ did for us and apply that to us, he will remember all our sins. We will be no more capable of covering our sins than Adam and Eve were. And God had to come then and shed the blood of an animal and use its skin to cover their shame. There Christ was pictured to us.

How necessary then that we sing this prayer:

My sins and faults of youth,
Let them forgotten be,
And for Thy tender mercies' sake,
O Lord, remember me.

For thy mercies' sake is for Christ's sake. He is the seed of the woman who crushed the head of Satan and made us a people whose sins are covered. And because God remembers not only that cross, but also who it is that Christ represented on that cross, he remembers that we are righteous in his Son.

Our calling is to remember all this and thank God for his grace.

Read: Psalm 130
Psalter versification: 61:1

THE BLESSED MEEK

The meek will he guide in judgment: and the meek will he teach his way. All the paths of the LORD are mercy and truth unto such as keep his covenant and his testimonies. —Psalm 25:9–10

Would it comfort you and give you peace of mind if you could be given a glimpse into God's book of life and find your name there, written in indelible ink? Well, you can and should do that. We have the Scriptures, God's word, and in them he tells us whether our names are in that book of life or not.

In Psalm 25 David is used by God to tell us that those who are meek, and in that meekness keep his covenant and his testimonies, have their names in that book of life, and that Christ blotted out their sins and earned everlasting glory for them.

For in Psalm 25:9–10 we read: "The meek will he guide in judgment: and the meek will he teach his way. All the paths of the LORD are mercy and truth unto such as keep his covenant and his testimonies." Our versification has it thus:

> The pathways of the Lord
> Are truth and mercy sure
> To such as keep His covenant
> And testimonies pure.

Keeping God's covenant and testimonies reveals true, sincere meekness before God. That meekness declares undeniably that these are those whom God is guiding on the way to everlasting heavenly bliss. Did Jesus not say that the meek are blessed, because "they shall inherit the earth" (Matt. 5:5)?

Meekness here means meekness before God. Such meekness is bowing humbly before his will. It means that by word and deed we say that he is God, and that we are creatures made by him for his glory, creatures who must do his will continuously. We must walk the path he designed for us here below. It is the pathway of love to him.

Every sin is an act of pride. In it we lift ourselves above God and say to him: "You cannot tell me what I may do!"

Do you find meekness in your life?

If you do, be sure to pray for God's grace to keep you in that walk of meekness. You will have the assurance of being one of his beloved children only while you walk in meekness before him.

Read: Psalm 37:7–34
Psalter versification: 61:3

KNOWING A PRECIOUS SECRET

The secret of the LORD is with them that fear him; and he will shew them his covenant. —Psalm 25:14

Keep God's covenant, and he will keep you enjoying covenant blessings. That awesome truth we find in Psalm 25:14, where we read: "The secret of the LORD is with them that fear him; and he will shew them his covenant."

The secret of the Lord is not information about one's name being in the Lamb's book of life. That is no secret, as we saw yesterday. A walk of meekness before God shows that one's name is in that book.

The word *secret* has in the Hebrew the root meaning of a divan or couch. Here it is a love seat where God and his people sit together and have a most intimate fellowship of friendship. God and his people sit in a private circle, where no ungodly may be. And here there is perfect agreement between God and that people. In fact, disagreement would make one get up and walk away. But the meek, of verse 9, agree with God and enjoy walking in love before him. They keep his testimonies and covenant. To him they say: "Thou art God, and we are thy people. We love thee and enjoy serving thee." And he says to them: "I am your God and Father in Christ. I love you and have prepared a life of glory for you."

They are friends of God, and he in Christ is their friend. They enjoy living with him, and he reveals his love in having them there with him in his house of many mansions. That beautiful truth we have in our versification in these words:

They that fear and love the Lord
Shall Jehovah's friendship know;
He will grace to them accord,
And His faithful covenant show.

A bond of fellowship, a tasting of God's love, will be enjoyed by those who love God and delight in fellowship with him. Showing his covenant is far more than making them know that there is such a covenant. It is more than causing to know that there is such a covenant. The devil knows that there is a covenant between God and his people in Christ. It means to know in the sense of enjoying all the blessings of that covenant. That is ahead for those who love God.

Read: Psalm 25:1–14
Psalter versification: 68:4

SAFE IN GOD'S COVENANT FAITHFULNESS

Mine eyes are ever toward the LORD; for he shall pluck my feet
out of the net. Turn thee unto me, and have mercy upon me; for I
am desolate and afflicted. —Psalm 25:15–16

If he could get his way, Satan would turn us all into covenant breakers. He is constantly devising ways of getting us to turn away from God and to go up against him, rather than to sit down in covenant fellowship with him.

Of that David speaks in Psalm 25:15–16 and also shows how miserably the devil will fail. He wrote: "Mine eyes are ever toward the LORD; for he shall pluck my feet out of the net. Turn thee unto me, and have mercy upon me; for I am desolate and afflicted."

Satan is constantly devising traps wherein he can catch us. But, as David declares, God will pluck us out of his net. We cannot do that ourselves. We have not the strength to escape Satan's crafty and powerful devices. David stated it correctly when he wrote that we are desolate, that is, alone in the midst of the innumerable host of Satan's army. He also states that we are afflicted, that is, poor. That is the basic meaning of the word. Being attacked, we are helpless, for we have no money to buy weapons of defense or of offense. In ourselves we are at the mercy of Satan.

That is why the child of God must and does set his eyes upon Jehovah. He will enable us to keep his covenant and his testimonies. He will keep us safe. In his mercy in Christ he will pluck our feet out of any net into which Satan had led us and caused us to fall. He will make us look with our eyes unto God for help and safety.

God's covenant will stand. It does not depend upon us. We are safe because of God's covenant faithfulness, not our own.

Our versification expresses it beautifully in these words:

My eyes are evermore
Tow'rd Thee, O Lord, Whose care
Shall surely save my heedless feet
From ev'ry hidden snare.

Take note of the fact that God will take care of us. That care will keep us safe. There is no one more careful than God. And there is no one more powerful than he is. We are safe in his mercy.

Read: Psalm 91
Psalter versification: 62:3

KEEP WAITING

O keep my soul, and deliver me: let me not be ashamed; for I put my trust in thee.
Let integrity and uprightness preserve me; for I wait on thee. —Psalm 25:20–21

There are times when we become very impatient because we are kept waiting for that which we greatly desire. There are also times when it is a blessing to be kept waiting. Of such a waiting David speaks in Psalm 25:20–21 in these words: "O keep my soul, and deliver me: let me not be ashamed; for I put my trust in thee. Let integrity and uprightness preserve me; for I wait on thee."

Waiting here is not waiting for something to happen. Rather it is waiting upon someone. In this case it is waiting upon God. And that means putting one's trust in him. It is waiting upon God in the sense of looking to him and expecting something from him.

What David wants is that his soul be kept from sinning against God. That is what we find in our versification also in these words:

> Defend and keep my soul,
> From foes deliver me,
> And let me not be bro't to shame:
> I put my trust in Thee.
> Be truth and right my shield,
> Because I wait for Thee;
> Thy Church, O God, do Thou redeem
> From all adversity.

He prays that God will keep his soul from shame and that integrity and uprightness preserve his soul. In other words, he wants to be kept in covenant faithfulness. He is not merely concerned about bodily comfort and safety. He wants to continue to walk as God's friend.

How about it? Are you as concerned about your soul as others are about their bodies? Are you concerned about living in integrity, that is, innocency? Is uprightness, being exactly as God wants you to be, your deep desire? Is that more interesting to you than to be kept from sickness, pain, and physical death?

Do you want to be kept where you will enjoy God's secret and enjoy covenant blessings? Pray then that you may be kept waiting upon God and his mercy in Christ. That is a blessed waiting. And that is a very important keeping. We must wait upon God; but he must keep us in that covenant activity. He must keep in us the new life Christ earned for us and has bestowed upon us.

Read: Psalm 121
Psalter versification: 63:3–4

December 18

MANIFESTING TRUE WISDOM

The fear of the LORD is the beginning of wisdom: a good understanding have all they that do his commandments: his praise endureth for ever —Psalm 111:10

Where we begin often determines whether we will succeed or fail. Begin to build a house in the sand without a good foundation, and the rain, the flood, and the wind will destroy it (Matt. 7:24–27). The same thing is true about obtaining wisdom. As we read in Psalm 111:10, "The fear of the LORD is the beginning of wisdom: a good understanding have all they that do his commandments: his praise endureth forever."

The truth we have here is that unless we have the fear of the Lord, we have no wisdom. Men may laud us and call us the wise men of the day. But we must fear God, or we just do not understand anything correctly.

Rule God out of his creation; fear men instead of God; and you are simply walking in folly. Attribute any part of salvation to man, and maintain that man begins it by letting Christ come into his heart, and you reveal that you have no true understanding of Christ and the salvation in him.

To fear God means to believe that he is God. *Fear* is the Old Testament word for faith. Merely to be afraid of God is not wisdom. Trust in him, rely upon him, and serve him, and you are wise. The psalmist here expresses that fear by stating that they who fear God have a good understanding. The words *his commandments* do not appear in the Hebrew text. And the psalmist explains it more fully by stating: "His praise endureth forever."

The idea is that he who fears God, he who is truly wise and has a good understanding, will praise God. That is what the fear of the Lord always produces. Our versification explains it thus:

In reverence and in godly fear
Man finds the gate to wisdom's ways;
The wise His holy Name revere;
Through endless ages sound His praise.

If you praise him by word and deed, you reveal true wisdom. Those who do not praise him reveal lack of good understanding.

How much wisdom have you revealed today? Do you understand your calling in the midst of this world? Are you wise as to why God placed you on this earth, and what your calling is before him?

Read: Psalm 111
Psalter versification: 304:7

ALL IS WELL

Surely the wrath of man shall praise thee: the remainder of
wrath shalt thou restrain. —Psalm 76:10

In days gone by it looked, and in days to come it will look, as though things momentarily slipped out of God's control. Cain killed Abel. Pharaoh placed all of Jacob's offspring in abject slavery. The Jews killed God's only begotten Son. And pretty soon the antichrist will wreak havoc upon the church of Christ.

But Asaph was used by God to assure us that all is well, and that all things always work together for good. He wrote in Psalm 76:10, "Surely the wrath of man shall praise thee: the remainder of wrath shalt thou restrain." And our versification states it thus:

When from heav'n Thy sentence sounded,
All the earth in fear was still,
While to save the meek and lowly
God in judgment wrought His will;
E'en the wrath of man shall praise Thee,
Thy designs it shall fulfill.

Absolutely everything that happens praises God, for it all is exactly as he eternally planned it. That cruel and arrogant death of Christ was not due to a momentary loss of control by God. He planned it, as we read in Luke 22:22. He went as God had determined. And therefore, God was praised in it as his work of blotting out our sins.

What will not serve God's church will never, no never, happen. Nothing in the future, no matter how terribly the church is persecuted, will not serve the elect children of God to bring them to heavenly glory.

Nothing in your life, no matter how painful and what a loss it may be for the flesh, will to any degree keep you from reaching the exact place in glory that God eternally planned and promised in his word.

The devil, the fallen angels, and all the unbelievers who ever lived on this earth are all tools in God's hand to bring us exactly what we need to be polished, so that we, in the day of Christ, may shine brightly with the glory of God.

All is well. And we do well to praise God for his constant care and loving-kindness which he shows unto us.

Read: Psalm 76
Psalter versification: 207:3

A PRAYER FOR VINDICATION

Judge me, O LORD; for I have walked in mine integrity: I have trusted also in the LORD; therefore I shall not slide. —Psalm 26:1

A man who lost a court case may appeal to a higher court, thinking that the members of the jury have, or the judge has, been influenced by emotion rather than facts; and he may desire to have a higher judge listen to his evidence and vindicate him.

But a man who is guilty and declared innocent will not appeal his case or want a retrial. It may seem strange then that in Psalm 26 David appeals to the highest judge that there is, namely, God, and that he prays: "Judge me, O LORD; for I have walked in mine integrity: I have trusted also in the LORD; therefore I shall not slide" (Ps. 26:1).

Now, bear in mind that this is David, a man of the fallen human race, and of whom there are many sins recorded in Scripture. Dare he sing:

> Be Thou my judge, O righteous Lord,
> Try Thou my inmost heart;
> I walk with steadfast trust in Thee,
> Nor from Thy ways depart.

The explanation lies in the fact that the words *judge me* are better translated as *vindicate me*. Vindicating is judging but in the sense of telling false accusers that they are wrong.

Quite plainly there were those who accused David of walking in sins that he did not commit. He did trust in God and was not an unbeliever.

How urgent and necessary it is for us today that we make this our prayer. There is much that calls itself church and many who claim to be Christians who accuse others of teaching false doctrines and of defending lawlessness. What counts is not what earthly judges decide but what God finds in man's heart and mind.

Not only does God's decision count, but it ought to give us confidence and assurance.

Never mind what men say. They so often are wrong. But God is never wrong in his judgments. And in the judgment day it will all become plain. Commit your way now then unto God. Keep trusting in him to set all things right in the day of Christ.

Read: Psalm 26
Psalter versification: 69:1

REQUESTED SOUL-SEARCHING

Examine me, O LORD, and prove me; try my reins and my heart. For thy lovingkindness is before mine eyes: and I have walked in thy truth. —Psalm 26:2–3

There are times when frightening experiences or the hearing of some very sad news hit us in the pit of our stomachs. At least that is the way we today, and in our country, explain the emotions we experience when we are frightened or given sad news. The Israelites, however, in the days of David would say that they felt it in their kidneys. And that is why David wrote in Psalm 26:2–3, "Examine me, O LORD, and prove me; try my reins and my heart. For thy lovingkindness is before mine eyes: and I have walked in thy truth." The *reins* here is in the Hebrew the word *kidneys*.

What David is doing here is praying to God that he will vindicate him before false accusers by trying, that is, testing, his kidneys and heart. He asks the sole Judge of the supreme court to examine him, knowing that from his eyes is absolutely nothing hidden. He is sure that God will find that, instead of enjoying these sins of which he is falsely accused, he is stricken by them with pain in his kidneys, and that his heart has by no means chosen to do these evil deeds.

Our versification puts it this way:

O search me, Lord, and prove me now;
Thy mercy I adore;
I choose Thy truth to be my guide,
And sinful ways abhor.

His heart chose to keep God's law, and sin strikes him in his kidneys. These sins of which he is accused he actually abhors. The evil of which he is accused was not chosen by his heart.

David is not here concerned about his name or honor, even though these are important, since he is king over God's people in Israel. But he prays because he wants to be pleasing in God's sight. He wants to be judged to be a faithful child of God by God himself.

That should also be our concern. What men think of us is not that important. What they call us is not so serious. What God finds in the innermost recesses of our souls, what hurts us and what we choose, is extremely important. If God finds the life of Christ in us, we have reason to rejoice and can stand the false accusations of men.

Read: Psalm 139
Psalter versification: 69:2

VOICE OF TRUE THANKSGIVING

I will wash mine hands in innocency: so will I compass thine altar, O
LORD: That I may publish with the voice of thanksgiving, and tell of
all thy wondrous works. —Psalm 26:6–7

It now becomes plain what sins David was accused of committing. In Psalm 26:4–5 we read: "I have not sat with vain persons, neither will I go in with dissemblers. I have hated the congregation of evil doers; and will not sit with the wicked." He is not a companion of evildoers. They are not his friends and companions. He does not walk with them in their deceit and godlessness.

However, he does know that he has sinful flesh and has in many ways sinned against God. Therefore, he continues: "I will wash mine hands in innocency: so will I compass thine altar, O LORD: that I may publish with the voice of thanksgiving, and tell of all thy wondrous works" (vv. 6–7).

Today he would write: "I do not deny that I often sin; but I flee to the cross of Christ to wash my sins away. I walk about his cross, typically presented by an altar in the temple. I encircle it with the confidence that Christ's blood washes away my sins. In all this I see God's wonderful work: and it moves me to tell and sing of my thankfulness to him."

How about it? All around us are Christmas lights and decorations. On the radio increasingly we hear Christmas carols sung. For weeks the stores have been displaying and advertising Christmas presents. You would think that Christmas is a wonderful day for mankind. It seems to be the greatest day in the year!

For all men that is certainly not true. For most men all this is vain, that is, empty, utterly devoid of thanksgiving to God and of spiritual significance. Let us rather sincerely sing:

My hands I wash in innocence
And seek Thy altar, Lord,
That there I may with thankful voice
Thy wondrous works record.

Is that not our calling on Christmas day? God's gift to us must speak to us. Without Christ's birth that altar in the temple had no meaning, and our hands would never lose their awful guilt. Our gift on Christmas must be thankful praise to God for his gift to us.

Read: Isaiah 55
Psalter versification: 69:3

GOD'S HONOR IN GOD'S HOUSE

LORD, I have loved the habitation of thy house, and the place
where thine honour dwelleth. —Psalm 26:8

What means more to you? God's house or the houses of worldly amusement? Where do you find more joy? Is it in God's house on the Sabbath and with those who sing God's praises? Or is it where you can watch, and have fellowship with those who watch, Sabbath-breaking heroes of this world? And when Christmas arrives, will you be going up to God's house with zeal and enthusiasm? Or will your heart be set on gifts and a sumptuous meal?

David said that he did not sit with dissemblers (Ps. 26:4), that is, with those who are only Christians in name, and that he hates evildoers. They then are not his heroes. He will not sit with wicked men. And then he states: "LORD, I have loved the habitation of thy house, and the place where thine honour dwelleth" (v. 8).

Plainly tinsel and decorations, feasting and exchanging of material gifts, did not set David's heart on fire. Instead he taught us to sing:

The habitation of Thy house
Is ever my delight;
The place where dwells Thy glory, Lord,
Is lovely in my sight.

It is true that Solomon built a beautiful temple and that David writes here of a tabernacle, which was a large tent with vessels of gold and silver and with beautiful tapestry. But that is not what brought David his joy. He speaks here of God's glory in our versification; and in the Scriptures he writes of God's honor. He had just spoken of God's altar, which he encircled and looked at with hope.

Christ and his cross were there in God's house. His blood was there sprinkled on the mercy seat of the ark in the holy of holies. And today in his house of prayer we encircle Christ and his cross in the preaching of God's word. There we hear—or surely ought to hear every Sabbath—of Christ and be moved to sing: "Glory to God in the highest, and on earth peace to men of good will."

We ought to honor God, not ignore him or think of him occasionally. And Christmas day should be a day we set aside to honor him. Honor him on that day with songs of thanksgiving.

Read: Isaiah 40
Psalter versification: 69:4

December 24

THE GIFT OF GOD'S TENDER MERCY

But as for me, I will walk in mine integrity: redeem me, and be merciful
unto me. My foot standeth in an even place: in the congregations will
I bless the LORD. —Psalm 26:11–12

Reversing the letters of a word can make it take on an entirely different meaning. Change *top* to *pot*, or *saw* to *was*, and you are mentioning things in entirely different fields. Change just one letter in a word, and again you radically change the meaning. *Coat* and *cost*, *smell* and *small* bring entirely new ideas to mind.

Tomorrow we should change one letter and not imitate the world. Many tomorrow will say: "Merry Christmas." Believers understanding the real meaning of Christmas will not speak of being merry but of God's mercy, which realized all that this day signifies.

If there is one thing that is usually far in the background or completely ruled out on Christmas day, it is God's mercy, even though in it he sent his only begotten Son to be our savior. A song we ought to sing every day but surely on Christmas is:

Redeemed by Thee, I stand secure
In peace and happiness;
And in the Church, among Thy saints,
Jehovah I will bless.

The word *mercy* is not literally to be found here, but in Psalm 26:11–12, upon which our versification is based, we read: "But as for me, I will walk in mine integrity: redeem me, and be merciful unto me. My foot standeth in an even place: in the congregations will I bless the LORD." And surely he will bless the Lord because of his mercy.

Did not Zacharias say in Luke 1:72 that Christ was sent "to perform the mercy promised to our fathers"? And then in verse 78 he states: "Through the tender mercy of our God; whereby the dayspring from on high hath visited us."

Today, and surely tomorrow, bless God for his mercy. Keep in your mind the salvation God realized for us through his Son. Keep your feet on even ground, not spiritual today and carnal tomorrow; not briefly considering things that make your salvation sure, and then brushing it all aside to have fleshly merriment. Let your greetings tomorrow speak of a blessed Christmas, not a merry Christmas. Let God's mercy shine forth, and praise him for his merciful gift.

Read: Luke 1:39–56
Psalter versification: 69:7

361

GOD'S WONDERFUL GIFT TO US

Many, O Lord my God, are thy wonderful works which thou hast done, and thy
thoughts which are to us-ward: they cannot be reckoned up in order unto thee: if I
would declare and speak of them, they are more than can be numbered.
—Psalm 40:5

The angel said it, and by faith we accept it and are comforted by it. He said: "Fear not: for, behold, I bring you good tidings of great joy, which shall be to all people. For unto you is born this day in the city of David a Saviour, which is Christ the Lord" (Luke 2:10–11).

David, although he did not see this truth as clearly as we do, wrote: "Many, O Lord my God, are thy wonderful works which thou hast done, and thy thoughts which are to us-ward: they cannot be reckoned up in order unto thee: if I would declare and speak of them, they are more than can be numbered" (Ps. 40:5).

Is there a more precious gift than God's Son? Can you think of a more wonderful work of God than this coming of his Son in our flesh, to represent us and take away our guilt, so that we can enter into heavenly glory? Did you receive any other gift today that can in any way and to any degree compare with this gift of God's grace?

In the measure that we see our sin and guilt, in the measure that we see our hopeless condition, the birth of the Savior is a most wonderful gift of God. And although there are a few Christmas carols that praise God, by all means sing these words:

O Lord my God, how manifold
The works which Thou hast wrought,
Ofttimes Thou hast bestowed on us
Thy care and gracious thought.
Thy works and thoughts most wonderful,
If I of them would speak,
Cannot be numbered, and in vain
To set them forth I seek.

What a wonder that gift is! Not only was it a virgin birth—a miracle we could never begin to perform—but this wonderful work of God did so much for us sinners! For us who wanted to become like God (Gen. 3:1–6), he became like unto us, so that he could save us from our sins and make us spiritually like unto his Son! What a loving thought of God to us!

You cannot measure this wonderful gift. You cannot weigh it or set a price upon it. But because of it, we can with the angels cry out: "Glory to God in the highest" (Luke 2:14). Fill the day with praise to him.

Read: Luke 2:1–20
Psalter versification: 108:6–7

REMEMBERING CHRIST'S BIRTH

He shall cry unto me, Thou art my father, my God, and the rock of my salvation. Also I will make him my firstborn, higher than the kings of the earth. —Psalm 89:26–27

As David wrote in Psalm 40:5, we cannot number all the blessings which God gives us in his Son who came into our flesh. But this does not mean that we must be silent. Rather we should daily sing:

> In vision to His saints God spake:
> From out the people one I take,
> A mighty leader, true and brave,
> Ordained, exalted, strong to save.
> Thou art my Father, he shall cry,
> My God, my rock of refuge high;
> My firstborn son shall he be owned,
> Above the kings of earth enthroned.

This is our versification of Psalm 89:26–27, where we read: "He shall cry unto me, Thou art my father, my God, and the rock of my salvation. Also I will make him my firstborn, higher than the kings of the earth."

That he would cry to God, "Thou art my father," the angel revealed to Mary when he said: "The Holy Ghost shall come upon thee, and the power of the Highest shall overshadow thee: therefore also that holy thing which shall be born of thee shall be called the Son of God" (Luke 1:35).

That he would be higher than the kings of the earth was also declared to Mary by the angel in verses 32–33 where he said, "He shall be great, and shall be called the Son of the Highest: and the Lord God shall give unto him the throne of his father David: and he shall reign over the house of Jacob for ever; and of his kingdom there shall be no end."

It will be an everlasting kingdom and in that sense have no end. He will conquer the whole world. There will be no end to the nations out of which he will gather his church. This day is called December 26, 1988 AD. All nations today count time by his birth. For AD means "In the year of our Lord." The ungodly nations also recognize his birth!

What a gift to us then that we have such a universal King, who is now at God's right hand with power over all things in heaven and on earth. Do not let the joy and significance of his birth fade away today. Consider and remember it and thank God for it. It has endless and unspeakable blessedness for us.

Read: Psalm 72
Psalter versification: 243:1, 5

A SURE COVENANT

My mercy will I keep for him for evermore, and my covenant shall stand fast with him.
—Psalm 89:28

One of the wonderful truths of Christ's birth is the certainty of God's covenant with us. For Christ is our covenant head; and that covenant is the relationship of friendship God establishes between himself and his chosen people.

Jesus was born in a stable, a place of abject poverty, fit only for cattle. But as our covenant head he realized for us a house of many mansions where we may live with God in a glory which eye has not seen, ear has not heard, and has never entered into the heart of man (1 Cor. 2:9). This is possible only because God's Son came into our flesh as our covenant head.

Of this God spoke in Psalm 89:28, where we read: "My mercy will I keep for him for evermore, and my covenant shall stand fast with him." This follows the statement concerning Jesus: "I will make him my firstborn, higher than the kings of the earth" (v. 27). That does refer to the birth of Christ, which always but especially at this time of the year we celebrate. Let us sing:

> For him My mercy shall endure,
> My covenant made with him is sure,
> His throne and race I will maintain
> Forever, while the heavens remain.

The sad thing is that at this time of the year we are so cluttered up with worldly things and put Christ's birth out of mind; and this past Christmas, most likely, is not still of great importance to us.

For the world, Christmas is long gone; and now there is the grief of all those bills for the gifts that were purchased. But is there really a good reason why we still should not sing of his birth and talk about it?

If his birth did not take place, the cross could never have happened; and we would still be in our sins. Then as covenant breakers we could only expect the opposite of covenant blessedness. But now we can be absolutely sure that God's covenant and its promises stand. We have nothing to fear. And Christ's ascension to God's right hand is the assurance that we will enjoy covenant blessedness in God's house.

Read: Psalm 89:20–37
Psalter versification: 243:6

PRAISE FOR GOD'S LOVING-KINDNESS AND TRUTH

I will praise thee with my whole heart: before the gods will I sing praise unto thee. I will worship toward thy holy temple, and praise thy name for thy lovingkindness and for thy truth: for thou hast magnified thy word above all thy name. —Psalm 138:1–2

It was two years or more after Jesus' birth that the wise men came with gifts of gold, frankincense, and myrrh. They made a long journey to bring these gifts. We ought to bring evidences of our thankfulness to God for his gift of his only begotten Son. And we ought not wait until next Christmas to do that. Do so today and sing from the bottom of your heart:

> With grateful heart my thanks I bring,
> Before the great Thy praise I sing;
> I worship in Thy holy place
> And praise Thee for Thy truth and grace;
> For truth and grace together shine
> In Thy most holy word divine.

If you turn to Psalm 138:1–2, you will read it thus: "I will praise thee with my whole heart: before the gods will I sing praise unto thee. I will worship toward thy holy temple, and praise thy name for thy lovingkindness and for thy truth: for thou hast magnified thy word above all thy name."

Were it not for the truth in these words, our future would be bleak. Without God's loving-kindness, and Christ's birth in it, there would be nothing that called for true thankfulness before God. And so quickly we set aside our thanks for that birth and for that Son and his cross.

But note that David praises God for his loving-kindness and truth. Where do we see these more richly than in Christ, who was sent in God's loving-kindness and who declared to us that he is "the way, the truth, and the life" (John 14:6)?

Surely we can see that the coming of Christ is the magnification of God's word, for he is the Word become flesh. If only we could keep these truths before our minds and in our hearts. If only with grateful hearts we would bring thanksgiving to God every day and be wise men who are interested in spiritual things and in our salvation. Praising God with our whole heart means that we praise him more than once a year for his gifts to us. But it also means that we do so more than once a day.

Read: Psalm 138
Psalter versification: 381:1

MERCY BASED ON JUSTICE

I will sing of mercy and judgment: unto thee, O LORD, will I sing. —Psalm 101:1

There are things that must be separated, and there are things that belong together and should not be kept apart. The wheat must be separated from the chaff. But that kernel of wheat must not be cut off from rain and sunshine, if it is to produce more grain for man.

Similarly, God's mercy and his justice go hand in hand. If we take that justice away, we make mercy impossible. God's mercy is only upon those whose sins have been blotted out by the blood of Christ. David declares this in Psalm 101:1 with these words: "I will sing of mercy and judgment: unto thee, O LORD, will I sing."

David had been stopped in his improper attempt to bring the ark back to the tabernacle. God slew Uzzah for touching that ark (2 Sam. 6:7). Here was God's judgment or justice. But there also was mercy. David made an arrogant, improper attempt to move the ark with an army rather than by the priests. God did not slay him, but in mercy saved his life. For David's sins were blotted out by the blood of Christ. God's justice was satisfied, and David could be dealt with in mercy. He could with thankfulness sing:

> Of mercy and of justice
> My thankful song shall be;
> O Lord, in joyful praises
> My song shall rise to Thee.
> Within my house I purpose
> To walk in wisdom's way;
> O Lord, I need Thy presence;
> How long wilt Thou delay?

Yes, the ark belonged in that tabernacle, and David was right in wanting to have God's presence typically there in the tabernacle. But justice always calls for punishment upon sin. And mercy can be shown only when sin is removed, its guilt being taken from someone.

Thank God then for the gift of his Son whose birthday we celebrated a few days ago. Thank him for the cross that blotted out our guilt, so that we could taste and enjoy God's mercy. Sing of God's mercy; but by all means sing also of his strict justice that makes his mercy possible for us poor sinners. Without the cross Christ's birth has no value for us.

Read: 2 Samuel 6:1–19
Psalter versification: 271:1

KNOWING OUR FRAILTY

LORD, make me to know mine end, and the measure of my days, what it is;
that I may know how frail I am. —Psalm 39:4

There are times when we are glad to have what we are experiencing come to an end. There are also times when we look up against an end to what we have been doing. What hurts and embarrasses we want ended. But what we enjoy and what gives us delight we want continued without end.

Tomorrow we come to the end of another year, which reminds us that we are one step closer to the end of our lives. Surely when the clock ticks again, we are closer to the end of the hour, the day, the year, and of our earthly lives. We can then understand these words of Psalm 39:4, "LORD, make me to know mine end, and the measure of my days, what it is; that I may know how frail I am."

That should be our prayer. To God we should pray:

> My end, Lord, make me know,
> My days, how soon they fail;
> And to my thoughtful spirit show
> How weak I am and frail.

Make that your prayer today; but make it your prayer every day. The year ends tomorrow, but another year comes the next day. Our days on earth are going to end; and then here below there will be no tomorrow for us.

Now, our frailty is not simply physical weakness of our bodies. We are so spiritually weak, even though we are born again with a new life in Christ. In ourselves we have absolutely no strength to keep ourselves from falling into sin or to keep our bodies alive. It is true that our souls go on; but we have no power in ourselves to keep them from plunging into the lake of fire.

It is so very important therefore that we know that Christ is so powerful. Having blotted out our sins on his cross, and because of it conquering death and the grave for us, we can, knowing our frailty, look to him at God's right hand with confidence.

Knowing our frailty, we can appreciate Christ's work and power. And we are ready to praise God and look for better things in the life to come. Learn your frailty: but look away from self and unto Christ for comfort and assurance. This life must end, if we are going to have the blessedness of the life Christ purchased for us.

Read: Psalm 90
Psalter versification: 107:1

LOOKING WITH THE EYE OF FAITH

LORD, thou hast been our dwelling place in all generations. Before the mountains were brought forth, or ever thou hadst formed the earth and the world, even from everlasting to everlasting, thou art God. —Psalm 90:1–2

Today we come to the end of another year; and every time Old Year's Day comes, we can and usually do look backward and forward. However, it is important that we look with the eye of faith when we look back at what happened and when we look forward to what we would like to have take place in the year ahead.

We do have a versification of Moses' words in Psalm 90 that we do well to keep in mind. The words are these:

> O God, our help in ages past,
> Our hope for years to come,
> Our shelter from the stormy blast,
> And our eternal home.
> Under the shadow of Thy throne
> Thy saints have dwelt secure;
> Sufficient is Thine arm alone,
> And our defense is sure.

Moses states it thus in Psalm 90:1, "LORD, thou hast been our dwelling place in all generations," and then later in verse 2: "Even from everlasting to everlasting, thou art God."

When by faith we look back at what happened, not only in the days of this year, nor in all our life, but from the day that God made man and placed him in the garden of Eden, we can and should say that God has been our dwelling place. When with the eye of faith we look forward, we can and should say that God will take care of us. For he is from everlasting to everlasting the almighty, faithful God of our salvation. He will not for a moment lose control of all creation. No one shall be able to do anything that will not work together for our good.

Our versification is not wrong when it states that God is our eternal home. Moses did say that he is our dwelling place. And the idea is that we have constant covenant fellowship with him. He has not left us but watched carefully over us. And since he is from everlasting to everlasting the Almighty One, we can look forward with confidence.

Not only looking back can we see how marvelously he defended and protected his church in Christ, and will do so in the future. But we can and should look up to Christ at God's right hand as our savior.

Read: Psalm 90
Psalter versification: 247:1–2

TOPICAL INDEX OF TITLES

F

faith, amazing, 86; constant covenant faithfulness, 51; in adversity, 264; knowing God in his faithfulness, 150; looking with the eye of, 368; our mighty God and faithful guide, 332; safe in God's covenant faithfulness, 353; the boldness of, 172; the silence of, 164

fear, 24, 231, 274

fed, 22

filled, 44, 320; *see also full*

first, 94

fitting, 18

fixed, 207

fleeing, 77

foe, 89; *see also enemies*

folly, 77

foolish, 69, 70

footstool, 288

foretaste, 57

forgive, 9, 211, 212, 345

formed, 235, 286

foundation, 136

fountain, 138, 184, 342

frailty, 367

friend, 89

fruit, 78, 346

full, 20, 105, 171; *see also filled*

G

Gethsemane, 88

gift, 135, 361, 362

give, 135, 245

gladness, 32

glorify, 38, 145, 251

glorious, 96

glory, at the end of the road, 3; established, 300; for the newborn child of God, 347; heavenly, 26, 92, 258; God of all, 36; kept on the way to, 127; seeing our redeemer's, 43; to God, 102, 116

golden, 63

good, 35, 301

grace, a cry for, 194; boundless, 213; God's abiding, 272; kept in God's law by,

254; saved by, 120; that conquers, 107; tried in, 338

great, 143, 302, 325, 336

guide, 5, 262, 332, 349

H

haste, 195

hated, 72

hatred, 238, 255

hear, 84

heart, a sound, 218; an understanding, 158; corrupt, 71; enlarged, 147; fixed, 207; of the matter, 29, 54; upright, 100, 190; *see also wholeheartedly*

heavenly, blessedness, 311; citizenship, 122; glory, 26, 92, 258; joy, 82

help, 125, 242, 305, 335

hide, 12, 232

holiness, 239, 250

holy, 74, 119, 296

honor, 360

honorable, 303

hope, blessed, 95, 202; for a sure salvation, 240; for spiritual safety, 278; quickened unto stronger, 185; that maketh not ashamed, 154; the believer's, 215; waiting in, 131

house, 256, 257, 360

humble, 228, 241, 281

humiliation, 303

I

immeasurable, 273

implicit, 323

important, 52

inevitable, 346

inheritance, 265

iniquity, 345

instruction, 263

instructive, 219

Israel, 191

J

Jehovah, 48; *see also Lord*

Jesus, 279

joy, an overflowing cup of, 25; heavenly,

82; judgment day, 329; of the church, 326; restored, 32; spiritual, 45

joyful, foretaste, 57; God's praises joyfully sung, 169; new creation, 252; singing witnesses, 248; the reason for joyful singing, 85

judgment, 166, 186, 280, 329

just, 242, 366

K

keep, 65, 354

kept, 127, 224, 244, 254

king, 277

knowing, a precious secret, 352; God, 150, 179; our dependency upon God, 75; our frailty, 367; the power of God's wrath, 297; the way to knowing God's love, 156

L

laughter, 44

law, appreciating, 39; delight in, 113, 205, 245; directed by, 99; kept in, 254; living in, 308; love for, 282; meditating in, 15; seeing the wonders of, 121; walking in, 97

led, 233

level, 226

life, blessed, 193; eternal, 342; fountain of, 138; light for, 343; momentary, 295; storms of, 283; that praises God, 318

lifted, 223

light, 200, 234, 262, 343

lips, 33

living, 6, 55, 217, 308

longing, 74, 291

look, to God in prayer, 73; upward, 40, 134, 228; with the eye of faith, 368

Lord, 289; *see also Jehovah*

loss, 101

love, abiding, 272; corrective, 213; for God's law, 282; hatred that reveals, 238; knowing God in his, 179; living in love to the neighbor, 55; living in love toward God, 217; of God, 165; revived with greater, 143; souls filled

with, 320; sweetness of God's, 90; turned in God's, 118; way to knowing God's, 156; wondrous, 225

loving-kindness, 365

M

maintained, 149

maketh, 154

man, 295

manifesting, 355

marvelous, 104

matter, 29, 54

meditating, 15, 142

meek, 152, 351

meeting, 256, 271

mercy, a cry for, 27; amid miseries, 275; an urgent prayer for, 229; based on justice, 366; encompassed with God's, 157; everlasting, 60, 276; immeasurable, 273; quickened in God's, 243; tender, 4, 361; the meeting of, 271; the way to cry for, 321

mighty, 18, 332

miseries, 275

mockery, 170

momentary, 295

mouths, 44, 171

must, 67

N

name, 174, 188, 269

necessary, confession, 281; conversion always, 46; guidance, 349; prayer, 198

need, a prayer for needful quickening, 307; a thorough cleansing, 28; an understanding heart, 158; fully supplied, 20; our greatest, 336; urgent, 144

neighbor, 55

new, 252

newborn, 347

O

only, 11, 53

overflowing, 25

176; deepest reason, 130; God's work, 108; hope for a sure, 240; humbly waiting for, 241; inevitable fruit, 346; sure response, 334; sure, 47, 64; understanding our, 333

sanctified, 195, 291

Satan, 340

save, 81

saved, by God's name, 174; by grace, 120; from spiritual shame, 348; in a marvelous way, 104; in awesome righteousness, 312; in righteous judgment, 166; that we may serve, 161

secret, 352

seeing, 43, 121, 342

seeking, 98, 111

serve, 161

shame, 92, 348

sight, 42

sign, 122, 285

significant, 93

silence, 10, 63, 164

sin, 10, 105, 112

sing, a call to, 19, 247; a most difficult song, 87; creation, 316; joyful singing witnesses, 248; singing God's praises properly, 151; the reason for joyful singing, 85; the singing pilgrim, 187

sleep, 324

smile, 117, 292

snow, 30

solid, 136

song, 96

souls, 38, 302, 320

soul-searching, 358

sound, 218

sovereign, 137

speak, 71, 84

speech, 251

spiritual, bread, 22; joy, 45; safety, 278; shame, 348; strangers, 175; time for the things, 306

state, 210

statutes, 142

steadfast, 261

step, 126

storms, 283

strangers, 175

strength, 170, 185

sung, 169

supplied, 20

sure, comfort, 280; covenant, 364; heavenly glory absolutely, 26; refuge, 284; response, 334; salvation, 47, 64, 240; sign of heavenly citizenship, 122; victory, 167, 209; *see also reassuring*

sweet, 90, 324

T

tactics, 340

talks, 114

tears, 292

tender, 4, 361

testimonies, 304

thankful, 7, 34, 59, 201, 267, 344

thanks, 182, 196, 249, 359

things, 94, 306

thorough, 28

thoughts, 237

thrill, 212

time, 128, 306

tomorrow, 331

transcendent, 260

treasure, 79

trees, 78

tremendously, 52

tried, 338

trouble, 178, 302

true, 13, 253, 355, 359

trust, a blessed, steadfast, 261; and thankfulness, 344; childlike trust in God, 153; implicit trust in God, 323; in and thanks unto God, 249; in God alone, 68; in God, 337; that is a must, 67

truth, 146, 171, 200, 230, 271, 365

U

understanding, 158, 299, 304, 333

unholy, 119

unite, 192, 193

PSALMS INDEX

PSALTER INDEX

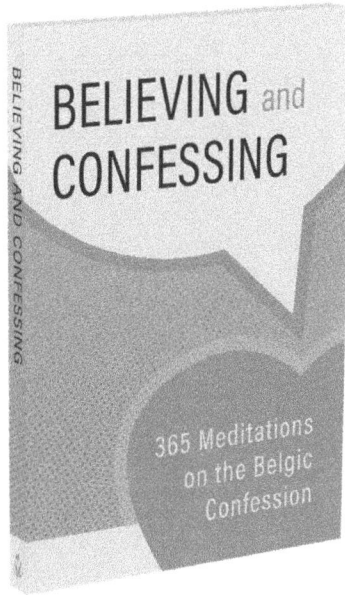

Believing and Confessing: 365 Meditations from the Belgic Confession

"Though we shall grow in the knowledge of God into all eternity, we shall never reach an end of our search for the riches of God's blessed being. Everlasting life is not long enough to exhaust the riches of the knowledge of God. Though we know what the Scriptures say of God, our knowledge of God is less than a thimbleful of water in comparison with all the oceans and seas on the earth. Yet, we know him—know him as our Friend, our Redeemer, our covenant God! What a wonder, for he shows us enough of himself for us to live in warm covenant fellowship with him. Let us exalt his holy name."

- excerpt of January 6 meditation, *God is Incomprehensible*

All books available at **rfpa.org**,
or by calling the Reformed Free Publishing Association
at **616-457-5970** or emailing **mail@rfpa.org**.

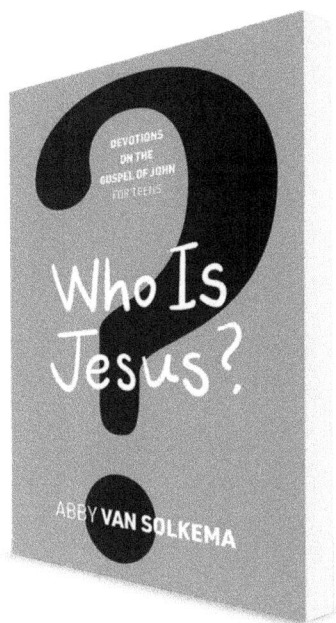

Who is Jesus? Daily Devotions on the Gospel of John for Teens: Book 1

"Jesus is not just light; he is the Light. As the Son of God, he is the source of all light. Even when he took on a human nature and came to this dark world, he shone as a perfect example of what is true, right, and good. Since the fall, the natural state of this world is death and darkness. All men are not only lost in the darkness, but they prefer the darkness and cannot even comprehend the light. Yet in his mercy, God uses the light of the gospel—the truth about Jesus—to draw out of darkness those whom He has elected before the world began. This light exposes sin and irresistibly draws God's children to saving faith."

- excerpt of Day 2 meditation, *Light and Darkness*

All books available at **rfpa.org**,
or by calling the Reformed Free Publishing Association
at **616-457-5970** or emailing **mail@rfpa.org.**

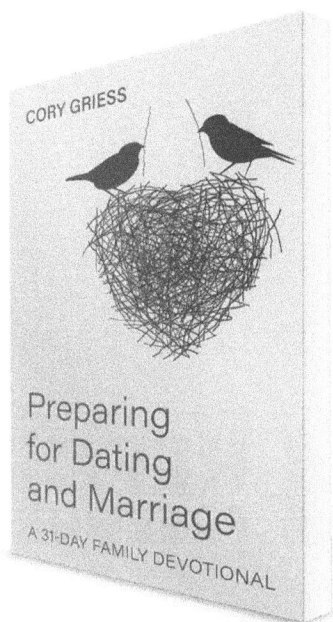

Preparing for Dating and Marriage: A 31-Day Family Devotional

"How does he bring to every man his wife and to every woman her husband today? Not the same way he did for Adam and Eve of course. He does so by his providence. As he leads us to seek the right kind of spouse, and as we learn the teaching of his word regarding what marriage is, the goal of marriage, what to look for in a spouse, principles to follow in looking for a spouse, dangers to avoid, and examples to follow—he providentially leads us to our 'Adam' or our 'Eve.' That list above is everything we will discuss in the next twenty-nine days."

- excerpt of Day 2 meditation, *God Brings a Spouse*

All books available at **rfpa.org**,
or by calling the Reformed Free Publishing Association
at **616-457-5970** or emailing **mail@rfpa.org**.

REFORMED
FREE PUBLISHING
ASSOCIATION

Our Mission

To glorify God by making accessible to the broadest possible audience material that testifies to the truth of Scripture as understood and developed in the Reformed tradition.

Reformed Free Publishing Association
1894 Georgetown Center Drive Jenison, MI 49428-7137
Website: rfpa.org

www.ingramcontent.com/pod-product-compliance
Lightning Source LLC
Chambersburg PA
CBHW051218150426
42812CB00053BA/2508

9 781959 515203